In the Life

In the Life
Versions
of the criminal
experience

by Bruce Jackson

Holt, Rinehart and Winston
New York   Chicago   San Francisco

Published simultaneously in Canada by Holt, Rinehart
and Winston of Canada, Limited.

Library of Congress Catalog Card Number: 74-155518
ISBN: 0-03-086575-1

First Edition

Designer: Winston Potter
Printed in the United States of America

A section of this book was previously published in *True*.

The author gratefully acknowledges permission to reprint from his previous works:

"Who Goes to Prison," *The Atlantic*, January, 1966. Copyright © 1965 by The Atlantic
Monthly Company.

"Exiles from the American Dream," *The Atlantic*, January, 1967. Copyright © 1966 by
The Atlantic Monthly Company.

"Prison Nicknames," *Western Folklore*, volume 26, number 1. Copyright © 1967 by the
California Folklore Society. Reprinted by permission of the Society.

"Our Prisons Are Criminal," *The New York Times Magazine*, September 22, 1968. Copyright © 1968 by The New York Times Company. Reprinted by permission.

A Thief's Primer. Copyright © 1969 by Bruce Jackson. Reprinted by permission of The
Macmillan Company.

"Beyond Attica," *transaction*, November/December 1971. Copyright © 1971 by transaction inc. Reprinted by permission of transaction.

"Prison: the New Academy," *The Nation*, December 6, 1971. Copyright © 1971 by The
Nation. Reprinted by permission of The Nation.

Wake Up Dead Man: Afro-American Worksongs from Texas Prisons, Harvard University Press. Copyright © 1972 by the President and Fellows of Harvard College.

For Susan

Contents

Acknowledgments

Over a four-year period (1963–1967) my research was generously supported by the Society of Fellows of Harvard University; without the support of the Society's Senior Fellows, especially the three men who were chairmen during my tenure—Harry T. Levin, Wassily Leontief, and the late Crane Brinton—I doubt I would have been able to do most of this work. Additional financial assistance was supplied by the Milton Fund of Harvard University, the Ruby T. Lomax Fellowship Committee of the University of Texas, the Research Foundation of the State University of New York, the Institutional Funds Committee of the Faculty of Arts and Letters of SUNY at Buffalo, and the Graduate School of SUNY at Buffalo. I used part of my year as a Guggenheim Fellow (1971–1972) working on final manuscript revisions; during that period the English Department of the University of California at Berkeley gave me office space and other courtesies. Professor George List, director of the Archive of Traditional Music at Indiana University, lent me recording equipment and tapes for my first prison trips in 1962. Members of the secretarial staff of the SUNY at Buffalo English Department typed most of the long manuscript, even though they were already overloaded with regular department work. My thanks to them all.

I also want to thank the officials of the various institutions I visited in Texas, Massachusetts, New York City, California, Indiana, and Missouri. Of these I especially want to thank Dr. George Beto, director of the Texas Department of Corrections.

Several other friends helped in several ways, especially Professor Frederic Fleron, Jr., Political Science Department, SUNY at Buffalo; Professor John Gagnon, Sociology Department, SUNY at Stony Brook; Mr. Ed Hall, SUNY at Buffalo; Warren G. Bennis, president, University of Cincinnati; Professor Al Katz, Law School, SUNY at Buffalo; Danny Lyon, Bernalillo, N.M.; and Joan Katz, Buffalo.

Finally, and most important, I want to thank all my acquaintances and friends in the life, the ones still in those joints, the ones I'm still in contact with on the streets, and those who have disappeared into the rooms and streets and roads of that world so amenable to those who have reason to disappear in such a fashion.

Berkeley, December 1971

You can't help what you are; if you could,
you would a been somebody else.
—Little Richard on a late-
    night talk show somewhere

1. Introduction:
About this book

This is the third volume in a series of studies about prison and deviant culture. In the first, *A Thief's Primer* (Macmillan, 1969), I suggested a typology for criminal behavior and prison social structure, and I tried to document the way one kind of professional thief located himself in the social spectra of prison and free-world criminal societies. The second volume, *Wake Up Dead Man* (Harvard University Press, 1972), documents the present status of one form of prison folklore—the work songs of the black convicts—and attempts to detail the social situations and the physical and psychological functions and needs that made the songs not only possible but necessary.

In the Life consists of statements about crime and prison by men and women I met in prisons in several states between 1962 and 1968; not all the interviews were done in prison, but the initial contacts were made there.

It is a book about some losers, about people who managed to get themselves put in prison. With a few exceptions, these are not criminals who go for years and years in the life without a bust; nor are they the people who manage to live a nice square life while hustling on the side for their real incomes. They aren't Mafiosi in big black Lincolns driven by white chauffeurs, they aren't jewel thieves who look like Cary Grant, they aren't hookers who look like Elizabeth Taylor.

It is important that you note I didn't say these people represented most of the criminals in this country, nor did I say they took most of the money taken illegally; that is done by another class entirely. They represent the population that gets itself caught.

With rare exceptions people do not go to jail just because they are guilty of something; they go to jail because they are too dumb or broke or clumsy or unlucky to stay out. And a few happen to like it there.

The people in this book have worked at a variety of occupations, all for money: turning tricks, dealing dope, heisting banks, peeling safes, writing checks, negotiating major and minor swindles, peddling hot merchandise and cold women, all that. Some are in here because I met them in prison and I think they are representative of an important

3

part of that population—people who aren't criminals so much as fuckups. A lot of fuckups are in prison.

The purpose of this book is somewhat simpler than *A Thief's Primer*: I want to let a wider spectrum of those who have been *defined* as criminal discuss in their words what seemed interesting or important aspects of being in the life (in prison or out). What I hope comes out of all this is not just a sense of what some aspects of the life are like, but also a sense of the ways the life generates its own expressive culture.

I have been curious for some time about the social dialectic in deviance—how does the process of identification as an outsider by important individuals or social agencies lead in turn to further changes in personality or behavior that are increasingly aberrant or deviant? Giving names to things really *is* important, and I think one could do a history of many complex deviant careers simply by noting the labeling sequence the individual actor experienced. A good portion of several of the interviews has to do with that labeling process—and how the individual reacted to each successive step.

I have not included much information from one-shot criminals. Nobody ever knows about the one-shot criminals who don't get caught; and the ones who do get caught and go through the law enforcement process and don't come back in are a very different group from the ones who get into the life; it is that latter group I'm after here. I wasn't interested in noncriminal murderers, for example, because I feel they are more fit for a study of rage than of crime. But when such people fit the world of prison, I did include them.

I have not included anything on drug use by students and older squares—a socialization process is involved there, several actually, but they, too, are another subject. For similar reasons, I have not included anything on political prisoners—draft resisters, Black Panthers, etc.

I have not included anything about organized crime by organized gangsters; I don't know any organized gangsters.

In the sections about pimps and prostitutes I have not included anything on the square ladies—like the ring of Long Island housewives who were busted a couple of years ago—who sometimes turn tricks, but who are in the business for a very different kind of kick than most of the whores I know.

And finally, I have not included anything about the biggest criminal group of all: all those squares who steal all the time by padding expense accounts, faking insurance accident and theft reports, developing phony neck injuries anytime anyone taps their rear fenders, taking home from the office or plant anything that isn't nailed down, fixing prices, advertising falsely. There are no abortionists, no police-men who take bribes or re-peddle confiscated dope or burglarize the apartments of raided junkies. None of these people is here.

It is hardly a secret that America is a criminal country. If by *criminal* we mean violating the criminal code, any criminal code, then we can expect to find few people who have not been guilty of some act of theft or fraud or sexual perversion or variation that could get them sent to jail for years. Most people do not get sent to jail, and there are reasons for that I shall have more to say about later.

The concern here is not with square people or people who look square or even people who pretend they are square. It is mostly about and by people who are consciously in the life, and that life isn't yours or mine, and it may not really be theirs either, but they believe it is. It is about the ones who got themselves tagged by the complex proce-dure our society has for naming someone a criminal; it consists of what they said about what happened to them, what they thought it was all about, and what they wanted to tell an outsider who usually came more or less well recommended, but was an outsider nevertheless.

The speakers talk about how they turned out in the life, what sort of things they did while in it, how they dealt with squares and with other people they considered like themselves, what they hoped to get out of it all; they also talk about what they do while they are in jail or prison and what jail or prison does to people like themselves and how they feel about all that. They talk about the different kinds of criminal one meets, the different kinds of convict one finds. They talk about armed robbery and murder and pimping and hustling and dope and gambling and conning and how to be a good or bad convict and what they think of their keepers and their fellows, what it is like doing time, what kind of social options there are and what kind of sexual ploys and roles they develop and adopt to make prison tolerable.

Several of the discussions and raps are with and by people whose main offense was being a little weird (some of the free-world homo-sexuals in the section on Queens, Punks, and Studs), being service rather than predatory criminals (the pimps Richie, Wilbur, and Jack), or being involved with dope. Dope turns up a lot in here—not only in the talks with Doc, Bebop, and the Three Ladies, but occasionally in talks with other people who got sent to jail for other reasons (several were also addicts, but Matt, for example, was a dope runner when he wasn't out using his pistol).

That is because dope turns up a lot in the life, too. There are a lot of people in the life who have been addicts or who have experimented with junk or have dealt it or had whores who used it or had crime partners or friends who have. Dope addicts tend to commit a lot of crimes, and the crimes they commit tend to be small ones because most addicts don't have adequate time or skill to work up planned and elegant jobs with grace and style; they tend to nickel–dime things like yanking the change box from a taxicab at a stop light or a purse from a subway seat through the window as the train is pulling out of the station, or boosting something from a store that can be turned to cash quickly and easily, or turning tricks. In addition, they're scoring for dope regularly, sometimes several times a day, and that means they are often walking around possessing drugs or carrying their works (needles and eyedroppers, usually), so they are doubly vulnerable. And dope addicts seem to snitch on one another a lot—that is because of the power-wedge the police can and do use against them. I don't mean the old business of dangling a shot in front of someone just going into bad withdrawal and promising him enough dope to ease his first few days in jail if he will inform on his friends (though that is done, of course), but the gambit of busting someone for dealing and offering to reduce the charge to simple possession, which in most states carries a far lighter sentence, if the addict will set up other people for arrests. This ploy doesn't work when police are after a safe burglar; a safe burglar can be snitched on only by his partner. Dope fiends can be snitched on by half the people they know, and they usually are. I know of safe burglars who have worked without a bust for fifteen years; I don't know of any dope fiends who have gone even two years without a bust.

At first I thought to set up separate chapters for matters of primary concern or activity: dope, jail, prison, robbing, hustling, punks, etc. . . . But it all melds together; they're not separate in the life and there seemed no way that wasn't completely artificial to separate them here. I have tried to structure the book so that discussions on more or less the same subject are located together. The stress in the first set of interviews is on outside activity, the life one leads on the streets; the stress in the second and third sets is on life in prison and jail. But in the first set there is talk of jail and prison, in the second and third there is talk of life on the streets. The street and prison are both part of the life. A few people appear in different sections—Ray, for example, appears first talking about work and life outside with his partner; later, he appears in the prison section talking about a sentence he did some years before in Louisiana for auto theft; Big Sal first tells about her work as a thief and madam, then in a later chapter talks about sex in a women's prison.

I remember sometimes hearing stories about good bars and pneumatic women, being told how we could go to these places and drink the good booze and groove on the groovy music and ball the pneumatic ladies. Sometimes I went with some people when they were on the streets and found the attractions depressingly grubby. It *is* a grubby existence, as a rule. And after you sit there and drink with the other characters and talk about other people you know who have disappeared or are locked up or on the run or dead or perhaps even making it somewhere, there isn't much else to talk about, so everybody gets high on booze or pills or grass and watches a pro football game someplace there is a color TV, or balls someone and *then* watches the pro football game on the color TV, or if there is no game and nothing else to talk about and you don't feel like balling anymore you drink or smoke or pill yourself insensate or even unconscious. In this world everybody seems to sleep a lot, sex is too often completely lacking in affect, and the kicks found the rest of the time never seem to satisfy very long.

The movies make such a to-do about the life, and television is even more fantastic. Crooks always have these neat apartments, lovely women, everybody is witty and knows which fork to use.

In the life, you don't live in neat pads, as a rule. Often you don't ever live anywhere for very long; you move and move and then move again. You live somewhere for a while, then the cops come in and bust the place up and take your bankroll and stereo and TV set (and sometimes don't even bother to charge you with anything after doing all that) and you go get yourself another place, another stereo, another TV set. The women you hustle are women who are willing to be hustled by people like you—second-run acrylic. The conversation is about booze and dope and getting laid and football and how much so-and-so took off such-and-such a joint last week and how somebody got busted. All that sophisticated, heady stuff. Yagh.

You hustle for a living and everyone you meet hustles you. The cops shake you down, the lawyers take what the cops didn't get, the women expect the money to be there and to hell with you if you're not bringing it in. In this world precious little is done for love. I think couples like Nick and Margie McMurphy, or the kind of sustaining relationship Big Sal kept with her men, even when they were sent off to do long bits or were on their way to the chair, are rare in the life—usually relationships are transitory, epidermal, and conditional.

And if you're a woman in this kind of world—good grief, the men you've got to deal with. The image of the Lady in Crime—again from movies and TV and the press—is that marvelous fantasy: the gunmoll Bonnie Parker who looks like Faye Dunaway; the wizard call girl; everybody has flashing hair and very good teeth.

Most women I know who hustle do it because they need the money. Many are addicts; a lot who aren't are between hooks; a few do it to keep some man happy. Of all the whores I've met I don't think I've found more than two or three who *really* liked the work, at least not consciously, and those two or three were middle class women on a very curious trip indeed.

In a way, this book came about by accident. I had started out collecting prison folklore—I was after the songs, stories, argot, and folkways of what I saw as a folk community of a special kind. The interviews were at first incidental to that, mainly to fill in background. If they happened to contain a lot of random material, I considered the time and tape worthwhile for my own information and because it was easier than stopping everybody to say, "No, not that, what I'm after is . . ." I decided it would be easy enough when I got home to pick out what I was after. I was not investigating social structure, the roles, the prerogatives, who does what to whom. Not at first, anyway. Then I understood it was impossible to understand the folklore without at least attempting to understand the society itself, without trying to find out something about the life as lived. Because I was not approaching people as a sociologist, the questions I asked were sometimes not the ones one "ought" to have asked, so I sometimes happened to get answers I wouldn't have gotten ordinarily.

Why did so many of the people talk as much as they did? First, there was a natural selection involved: many inmates never came near me; some types, even in prisons where I am well known and get on well, still won't—they don't ever talk to outsiders. Others, after my first visit had passed and no one got in any trouble for anything that was said (and someone always said something he shouldn't have), decided I was all right and let it be known that they would talk with me if I wanted to talk with them. I wasn't a cop, I wasn't a lawyer, I wasn't a newspaper reporter—I was just someone who was interested, without passing judgment, without wanting anything anyone didn't want to give. So we got on. (Once I was even checked out. The first time I visited Missouri Penitentiary I was still in graduate school; I went with a friend, Frederic Fleron, Jr., who was a grad student in political science at Indiana. To avoid difficulty, I had written the warden beforehand that Fritz was going to come along. The second day there, one inmate asked if I still lived on that second-floor apartment on 5th Street in Bloomington; he turned to Fritz and asked if he was still in his South Fess Street apartment; then he asked me how the new baby was. Fritz and I were astounded. The man said, "We had you checked out. You checked out okay, so we'll talk to you." We never found out how they had managed it.)

While working on these manuscripts I noticed some differences in my own techniques over the years. In the early tapes (1962–1963), I seemed to talk a lot. I occasionally gave opinions. These were often more conversations than interviews. Later on, I tended to adopt a far more passive role with all save the most taciturn informants. I learned along the way that the questions you ask structure the statements you get, not only in form but in content and focus, so I decided to ask as few questions as possible and to make those as general as possible so the speaker could decide what he considered important enough to talk about. That is necessary if you want to get what *he* thinks important, rather than what he thinks *you* think is important. I usually found, after the conversation started, an occasional "Hmm," or "Oh" or a puzzled expression was enough.

There are stages for anyone doing work like this. In the beginning you know so little you don't even know what questions to ask, so you must be silent while you learn the language. Then you learn what you think is the language and go off chatting with it, trying it out, refining definitions, poking into gray areas. Then comes a period of diminishing returns, for you are focusing on your questions rather than their concerns. That's when you shut up and just listen again.

When people talk to me about this work—students or other faculty people mostly—they rarely ask me why someone spoke to me the way he did (which I was always curious about), but rather, "How did you get them to let you in?", "them" being the prison authorities. There is a queer assumption in America that our official institutions are closed to us even when our purpose is completely legitimate; sometimes I suspect one of the main reasons so many things do get kept secret is simply because we are willing to believe there is some reason why they should be secret.

I got into prisons simply by writing a warden or prison director, telling him I was studying prison culture, and asking if I might visit his prison with my tape recorder. The farther north I was, the more restrictions seemed to be imposed on my movements; the most open prison, the one in which I had complete freedom of movement and complete access to documents, was in Texas, and I therefore did the majority of my work there. I have been kept out of only three prisons: New York's Sing Sing and Attica prisons, and California's San Quentin. Warden Denno at Sing Sing responded to my inquiry with a letter I still cannot translate fully, but his main objection to my visit seemed to be that since the prison was full of criminals it was no place for anyone to be doing research. San Quentin's Warden Nelson refused to let me speak with any of his inmates in 1971 (after the San Quentin shootout and the Attica massacre) because, he said, he didn't want to jeopardize them; I was working for *The New York Times* then and pointed out I'd never heard of anyone getting in trouble with other inmates because he'd talked with a reporter—in fact, one of the demands in all the inmate riots during the previous two years had been access to representatives of the press. He shrugged his shoulders and said he wouldn't risk his inmates. I never tried getting into Attica, but in the spring of 1970 I got a smuggled message from an inmate who said some inmates had me on a list of people they wanted to invite to give seminars and lead discussion groups. But Warden Mancusi crossed my name off the list, presumably because I had previously written about prison problems in *The Times* and he didn't want anyone writing about problems in Attica. Other reporters managed to visit the place later, however.

I went to the prisons and wandered around inside and talked with people. Usually I found some private place to talk—under a tree, in a corner of a work area, sitting in someone's cell late at night, in the kitchen—places the guards weren't and where it was unlikely we'd be overheard even by electronic listening devices, if there were any.

I was in only one women's prison; it was too difficult for me. I got on fine with the inmates, there was no problem or silliness about there being a man around, but the administration and guards nearly went bananas every time I walked up and down the hall. I remember sitting in a counseling room with three women talking about dope; the side of the room facing the hallway was glass from about knee-height up. The table was wide, easily four feet. Two of the women sat on one side of the table, one sat at the end. I sat on the side against the wall. About every ten minutes a guard came by, pretending not to look, and found some excuse to bend over and make sure there was no hanky-panky going on under the table. We were all sitting back in our chairs, and the table, as I said, was about four feet wide. Not nearly so wide, it turned out, as the flaming imaginations of those guards.

In Massachusetts the helpfulness was counter-productive. Walpole Prison had in the past cooperated with a number of local colleges—it had been visited by many students working on theses, student trainees, professors working on articles, surveys, studies, experiments, everything had gone on there. They had set up a procedure: I was allowed to use an office in the psychology section of the front building; it was as if I were one of the staff. Which, of course, was no good at all: rather than a help, this was a hindrance, for it was almost impossible to establish rapport with inmates except in a very few instances. I couldn't wander around the work areas and cellblocks the way I usually do. (I remember one incident, sitting under those fluorescent lights in that air-conditioned room, talking with an inmate about an escape plot that had just been busted. He leaned against the microphone in front of him and whispered, "We should be careful what we talk about. This room might be bugged.") But that physical restrictiveness was only half the problem in Massachusetts: most of the inmates who would talk freely seemed to be men who had had experience with sociologists in the past. Most questions elicited answers that sounded as if they had been culled from standard criminology textbooks. I asked a few why they talked like that and they said they had read a lot in standard criminology textbooks they had borrowed from the students. Some of the Massachusetts interviews are very good—I have included two here—but after a while I found working there so frustrating I spent more time in Texas where there were no restrictions on my movements and no sociology students to give everyone all the right answers.

Usually the work was like such work on the outside: relaxed and interesting. I can think of only one spooky incident. It happened in Missouri Penitentiary in Jefferson City.

It was a summer night full of mosquitoes up from the Missouri at the far end of the lower yard. I stood on a pile of rubble separating a pair of long, low buildings that looked as if they should house rows of lathes or drill presses. One was the prison chapel, the other the band and athletic equipment storage building. The rubble was a reminder of a riot that had taken place several years before. It had lasted several days, cost several million dollars, resulted in several deaths, scores of injuries, and a change in the prison's administration. I had heard about the riot on other occasions, but just a few hours earlier I had spoken for some time with a small man in his early thirties, said to have been one of the ringleaders. His sentence had originally been a short one; his sentence was now life because of a murder charge for something that had happened during the riot. Without discussing his part in it, he told me how the rioters had ripped out the brick wall of death row to get to an informer who was kept there in protective custody because it was the safest place in the prison. Anywhere else, the administration feared, the man would be killed, but death row was impenetrable; no one could get past the guards or the multiple sets of special steel doors. No one, of course, ever considered that anyone would simply bash down the brick wall. Almost no one.

The men on death sentence were invited to join the riot. One, awaiting the chair for a killing spree, refused, saying he'd rather take a chance on a last-minute reprieve; he got it, reportedly in part because he refused to break out. The rioters went on down the line and found their man. They cut out his tongue with a straight razor and held his head back until he strangled to death on his own blood.

The man described it to me in a flat voice. It was a long time ago, another world.

But much of the rubble was still here, some of the destroyed buildings had yet to be rebuilt. He shrugged, as used to the rubble as he was to the wall and gun turrets. Shifting back, he told me he had caught a bullet in his foot the second day of the riot, walked with it until the riot was starved or burned or blasted out several days later and the troopers came in and began rounding people up. During the interrogation, the police didn't hit him as they did some of the others; they only stepped on his foot from time to time.

Then it was time for him to make a count and we did not talk anymore. I recorded some men in the chapel. A large man with a mattock wandered in while we were making the last tape and said, swinging the mattock as one might gesture with a cigar, "Why you recording them creeps?" I told him. He said I'd do much better recording two other men.

"Go over to the band office and tell them I said send them over," I said.

"I can't."

"Why not?"

"They don't let me in there."

"Tell them I said it's all right."

"No. No. Better not. They don't let me in there after what I did."

"Well, call in through the window." He went off, swinging his mattock.

"Who's he?" I asked the men in the room who had said not a word all this time.

"He's a fucking nut, that's who he is."

"Yeah," another man said. "That's why they don't let him over there."

They were obviously discomfited. I had seen them called creeps and they had not responded. Nuts have prerogatives in prison, but they didn't know if I knew that or not. Our session broke down into awkwardness and we decided to resume the next day.

I looked at my watch. It was almost time for me to leave. But I had only one more day; what if the mattock man really did turn up someone good? I knew the day shift would go off soon and the third-shift guards didn't know what time I was supposed to leave, so I decided to stay where I was and finish up.

Soon he came back with two men—a fiddler and a guitar player —and he was right, the recording session was excellent. Then it was time for another count and they went back to their cells. I began stowing my equipment, taking with me only the tapes recorded that day, which, even though I doubted anyone would do anything with them during the night, I always took with me when I left and locked up outside the prison.

It had just become night and between the two low buildings where the riot had in part exploded it was very dark. I picked my way among the stones and cracked bricks. Except for a silhouetted guard in one of the towers on a far wall I saw no one. Below me the great prison yard was deserted, bleaker and more desolate than it was in daytime.

The quiet was suddenly splintered by the wail of a siren. It hung over the yard for a moment, then found its focus and pierced everything. I felt it in my teeth. I froze, thinking, "Now the shooting will start."

It did. First a couple of single shots, then a long burst from a machine gun.

I saw it all: what an end to a moderately promising academic career. How would my wife explain it all to the family—after all, I was teaching freshmen how to read and write, innocently vacationing and making tapes. I knew most of my colleagues would be too busy to attend the funeral. Alas.

And should I survive? The thought crossed my mind and I considered for a moment going back for my tape recorder. What a set of tapes that would be! But I'd need a power outlet, it wasn't a battery-operated machine. I was too far away from the action to do any taping. I decided I'd best turn my attention to getting myself somewhere

where the action wasn't. Then it occurred to me to determine just where the action *was*. And I noticed it was quiet again. How long? I couldn't tell if I'd been standing there twenty seconds or half the night.

I heard the siren again. Not so loud as before. And another noise. Applause. Applause?

I came round the longer of the two buildings and found what I now knew must be there: about two hundred inmates sitting in folding chairs watching a cops-and-robbers movie. The projector operator saw me and came over to say hello. I hoped it was dark enough so he couldn't see how red I knew my face was. The men clapped at something.

"Them guys," he said. "They know how it's going to end. Just like the Indians. Our side never wins."

I bade him a fair evening and went off to consider my callowness and the dangers of too long a working day coupled with too vivid an imagination. In the future both would have to be restrained.

I should say something about how the information in this book is stacked.

First, there is the natural selection: the people with the intelligent raps here happen to be people who can rap intelligently. I have no idea what portion of the free and imprisoned criminal population they represent. For all I know, 90 percent of the convicts in a joint and 90 percent of the hustlers on the streets are inarticulate and un-self-reflective. But I don't *think* that is the case. I can't prove it, but I don't think it is so. Too many people, it turns out, really can tell their own story well; they can't tell any others well, perhaps, and they can't extrapolate very far from their own experiences, perhaps, but they can run down that one story with a splendidness that is theirs alone. I try to let them do that in here.

Second, there is the editorial work done on the transcriptions from the original tapes. I selected from among many conversations the ones I would print, and that selection no doubt reflects certain biases. It clearly reflects a bias toward the articulate. It probably reflects a bias toward what must evolve as a certain sense of what the criminal and convict milieus are like. I admit to that: I do think I know what the convict milieu is and I do think I know what the criminal world in the streets is like, and I think the voices heard here represent and articulate or challenge those ideas. It is from these people I learned most of what I know about the life. The loading is in the direction of my teachers' perceptions and experiences and interests; all students do that.

There are editorial doings of a somewhat more prosaic nature. I have corrected some grammar—mostly when I felt a printed error would give an unfair or unrealistic impression of what the person sounded like (given the difference we all demonstrate in spoken and written English), and I have excised some of those false starts we all make when we speak.

When I found statements I thought might lead to trouble for the speaker or someone else, I fuzzed enough of the facts to make sure that trouble didn't happen; I tried to make sure I did not also destroy the import of the remarks. When it was a choice between endangering someone and introducing an egregious distortion, I dropped the bit of data. I edited out a lot of my questions when they didn't have any appreciable effect on the data coming across; I left my questions in (they are the lines in italics) when they are important, where they have content, or where they redirected the conversation. I changed all the speakers' names. That was to protect the guilty; the innocent, as Kurt Vonnegut has pointed out, don't need such protection.

I shifted around some sections of the discussions so they seem more coherent than they in fact were. I feel this is legitimate—in conversation we have the option of reintroducing topics dropped earlier; we have the tangential urge that sets us off on Homeric appositions; we have the vocal inflections and hand and face signals that let us bring things back after a long excursion elsewhere. In print these things are distracting and confusing, in speech they are perfectly natural and comfortable; conversations enjoy a Brownian motion print can't handle very well. So, if we talked about something for a while and then wandered off to something else and then returned to the first subject, or if we talked about the same topic on different occasions two or three times over a year or two, I may have shifted sections so it seems that we talked about one thing all at once.

It will be obvious to you when the speakers are rationalizing or posing or bullshitting. I think these rationalizations or affectations are important. If we are concerned with what moves people to do the things they do, then facts are important, but perception of facts is often more important, and interpretation of perceptions can be more important still. Even lies—however transparent—tell us something: people only lie about what matters, or what they think matters. But most of the talks are fairly straight—given the slight twisting done by people to make themselves decent in motive to themselves. In any personal account—criminals here, but also in the autobiography of a president—you must remember that in one's own scenario one is never the bad guy.

People do that realigning all the time, and the way they present themselves is as much a social fact as any deed they may have done at any concrete place and specific time in the past. If nothing else, it gives you the way they prefer to regard their experience, their track in this world. And there is some importance to that.

Some things are deliberately left out of this book. I haven't tried to tell much about the contexts in which we talked. Most of the conversations were in prisons, as I said, places where I usually had a free run and there were no guards around. But it was prison nevertheless, and that influences what talk goes on, however much one is trusted. Some of the conversations took place outside. It didn't seem to make a great deal of difference, really, but I thought I should mention that for those for whom such qualifications are important. I might have written here about steaming nights on the Houston docks with Red chasing down a Mexican whore with whom he'd been living but who was now giving him a curious runaround; about meeting Doc between commitments; about meeting a girl in one town who had been a freak-trick whore in another and how we had, on the spot, to conjure up an imagined relationship in San Francisco five years earlier when I was a student there (I never was) and she was a dancer there (she never was) to explain to her new square friends and her unbearably square husband why we should happen to know one another and be greeting each other like long lost friends and why we had those silly smiles when we talked about people we knew (other "students" and "dancers"); about sitting on a curb in an East St. Louis alley rapping with a funny man named Radio who sang one song over and over and over again and his friend Johnny Hondo (really: Johnny Hondo) who carried in one hip pocket a pint of rye whiskey and in the other a pint of 7-Up and he alternated swigs as people went in and out of the shooting gallery behind us; about sitting on the beach in Venice with a dozen addicts and ex-addicts talking about the life, in and out, while a bunch of kids gathered about us and we wound up with $34-worth of Chicken Delight. All that is another book, I think, not really this one. My book. This one is theirs, so except for introductory comments I shall keep out.

2. The street

Sometimes I find crime a lot like door-to-door selling: it seems easy, it seems to require little talent, yet few people ever do it well, and few manage to stick with it very long. In both fields there are mobs of amateurs trying to make it, many because there seems nothing else to do; there are also losers who haven't made it doing anything else. But door-to-door selling and crime are hard work. To do either well requires intelligence, adaptability, and perseverance. Not many people have those qualities in abundance, and most of those who do have them find remunerative employment with more job security than either crime or door-to-door selling has to offer.

Most people who do well at criminal activity are called businessmen; they are called businessmen because that is what they are. We don't call them criminals because, for a variety of reasons, they escape the labeling process. More and more I have come to believe that a criminal is not someone who has done any act, however gross or heinous or grabbing, but rather someone who somewhere along the way has been *named* as criminal, who has had the Finger pointed at him and the Magic Marker make its perfectly indelible X in the center of his brow.

A criminal career comprises not only acts of crime, but a style of living. Distortions in any criminal's account of himself tend to occur most when he relates aspects of his relationship with the style. The acts themselves are verifiable (with minor discrepancies allowed: a thief might claim more jobs than he actually pulled, he might exaggerate the size of his income, he might minimize his terrors), and the crafts involved in obtaining other people's money without their consent are well known. What cannot be known is how a specific thief or a specific hustler really relates to the perquisites and requisites of his life situation; there is not only the problem of his relationship with his listeners, but also of his honesty with himself.

The speakers in this chapter worked at a variety of occupations, they filled a variety of roles—killer, robber, con man, dope dealer, madam, burglar—and they tell us the way they remember some of the facts about their working lives, or what they would like us to believe

19

were the facts of their working lives, and what they would like us to know about their attitudes toward those facts. Each presents the self he considers or wants considered his outside self, and that is a *fact*, one not open to adjudication.

I mentioned in the Introduction that dope is one of the paradigmatic elements in the life. Several addicts in this chapter discuss different kinds of involvement with dope. Bebop, the jazz musician, talks about how he would love to live in peace with it forever; the three women talk about how their inability to escape dope kept them from any life-style but the criminal, and Doc, the dentist who went to Yale, talks about how drugs gradually took over his world.

Doc's is a classic story, but it is one rarely told in public: the professional man who for a while gets his drugs through legal channels (Doc used drugs he had around his office at first) and treats himself for a real or nearly real painful physical condition, who stays on dope after that physical condition is past and for a while uses squares' channels for moderately illegal scoring (false prescriptions in his case), but still functions professionally, then, when those channels close down, turns to illegal sources, and involves himself in the entire criminal cycle.

Bebop—in his conversation if not in his life—is committed to dope in a way none of the other speakers here admits. The others either pretend to themselves they are not really addicts or would do anything not to be, but Bebop has it all worked out: dope, he tells us, won't make anyone do anything he wouldn't ordinarily do, but withdrawal gets many dope fiends to act in ways antithetical to their real character; for him the enemy is withdrawal, not dope. There is some truth in that: the junkie doesn't steal when he's in the corner nodding, only when he's scuffling for enough money to buy enough dope to get back in the corner nodding again. Bebop several times claims he is just talking, he isn't arguing with a "reformer," or someone like that, but that isn't really true: Bebop is *always* talking to a potential reformer and always comes out with that elaborate rationale. As a kind of idealization of the dope fiend's world his rap is important, but it is also important that Matt, the closemouthed gunman and dope runner, agreed to tape an interview mainly because he was so annoyed when he heard Bebop carrying on about junk's virtues when I was talking about dope with four inmates one afternoon.

It is usually said that junkies are mostly people who have flopped in everything else they've done, and dope for them is the final copout. I find that an oversimplification. It is true that many dope fiends haven't made it elsewhere (the crop of addicts coming home from Vietnam are a new aspect and I don't include them in these generalizations), but we shouldn't forget that being an addict is very hard work indeed. One must hustle every day, all the time. I suspect one attraction addiction offers people who have failed in large ways or who have failed to integrate themselves into the large system is that addiction consists of a series of small successes and offers a compelling smaller system in which the addict makes out very well. Each day a junkie must score enough dope to shoot up four times or so; he may do that all at once, he may have to find four dealers; each day he must get enough money for those scores; he may do that at one shot, he may have to score money several different times in several different ways. A lot of needs, a lot of need fulfillings, a lot of little successes. That is an important aspect of the life, one that is sometimes as hard to kick as junk itself; success is always hard to give up wherever you are in the system.

The other speakers in this section illustrate different kinds of relationships with the life. Some are professionals, some are aberrant, some are still incapable of understanding why they got into trouble, some considered trouble a risk just like the risks a regular businessman takes. Bob and Ray are professional robbers; they studied, planned, weighed alternatives. Slim Wilson—gambler, pimp, hobo, soldier—isn't so much a criminal as a roustabout; his life-style leads him into situations in which he gets into trouble, his world of chasing the dice and running his whores, a world in which there is no moral center but making it, no tomorrow, no basic plan other than that somewhere each night he will lay his head down for some rest, a world in which anything is possible.

Matt is black middle class. He ran dope, but only for the money; he never used dope and doesn't sympathize with people who do. He worked as a robber and gunman for the same reason he carried those packages of narcotics across the country: money.

One law enforcement official who has known Chinaman for over thirty years told me he felt Chinaman was one of the most dangerous people he'd ever known, but Chinaman has a perfectly logical rationale for each of his three attempted murder convictions and his one homicide. All those events make perfect sense to him, and the notion that perhaps one should not be in situations where one is shooting at people never intruded on him. He considers himself unlucky, but he is only partially right; had he been lucky enough to be a good shot he might have gone to the chair thirty years ago.

Larry Kent is a con man, he tells us that much. The problem with a con man is that you—and sometimes even he—never know quite how much of his rap is true and how much is con. It may be true that Kent had a driver and wore civilian clothes when he first went to the Texas prisons, but I haven't been able to find any corroborating evidence for this; his remembrance that the old days were rather nice is nonsense: Texas prisons in those days were utter hell: the food was bad, the buildings wretched, the guards brutal. It may be true that he is an electrical engineer, but Newark College of Engineering, where he claims to have taken a degree, never heard of him. But a lot of what he says does check out. I looked at his file and found he was on Federal probation, which was revoked once; he was in fourteen separate jails (with one escape); he was in seven different state prisons. He admits to forty-five arrests; his FBI check turned up only forty-one of these. His record lists convictions for mail fraud, vagrancy, bad checks, embezzlement, con game; the only entry about his military career is "Deserted U.S. Army, never caught." His present sentence is for bad checks he dropped at a gas station. I included the entire conversation with him because the important thing with a con man isn't the particular truth or falsehood he may be delivering at any particular moment, but the style of the rap he lays down. And the style is apparent in Kent's interview.

Except for Jack, the other speakers need no introductory comment; they tell their own stories directly and clearly. Jack is anomalous as a pimp: he really grooves on having sex with the whores he runs, and I get the feeling about him that he is like the candy lover who buys himself a candy store. In theory the latter is in business, just as the man who sells fertilizer or auto mufflers, but there is a difference—he has a relationship with the merchandise the others cannot share. Jack has a relationship with his whores that most pimps do not —he seems to groove on them sexually *because* of the work they do, rather than in spite of it. The other two pimps, Richie and Wilbur, both present what is probably the norm of the whore/pimp sexual relationship: you avoid it when you can, because, they figure, having the woman see the man as dependent on her in *any* way—even if it is a result of her craft and art—reduces the man's ability to control her. I know many people in the life who are with hustling women, but I would not classify them as pimps. A pimp is someone who keeps the woman working, who takes her money, who presumably handles her little hassles for her. I know characters who have women who occasionally go out and turn tricks—especially when their man is in jail—

or who run up on a whore and have a relationship with her and happen to take her money. But taking the money is secondary there, it is the sex and company the character is after, the money is a bonus; the man does not define himself as a pimp and I wouldn't either. To be a pimp requires that one perceive oneself as such, and because of the role's low status in the white criminal world and its high status in the black street world, no one makes the claim casually.

The word "criminal" identifies not a specific kind or style of behavior, but rather the way certain actions and kinds of actions are formally evaluated in a specific culture at a specific time. *Crime* is not so much a physical fact as it is a relationship, one between act and attitude toward the act. The label of *criminal* is affixed to the actor not because he acted in a certain way but because his society makes certain inferences about his motives when he acted.

This is most clearly illustrated by the various ways our society regards the killing of one human being by another. Killing is murder in a narrowly defined set of circumstances only; in most cases killing goes on with the endorsement of one's society and is regarded as proper and perhaps even laudable; in many cases it is considered an unavoidable accident and no culpability follows.

If one kills another person without intent and through no fault or carelessness of one's own (a drunk runs into the road from between two parked cars on a rainy night and is hit by a driver going under the speed limit; a boxer kills his opponent in the ring; a construction worker dumps a load of steel on a place where a fellow worker wasn't supposed to be standing; a doctor makes a defensible error in judgment in the operating room), our society does not hold one liable. There are many circumstances in which one may fully intend to kill the other person but that killing is defined as justifiable or even socially desirable (the police officer defending himself or others against an armed felon, the homeowner shooting an armed intruder, the husband shooting his wife and her lover *in medias res,* the pilot dumping high explosives and jellied gasoline on what he was told are enemy camps, the state's professional executioner killing a condemned man). Sometimes the killing is technically against the law but popular sentiment rejects the definition (such as police in Chicago who entered a Black Panther hangout with guns blazing, or police in Detroit who shot up blacks in the Algiers Motel). Other kinds of killing, depending on the intentions of the killer and the posture of the killed, have been negatively sanctioned by our society in a variety of ways, ranging from relatively brief or suspended jail terms (for vehicular homicide, say), to execution (for premeditated murder, which is deliberately causing the death of another person without legal justification or social approval). The specific overt *act* in all these situations is the same—one individual directly causes the death of another—but because of the perpetrator's intentions, the victim's actions, both persons' roles in society, and the circumstances of the death, society attaches different weights and offers different responses.

We often read or talk about the *criminal* as if this were some homogeneous category, as if the word defined a personality type. It is no more useful than the word "killer," which could, given the proper circumstances, cover any of us. And it hides an important point of discrimination: one man might be noncriminal his entire life except for two minutes (when he decided to dip in the till or do in his wife) and another might engage in activity defined as criminal from puberty through senility, yet both can earn the same label.

There are many different kinds of criminal actors. Some are not at all involved in the criminal world and they earn their label by an act that is in their experience anomalous, one resulting from extraordinary conditions; these are usually called *impulse criminals.* There is a large group of technical offenders who might be called service criminals; I say technical offenders because their activities have no victims in the usual sense of the word. Though the activities are proscribed by law, the lawbreaker works with the consent and at the request of the citizenry he services; in this group would be bookies, prostitutes, dope pushers, abortionists, pimps, etc. There is also a group that offends against morality, such as homosexuals, sodomists, drug addicts, etc., and there are politcal deviants such as civil rights organizers, draft resistors, etc.

The people who make their living by criminal acts of other kinds may be classified in four categories: *habitual* or *compulsive, organized, professional,* and *career.*

The *habitual* or *compulsive criminal* or *thief* is one who steals, but for whom neither the acquisition of property nor the style of criminal life is particularly important. For this person, the act is an end in itself, though, like sex for the victim of satyriasis, it never satisfies, so he is condemned to do it again and again and again.

Organized crime covers an extremely wide range of behavior. It includes everything from the so-called Mafia or Syndicate operation to price-fixing by large, otherwise respectable, industrial concerns. The term refers to the *mode* of business activity.

Professional crime refers to the nature of the individual actor's commitment. The standard description of this kind of actor was given by sociologist Edwin H. Sutherland in *The Professional Thief* (University of Chicago Press, 1937), an autobiographical account by one thief and an interpretation of that account by Sutherland. Sutherland's definition of professional thief requires two essential elements: recognition and tutelage by other thieves.

There is a problem with that definition, for it excludes the full-time thief who was self-taught, it excludes check writers who work alone, it excludes many armed robbers who—like Bob and Ray—are especially careful to avoid other thieves. If we are to keep Sutherland's characteristics of tutelage and peer recognition as the qualifications of the professional thief, and if we want to continue using that term, we need another term for relatively successful thieves like Bob and Ray, a term that will distinguish them from the rums, the incompetents, the career convicts, the amateurs, the impetuous. I call their role that of *career thief* or criminal. The term is certainly not new—I discuss it in more detail in *A Thief's Primer*—and the above discussion suggests its most useful limits.

Life, for some criminals, is extremely discontinuous, more so than for the organized criminal or vice offender. Organized criminals have life continuity just like any other businessmen; addicts and prostitutes have sustaining symbiotic relationships with police and other criminals with whom they must deal, and the very nature of their illegal acts demands a certain regularity of movement and sometimes even clients. The prostitute has a relationship—albeit antagonistic—with her customers; the addict has to maintain his connections and he must have his daily source of dope, he must deal regularly with the police.

But the safecracker never confers with his victim, the check writer and robber confer a brief and artificial moment only; all are highly mobile; none deals with police except when he is arrested, and any relationships developing then are transitory. Some may frequent bars where criminals congregate, but meetings in such places are usually rare and unplanned. At most the working safecracker or check writer or robber has sustained contact with a very few people with whom he may be working at a particular time, his women, and with his lawyer. This relative isolation contributes to his dependence on externals for status, his tendency to spend a lot of money quickly and obviously, his attempt to make an expensive rather than "good" appearance.

In the middle class world, money is spent on things that are permanent (house in "good" section of town, art) or socially approved (gifts to charity, vacations, private schools for the children, clubs); the criminal world spends money quickly and obviously.

The successful square must be relatively stationary to make his money and exercise his class options, and his job is related to his status (money isn't enough—he must make it in a "correct" way); the thief must be mobile and ungrounded if he is to survive. The square evidences his success, and concomitantly his status, by his occupational role and his concrete possessions; the thief by visible spending. Half the thief's status parameters are not verifiable (he cannot brag about his jobs, he cannot have witnesses to his expertise), while the square can have his professional status inspected at any time (e.g., the doctor with his diplomas and certificates and licenses arrayed for your view, or the professor with his shelf of publications; thieves have no offices, they don't get certificates for jobs well done or courses passed, and they don't write for professional journals).

For most successful criminals, life is terribly lonely. Anyone you trust enough to tell the truth about yourself knows enough so that he can't really trust you. The unsuccessful criminal, of course, gets more attention than he knows how to handle.

It is curious that the image connected with crime in America, the image one gets from the press and from politicians, has little to do with what most of the people in this book did with their workaday time; the image has to do with violence: rape, murder, things like that. I find that curious because America has always been violent and convulsive; the only differences now are that minorities sometimes articulate their suffering with more success and the media reveal to us more of the evils we do or help or do not fight. Life in the ghetto has always been violent, but we did not pay much attention to that before. We have always defined out of the moral scheme those whose marbles we wanted: the Indians did not simply wander away in joy when the white man came for the land, they were driven off or shot off or carried off; the labor unions did not grow pleasantly and nicely because there was a clear need for them, the organizers had to fight everyone from the employers to Federal troops. For a time there was perhaps a wilderness edge to this country where violence was a norm, a sense of violence a survival factor, and this violence could go unnoted in the polished urban centers. Now the wilderness is in our cities. It is not new, it has just finally come home to roost.

Jerry: "The only sonofabitch around . . ."

I was in Memphis and there was a little fiasco you might call it.

I was staying with a young woman, shacking up, so to speak. Anyhow, I didn't know she was married. I was, but that was immaterial, and she was very despondent when I met her and I brought her out of the dumps.

And she brought me out of the dumps too, until a certain day when her old man showed up.

I was down in a bar just two doors over and downstairs from where she lived, and in he came waving this pistol, you see. He says, "Where is that sonofabitch?" I'm looking around for this sonofabitch and everybody is looking at me.

Knowing that you're the only sonofabitch around?

Exactly. He heads for me, you see. And he says, "You're the guy's been shacking with my wife!"

"I beg your pardon," I say, one thing and another, trying to play the cool bit, you know. The cool bit wasn't going to work—he had this pistol and was going to blow my damned head off.

So one thing led to another and he got shot and I didn't have a pistol.

I got a little charge out of that. They called it third-degree murder and that landed me in Nashville for a while.

Bob and Ray: "If it's a case of me or you . . ."

BOB: Oh that Kansas City, they'll go and make a nervous wreck out of you. Oh, those sirens.

RAY: You talk about a couple of nervous characters. I think I told you once that in Los Angeles they never use sirens except on a Code

Three, and the only other time you hear it you know it's an ambulance. The fire trucks have big claxon horns. So when you hear a siren you just don't worry about a thing, you know that it's an ambulance, or you know that there's a cop in trouble somewhere and you better move out of the road.

In Kansas City, if they're going to arrest you for jaywalking, they turn on the siren. Coffee break: *aieeeeeeeeeee*. We almost had a nervous breakdown the first two weeks we were in Kansas City. We wound up on a well-traveled corner and boyohboy . . .

One day we had a hell of a time. Bob's gone, and usually when we're separated like that, if he was downtown say, we made it a point to call every two or three hours or so. You know, checking to see what's going on. Well, I hadn't heard from him and I knew what it probably was, I knowed he was tied up with this gal, but still I was a little bit worried.

BOB: How can you quit in the middle and go to the telephone to call?

RAY: And at that time I heard *aieeeee* coming closer and closer. Well, the front of the apartment had this little horseshoe drive, and the window from our bedroom, the bay window right over this drive, and I look down Farmer because it looks like that's where the sound is coming from. I'm looking down and it comes closer and closer, and it slows down, pulls up in front of the driveway.

I head for this .380 of mine, it's over in a holster just by the bed. I come up with that thing and I bashed one into the chamber and I headed for the window again and I thought, "Shall I stay here or shall I head for the roof?"

I look out the window again and all they've used the driveway for was a U-turn. They're gone back in the other direction.

BOB: Normally, when we're just home from a robbery the police cars are out looking for the car we used on the robbery, if they're looking for anything at all, not for the car we owned.

We would steal a car and use that, and then we'd ditch it after the job. We'd drive it six or eight blocks away and get into our own car. Sometimes I'd actually back into the place so they'd be sure to get the license number, I'd pull in hard so they'd get a good look at the car, and then by the time they found that car we're back home.

Our getaway car was a ten-year-old Plymouth. It had a hand paint-job on it. We bought it on time payments for $150 to be paid off weekly and we never did get it paid off.

Who would look for a pair of robbers like us in a car like that?

We'd steal a nice big Ford or Mercury or something for this robbery and then switch back to our car on the way home. We've had to pull off on the side of the road and let the cops pass on the call they were on and wonder if maybe it was us they were after. We get home and turn on the transistors and listen to the police calls. Usually they find the car about the time we get home. They'd spot the car and just close in on it. We never got into any trouble at all.

What we did was, we never got in or out of a car both of us at the same time. One would get out, cop the car, the other would drive our car somewhere, get out, the first one would pick him up, and then we'd go off and do the holdup, then afterwards we'd reverse that. So nobody ever saw the two of us together getting in or out of a car except at the scene of the robbery.

The only time we had any difficulties at all was coming back from a place one morning and we were on the Hollywood Freeway and we timed it so we'd beat the traffic but we were late and we hit right in the middle of the traffic and so I'm trying to get over on the right side to make this cutoff. We'd already switched cars and were in our own car. So I cut up close a couple of times. Now Ray's got all this money sitting there on his lap, he's got his gun laying over there on his leg, I got my gun in my belt, and I hear this guy yell, "Hey!"

So I look out the window and he looks out the window, and there's a cop right out there. A police car has pulled up right beside us and he says, "Next time I see you cutting traffic like that you're going to get a ticket." I reached down and pulled the hammer back on this thing. There's only that one cop in the police car. "I could stop now if it wasn't so busy," he says, "I'd stop right now. You watch it."

I says, "Yes, sir," and switched the gearshift.

He'll never know how close he came. Just because we were a little late coming home from that robbery.

Would you have shot him?

If we couldn't have broken through, I'd have had to. But we made it. The point is that we didn't want to hurt anybody, but if it's a case of me or you it's going to be you.

I was on the Marine Corps rifle team, I'm an expert pistol shot, at least I was at that time. And I'm afraid that it's yes, I would.

Had I ever come into a place and the guy tried to play hero with me and grabbed a gun, I would have killed him. I always figured that if I shoot somebody I'm not going to shoot him to wound him or let him point me out later. They always say there's more of a chance to getting more time if he's dead than if he's alive, but there's also more of a chance of going to jail if he's alive and there's been a shooting and you'll get a long time away on that. I didn't want to hurt anybody. And we tried our best not to, which means we never did. But if it ever comes up or down to the brass tacks, I'm afraid I would have to.

RAY: We pulled a little thing one morning.

The woman working there had a heart condition and her lips turned purple. *Purple!* She was really scared, and it nearly scared me to death. I knew that if she would die it would be the same as if I had put that gun up to her head and pulled the trigger. I asked her what the trouble was right away and she couldn't talk and this other guy told me, "Well, she has heart trouble." I asked if she had any pills and he said, "Yeah, I think she does." I snatched her purse and I got her out some glycerine pills. I took her over to the couch, set her down, patted her hand, got her a glass of water. Believe me, I worked over that woman.

BOB: I'm spending all this time working on opening the safe. I say, "Is she all right?" And he's patting her on the back.

RAY: I was there about half an hour with her.

BOB: It was a public place, I mean the public could walk in and out. But nobody came in.

RAY: If they had, they just would have had to wait. Boy, I just wasn't about to let that woman die.

As Bob said, we've been at this for quite a little while. This is the first time we got caught and we got two five-year sentences run concurrently. In other words, we do the five years together. It's just like having one five-year sentence.

Now Jack over there, he's never been in any trouble at all before this time, never done anything wrong before this time. He was married, had a couple of kids, lived a pretty decent life, got himself tied up somehow and had to have some money. Picked up a gun, went out to a tavern, held the tavern up, ran into a hero. A drunken hero. Come running out of the place and tries to jump Jack, screaming at him and jumping. So Jack comes up with his gun, shoots and kills the guy.

He's doing life. Now I, being a part of all this, I don't see the fairness of something like that. True, we didn't kill anybody, but all in all, I just can't see it.

You're in on armed robbery?

Yes.

The usual sentence for that is ten to a quarter. How come you got only five?

Pictures. The secret of getting less time is pictures [money].
Other professionals I know take care to have some money salted away.

We got two fives and they were talking twenty-five. That was on two armed robberies. It cost us what we had, plus I owe my grandmother some. I can always pay her back—that's one good job.

BOB: Pictures, they work very good. Other things help, too.

When we got arrested on this, California comes in and they want to talk with us about sixty-seven armed robberies. So they called us down to this room and this guy comes in and says, "I want to talk to you guys about a job in California."

I figure he's going to set us up with something, so I say, "What do you want us to pull?"

He says, "No, it's not quite that way. I got a small list here"—and he takes out a stack of papers about three inches high—"and they want you to go down and check off the ones that you did."

Well, I just cracked up. I said, "What are you, some kind of nut or something? You just want me to check them off for you and initial them too?"

"No," he says, "just check off the ones."

"Well, what's going to happen? Are you going to drop the charges on us?"

He said, "Well, I don't know what they're going to do. They just want to know which ones you've pulled."

I says, "Yeah, you and Kansas and Missouri and a bunch of other states would like to know that. I don't recognize any of these as ours. Nope. Sorry."

I think there's maybe two on the list we didn't pull.

After a couple of visits he finally says, "Cop to certain ones and we'll drop the charges." Now we already had a detainer on us from St. Joe, Missouri, and one from Kansas and a Federal detainer. So I said we'd do it and I copped nine of them. My partner gave him a couple that weren't even on the lists to show him we were in good faith and everything.

RAY: But we never initialed anything. We just told him, "All right, you want some: these are the ones."

BOB: We said, "We'll go down the list and check them off for you." And of course we could've just started with the first nine, but we went through picking here and there to make it look good. So they did it. California dropped all its charges. We've got no charges against us whatsoever now.

RAY: They're very good about that. Some states are very good. If they tell you they'll do something, they will. This Federal man, the time we were picked up on this charge—we were picked up for a bank job we didn't do and then got convicted for some things we did do—we also had a stolen car that we'd brought from California.

BOB: It was a Chevy. A very nice little car.

RAY: So of course we had mickeymouse papers on it. They were false but they were good. I mean, they appeared good.

This friend of ours in Los Angeles, he takes the body plate off the door and makes a new plate. And he makes the registration to match that plate. He leaves the motor number and all that the same. Now you can't sell the car because when you do that the motor numbers are checked, but for $85 you get all the papers you need and so long as you pay your parking tickets you're clear. They can tag you a thousand times and it doesn't matter. And you have a new car every year for $85. You get tired of it, you just drive it off a cliff into the ocean and what have you lost? Just $85 and what else can you do with $85 nowadays.

And for an extra $100 he'll even steal the car for you.

BOB: Let me talk about the police station in Kansas City. He comes home drunk in Kansas City and we're driving a stolen car we got in Santa Barbara, California. It belonged to some gal in Palm Springs. He comes home drunk one morning, parks it, and they tow it away. We went out in the morning and I said, "Where did you park it?"

"Beats me," he says, "I think I parked it there." We got a cab and went all over the neighborhood looking for our car. He might have parked it anywhere within six blocks.

So we called the police station and gave them the license—the same as we got on it in California. We never changed the plates. And they said, "We got it, just bring proof of ownership."

So he goes there and he's got to go up to the auto theft division to get the car. They say, "You got proof of ownership?" And he hands them the registration. What I did was take the registration off an old car we had and just tore it evenly with another one and put the two pieces together. Which gave all the information on her car on top with the motor number, and at the bottom was our names. I put a piece of white tape across the back because the printing on the back didn't match up. But this white tape didn't match either, so it was fine. So the guy says, "Yeah, what's your license number?" And he says, "Well, it should be on there somewhere," and he takes the registration out of its folder, opens it up, turns it over, and says, "Oh yeah, here it is in the corner." The cop says, "You can pay the fine here. The car's at the garage."

He pays the fine and then they *drove* him down to the garage and he got our car and came home.

RAY: But this Federal agent, when they were talking to us about this bank robbery, he said, "Now I *know* you did that." What had happened, they got a partial little fingerprint at this bank job. There's two other fellows and myself that it matched up on. They eliminated the other two real quickly and they can't find me, so right away they think it's me. So then, checking further, they find out Bob's with me. We both fit the general description and so the FBI thinks, "Aha, we got these two." But I'm telling you, man, we *never* hit a bank. Never.

BOB: We stayed away from the Federal whenever we could.
They get serious about it.

Well, they got all the money, you know. The state, you can really beat the state. You got a chance against the state government, but not against the Federal.

RAY: So I told him, "What day was this supposed to be pulled?" He tells me and I tell him, "Well, you can forget about me. I was in the Los Angeles county jail." Which I was. And I say, "And my partner, he was working a job every day where he had to hit a time clock." So he had that. Before he left he said, "Well, I'll tell you, if you're telling me the truth I'll see to it that no charges are added." So after we were up here about a month here comes a big fat detainer from the Federal authorities. We fired him a letter back real quick and he didn't even answer, he just dropped the detainer like he said he would.

We had another detainer in St. Joseph, Missouri, for a supermarket holdup and we never been to St. Joe. They got a 188-day law where they got to try you within 188 days in the same state or drop it. They wrote back, "We know you're guilty, we're just closing our books on it by writing in you're guilty." They cleared up their books. Charged us with it and as far as they're concerned we're guilty.

We still got a detainer on us in Kansas for armed robbery. But they couldn't extradite us on it because there's not enough evidence. The reason there's not enough evidence is we didn't do it.

RAY: We almost had it in Kansas City. They converged on us as if we were Al Capone. We were driving down the street and all of a sudden there's all these city squad cars. One down in front, one in the back, one alongside. And there's this one guy right outside the window.

BOB: He sticks his shotgun in my window and says, "Don't move!"

I says, "Man, are you kidding?"

RAY: There was another one laying over the hood, pointing his shotgun right through the window at me, and he says, "Don't move." And this clown says, "Something wrong, Officer?"

The cop said, "Leave your car here."

I said, "You're crazy. That means we'll have to come all the way back here to get it back."

He kind of hesitated a minute and said, "Well, what you want us to do?"

I said, "I'll drive it so we can just leave the station with it." So he lets us both get in the car and we start off with one police car in front and one in back.

All we're doing is looking for the first side street. We're going about a block and, all of a sudden, sirens screaming and yelling, they pull us over to the curb and this one finally comes over to me and says, "You get on and come back here with us."

The first light and we would have been gone; they left us both in the car, can you imagine that?

What made me mad is we almost got away from them. We talked our way out of it damn near after they stopped us, convinced them we weren't who they wanted. But they looked through the car. The woman we stole the car from was a thief, see. In the trunk was about three pillowcases full of towels that she'd stolen from all the motels she'd stayed at, all these towels with motel names on them, and there were so many it looked suspicious and they took us in because of that. I hate a thief.

BOB: We didn't want to hurt anybody. We've had plenty of opportunities to hurt people, but we never did. That's one thing that Brown has always said to us: "Go ahead. One of these days you'll slip. You have yourself some fun, so long as you aren't hurting citizens. You hurt one of my Los Angeles citizens, you sonofabitch, I'll put you in jail."

RAY: They won't look for you for twenty-four hours after a holdup. They haven't got enough men on the police force.

BOB: But they will arrest you and make you quit.

RAY: They have to catch you for that. They know that you're not going to quit and that they'll get you eventually. But if you hurt somebody, kill somebody, hit a cop or anything like that, then all the stops are out. It's all out to get you. As long as it's a straight holdup and nobody gets hurt and nobody's feathers are ruffled, they don't bug you about it.

BOB: They've pulled some beautiful stakeouts there. They've killed some eleven holdup men out there in seven days.

RAY: They were staking out these liquor stores because so many liquor store robberies were happening out there. They started to set up cops in the back rooms. A guy walks in and tries to pull a gun, the first thing he sees is *boom*. This one guy, he killed four stickup men himself. He actually outdrew them, outdrew and killed all four. And they gave him a good citizen's award. Got in the papers and everything. One day a customer was in and he was telling him about it and this guy comes in and says, "Are you Mr. So-and-So," and the storeowner says, "Yeah," and the guy goes *boom-boom-boom-boom-boom*. Walks up to the cash register and leaves him with five bullets in his chest.

BOB: You'd be surprised. Some of them do bad things. I mean bad things you never hear about. This guy held up a place one day and he was spotted by a cop on a three-wheeler checking around downtown. The cop took off after the car. The guy pulled into a side street, did a quick turn, and comes up broadside into this three-wheeler, he gets out of his car, beats the cop up, pours gas all over the cop, and sets fire to him. And not a soul came out of the house where people were watching.

RAY: How about that guy who came into a liquor store in Los Angeles with two .44s strapped low on his leg. They looked innocent, so silly, like kids' toys. And when the old clerk asks him, "Can I help you," he says, "Yeah," and goes *boom*. So there's a customer standing there and the guy looks disgusted at the customer and goes *boom* at him too. Goes up, cleans up the cash register, and drove off. And they never did catch him. Two of them .44s strapped low on the leg. Like Wild Bill Hickok. He come in and whipped out both of them. Hit them right on the head and yelled *boom* and cleaned out the till. They got some lulus out there in California, I tell you.

To show you how stupid people can be, let me tell you about this one job.

The Hibernian National Bank in New Orleans was held up by four armed men and they got away with about $42,000. Two of them are still serving time—nobody you know, by the way. One guy I met in L.A. claimed he was a part of it but I know the other three and I don't think he really had anything to do with it. But he tried his best to convince me. Some guys are like that.

Anyway, these four, none of them had a record for felony. A few minor arrests, but nothing serious, no real records. Just to show you how stupid people can be, even though they were able to pull this job off successfully and not hurt anyone in the bank, they didn't have to hurt a soul and got away with the money and weren't even chased.

Police threw a cordon around New Orleans and tried their best to keep them in the city. One of them who wasn't from New Orleans, he talked his uncle into putting him into his trunk and his uncle drove him across the bridge all the way to Biloxi in the trunk. And he got out of town pretty quick without difficulty, so he's laying low.

They gave him their permission to cut and said, "Go ahead if you want to leave." But the rest of them was sitting tight. One of them was a cabdriver. He got in his cab and went to work. One was cooking in a downtown hotel. They all went to their jobs. Cool and real nice.

This guy in Biloxi gets to drinking and picks him up a whore. Whore sees he's got some money and says she'd like to go to Chicago. Okay, now up to this point, even this isn't too bad. Anybody's liable to feel a little excited at the moment with all that money. That was $42,000, which meant each guy had about ten grand.

So he says, "Okay, I'll take you to Chicago."

But instead of taking a bus, a train, or a plane, he hires a *taxicab* to drive him to Chicago, Illinois, from Biloxi, Mississippi!

Now everybody in the South knows this bank has been robbed. So the driver goes ahead and drives him all the way to Chicago, collects his fare, and goes straight to the FBI.

The boys got twenty-five years in the Federal and twenty-five years in the state pen. They did their state time and one of them is now doing time in Leavenworth and the other is in Atlanta. I guess they're in separate places because they're a little rough on each other when they get together.

(It's not double jeopardy by the way. The state can try you for armed robbery and the Federal for holding up a bank.)

RAY: I've noticed that with holdups men get more excited than women. I remember the cutest old thing in a supermarket. She didn't get shook up at all. When they go, when they *do* get excited, they get hysterical, but on the whole I think women are a lot more calm than men.

BOB: Once we were at a counter and I'm standing by the register and Ray's behind me and there's a guy behind him reading a *TV Guide*. When we left he was still standing there reading the *TV Guide*. Never noticed a thing.

RAY: And so Bob was getting the money and he tells her, "It's a holdup."

You know what she says? She says, "Oh, shit." Twenty-four, twenty-five years old, you know, and giving it out, she says, "Oh, shit." And starts taking the money out. Now is that any way for a nice lady to talk? So Bob goes out and gets in the car and I waited until it was started up, then I told her, "Now you just stay where you are, honey, until I get out of here. Don't worry about a thing."

BOB: I was checking traffic there and when I was ready I tooted my horn for him to come out.

RAY: And this guy, he's still reading his *TV Guide.* He never did know what was going on.

So we get into the car and I just happened to turn around and I says to him, "Look, look back there, Bob." And he slows the car so I could turn around and look more and here's this cute little old head sticking around the corner, looking at the goddamn license plates. All she had was her head, just part of it, sticking around the corner trying to get a license plate. She was cute; I wanted to go back and see if I couldn't date her sometime.

BOB: We went into a bar one night and this old broad was behind the bar and she said, "What do *you* want?"

"This is a holdup."

She says, "Oh, Jesus Christ!" She threw a beer bottle in the back.

Ray says, "Where's the money?"

"The fucking money's in the safe."

No manners whatsoever. She's just storming, heaving beer bottles. About fifty years old.

And then she gave descriptions of us. Said we were both five-foot-seven—and we're both over six feet—and weigh approximately 140, and had on Levis, white T-shirts, and black leather jackets. And we never owned that combination in our life. And then she put in a claim for about $2,000 more than we got.

You'd be surprised how much more money is claimed than you actually get. About the only one we found that was definitely honest is Safeway. They got us for $1,665.10. And we didn't get the dime, we didn't take change at all. We just took the cash. Sixteen hundred of it in ones. Have you ever tried to spend $1,600 in $1 bills?

RAY: Oh, we were mad.

BOB: I thought we were hitting the jackpot. This guy just put handfuls of the stuff into bags.

At first we couldn't get the safe open. It was his first day as manager and he's got the combination in his wallet. He's got to turn it like this—he turns and misses it. We say, "What's the matter?"

The man says, "This is my first day."

There's about seven cash registers and I got about half of them empty. An old lady about sixty years old comes up with her cart, so we interrupt what we're doing and check her out, we let the guy check her out and she goes out the door—

RAY:—she never did know what wa going on.

BOB: So I'm on the last cash register and this Falstaff man comes up. He's been loading bottles in the back and he says, "Hey, what's going on?"

I say, "Just stand right there."

"What for?"

"It's a holdup."

He says, "Oh. *Yeah.* Right." And he stops, you know.

I'm looking over at the manager and see he's taking money out of the safe, his hands are full, it's all in bundles, you know. Jesus Christ, we done hit the jackpot. We are going to retire. So we get into the car and I ask Ray, "How'd we do?" And he says, "I think we got enough to retire on." That sack was just bulging with bills. So we get to the apartment, up it down on the couch, and it's all ones. Goddamn $1 bills.

RAY: We sat and looked at each other for about fifteen minutes and then we started cussing. And all that night we were trying to get rid of ones.

BOB: This is funny. We go out to a bar, see, and he heads one way and I head the other. Go out and get a drink and you say, "Hey, can you give me a ten for these singles?" You can't cash too many, maybe at most twenty, of them at a bar. You can't take them to the bank. You can't run down to the bank and says, "Hey, how about giving me some twenties for these sixteen hundred singles?" They'd arrest you right there. So I buy a drink and I get something and I get tens and twenties and he's out doing the same thing.

I get home about two o'clock in the morning. I still got a lot of ones left. He comes staggering in about two thirty and I says, "Did you get rid of many?"

He says, "Who the fuck *cares?*" He couldn't even see.

RAY: And I passed up some real nice little thing that night because all I kept thinking was, "I don't dare let her see me with all these ones." My pockets were full of them, bundled in here and there, about six hundred of them.

BOB: He comes in and I say, "Did you get rid of many?"
He says, "Who the fuck *cares?*" Boy, he's drunker than a skunk.
Just staggering around.

RAY: I tell you, the whole thing depends on the first impression
you give. We found that out within the first four weeks.

BOB: We were always very polite. We hardly ever cussed on the
job or anything like that.

RAY: And if you're very determined you don't even have to pull
that gun. He almost always shows his gun—

BOB:—but he very seldom shows he's got one.

RAY: I'll just open my jacket so they see it and that's it.

BOB: And we're usually very polite about it. I always say, "Yes,
sir," "No, sir," and "Thank you." And I tell them, "Sir, this is a
holdup. Now I hate to cause you any trouble but if you cause me any
trouble I'll blow your fucking brains out, sir." It usually works out real
good.

RAY: Every once in a while we'll do something just to throw them
off. Like we'll go into some jive talk.

BOB: One supermarket in Kansas City we did that. The manager
was in the back. We figured he'd be there. Back of these swinging
doors. So I walked up to the clerk and said, "My name is Johnson.
They called me that I had a check returned here. Could I pick it
up?"

"Well, you got to talk to the manager, sir." Which we knew. So
he buzzed the buzzer and the manager said to send me on back there
where he was.

I went through the swinging doors at the back of the store—you
know how they are in those big Safeways—and there are these two
Falstaff guys loading bottles on a truck, they're on my right. The manager and the clerk are on my left with their backs to me. I put my gun
out right in front of me so those Falstaff guys wouldn't see and I
tapped them both on the shoulder and I said, "Hey, daddy-o, like
man, this is a heist. Now step back, dad." And I headed them toward
the front. "Now no noise, please, cool, man." We got up to the front
and I said, "Okay. You, big daddy, you're the wheel. You hit them
over the safe, you help that cat over there. Make it with the cash register there." And we'll do that just for kicks, it throws them off a little
bit. They go off looking for somebody else.

We never talk like that ourselves, but it helps once in a while. I
used to call him George every once in a while. "Hey, George."

RAY: And I used to call him Clyde. I used to say, "What do you want, Clyde?"

BOB: Clyde Pugh. We used to have a ball. You think up things as you go.

RAY: Oh, we had us a ball. We used to tip good at restaurants.

BOB: Diamond Jim is a big one over on Hollywood Boulevard. He had about 180 people waiting for a table one night but he spotted us coming in and so we were first. I always slipped the man there some money and he knew us.

RAY: The whole thing's kind of juvenile in a way; I mean, it's just a way of getting recognition.

BOB: We're trying to keep the depression from setting in. You see, we get the money that's stored up and we spread it out thinly, and then it all gets stored up until we grab it and spread it out again. It keeps California from getting a recession. We're strong believers that nobody should accumulate all the wealth.

BOB: When we started with our first robbery, if it hadn't been successful we would have probably quit. A lot of times people will hit a place and get just $40 or $50. We got $7,200 on the first one.

We were broke at the time. If it had been someplace where we got $30 or $50 we might have hung up right there and said, "The bother isn't worth it." I don't know. Have you ever had $7,200 in cash in your hand at one time?

RAY: And no bills to pay . . .

BOB: . . . no taxes . . .

RAY: . . . just the money, there in your hands?

BOB: We had $15 to pay for room rent and that was it, that was all we had.

You'd be surprised how something like that will change your outlook. I seriously think if you had been with us or if I could take you out to California right now and put this kind of money in your hands, take you out and let you rob somebody and see how easy it is, and show you how it is twice as easy the next time, I mean, you'd be surprised how much money is out there, you know, if I could show you that stuff, your attitude would change too.

Of course we got busted. We were at it four years to the month before we were ever busted. I'd been arrested numerous times, questioned, but no convictions. That's all it was. They say our record looked like a Mickey Spillane novel, but no convictions. When you get that kind of money it's awful hard to do without it. Especially when you can spend it however you want and you don't even have income tax to pay. You want to go down and buy yourself a cashmere sports coat, like I did, for $200, you run down and buy yourself a sports coat.

BOB: When my partner and I first decided to go into crime, the first thing that we had to decide was just what branch of crime to go into. You've got car theft, you've got burglary, stealing, stealing money or rolling drunks or whatever you call that, armed robbery, what else . . .

RAY: A number of things.

BOB: Checks. Having past experience in them which was rather disastrous I gave that up.

RAY: Backtrack here. You might be interested in our mental attitude at this particular time. I mean why we even considered going into crime at all.

I had been separated a few months from my wife; Bob had left number three or four at the time. I'd lost an exceptionally good job and had been blackballed for a year in my field because they'd found out I'd done time some years back on auto theft. Had a little trouble over a little bit of embezzlement that was embarrassing and pulled out. We were at a pretty low ebb, because we knew that using our own names and giving our own backgrounds and everything we couldn't do what we were used to doing and have the amount of money that we were used to making. So we were forced to do something in order to live in the manner to which we'd become accustomed.

BOB: Not actually *forced* of course. We weren't broke, we were far from out. We had a little bit of money and I had a job at the time. And I think you'd just lost one?

RAY: Yeah.

BOB: I've never had any trouble getting a job. Anybody can work, but of course I don't dig working. I mean, not that type of manual work. And then when we got together and talked it over and decided that in order to get the amount of money we wanted in the shortest time, that crime was the way to get it.

And crime, we feel, is just like any other business. In other words, there's setbacks in crime and there's deficits, just like you run a business and there's a chance that you might burn down or you might go bankrupt or your employee might have embezzled everything you got without the insurance to cover it, and it's the same way with crime.

Of course the penalty for going bankrupt in crime is much stiffer, but at the same time your material gain is much more than it is in a regular business.

When we decided to go into crime, we were both what you might call inexperienced criminals at the time, so we decided that to decide what branch we wanted to go into we should first do as much research as we could and find out which made the most money the fastest and percentage-wise was the safest.

I think you'll find that every public library in the city has the statistics on the number of crimes committed the previous year, approximate value of each crime, and you could figure out from the number or amount stolen, the number of crooks caught, the number of convicted, all types of things, what was best for you. We spent four days at the public library and researched and we come up with armed robbery as the best.

Now you've got to take this into consideration: there are crimes that are pulled and got away with, but one man might have pulled twenty armed robberies before he's caught, so they got him on one and there's nineteen unsolved. Statistics-wise it looks like everybody's getting away, but actually they're not. And you've got to take that into consideration when you check into it.

RAY: We found that armed robbery is by far the best as far as getting away with it is concerned. Unlike burglary or breaking and entering, you don't take anything that you have to convert into cash, thereby putting something into somebody else's hands, and you're taking nothing but money, which is spendable any damn place, I don't care where you go, that money's going to be good. And unlike stealing cars, you don't have to worry about transporting the car to wherever you're going to sell it, and unlike strong-armed robbery—which I tried once—you don't have to worry about knocking some sonofagun in the head and maybe causing him a hell of an injury or maybe even killing him when you didn't even intend to. But still, there is always that chance.

BOB: There's that possibility in armed robbery, too. Of having to shoot somebody.

RAY: We discussed this a great deal. What we would do if and when. And luckily, in all this time, there's only been one or two slight instances where we've had to worry about it. And I think we came out with flying colors. We could have very easily killed a couple of people, but we never did.

BOB: We made up our minds to begin with: if we ever got surrounded and in the position where the police said, "Come out with your hands up," that we would come out with our hands up. There's none of this Custer's Last Stand type bit. If I walked into a place and the man actually got the drop on me where I knew if I tried to shoot him he was going to shoot me, then I'm giving up because I can see no point in getting killed. And I'm not the hero type. In other words, I'm somewhat of a physical coward or I wouldn't pick up a gun in the first place. That's the way I look at it.

But we're not heroes and we took all this into consideration before we ever went into it. And as I said, after we did our research and we settled on armed robbery, then the thing we decided was we had to have some weapons. I mean, if you're going to armed-rob somebody you're going to have something to armed-rob with. Neither one of us had any weapons at the time. And the easiest way to get them was to go buy them. So we did that. We went out and bought one to begin with, one between the two of us.

RAY: That's interesting too, especially with all this gun-control talk nowadays.

So many people say it's hard for a man intent on something like this to be able to arm himself. It really is the simplest thing in the world. We got our first weapons on the West Coast. Both of us had records in Los Angeles, in the city. Yet we went to a town out in the county and there was a very thorough check made in the town where we bought the guns, but simply to see if we'd ever been in trouble in *that* particular town. That's as far as they checked.

BOB: We went in and we bought the gun and we paid for it. It was almost our last dollars at the time. And we bought a box of ammunition. The ammunition they let us take with us. The gun they kept for seventy-two hours. So we had to come back three days later to pick up the gun. Three days later I came back and they said, "Here's your gun, thank you very much." And that was it. That was a Friday. Friday night we pulled our first holdup.

Another thing that came up when we were discussing crime and stuff is what we were going to rob. After we decided to go into armed robbery and decided we'd need a gun and went out and bought the gun, we had three days to wait. So then the question came up, who and what we should rob. Was it your idea or mine to pick the place?

RAY: I think the first one was yours. We decided from the first that we wouldn't limit ourselves for several reasons. But mainly because that's the simplest way to get an M.O., modus operandi. If you stick to just one type of place that's where they're going to be looking.

BOB: In other words, not one robbery, but one type. If you run around robbing all liquor stores or all supermarkets or all hotels. Our first one was a service station that cashed payroll checks. I happened to be in the place two or three times before when I'd worked as an accountant nearby, but time enough before that the new man wouldn't know me. We looked it over three or four times, we went down and checked it out, and of course we knew he picked up his bank deposits for the bank money on Friday to cash payroll checks Friday night, Saturday and Saturday night, and Sunday. There's a lot of big businesses around there that get paid on Friday and they'd come in there and cash their payroll checks. From being in there before I knew approximately what time he came back from the bank. So we just waited for him.

That day he came back and we relieved him of his money in the same bank bag he'd brought it in and we left.

It wasn't a spur-of-the-moment robbery. Nor was it a real planned robbery, I mean one that was rehearsed. We played it by ear. Every robbery—no matter how much you've rehearsed it—you've got things come up you didn't look forward to or into. And you've got to be, I guess you'd call it cool enough to play these things by ear and handle them as you go.

Each one of us has more or less a certain assignment in a robbery. In one particular supermarket we robbed my job was to get the manager and get the money. Ray's job was to keep an eye on everybody else. I was so intent upon this manager when I was getting the money that one of the clerks walked up from the back room and he walked not ten feet from me and I didn't see him. Of course my partner did, and he proceeded right there to take care of him, keep him at bay, so to speak. But I was so intent upon my job there and I know my back was taken care of that I didn't have to worry about anything else that I never seen the man and he wasn't ten feet away from me and almost in my line of sight. I had no idea at all that he was there because it wasn't my job to watch him. That was his job.

RAY: One thing that kept us out of trouble all those years, probably the main thing, was we never once went back to any old hangout. We never went back to the old bunch we used to hang around with.

BOB: You'll find in crime you move in different circles. In other words, when you first start off, you're a working man and you're accustomed to $70 or $100 a week take-home pay, whatever it is. And when you get the extra amount to where you can afford to spend $200 a week, well, you're way up. But it don't last long, maybe six weeks or two months. And then you get accustomed to that $200 and you start looking for something a little bigger and better to hit. Which you do. And then you move up into the $300-a-week spending bracket. And this continues, there's no stoppage. It's a plane that just keeps advancing. And as you advance, your mode of living and your clothes change in accordance with it, and your apartment changes. And you can't go back. In other words, if we went back to the first places we hung out, the first cocktail lounges and stuff when we were making $100 a week, and were going in there in a $500-a-week suit, somebody says, "Mmm, what's going on?" We're driving a new car, wearing new clothes, we got tailor-made clothes on, I got a monogrammed silk shirt on, and right away you get raised eyebrows.

So you got to drop your friends, too. What friends you make at each level, you got to leave at that level. You just disappear. That's what we always did and I think that's one of the things kept us out of trouble so long.

Of course, at the stage we were living at when we left Los Angeles, about the only way we could of got any higher was to rob Fort Knox. But I couldn't find a way to get in there.

RAY: We never even associated with thieves or anything. If we had to have anything to do with them, we did it and that was it. We never ran around with them.

BOB: If we needed a third man or something, we'd call Eddie and Eddie would fix us up with somebody.

RAY: But we never socialized with those people.

BOB: We got this one idiot for a driver, but he couldn't even drive. Oh, man, what a waste of time he was. Scared, nervous, pale. He come over with the car and squealed around the corner. I said, "Man, we can't speed or anything like that, we got to take it easy. What's the matter, is the car acting up?"

He says, "No, I don't know how to drive."

I said, "I figured it was something like that." I moved behind the wheel and we gave him his cut for doing nothing. All he did was sit in the car. And I had to move him over and drove myself. So he watched the car—big deal. Anybody can watch a car. Got $250 for it.

There was a supermarket out in Santa Monica. It's a square market and there's a door on two sides with the parking on a side and in the back. The reason the doors are where they are is right between them is a big L-shaped magazine rack.

We found out from a friend of ours that this guy cashes payroll checks for one of the big plants near there. So we went down about nine thirty one night, parked in the parking lot right by the door, and there wasn't anybody there but the manager and one clerk standing at the cash register. We knew all the money was in the cash registers. We walk in and there's a man over there reading magazines, flipping through the pages. So I told Ray, "Be sure to watch him." He says, "Okay, and you keep an eye on him too."

I walked up to the manager and he says, "Can I help you?"

I says, "Yeah, this is a holdup."

And he says, "No. No, no!"

I says, "Yes. Yes, yes!"

And he goes, "No, no, no, no."

And I says, "Yes, yes, yes, yes."

So Ray says, "This is getting silly. You open up that cash register!"

So I pushed him aside and Ray went around to the other one and he's holding the gun on the clerk. We had trouble getting our hands on the money. You get it out of one drawer and I'm stuffing it in my shirt and I couldn't lay my gun down. I got both pockets full and my shirt's stuffed full, and Ray's got a handful, and we start backing up and I turn around, and the guy at the magazine rack is gone. I told Ray, "Let's get out of here." I figured that guy went to call the police.

So we hit out the side door real quick and he's not five feet in front of us, he must have just left, see, and he's walking down the side-walk and going, "Wishh, shh, wishhh," his old arms just swinging and him trying to whistle and just getting these funny hissing noises out, not whistling a note but he's trying like hell.

We get in the car there and he walks across and he gets in his car and he turns on the overhead light when he gets in and he folds his arms across his chest and lays his head back on the seat and sits there real still, not moving, his eyes closed.

RAY: He's letting us know he's not going to do anything wrong.

BOB: We drove by him and we turned left on up the street and went on, and I heard these tires squeal and brakes go and I look back and there he is, turning right. Really hitting them. I thought sure we'd been had when that guy left, I thought he'd call the fuzz for sure. But he didn't want nothing to do with us, he just kept moving.

RAY: And the sneaky sonofabitch didn't pay for that magazine either.

BOB: He stole that magazine, too. It was *Argosy*.

RAY: He walked out into the heat of the night with that *Argosy*.

BOB: It's been funny out there. This one guy we robbed, it was at a hotel. He was only the clerk there and it was his first night on duty. Walked in and pulled out the guns and said, "This is a holdup."

He said, "Oh, yes, sir." He opened the door to the back room, turned the light on, put his hands behind him in just the right position. Ray went on and taped him up, we took the money and left. Wasn't in there a minute. He was very cooperative, a fine fellow.

We had a pretty good way of splitting money, Ray and I. We had a drawer in our desk at home and we usually kept about $2,000 in it. We had a safe deposit box too. When he'd go out or I'd go out at night, we'd take what we thought we needed, anywhere from $50 to $200 usually. When we came back in the morning, what was left over we'd put back in the drawer. When the drawer got down to $200, we'd stop down at the bank and bring it up to $2,000 again. And that was it.

I never knew what he spent, and he never knew what I spent. We never knew what we spent. The only thing we discussed is when he wanted to buy his girl a $700 stereo set she wanted, something with stereo hi-fi and FM and tape. Fine: we went down and bought it. And I bought mine an outfit to go out in. And so on. That sort of thing we'd discuss. But our evening's expenses, a date, always ran from $50 up, but usually it wasn't much more than $60 or so. A lot of times we didn't go out, we'd stay together. But that's the way we handled our money. That way we were never worried about "Did he get his cut?" or "Did I get my cut?" or "Is he spending more than me?" Really, we didn't know.

When you're going out three or four nights a week, you can't keep track of how much you spend anyway. And there was no reason to bother with it. When we got low, we'd get money from the bank safe deposit box, and when the safe deposit box got low we'd go out and get it filled up.

We got three places in one day one time; I robbed one at eight thirty in the morning and one at two o'clock in the afternoon and he hit one at nine o'clock that night.

RAY: We were busy that day.

BOB: We were in three different parts of town. Three different places and three different cars. All three of those places had the money on the same day and it was either hit them now or wait a week. Financially we couldn't wait, so he hit one and I hit the other two. Boom, boom, boom. I was tired that night. It takes a lot of energy.

RAY: It does. There's a certain strain that you feel physically when it's over with.

BOB: Actually the physical labor was very slight. But it was exciting. A very exciting day.

RAY: It's kind of nerve-wracking.

BOB: Next day we went to Santa Barbara for the yacht races. We'd meet a lot of people. We met Billy Wilder, the producer, at a cocktail party. And Jeannie Crane. And this mystery character, what's his name—Vincent Price. We'd never seen movie stars before those days. It was the money that did it. It was all the same color. Live it up was what we did.

RAY: It's like a kid at camp, you know.

Once we hadn't been back but fifteen minutes from this robbery, an early morning thing, and all of a sudden there's all kinds of commotion in the neighborhood. There's sirens, and in Los Angeles they never use a siren unless it's a Code Three, which is "Come to the aid of another police officer." That's the only time the police ever use a siren in L.A.

I thought, "My God, man, something's happening. The Martians must have attacked or something." They're converging from all over the place and right down at the corner. There's a big Catholic church and they're right in front of the church and the service station there and everything. And we're wondering what in the hell is going on. We think, it couldn't be us because then they'd be down here, they wouldn't be down at that end of the block. So we scoot on up to the apartment, we're sitting up there, and all this commotion is starting. We hear whistles blowing, people running around and everything.

And there's a big knock on the door. We just look at each other: we don't know what to do. Bob looks at me and I finally say, "Well, you better go answer the door." He goes to the door and there's a uniformed cop standing. I ease back in the bedroom real quick.

Had you taken your guns off yet?

I'd just put them in the bedroom, they're hanging up in there. So I cruise back in the bedroom real quick. I hear this cop panting, all out of breath, and I hear him say to Bob, "Did you see two fellas?" And I think, if it's us he's after he wouldn't be *asking* us. So I stick my head around the door and what it turned out was, there's this little greasy spoon right around the corner, little hamburger joint and chili parlor. Two sonofaguns had gone in and held up the place with double-barreled shotguns, ran off on foot! They got a total of about $8.40.

BOB: No car, no nothing, they just headed on down the street.

RAY: Right behind our apartment building the Hollywood Hills begin. And they had taken off, as the old saying goes, they headed for the hills. What the police wanted, they wanted to know if we saw any-body and if they could have our permission to check our garage downstairs in case they were hiding in there.

BOB: I was twelve years older when he left.

RAY: We were nervous, oh, man.

There was always something happening in that neighborhood, and it was a very expensive neighborhood, too, that's what used to get me.

BOB: We lived in a thirty-unit apartment building there, and twenty-three of them were filled by women, with one or two women in each apartment. I don't know of two that were working, I mean that I ever seen go to work and come home. We had Dutch doors on the front of our apartment and the first thing you'd see when you walk in our apartment was a bar that was on the right, a cocktail bar there with five stools on it. We were home most of the day and the landlady thought we owned a restaurant. When we got the apartment I was managing one at the time and I took her and her husband down there a few times for dinner, and then we "sold it," and was then getting our finances together. And everybody seemed to stop in there for a drink. Our door was open and we had liquor there all the time and they'd come in and help themselves.

One Saturday morning about ten o'clock the two gals that lived down the walk from us, they stopped by and had a drink. About that time Phil come up, he's a guy that lived down there, he's an ex-bookie. And Shirley and Marty come over and then a couple of others. And by two o'clock in the afternoon there's about fifteen people in the apartment all living it up and having a ball. We had dates that night and nobody seemed to mind when we left. They were still there. We got home about two o'clock Sunday morning and the party's still going, only they've added about six people. Ain't missed us a bit. They're drinking up all this booze we'd stolen, you know. We went in the bedroom and there's about six people crapped out in the bedroom, everybody's asleep just having a ball. So we went down to the Holly-wood Roosevelt Hotel and got us a room, stayed all night, come back home about eleven o'clock Sunday morning and the party's still going on.

RAY: They hadn't even missed us that night.

BOB: They didn't even know we was gone. So about five o'clock that night we kicked everybody out and got the maid in to clean up the apartment. And they didn't know we'd been there and gone. They really enjoyed it.

RAY: The two gals we were going with. They didn't have any idea what we were doing. They knew there was something—

BOB:—they knew we were crooks, that's what.

RAY: Everybody out there is into something anyway. They usually find out by experience if somebody is putting out the money just keep the mouth shut and let it go at that.

This one he was going with was a cute little old thing. Had a fake ponytail and when she had that ponytail on she looked like she was about sixteen years old.

BOB: Built like a brick pagoda.

RAY: And of course anybody that laid down that $25 or $50 Shirley would turn over real quick. We were all pretty close. I'm down at the pool one day and she comes storming across the walk and madder 'n hell, and I says, "Where you heading to?" She come around to where she could talk to me.

Now there was this queer hairdresser she had a deal with. He'd fix her hair and she'd give him a little bit. A weekly deal.

Give him what, I thought you said he was queer?

Well, he was, but he's not *that* queer. You should have seen Shirley.

Anyway, he'd been working on her phony hairpiece and he'd ruined it. He'd put too much something on it and it all frizzled up and she's mad. "And he's not gonna buy me a new one." He won't put out that $50 to get her a new ponytail.

She was always bringing her troubles to me anyway. So I said, "Well, Shirley, what in the hell can I do about it?"

She said, "Well, if you aren't any friend of mine, just forget it." She stomps off and gets about ten feet away, she turns around and comes back and says, "I had this thought."

"What's that?"

She says, "I know how I can get even with him."

BOB: Oh, this is a nice little gal.

RAY: I said, "How?"

She said, "Well, he's a hairdresser."

I said, "Yeah, you told me he's a hairdresser."

"He makes his living with his hands."

"Yeah?"

"I want you to break all the fingers in both hands."

Oh, she was a sweet thing.

Shirley comes over to the apartment one day and she's all down in the dumps. So I had to play daddy and drag it out of her. This will kill you, this is typical of this type of girl.

BOB: What we consider a dumb broad.

RAY: I said, "What's a matter, Shirley?"

"Oh, I don't know. Nothing."

"Oh, come on, something's the matter, tell me about it."

"No, well, no, I don't think I better."

"Come on, you know you're gonna tell me before the morning's over, so come on and tell me."

"Well, I went to the doctor this morning."

"So what's the matter?"

"I got this little inflammation. You know, female troubles."

"You been laying down too much?"

"No, no, no, just an inflammation."

"What you gotta do about it?"

"Oh, he gave me some suppositories and things. And I've gotta go back."

"What caused it?"

"Nothing important."

"Come on now, tell me. What caused it?"

"Well, about a month ago I ran out of douche powder. I didn't have anything and this trick just had left and I wanted to clean up. There was some liquid Lux and Lux is supposed to be good for anything. So for the last month I been using liquid Lux."

Now there's a testimonial for you, somewhere in there is a testimonial.

Shirley had a girlfriend and I went with her sometimes. We'd just gotten in one night about four o'clock in the morning and there's a scratching on our windows. We were just dozing off and we tried to ignore it, but they kept making so much noise we were afraid they were going to wake up everybody in the apartment house. *Bam bam* on the door. I said through the door, "What do you want?" But they keep it up: *bam bam.*

"Let us in, let us in."

I open the door and they're dressed fit to kill. All decked out.

BOB: See, their hustling must've been very poor that night.

RAY: And we told them, "You two went out to sell some of yourself and nobody was buying and so now you're back here still wanting a buck or two so it won't be a completely dead evening?"

BOB: Shirley was really money-hungry. That broad would do anything for a dollar.

RAY: A real cheer. But she was a doll, believe it or not.

BOB: Beautiful.

RAY: So anyway, Shirley as usual starts crying.

BOB: It was about like screwing a ditch, about that tight. Just awful.

RAY: So anyway, she starts crying and she says, "Oh, can I have some money, can I have some money?" And this got me, the fool.

We'd just made a hit that afternoon and we had about $10,000 in this drawer in the bedroom. So all he does is he goes in and comes out with it in his hand and he says, "You mean this stuff?"

She left the floor and leapt over to him—which was a good eight feet away—and was slurping all over him and saying, "Oh, honey . . ." He's standing there not even holding onto her, with two handfuls of fresh money.

BOB: She says, "Honey, I need $50 real bad."

I says, "I'll give you five."

"Aw, come on, Bob."

"Six."

So we finally settle on $25. We go down to her apartment so Ray and the other one could use ours and she goes to the john. I'm laying in bed there and I got the sheet up over me. She comes in and says, "Where's the money?"

I says, "Oh, I laid it around here someplace."

There's a five on the coffee table, she picked it up. She got a five off the bar and another one out from under the radio and there's one laying in the ashtray. She says, "Where's the other one?"

I pulled back the sheet and I had a rubber band around the bill strapped to my dong. "Here it is."

Boy, was she mad. She thought I was making fun of her.

The one with Ray said, "Did Bob tell you I was pretty good?"

He said, "No, to tell you the truth, he said you was pretty bad. I just wanted to find out for myself." She got mad too.

Then she said to him, "Where's my money?"

RAY: I said, "I'll pay you later." I never did pay the girl. I feel real bad about it.

BOB: She wouldn't take a check.

RAY: I felt real bad.

BOB: I'll bet you did.

Anyway, I gave her about $300 a week. I just gave it to her because she said she needed it. When we first met her I felt sorry for her. Hustling like that. But she'd spend it on nothing.

She got this one idiot to give her a credit card, one of those things that's good anyplace. She goes down and she buys a little deal that holds Kleenex, a wastebasket, and something else, and it's $43 for the crap, it was a three-piece set.

RAY: She comes in all dressed and says, "You guys need anything?"

"No," I says.

"Suits? Need any suits?"

"No," I said, we didn't need anything right then.

When she comes back in she says, "You sure you don't need anything?"

"Well, we can always use some shirts." So she goes right down and gets some two dozen shirts on this poor bastard's credit card.

BOB: Buys herself two dresses, one's $165 and the other's $120.

RAY: And I says, "That sonofabitch is going to *kill* you when they catch you."

"Aw," she says, "I'll sweet-talk him."

Next time I saw her she's got the biggest shiner I've ever seen. "See," I said, "I *told* you that somebody's going to catch up with you."

She says, "I may have to get those shirts back."

I said, "Fuck you."

This is the one I was going with. She was going to move from this Shirley. So she was afraid that Shirley might steal some of her clothes, so she gives me all of her clothes to keep in our apartment. And she's got a fabulous wardrobe.

BOB: There's two closets full of women's clothes in our place and I'm going with another girl. You ever try to explain something like that?

RAY: She was supposed to come over one night and I'm about half-tight, and she didn't come, she didn't come, and I kept waiting. I had told her before, "Now look, when you're out on a trick all you got to do is say so, don't lie to me. I know you're working for a living, you got to make a buck. Just tell me, don't horse around and give me all this bullshit."

She didn't understand how I felt about this, we hadn't been going together too long and she didn't understand how I thought about it, which was nothing to speak of.

So I wait and I wait, and I'm no Marty, so I go over and I pound on her door and I say, "Look, you told me you'd be over several hours ago. There hasn't been one peep out of you." She wouldn't open the door and I'm yelling at her through the door. I said, "Either you're over here in five minutes or every goddamn stitch of clothes is going from here to that pool."

The walk along the third floor went right over the swimming pool, so I went right over and I got as much as I could carry and went back out in the hall to that part of the walk and I started a countdown, and before I got to ten her door opened and here she comes. She didn't even stop for me. She's almost naked and heading for our apartment and stands in the door and says, "Come on, I'm here! I'm here!" She didn't want anything to happen to those clothes. She did have some fine clothes, though.

She was always something. She was from Missouri, too. And the other one was from Kansas. I don't think mentally she was above twelve years old. She had some notion that I should be *mad* about what she was doing.

BOB: 'Cause she was always turning tricks, you know.

RAY: 'Cause she was a whore. And she always felt that I should be mad. And because I wasn't she couldn't understand what kind of a person I must be. I never could get it across to her. I used to sit for hours and talk to that girl, but she never understood that I just didn't care what she did.

BOB: We didn't carry guns except when we was on a job. These two-bit hoods, they pack one around all the time and you can always see them looking out of their eye like some bad movie. We never carried a gun unless we were going out to pull a robbery.

RAY: We've always had very well-satisfied landladies and people like that.

BOB: That landlady, when we checked out to come back to Kansas City, she said, "Boys, I sure hate to lose you two. You're quiet, you don't cause us too much trouble." We had a few parties now and then, but nothing real riotous, you know. She said, "It's hard to get young businessmen like you anymore."

I told her, "Yes, ma'am, I guess it is."

She said, "If you ever come back, you be sure to look us up."

I said, "I'll surely do that."

That reminds me of the guy we robbed and had to tell him to keep the checks. We robbed a supermarket one night. There were two cash registers. One was just closed, the other one had a big line of people, so we went to the one that had just closed and the guy said, "Can I help you?"

I just opened my jacket and showed him the gun, closed my jacket, and I said, "This is a holdup. Now, no trouble or I'll be forced to shoot you."

"Oh, no trouble, sir, no, sir." *Zingg!* he opens it up.

I said, "Just put the money in a sack." Well, he's got a sheath of twenties a couple of inches thick with a whole bunch of checks in there.

And he says, "You want the checks, sir? Or can I keep them?"

"Nah, I don't want the checks. You want the checks, Ray?"

"Nah, I don't want them either."

The guy says, "Well, can I keep them? I sure appreciate that, sir. That's mighty nice of you, sir." He lays them off to the side. He says, "Not many men would do this. I sure appreciate it, sir." He's shook, you know. He puts the money in the sack and says, "You're sure I can keep these?"

"Yes."

"Well, I sure appreciate that," he says, "thank you and ya'll come back again now."

RAY: We hit this one and it was a little family affair. He had a big butcher department and a grocery department. The butcher department he leased to another fella and it was way back in the back, you couldn't see the front at all from the back. He'd just opened up and he had a nice liquor setup and everything and he'd just finished putting money in the register over at the liquor part when we come traipsing in. We'd hit him then because we knew he'd be by himself for about fifteen or twenty minutes until his wife come in.

So we got started a little bit late and mama comes trucking in. And the minute she hits that door she's yakking. She's running her mouth to him. She can't see that we've got guns. We're standing there right in front of him. She's in a little room an aisle away, she can just see our heads. It's just a little cubbyhole for hanging up galoshes and coats, you know. And he's looking over at her making all kinds of faces like he's in trouble and she just goes *babblebabblebabble*, just running off at the mouth and not paying a bit of attention to this poor sonofabitch. And he's trying to let her know that something's happening.

He has this little floor safe and he finally gets it open and takes the money out and starts counting it for us. "Five, ten, fifteen . . ."

We tell him, "You don't have to count it, sir, we'll do that. You just put it in a sack." He does that, then we say, "Now the cash register." All this time he's trying to give her a sign and she's still yakking and not paying him a bit of attention, and she was still going when we walked out. I'll bet he killed her later on.

We robbed this mortuary one morning. Why are you laughing, what's wrong with robbing a mortuary? You see, when they have a bunch of funerals over a weekend they often make people pay by cash, so you figure they're good for $2,500 or $5,000, depending on how many funerals they've had.

We went in this Sunday morning and the man had just come in and opened the safe. We walk in wearing business suits like potential customers. Ray taped him all up. Now they had this big casket laying on the floor on display there, all red velvet and plush. I wanted to put the guy in there, but Ray wouldn't let me. I wanted to lay him out. It was plush and red, beautiful red velvet and painted all pretty white. Anyway, Ray talked me out of it. I thought it would be so cute if his boys came in later and saw him all spread out like that.

Hey, you want a mink stole for your wife? For three hundred bucks? We saw this most beautiful mink stole this petty larcener had. He wanted three hundred bucks for it. Only thing is, you couldn't have worn it on the coldest night it was so hot. It would have heated up and burned.

There was this little place where we robbed a little Jew one time. He wasn't but five feet tall. He's got one of these big old safes, the big double-door things, so one day we held him up. I got the money out of the cash register and I said, "Open the safe." He runs over, wraps his arms around the safe, shaking like a leaf and as white as your shirt is in this sunlight, and says, "You're not going to take my money out of the safe."

I say, "Move, goddamnit. You gonna get hurt."

"No, I won't move."

"You gotta open it," I say.

"Knock me out," he says, "but I'm not going to open it. Shoot me, I'm not gonna open it. I'm not gonna open my safe."

So I stepped back and he just hung there on the safe and I got my gun and my partner says, "Well, what you wanna do?"

What am I going to do? I can't open the safe. If I knock him out or shoot him he can't open the safe. If there was somebody else around I could have threatened the other person and got him to open the safe, but he was the only one there.

So I says, "Fuck you, Jew," and we went home.

I think the funniest one we ever had, we hit this place one night and we missed one of the cash registers. There was just $300 in it, but it made me mad because they wrote it in the paper that we missed it. And I don't see how we overlooked it, only five feet away from the one we got and the safe. So we went back and got the place again, to pick up what we'd missed, about a month later that was. We went at six o'clock in the morning when the manager opened up and he's the only one there. Ray took him in the back room and taped him up back there and I put a white apron on and come up front to clean out the cash registers and the safe.

Just as I come out of the back room this gal comes in with a white apron on and I figured she might work here. I had a story I was going to put on her that I had just come to work that morning. But she worked at the restaurant down the street. She gets a pushcart and starts through the market, throwing stuff in the cart. I'm standing there watching and another gal comes in and says, "Give me a pack of Luckies, please." I give her the Luckies and ring up the sale and give her change. About this time the first girl comes up to the register and starts pulling groceries out. I read the prices on them and start ringing them up, about $10 worth of groceries. Well, she wants a receipt. I tell her I don't have any receipt books, the manager's gone home but will be right back.

"I'm at the restaurant down the street," she says, "and he always gives us a receipt. Will you tell him how much it is?"

"Yeah. I'll have him bring it down."

"No. I'll come back and get it in about an hour. You be sure to tell him that it's $10.30 worth of groceries."

"I sure will."

I took her money and rang it up and put it in the sack with the rest of the money. So I went in the back and he's laying on the floor so I kicked him in the side and I said, "Hey, that broad from the restaurant got $10.30 worth of groceries, she wants a receipt for it." He just mumbles away. Ray's sitting on him back there with a gun up to the side of his head so he won't try to make any noise when the customers came in. Just as casual as you please. I don't know if that girl ever got her receipt.

We filled up a couple of sacks with liquor—we were short of liquor at home—and took our sack of money and left.

I bet he figured that when those customers come in he was going to get some help then, but I just went ahead and waited on them. What would you do? There's no sense in sticking them up too.

RAY: That wouldn't be right.

BOB: No, it wouldn't.

The time before when we hit him we hit him at night. There was another guy on duty about one in the morning, he was closing up. Ray took him in the back room to tape him up and I put the apron on that time too and I went out and brought the papers in off the sidewalk, pushed the Coke machine in, like I was closing up.

Ray calls him back there and says, "Look, I want to know which nightlights to turn off and which ones to leave on." There's about three rows of switches there. And he says, "I don't want no bullshit."

The guy says, "Fourteenthirteeneleventwentyfiveseven and . . ."

"Slow down. One at a time." So he got all the lights out and he hollered at me, "You ready to go?"

I said, "Yeah, I'm all ready." So we go out the door and throw the night latch so the door locks like it's supposed to and just as it locks I see I still got this apron on. All of a sudden this spotlight hits us from the boulevard, it's a Los Angeles police car. I looked right into the light and we're both standing there with a sack in our hand and the cop stares at us and we stared back, and I waved and he waved back and he drove on down the street, and we got in our car and went on home.

They found the clerk about five o'clock in the morning. He was staring out the door all taped up. Some drunk coming along spotted him, he couldn't get out.

You must have used a lot of rolls of tape.

RAY: I used to be fast.

BOB: He could tape a man up in thirty-five seconds. And I could steal a car in less than a minute. He used to drive around two square blocks and by the time he'd get back I'd be pulling out. That's all working under the dashboard, not under the hood at all. A guy in an auto parts store made me clips for the wires.

We always used a stolen car. A cop told us that if they got us on the stolen cars alone they'd give us about two hundred years.

RAY: Where we live, as we said, right behind us was the Hollywood Hills. The street beside our house went up the hill and dead-ended there, it made a real sharp turn at the end. And that's where we used to hide our hot cars.

BOB: We'd pick up two or three in one night so we'd have them in case we wanted to use them. Just leave them parked there for any time we wanted one.

RAY: I did Louisiana time for '46 to '49 [see pp. 241–255 for his comments on that prison]. For a car. I was just a youngster then.

BOB: He jumped parole and his old man turned him in.

RAY: We don't exactly have a father-and-son relationship. Never have.

BOB: We left Los Angeles on that trip when the FBI picked us up. They had his folks' address in New Mexico where they live and when they went looking for him first place they went was Albuquerque to see his folks. We'd been there that morning, night before we'd pulled in coming back west. They come in there about eleven o'clock that day and we'd left about six that morning coming to Kansas City. We'd told his folks we was coming to Kansas City. We didn't know the FBI was looking for us. We knew we was cold in the state, the state wasn't looking for us; somebody was wanted for the things we'd been doing, but they didn't know it was us they wanted. At least I don't think they did. So we was going to stop in Wichita and see his sister. So his folks told the FBI that.

So we pulled into Wichita and the FBI had already been there talking to his sister, and his sister denied any knowledge of knowing where we were at. We found all this out from the agent after they arrested us. They'd no sooner left the sister's house than the sister and her husband came out and jumped in their car and took off someplace. Natural thing you would think was they were going to warn us, so the FBI followed them. They no sooner left and we pulled in to the sister's house and of course there's nobody home. So we left a note in the door saying we'd probably be back in a couple of weeks, we was going to Kansas City, and we no sooner pull out and they all pull in again.

RAY: It was like the Keystone Cops. Nobody meeting anybody.

BOB: They had a warrant out on us for twenty-nine days in Kansas City before they arrested us. We got picked up by the license plates. His half-brother had worked on the car and remembered the license number and told the FBI. It was a rookie cop that spotted us, he'd just read the flyer that morning, didn't even have his badge yet. He just spotted the license plate going down the street and called for help, I guess.

We were going with these two girls there. The weekend before we got arrested we went down to Lake of the Ozarks and rented one of the lodges out there and rented us one of those big sixteen-foot Cris-Crafts with an inboard engine, having a ball.

RAY: First you got to realize this: these were two very square young ladies. No idea what was going on at all. Of course we had a nice little story all strapped on them.

BOB: Yeah, we were working for International News Service. We had all the paraphernalia and all. Of course it had been defunct for several years at that time but nobody knew it. Not even us. Where we first met them was Oscar's in Kansas City, a dance place, and we took them from there up to Eddie's, which is the only big nightclub in Kansas City, and we'd wined them and dined them that whole month. Had bought them a couple of pearl rings, I think Ray bought his a locket, trinkets like that, and we got them records and stuff, out to dinner almost every night at the best places there in Kansas City. We went down to the Ozarks this one weekend to that lodge and got us the speedboat and stuff. So we're sitting around the table that Sunday and she says, "You want to know something funny?"

"Yeah. What's that?"

"You know, when we first met you, we thought you were a couple of hoods of some type."

"You *did?*"

That just busted us up, we just cracked up.

"Yeah, you were spending money and it didn't seem like you worked at all. Of course after we got to know what you did and that you only worked at certain times when they needed you we could see how everything worked out. But we were afraid of you that first week or two."

Funny thing is, the Tuesday we got picked up, we had a date with them that night; we heard from them afterwards, they told us about what happened. We were supposed to pick them up at eight o'clock but we got picked up at two o'clock in the afternoon. They turned the TV set on when they got home from work, six o'clock news was just coming on. They turn the TV on and there's our pictures. She said, "We just set there looking at each other for two hours, didn't know what to say to each other."

Chinaman: "He had the pistol in my face when I killed him . . ."

The first time I was down I come down with assault with attempt to murder. All three times I've been here for assault with attempt to murder.

Of course they put that assault with attempt to murder on me, I didn't exactly do what they said. That time. I did *this* time because when I got in the car, the fella's car that I drove off, when they drove up on me I went to get out of it and my gun went off. I hit the gun against the steering wheel and the gun went off. Well, quite naturally they put assault with attempt to murder.

Who was it the gun went off against?

A deputy sheriff.

See, as I was on my way back home—I'd been hunting and I had carried some whiskey with me hunting and I got drunk and on my way back home I come up by a store on the outskirts of town and I seen a Model A Ford sitting there. I didn't know whose car it was. I done got sick drunk and I thought I'd just get in the car and drive it on over to my brother-in-law's house. And just got in the wrong man's car.

What year was that?

1940. I was tried in '42, the fifth of May. That's when I got this life sentence.

And what were you in for the time before that?

Assault with attempt to murder. I shot a colored guy. Then I shot at another white fella.

Was that the first sentence?

The first time I was down I shot a colored guy.

What kind of sentence did you get for that?

I got a five-year sentence. That was 1935, I was twenty-one then. I spent one clean year outside since 1935, and that was the year of '41. I got this sentence the fifth of May 1942 and I been in prison ever since.

And what did you get for shooting the white guy?

I didn't shoot him. I shot *at* him. So he said. I got three years that time.

And who was he?

Who was he?

Yeah. I mean, why did you shoot him?

Claude Skelton, a white fella called Claude Skelton. I didn't exactly shoot at him. I had a old raggedy pistol and I was going to soak it to him [use it as collateral for a loan]. Well, me and him was kinda in a little argument. I wouldn't say no argument either, we was talking, and I pulled out this old pistol, one a them little old .38 breakbacks, I was gonna soak it to him for about a dollar to get me some whiskey with, but now as him and me was talking I went to unbreech it and that little old piece behind there what raises up, it hung and I took me a brick. I was drinking. I took me a brick and I hit on it and it went off and he thought I was shooting at him. And he run and I run. So the laws [police] heard the shots. And when they had my trial he told the law that we hadn't had no kind of misunderstanding—and we hadn't just exactly—but we were standing up there talking a little rough to each other. Wasn't exactly a misunderstanding and I wasn't even shooting at him. But now, as it got in the law's hands, well they put it like they wanted to put it.

Have you ever actually killed anybody?

I killed one fella.

Where?

In Robertson County.

Did you get a sentence for that?

No. The grand jury didn't even bill [indict] me. The high sheriff of that county told me wasn't nothing could be done about it because those guys was about six of them at me and they run me way down in the field where I killed that fella at and they was shooting at me. I had a shotgun, but when I made my first shot it hung up on me and I started to running. Well, I run, I would say, about a mile down across the field and when I knowed anything it was about six of 'em in a car coming down across the field at me. Well, I run on down there and I got my gun unloaded and got that hull out and I reloaded it. And about that time he was thirty feet from me, I guess. That's when I killed him. He had the pistol in my face when I killed him. But he had done shot at me a bunch a times. He had taken the first two shots at me in the beginning.

Why were they shooting at you?

See, I come from West Texas down there after some cottonpickers with a white fella. And while I was down there a boy that I know, Buddy Boltz, we went to his father's house. This colored boy's father's house. This white fella I was working for out there in West Texas, well, he was going to come down there to Calvert, Texas, to get some cottonpickers.

The boys was having a crap game at some people's house there and one of the boys was having a squabble with this boy, with Buddy Boltz, the boy that come down there with me.

And so I had my pocket knife and I was cleaning out from under my fingernails and so a guy over in front of this guy what was squabbling told that boy, the one that was sitting here under me squabbling with the boy that I come down there with, told him, "You better get up from there. That nigger behind you is going to cut you."

And so he gets up and I didn't say anything and so one 'em walked out behind me and told another one, said, "Come here," and so when he told him to come here I thought he was speaking to me. I asked him if he was speaking to me and he said, "Hell, no. The best thing you can do is get your goddamned ass away from down here."

So he broke off from the house after a pistol and I run.

I went on into town that evening and I come on back down to Miz Boltz's house. See, Miz Boltz's daughter was gonna go with us on the cottonpick. Well, these fellas that I had the round with, had the few words with, they was in town, but they was brothers to this other guy who wasn't even there when the round was.

Well, when I come back to Miz Boltz's house she told me, "Henry, I want you to go down and get Tit's things"—that was her daughter—"and bring 'em up here so you all can be ready to go in the morning."

I told her, "Okay." I said, "Miz Boltz, I'm gonna carry this gun with me just in case them guys come back from town and cut me off before I can get back. I'm going be right back as quick as I can."

So as I goes on down there I knowed these other fellas wasn't there, but I didn't know nothing about they had a brother. So as I passed the house I told this lady, there was a lady there, I told her that I didn't think them guys done me right, that I wasn't bothering none of 'em. And so I passed on. Me and her stood there and talked a few minutes. I passed on, I went by the house.

I guess I got about fifty or seventy-five yards and this other guy come out from behind the house, or come out from in the house somewhere, with that pistol. He hollered at me and told me to wait a minute. I stopped. I thought he was just gonna come down there and talk with me, you know. And he walked up for a certain distance and he come out with that pistol and told me to drop that shotgun. And I told him, "Man, you go on back to the house and don't bother me. I ain't gonna bother nobody. I ain't gonna bother you or nobody else."

So he told me, he said, "I said, drop that shotgun."

I turned around and went to walking off from him and he shot at me. And I turned around; just as I went to turn to face him, he shot at me again. Well, I had a shotgun there, wasn't no use a letting him kill me. And so I shot at him. I shot him. I shot him down the first time. Well, he gets up and started shooting at me again.

I unbreeched that old gun and that old gun hadn't kicked out hulls in years and there I was with a hung-up gun. Wasn't nothing for me to do *but* run. And I started running. And I run on by this girl's house where I was going to get these things at, the things to bring 'em up to her mother, and so before I knowed anything there's five or six of 'em in a car after me. So they run up on me down there in the field and I happened to manage to get my gun reloaded. That's when I killed this guy.

But I never done no time for it. High sheriff told me wasn't nothing could be done on that but just a dead man.

Big Sal: "I'd saw off their shotguns for them . . ."

I first turned out [went into the Life] when I was nine years old. A little tramp is what I was, really and truly. I would pick up men and go out in the country with them like I was going to fill a date and in the meantime there'd be about seven or eight little hoodlums in back, in the car following us. I'd get out there and I'd tell the old man, I'd tell him, "Look, I'm a virgin and I'm going to holler for my father." So naturally the guy is thinking, There ain't nothing I can do about it. If he's scared, if he's a family man, he's going to up with what money he got, and if I waved or anything, all those boys would come rushing up to the car and scare him half to death and then he'd have to up his money. It was more or less just robbery, that's all, but it was legit. This took place when I was nine and went on until I was thirteen.

We was living out on Beaumont Highway then, we'd just come to Houston. My downfall. I know myself was my downfall, but you know, there was the environment. I really believe in environment.

These two boys and I, we were very close, and what one of us couldn't think of the other one would. So finally there was three more boys joined the clique, club, or whatever you want to call it. We didn't have no name, we was just all friends.

When I was twelve years old we were all sitting around this beer joint one night. One of the boy's mother worked there, so we were allowed in the back room. We were all drinking beer. I would drink two beers and I was pretty well on my road, one of the boys never would drink nothing, and this other boy, he never would go out with no girls or nothing. This other boy kept saying, "What are you, some kind of queer? You don't want to go out with no girls or nothing." And he says, "How come you don't want no girl since you came home from reform school?" We were like brothers and sisters, you know. "Since you came home from out there in the tree army [forestry camp] you don't want to even associate with women."

So finally he got mad and he jumped up and said, "Well, you sorry little bastard you!" And he jerked him up by the hair on his head. He was drunk by this time. He jerked him up and says, "If you ever get high on marijuana, you sonofabitch, you wouldn't want to be going to bed with no gals either."

Hah!

So I break them up and I tell him, "You mean you just smoke marijuana?" Incidentally, at that time it wasn't against the law, it wasn't on the Harrison Act, this was in the middle thirties. You could go to jail for it, it was a state law and it was in the process of becoming Federal.

One of the boys says, "Why don't you turn me on, man?" And they told me, "You just set in here and wait." And they wouldn't let me participate. Well, I was going to whip them all or else I was going to get high. They jerked me around and told me, "Come on in."

They used to get mad at me. If they'd get mad, they'd throw me in the bayou. But they never tried to get in my pants or nothing like that. Nothing like that. They just considered me like a sister, but yet they treated me like a hoodlum, you know? If I got in a fight with somebody, they was there—girl or boy. They always fought my battles for me.

So anyways, he says, "Come on." So we go out in the car and he shows us how to smoke this weed and I liked it right off and I dug a kick. So I quit drinking beer and started just getting high. And about two weeks later this same boy—I won't mention his name because he's in the penitentiary now—he says, "Well, why don't you take a pill?"

I told him, "A pill?"

And he says, "Yeah, it's just a pep pill." So he gives me this benny [Benzedrine] and he says, "You'll like them."

I didn't sleep for a week. And I'm still trying to go to school, though, because I have a very strict father and he's German-Jewish, you know. So he's raising hell at home all the time, threatening to kill himself because I wouldn't stop running around. My mother was working. Daddy had this old stallion horse and every time Daddy would turn his back I'd get on this stallion and I'd take off. I'd run away from home on that damn horse.

At this time we're living in Lindale, we'd moved off the Beaumont Highway. We buy a home out there and my daddy's got a little grocery store and vegetable truck deal he'd drive around. Daddy threatened to send all those boys to the penitentiary if they didn't leave me alone. And *I'm* the one that's bothering *them*. I'm running after them, they ain't enticing *me*. I'm about twelve years old, I guess.

So it's in all the papers, about a bunch of teen-agers hijacking places. There's a gang of teen-agers and they don't have no kind of identification on them to go by or nothing else. It's us.

I would get in with some old man and then I'd go and tell one of the boys, Billy or one of them, that I know this old man and he's got some money and he doesn't have a safe. Nobody knew how to knock a safe at that time. We knew all these safecrackers but we wasn't that old, they wouldn't have nothing to do with us. So it was the boys and their little old sawed-off shotguns. I'd saw off their shotguns for them and we'd wrap them with tape and we'd take off. Sometimes they'd let me go with them and sometimes I'd have to wait at the house. I'd come home in the afternoon and go over to this one boy's mama's and they'd come home about one o'clock in the morning and we'd count the money up and split it down. I'd always get my split because I was the one that got the job for them and spied the old man or something.

One night they made a pretty big haul, bigger than was usual for kids. About $2,000. I say approximately that much because I don't remember the exact amount, I've seen too much of it since then. When they came home that night I noticed that Chuck and Jake were real nervous. They came by themselves and they was cussing these other boys, said they hated to see Billy go with them. (Incidentally, Billy's dead now, the prison guards killed him.) So we went home. We had a little room at this old house and we went there. They're telling me that they're worried about Billy. "Why don't you go by the hotel and see about him?" I said.

"No, trick him, man. If he ain't capable of taking care of himself now, well, he never will be." He didn't live with his people; he had people, but he didn't live with them.

These other two boys told me that something had happened with the deal, they got in a fight in the damned joint.

So about three o'clock the next morning the police busted in the house and got these two boys, Chuck and Jake, the two cousins, and carried them off to jail. I was home then. They had the other three boys. Billy had been whipped unpitifully. They're of age by this time, seventeen and eighteen years old, so they had been whipped unpitifully.

Gerald and this other stud, Dago (he got killed in the penitentiary later for snitching), they're not even touched. Chuck and Jake asked what happened and Dago says, "Man, they tried to whip me and I wouldn't tell on anybody. Wouldn't tell nothing." Started hollering that.

Billy spoke up and called him a lying sonofabitch. "You said *some*thing. This boy here's done been whipped, but not you." By this time these two policemen had whipped the hell out of them for even mouthing off at them. So the three gets whipped, Gerald signs statements and gets two years, and Dago tells them that I'm involved but he won't tell them my last name. But of course the police found who I was because I'd run around with these boys all my life, especially these two cousins. So Dago signs a statement on me, says that I was involved, that I was the one that told them who had the money and where it was kept and if it was on the man.

What I was doing was I'd stay at a lot of places until they locked up and I'd see where they'd hide their money. I'd talk to the people and I'd tell them we was going to party. I'd just stick around the store. Or I'd say I was looking for a job. I'd always think of some kind of story, and they'd say, "Why don't you stay here and we'll go out and get a drink after, we'll go to the drive-in and I'll buy you a malt." I was thirteen then.

So Dago told all of this. Then they all went to the penitentiary. Gerald got two, Billy got five, Chuck and Jake, they got seven apiece. And I got sent to reform school, Mary Burnett, a place for the correction of young girls. It wasn't considered a reform school, but that's all it was.

It was out there at Mary Burnett that I got introduced to narcotics for the first time.

Let me explain about the place. There was four cottages—Brian, Balen, Claxton, and Grey. Brian and Balen was for virgins, Grey was for the girls that ran away, you were still a virgin but renegades. And in this other one, Claxton, it was for the bad girls, for the whores and older girls. I wanted over there. They kept me in Brian and then they put me in Balen, and I kept getting in fights and I'd run off. I think I ran off 126 times as long as I was there—that was until I was eighteen, off and on. Anyway, I went to Grey. They finally put me in Grey after I was there about two months.

One of the girls, she was an Indian, she was a hustling gal, but she had squared up, was really trying. She had the wool pulled over these people's eyes. Miss Claxton and Miss Valentine really believed in her. Virgie was her name, I'll never forget her name. She tells me, "Hey, have you ever shot any horse stuff?"

I told her, "What do you mean, horse stuff?"

Incidentally, you didn't shoot dope back in them days. If you shot dope you was a sorry, rotten, no-good bitch, it was strictly uh-uh, you didn't shoot or sniff dope or anything. If you did, you wasn't no good. That's the way the characters (police give us that name, characters. In them days we was called people. Folks was squares and we was people. The police had a lot of respect for the characters, they only rode the people that shot dope. Characters tended to their own business). Anyway, I never messed around with dope fiends, I wasn't allowed to. The old boxmen [safecrackers] they was not dope fiends. They didn't start shooting dope till much later.

So Virgie says, "Well, do you want a shot of dope?"

And I told her, "God, no!"

So there was about five or six in the room one night. They pulled out the rig, the needle and the hype and everything, and started fixing. And I got to watching it.

Well, at the early age of nine I made up my mind that before I died there would be nothing I wouldn't do. I was going to do everything. There's only one thing I haven't done yet: go to bed with a Negro. I haven't gone to bed with a colored man yet. That's the only thing. I don't know, I just can't get above it or below it or something. But I just never have. And I've met some pretty ones and I've shot some dope with some pretty ones, but I just never have been moved that way.

I had made this brag at school—you know how kids are at that age. I sat back a lot, I didn't pop off a lot. I'd sit back and listen and I'd learn everything and if I approved or if it was my way of thinking, then I'd go along with it. If it wasn't, then I'd just go away, walk off. I wouldn't tell them they was wrong. 'Cause I believe that any way you want to believe, that's a kick with me, but just don't knock my kick and I won't knock yours.

And so she says, "Why don't you try it?"

And I says, "No, I don't think so."

She says, "I thought you'd try anything once."

I says, "Well, give the sonofabitch here."

So I went ahead and skin-popped, I wouldn't go with it in my vein. I just skin-popped. I was just turning fourteen then. I got sick. I was so sick I prayed to die, and they was all laughing at me. Well, it made me mad because they laughed and I said, "I believe if you give me another I'll quit throwing up." So they give me a little bit more in my skin. I passed out. And I got put in punishment.

Our punishment out there after they quit whipping us and quit shaving our heads was to put us in a turpentine room. They'd scrub the floors and everything with turpentine and let it soak up real good. They'd shut the windows down and nail them behind the bars, the grate. And then if you griped or anything they'd send one of the big girls in there to whip you. Hogs we called them.

I got myself locked up three days later. I had resentment in me, a lot, at myself mainly, because I went for the story. So I burned up all the matrons' uniforms, I think about six that I ironed that day. I just burned hell out of them. And I got ahold of Virgie's dress and blouse that she was going to wear to the dance and I burned that up. We got in a fight and I whipped her. She was bigger than me, so I really felt good because I whipped her without cheating. Then I was in with all the bad ones because I whipped the leader. So that made me a leader and I guess that's what I've been all my life now.

Just because I started that way and I reared myself that I could do anything I wanted to do. Anything that I think I can do and believe in myself, I can do it.

I ran off about three nights later, four of us did, on Miss Claxton's birthday. That was my first run-out. It was a funny thing, but every time I started to run off I'd go to this Mr. Smith and I'd tell him, "I'm fixing to go visit my mama, I'm going to run off." I've always idolized my mama; I did my father too, but he's disowned me now.

And he'd say, "Don't run off, we'll do something." I'd go ahead and run off. I did this from the time I was fourteen till I was eighteen.

Each time I'd run off I'd go home all right, but I wouldn't stay. Then I'd run into these little Mexican studs over in the ward in Houston and I'd tell them, "Why don't you fix me?"

They'd say, "Fix you? Hell, no. I'm not having Chuck come out of the penitentiary and kill me." And they'd run me back over to my part of town. They'd get me high on weed but they wouldn't fix me with dope. So every time I'd go back to that school I'd joy-pop, I'd just fix and that would be it. Maybe once a month we'd joy-pop. There was an old pimp came out there and gave Virgie her supply of narcotics. The grounds were open, like a home. But it was still a re-form school.

Finally, when I turned sixteen, I went home on trial. I didn't stay but a week, and my daddy carried me back because I didn't want to stay at home and I didn't want to go to school. And once when I was seventeen I got out for about two weeks and I stayed with my uncle in Dawson. Jake was getting out and Chuck was still in—the two cous-ins. Dago had gotten killed and Gerald was already out. Billy was still in the penitentiary.

They kept Dago in maximum security. I don't know if it was for snitching on our gang that he got killed or just snitching in the peni-tentiary, or just because he was wrong. He was out in the open, at the movie I believe, and they killed him.

Jake was released and he came out to the school to visit me, came with my mother and uncle. He told me, "When you get out of here we're getting married."

I told him, "I don't want to, I'm not in love with you."

He said, "We're getting married anyway."

I says, "Why?"

He said, "Because we're going to straighten our life up."

So I told him, "Yeah, okay." I was fond of him and that was all, but we were like brothers and sisters.

I had been touched only one time by a boy. When I was fourteen Chuck thought that I had been laid, and he was just a kid so he raped me, you know. He had really got to me, then he left town for a while, but I didn't snitch on him, so he came back. That's when I was four-teen and that was the only time I'd been touched by a boy and I was deathly scared of boys. In the meantime I had been introduced to ho-mosexuality. You was wondering when that was coming in, huh? You find it anywheres you're locked up.

I was just wondering which was going to come first.

That thing with Chuck don't count—it was the woman came first.

It was in the school. She was a schoolteacher.

I didn't expect it from that side.

I knew you wouldn't. She was my schoolteacher and I thought I was madly in love with her. Because, you know, she did introduce me to a kick. It was a better kick than any kick I'd been on. She left there and that's when I ran off. When I was on the run I stayed out about six months. I got with this butch gal. I met the gay people. I met this lesbian and this butch and a clique of them, and I started living with Fern there in Houston. I guess I love her today, I don't know. To me a man was always to be used and that was it, just for a kick. When Fern and I busted up, I went over to my mama's. I was eighteen. I get carried back and then I get out and I go ahead and tell Jake all about my dealings in homosexuality and everything.

It didn't discourage him. He said, "Hell, I had little flirtations in the penitentiary."

And I told him, "This was more than a flirtation." I'm trying to discourage him.

Finally he says, "Well, you're going to marry me."

So I told him, "Well, all right."

I came home in October of 1943 and we got married in December. We stayed together two months and I went home. I was eighteen, I was a married woman and I'd do as I damn pleased. Finally I went back to Jake. My daddy said that was my bed and I was going to lay in it, so I went back to him.

Then he told me about another cousin he and Chuck had, Dan, who was a gambler like Jake turned out to be, but Dan was a pimp too. So Jake tells me, "Why don't you start hustling [turning tricks]."

I tell him, "You been listening to that Dan Rogers and I'm not going for it." I blowed up.

He said, "No, I haven't been listening to nobody."

I told him, "I hustled as much as I'm ever going to hustle when I was a kid. There isn't no other man who's going to touch me and that's it."

I left him and went back to Fern and back into the gay life. I lived in the gay life about two years. I ran into Jake downtown and he was all pilled up and everything. He didn't shoot dope. This was in 1945. He tells me, "What are you doing?"

I said, "Shooting dope."

And he knocked the shit out of me. He told me, "You dirty little tramp." So he throws my ass into the car, takes off and gets Dan and all these gamblers around where he hangs around, and he tells me,

"You sonofabitch, if you can't sell pussy you're not going to shoot dope."

I told him, "You're not supporting my dope habit."

And I did have a habit. It was a skin habit, see, which I got in the last part of '43, and I had to live with him then and he never knew I was shooting dope.

So he told me, "I'm going to show you what we think about dope fiends." Here's all these hard-faced gamblers that I thought I really knew. And I had seen them put men on the barrel and roll them down the hill with rocks on them with chains wrapped around them and everything. I had seen all this and I knew what they were capable of and I was scared, scared half to death. I'd seen that Coke bottle thing.

Coke bottle what?

A Coke bottle will suck your guts out. I've seen that done, too. To a whore. That old gal got on down the block and these pimps got mad because she was cut-rating and they just put that Coke bottle up her and sucked her guts out and killed her. That's $3 and $5 whores. If they didn't run them off the block and make them stay off, they'd just kill them or do something drastic to them. And leave them that way and that way the police would find them. All they'd say is, "Well, some old trick got that old whore that way," then they'd blow it off. There wasn't nothing ever thought about it.

They took me out to the San Jacinto River and Jake throws me over the damn bridge, then he snaps that I can swim better than he can, so he jumps in on top of me. What they're trying to do is make me talk. They say they're going to kill all the dope fiends in Houston, they're going to kill all the whores and everything else until they find who turned me out on dope.

Finally Jake says, "This sonofabitch ain't going to snitch on anybody anyway."

It was a doctor who was giving me my medicine, I was shooting M [morphine]. So they put me on a cold-turkey kick. I had been skinning morphine and that was the worst habit I ever kicked, believe me. I couldn't even get up out of bed. And it wasn't in my head, either. They took me to the country, to this little old place they had, a deer lease up there, and they carried me way back in the woods. They set out there and they gambled and got in a fight or two, but they kept me there till I kicked the habit. When I came back to Houston I was going to square up. They was going to keep me away from everybody.

Back in those days, if they seen a dope fiend coming down the street, they'd cross. They didn't mess with narcotic addicts. No.

Because they're supposed to be unreliable thieves?

That's right. You cannot put no confidence in one of them whatsoever.

Now this was the first part of '46 and we go back together and he tells me, "Sal, why don't you start hustling?" He is still trying to talk me into that.

Now so far the only men you've had sex with are Chuck and Jake?

Right. So I told him, "Okay, goddamnit, you've talked me into it. It took you a year. Now I will be a whore but I'll tell you one thing, I'm going to be the best one that ever walked."

He told me, "Just for two years." Dig this. And I believe he was real sincere when he said it: "Just for two years till we get a home and get on our feet."

Why didn't he go out and steal or something?

He *was* stealing. But he was gambling it all away. Getting high on weed. He was blowing weed all the time then. Of course that really isn't expensive.

Every morning we'd get up and we'd go to the weed connection and ride around and get high and go eat and we just never did go to jail. We didn't have no problems.

When I turned out hustling, a stud I had met at a joint who had tried to pick me up turned out to be Dan, Jake's cousin. And I didn't know him and he didn't know me. So first thing off I meet him and he nearly gets me killed telling Jake that I had been in Galveston with them pimps and everything. He said, "What you do mean, you turned her out? She's turned out already." And Jake thought I had been hustling all that time we wasn't together and I had to convince him that I wasn't, that I was in jail, and I had to get my own mother to prove it before he'd believe it.

So finally I went ahead and I turned out on North Main in Houston, walking the street. They had whorehouses then in Houston, in this red-light district, but I wasn't halfing my money down with no landlady. So I had been on the streets hustling about two or three weeks and the vice squad started watching me. I pulled up from off North Main and went on to Root Square Park where they all was, all the whores in Houston worked Root Square Park.

There was a guy in Galveston, he was with the syndicate. I wasn't but twenty-two then and he was trying to get me to go to Chicago and get in that syndicate deal, but I told him, "No, I'm staying in Texas." I was always leery of him.

Shit, I'd meet different girls that was in that syndicate and they couldn't get away from them. They'd say that they'd send you to Pan-ama, they'd send you across in Europe, they'd send you places like that, to work and hustle. Shit, man, I can fuck and suck right here in the States, why am I going to catch a boat to go across? I just couldn't see it.

Then I left Root Square Park and I started shooting dope again, but this time I was mainlining. This is the first part of 1946. I started real heavy and I just finally told Jake, "I don't want to be with you, man." He asked me why not and I told him, "I just don't."

I quit hustling and went to Galveston. I ran into this girl and went to work in a drive-in, hopping cars. I just could not see hustling. Finally I ran into this stripper, Barbara, and she tells me, "Well, why don't you start stripping?"

"No," I told her, "I don't want to strip."

But she's going to teach me anyway. And her friends, they all taught me. So I started trying to pull off my clothes in front of some groups of men. I did one night and I blowed it, I couldn't go that one. Hell, it's hard for me to pull off my clothes in front of one man, let alone a whole group, a whole roomful of them. So I started messing around with the gay kids again at this drive-in. Shooting dope all along. Then I started running around with the show people, and prac-tically all of them was homosexuals and weed-heads.

Then Barbara tells me, "Hey, Sal, why don't you come down here and meet old Mary R." She had all the whorehouses in Galveston at one time.

I said, "I don't want to meet that gooch-eyed bitch." She's one-eyed. "I don't want to meet her."

So we go down there. I meet Mary and she gives me a spot in her house and I go back to hustling.

I started running around with this little old Greek boy who is just a weed-head and working stud, he's not a dope fiend or nothing. I told him that I'm on dope and he said, "I might get on it."

I told him, "Not from me you're not."

Incidentally, I've never turned nobody out on dope as long as I've shot it.

Barbara and Mary, they take off to New Orleans to work on a show. They leave me there in charge of the whorehouse. I knew how to run it because I watched her. I knew how to take books, I knew all the gals, they all knew me. Six girls were there. So that was my first whorehouse.

Then I went back to my old man in Houston and I quit working. In fact, when I became landlady I'd quit working. Then I went back to my husband and I got *pregnant*. Then I had a baby. I squared up after he was born, then I started hustling again out on Root Square Park. As soon as the baby was born I quit him because I didn't want no kids. I tried to find an abortion and everything. Now I'm glad I didn't because I have a fine son now, I have two of them. But then I didn't want no kids and I got mad at Jake and went back to New Orleans and the gay life. This kept on until the middle of '49 when I went back to my husband and got pregnant again. I stayed with him until I was two or three months pregnant and went home.

You know what, I never have had a man that when I came home from work tried to go to bed with me. Because they knew how I felt. They knew how I hated men, period. I've have to be so goddamned knocked to even trick a man in the first place. That's when I had my only pill habit, because I had to be so knocked out and goofed up and everything to even hustle a man.

So you were never making it with a man the same time you were hustling?

Take my first old man, this boy that I married the first time, Jake, he wanted me to start. He didn't turn me out, I turned my own self out, but he wanted me to start. Okay. When I'd come home and I was living with him, we didn't talk about trimming or nothing, you know, fucking. He'd kind of pull away, you know. It made him sick because I turned out hustling. I know it did. Because he wasn't a pimp. He's a newspaperman now, incidentally.

When my baby was born in December of '49 I told my mama that I didn't want my kids because I wasn't going to live square, I couldn't raise them right. I'd want to let them know what a hard cruel world it was and that wasn't right, they should find that out on their own, and that's all I'd be good for, to teach them that, the hardship of everything.

In the meantime, all this time between '43 and '49, I was helping burglarize, I was going along on jobs, I was helping haul out safes. I got picked up every time I turned around. My record will prove that. In Houston, I got picked up with I guess every character that ever was put out. A few of them's got killed in holdups, I lost one old man in the chair, I lost one to the police under gunfire, I got a scar on my leg to show where I got shot. I went through all this shit and I never run around with no women in crime. In stealing, hijacking, and all that, and I didn't associate with no women in that kind of life.

In '47 my little sister and I was running around together with all these thieves and box men. She got sent to Gainesville, but they first put her on probation to me. What happened was I ran up there and told Miss White that she had ruined my life by taking me away from my mother. I was all pilled up—I had a pill habit at that time with the dope habit. I told them, "You'll release her to me or else I'll kill her before she gets on the train." Miss White knew how crazy I was because in '48 I had went berserk and they put me in a nut ward. So she thought really and truly I would kill my sister. And I might have. So she thought it over and she went and talked to Judge Allen and they decided to give her one more chance. It lasted about two months.

We was in the apartment with my husband and another man who got killed by the police just after this happened. They had been burglarizing and their tools were across the street from where they lived. We were just visiting; I didn't go back to my husband, we were just chipping with them. So Hank and Jake were there and we went in and got high. Next morning, when we left, this little old boy come running by and says, "The police is all over the house, you know that?"

I turned around and looked at Jake, and I said, "We're going to jail, baby."

It was winter and he gives us the sawblades, the only thing they had in the house. I put them under my coat and my sister and I cut off down the street. Here comes a detective. He says, "You sonofabitches, I thought you'd never come out of that house. We been freezing our ass off all night long. And old Woody Stevenson's raising hell too."

I told him, "It will do old Woody some good." Hell, I grew up with Woody and he was as big a thief as I was when we was kids.

While we're talking I'm putting the hacksaw blades under his car seat.

He carries us to jail. He carries Jake and Hank out to the Northside precinct and they whipped the dog hell out of them. They present these tools to them and everything, but they couldn't prove nothing, because all they have is them tools and that was away from the house.

They took my sister and sent her to Gainesville, just like that. She was on probation to me. I failed and she failed. She stayed out there about a month and we had it made up to run off. This girlfriend of mine, Margaret Reynolds—she's dead from dope—she says, "Well, we'll just go out there and get her. And she can marry my little brother, by God."

They hadn't even met and we done got them married. But we wanted it all kept in the family. We was married to cousins so we thought they should get married.

So we went out there and found that she had ran off the night before, she beat us down. The old woman said, "She jumped like a squirrel and run like a rabbit."

That was my little sister. She had turned out hustling and she went up to Wisconsin and all the other states hustling, and finally got to California. And she married this pimp out of Dallas. He had been a policeman first, then a pimp. They're squared up now and they're doing real good.

She never shot no dope. She started to one time. She was ribbing me and telling me she's going to shoot some dope and I run in on her and kicked the hell out of her. I've never let her get on dope. Because by that time I really knew the hardship of it and the heartaches.

The baby was born in December and I stayed at my mama's. I got an apartment. I had these three men that I had been going with and when I found out I was pregnant I told all of them they got me pregnant. This Jewish fellow, he still thinks he's got a baby by me. So he pays my rent, he buys me a car, buys me a house full of furniture. Each one of them takes care of me and I don't have to do nothing but sit on my butt all this time I'm pregnant.

Then in December, when the baby was born, this stud walked in my front door and I like his looks. My sister was there, she came home from Wisconsin, and I said, "You know, I like that guy."

And she says, "Why, Sal? You don't like that sonofabitch. All he is is a little old booster and a dope fiend."

I says, "That's okay. I like him."

And I married him two months later. It was just something I had an urge to do. I just wanted to do it and I did it.

Did you ever get a divorce from the first one?

No. He won't give me one. He says he's going to kill me someday. When the kids got grown and my mother died, he's going to kill me.

So this guy, we got married and he went to the penitentiary. We got caught with a tow sack full of weed and he took the rap off of me. Baby was about three months old. He got two years. He'd just done ten for murder, he had murdered some guy at a filling station, beat him to death or something. He had just got through doing his ten and he came back with two years for that weed. That's when they was pretty lenient for weed. I stood by him that two years. But in the meantime I was running around with this other boy that is now dead from dope.

I had a whorehouse on Hardy Street there in Houston. And I pushed dope, I had pills, I had weed. Anything you want, just come to Sal's. That was the rumor around town. But, hell, there was a dope connection on every corner, it wasn't nothing to have dope. So I run that whorehouse. It was a real big house on Hardy Street. I had nine girls. And I had a payoff. It was $125 a week.

I was real funny about that. The Federal man came down here when I got my time and tried to get me to go out and testify against the men that I had the payoff with. I told him, "I don't know what you're talking about." These same policemen had helped me get out of a lot of scrapes, because I did them a favor by saving their reputation as policemen. And what good would it have done me to send somebody, even a policeman, to the penitentiary?

I've never been bitter toward the police. Hell, if we didn't have police we'd have an animal world. Really. We've got an animal world anyway. Dog eat dog.

Whatever the girls made in that place, I took $2 off $5. If they lived there and paid room and board, they'd pay $10 a day and the same $2 off each $5 they made. But there were no $5 dates in my house. I lived by the railroad yard where the railroad men got paid twice a month and came down. It was a good go. Girls who walked the streets and wanted a room for an hour or two, whatever they made was theirs, they just paid me for the room. But there wasn't but two girls I'd rent rooms to like that. If any others come off the street, I didn't know what they was talking about. I wasn't allowed to. We had rules on my payoff. I had to operate in such a fashion and keep it like a family rooming house.

When I got the house it *was* a boarding house. This old woman had died and her son had just kept the roomers there. They'd been having roomers there for years. The same ones. There was one gambler that knew me, and when I moved in, he said, "Sal, what are you up to?" He knew.

I said, "I'm fixing to open this sonofabitch up."

And he told me, "I thought so. Well, I can't stand the heat, baby."

And I told him, "I need your room anyway." It was understood. So he moved. He left the front room for my hustling parlor; that faced the street, which made it convenient. Upstairs I had six roomers. I got them all together in the parlor that night and I told them, "I don't know who's going to stay and who's going to stay and play, but it's going to be a playhouse from now on."

And this little bitty guy, I never will forget him, he was about nine hundred and twenty years old, he says, "Well, I can't play—I gotta work tonight." Just so serious.

I told him, "Well, we're going to play every night, honey."

And he told me, "Are you going to sell beer?"

I told him, "I don't have no license to sell beer."

He got mad and he said, "Have you got a license to run a whore-house?"

I told him, "Honey, I'm not running a whorehouse. It's a play-house. Don't you understand?"

We made friends before he left. The rest of them, they all said, "Well, if we want a girl we'll come back and see you." Laughing. I never did have no rumbles out of them. They never did run and call the police like a lot of people would. I don't know, maybe it was the neighborhood. Around there there was a colored house on one street and then another one that was all Mexicans. And there was so many connections around there. Even the drugstores—they sold pills. It was just a real regular whoretown, I guess, right in that vicinity. What made my place look good, I had my kids with me.

You know, that's why I think my kids turned out to be squares, both of them. The oldest one married a policeman's daughter. I don't know, they just don't want no part of that kind of life. They've seen it with me. They've seen what kind of hell I went through.

I got mixed up with a gal that's writing checks. It's her racket and she was out on appeal bond. She wrote a check for me to go in to cash and I got busted. She got me out on bond that night. The only reason the sonofabitch got me out on bond was because I had the money and I knew where the stash was. This stud that was in jail had our dough, and when I got in jail I got a visit with him and he told me where it was. So she got me out on bond. We went and got the dough and everything and fixed, and I stayed out about three weeks. Then I got some more checks on me. She wrote the checks and I was with her. I didn't cash one or write one, but I was there, I was involved. They put passing forged instruments [checks, bonds, drafts, etc.] on me. I jumped bond and I was on the run for about four months.

I went to West Texas and was working that area. I had a little thing going—appointments with all the porters. They all knew that I was wanted. One day in Big Spring this bellboy came down to the hotel, the Crawford, and he says, "Hey, your picture's in the post office."

I tell him, "You're ribbing. I go there every day for my mail, man. What am I going to do?" I was using my sister's name, but still . . . So I decided to blow. We went over to Lubbock and got all pilled up and then we come back to Big Spring and I went to the post office. And this big stud—I don't know where that big sonofabitch could've come from but he was the biggest thing I've ever seen—says something. I turned around and looked up beside his head. I'm tall with heels on and I looked at him and he was a whole head taller than me. I told him, "Yeah, what do you want?"

"What's you name?"

And I says, "Man, I'm who you want. That's all that matters." But I was tired, you know? Really and truly tired.

And something else. Back when I was a kid I worked at this carnival and I read cards for a kick. I ran around with these Gypsies. I had a superstition about reading cards: every time I run the cards I get in some kind of shit. Every time. It was just a superstition, but even so . . . I think superstitions are ignorant, don't misunderstand me. But I had run the cards that morning and I seen the police. When he walked up I didn't ask him no questions, I just told him, "I'm who you want."

These three bellboys came down to the jail and brought me something to eat. It was an old jail and they just could have pulled on it and the side would have fell out. They throwed me in there with all them men and I was the only woman in there.

There's one stud in there who's wanting to get to me. And I'm telling him, "I've never been raped but I'm ascared that's what you're going to do. 'Cause I'm sick. I got a dope habit."

And this little old Indian took a liking to me and he says, "Nobody's touching her." He's a little bitty sonofabitch and I don't know how the hell he stood his ground, but there wasn't anybody that touched me.

I didn't sleep all night because I had the habit, you know. In the middle of the night this jailer, I guess he got the word or maybe he thought everybody had got me by then, he comes and locks a steel door between the men and me.

Next morning, at nine o'clock, Houston police were there. They was ribbing me on the way back. "We heard there was a pretty weak jail there and you'd probably break jail." I've got running on my record. Even now, they won't let me out on the yard crew.

Then I finally got with Chuck, Jake's cousin.

He had been in prison and he got out. For nine years he had been in. He didn't shoot dope. If I even thought about it and he thought that I was thinking about it he'd knock the hell out of me. He just didn't allow it. Now he blowed weed and he's a jazz fan. If he's listening to some jazz you don't talk to him because you can't reach him.

It's really spooky the way he is. He wouldn't even have to be on nothing. Just the music would be his kick. He lived it so long.

I guess up until Leo that was the only man I could really say I really loved. And that's the boy that got in my pants when I was just fourteen with force. I don't know what it was. Maybe it was the aggressive part. Every butch I've ever been with has never really been aggressive, they was always tender and everything and I was more aggressive than they was.

In 1954 he was in jail and I made his bond the night I got out. Had him out for Christmas. Nobody in Houston would touch his bond. I got out and I went to this bondsman and told him, "I want Chuck out of jail." He got him out. I didn't have a penny and he got him out for me. I told him, "I'll pay you." I paid him his bond in two weeks.

We started living together and then we got married. We stayed out until March and we got put in jail and he got sent to the penitentiary with six years. I was burglarizing then and when I got back out found that I was pregnant. But I was pregnant in my tube and had to have this operation.

I got out and got me a habit. I had sackfuls of narcotics that we got boosting these drugstores and everything. I had this habit, a real bad oil-burning habit. I was running around with these four thieves—burglars—and we was knocking safes from everywhere. I was with this Dallas thief then.

I got in the hospital and I stayed about a month, come out, and I started living with this gal. I wouldn't go with men. I was pulled up from hustling now. I got this house over on Canal and I started a call service and had three girls working for me. But I was still burglarizing at night.

I had moved to that part of town because I had to. I'd shot at my old man. He wouldn't get in the car when I told him to. So we moved. We was in Mexican town. Chuck never did get out of jail on bond anymore. He come to the joint with six years. I stood by him all the time that I was out. That wasn't but about three more months.

I got out of prison again in June of '59. I met this boy at the bus station, this Dawson boy, and we got married. I just met him at the bus station and we got married. Some dope fiends picked me up. We started shooting paregoric at first. I didn't want to get back on dope. So the third morning I got up and I had a kind of hangover from that paregoric and I thought, "Oh, God." I looked at it and I started to put it in my arm. It started burning. I just throwed the goddamned bulb and needle and everything over in the corner and I says, "Fuck it. If I'm going to be a dope fiend, baby, I'm going to be a *dope* fiend." So I went to the border and got me some dope and I started pushing it. I went to Oklahoma and we were pushing dope up there. We come back down and we got picked up in Tyler.

Now Dawson was on parole and he was supposed to be in Oklahoma. We ribbed the policemen there in Tyler, told them that this goddamn place would never give us a chance, all that shit. Which they hadn't, but we hadn't give ourselves a chance either. So he said, "Well, I'm going to show you that here's one policeman that's not a sorry sonofabitch. I'm gonna give you another chance. Now get your ass on to Houston."

I was hustling there in Tyler and they had caught me dead in the act of hustling. We was shooting stuff but they didn't find the needle or nothing 'cause I ditched it in their trash can as I went into the police station.

So, anyway, he says, "Get on back to Houston or Oklahoma, where you belong."

So we did, we went on back to Houston. I got some dope. I got me twenty papers of H, and I started pushing. There wasn't any dope pushers in Houston then, I was the only connection there.

We lived at this one place for a year. I was doing things, boosting and all, but he wouldn't do nothing. He wasn't even a thief. I would get hot, I'd tell him, "You are the laziest no-good sonofabitch I've seen." He'd work, but I'd still cuss him for not stealing. He'd jumped his parole and everything, but he still would not steal and I couldn't understand it.

What had he been in prison for?

For one marijuana seed and a stem. That's what he got ten years for. The first time.

So he says, "You wait for me if I get caught."

And I told him, "Yeah, I'm going to wait for you. I stand by every sonofabitch that goes to the penitentiary." He had seventeen months to back up when he got picked up in June of '60. I stood by him and I went to see him until I got on the run myself.

Around Christmas of that year me and a friend was going to go up through Oklahoma bipping—scallybipping [burglarizing a house when they saw the wife out back hanging clothes], you know. We had been doing it around Houston, Dallas, places like that, but now we was going to go up through the States. She always went by herself, but I was going to go with her this time.

So I told her, "Wait till my man comes back." The man I was pushing for. I said, "Wait till he comes back with the dope. Let's don't leave dry, man, 'cause we've got this habit."

I got my boys from my mother and spent Christmas with them. I had this little house. I moved three or four times because I knew the narcotics boys was watching me, so I kept moving around. I was stealing in the daytime and half the night and pushing dope on the side. I had never hustled in years now. And I was still going to see Jake all the time and all them guards thought I was a jam-up old gal because I'd be down there rain or shine, sick or not, I'd be there. That is unusual, for anybody to come up for you in the penitentiary. One time I visited him and he said, "Why don't you quit shooting that goddamned dope?"

And I'm telling him, "You're behind the goddamned bars, man, and you're telling me to quit shooting dope? Why didn't you quit when you was out there?"

I gave him his Christmas box on the 27th. I counted my dope down and my man left and he was going to be back on the 28th. He didn't get back on time. And he even took my big pistols, my .38's and my .45 that I had, and left me his little ones. That was in case something happened to him on the border and he needed them.

So at eleven thirty on the 28th of December 1960 I didn't have a cap of dope on me. I was sick [withdrawal symptoms]. I woke up sick, I couldn't even stand. Had no goddamned clothes on. That's how sick I was. I came out of the house and I told the boys, "Come on, get in the car." They got in my station wagon and we backed out of the driveway into the street, and goddamn but I thought I was in little Mexico. Honey, there was six police cars that come up from every direction and surrounded my car.

J. J. Strickland was there. He had, about three or four months before this, picked me up and tried to make me turn some people over to him, tell him about them, snitch on them. I told him, "I don't know the people. That's what you got the badge for: earn your money." So he was pretty hot about it.

All the other policemen had told him, "Man, you wasting your time. If she tells you she's going to do you a favor just to get out of jail, don't go for it because she ain't going to do it. She ain't going to do you no favors."

He wouldn't listen to them. He thought he was a little con artist, he was going to con me into doing these favors for him. Well, he was hot because he lost the bet with some old policeman, I guess.

So he comes out there that afternoon. I had one little bitty piece of dolly [Dolophine] in my aspirin box. He says, "Give me your bag."

I told him, "You don't search me. A matron shakes me, but not you."

He said, "I said give me that goddamned purse."

It had been raining and that rain ditch was full of water and he started jerking on my purse and I let go and he went in the ditch. So him and I had a fight. He was fixing to hit me over the head with his pistol, but my landlady ran down and said, "Don't you hit that lady!"

Shortly, one of them runs up and says, "What's wrong with you, you gone crazy?"

See, I never fought with policemen. I always conducted myself as a lady. I didn't cuss them out or nothing. So they couldn't understand why I was fighting the sonofabitch.

I says, "I know what he's up to and he's not going to go it." I don't know why I even said that, to tell you the truth, because it didn't enter my mind that he was up to no good, you know. Then he shook [searched] my purse. He went on in the house and came back out with this gal that was in the bed and he put her in the car. He shook my purse again. This time when he went down in it he came out with the cellophane still rolled up. We fought over the purse and he shook it and he come out with this cellophane. Didn't even unwrap it, mind you.

I'm standing there, sick on a habit, and he tells me, "Here's your ticket back to Goree [Texas women's prison], bitch." Just like that.

I looked at him a few minutes and it didn't dawn on me that maybe he can't do this. I tell him, "Well, baby, if you can put me there with that piece of paper, well, go ahead on." He still hadn't unwrapped it, he didn't know what was in that paper unless he put it in there. And, baby, after all these years I'm going to start *carrying* a cap of dope? Sick? In my purse? You know what I mean. So I told him, "Well, go ahead on." We went on down. Strickland threatened to take my kids away from me if I didn't tell him who my man was and what time he was going to be back. He told me how many caps of dope I had the night before. I'd counted it out in front of one really good character. That punk. But I didn't have any of it then. They tore up my house and stole my diamond ring—it wasn't hot, someone got it for a hot check, but it wasn't from a burglary—that I'd got for some narcotics.

Strickland said, "Go call the juvenile department to come get her kids."

I told him, and I meant it, "If there is a God in heaven," when he told me he was going to take my kids, "if you take my kids I will blow your motherfucking house up. With your kids in it. You take my kids and see if I don't do it."

So he says, "I don't want your goddamned kids. All I want to do is get your ass in that penitentiary."

I told him, "Oh, you'll probably get me there, but you're not doing it fair."

So I made them take me to my mama's with the kids. I wasn't about to let them take them there without me. Chavez said, "Sal, don't you trust me?" Chavez I knew before he ever was on the narcotics squad; he's a pretty fair shooter. He said, "Come on, Sal. You're about the hard-headest woman I've ever met." He said, "Don't you trust me?"

I told him, "Man, I don't trust nobody. I don't believe in nothing, I don't believe in nobody. What I can see is a fact, that's all." So when I seen that my mama had my kids, then I rested all right. Sick and all, I was all right. That's how I won my kids in court from my daddy and his people, because the police got up and said I was a good mother even though I was an addict.

I was out on bail in about three months. They filed the habitual on me and I jumped bond. That's when my hell really begun. This boy that I had known back in the early forties had shot this woman in Dallas and he was in jail facing the chair and I was still pretty crazy about him in them days. I went to Dallas and tried to see him, but I couldn't because I was on escape from Houston. Finally I said fuck it and went to Galveston and got with this boy I had been pushing dope with, him and his old lady, and we went to Canada. I was on a big rib, I thought they wouldn't deport me from Canada, even if they found out that the States wanted me. Come to find out that they escort you to the bridge as an unfit citizen and they give you to the States. So I thought, "Well, that's it." I come back to Fort Worth and I run into a gal I was looking for who was married to Raymond Hamilton's nephew. All this bunch, I knew them all. It wasn't hard. I got right in.

I still had kind of a yen but I didn't have a habit. We was shooting dope and I started stealing with this clique, the Belands of Fort Worth. I got in with them and we started stealing jewelry and running it to this fence in Kansas. We started boosting. Then I got in with this burglar and we started burglarizing. I'm still on the run from Houston. There was this old thief I was with, he had plenty of money. He was broke if he had under a thousand dollars, that's the kind of thief he was. He'd get out and get some more, it was his security. For me, as long as I had what dope I needed I was happy. Satisfied anyhow. And Richard Lee Whitefield walks into my room.

When he walked in I thought, "Hell, I'll bet that's a thieving son-ofabitch." That's the first thing I thought. Later on, I asked him, "What you think about when the first time you ever seen me?"

He says, "Oh, I thought you was real sweet."

I said, "You're a lying sonofabitch. You were thinking about how much dope I had." But he was romancing me and I'm a romantic.

I told him I was with Robert and I said, "You want to make a trip with us?"

He looked at me, kind of smiling, and says, "Yeah."

So the three of us took off and went to Kansas, Nebraska, and all up through the States, and we made some money. In the meantime Richard Lee and me was slipping around in back of Robert's back and romancing. Whenever he'd go to bed we'd just get romancing and get knocked out together. He was watching out for me more than Robert was. Robert knew there was something going on, but he didn't have the guts enough to come up against Richard. We got back to Dallas and drove up in front of Richard Lee's mama's to let him out, and Robert said, "Well, man, we'll see you."

And I says, "Yeah, I guess so, man."

He looked at me. "What's happening?"

I told him, "I'm staying with him."

He said, "You don't want me to carry you back to Hazel's?"

And I said, "No, I don't want to go back there. I want to stay with Richard."

So him and I start stealing together. I guess we made every state in the union. Every state we was crossing he was trying to get me to marry him in it. All this time now I'm still sending money to Jake in the penitentiary through his mama and through my mother. I couldn't go around to the joint because they was waiting on me. They had picked up my brother and whipped him unpitifully, trying to make him tell them where I was. But my people didn't know anyhow because I was on the run. We went up to Kansas and we pulled this heist and this other boy went with us. They had a shoot-to-kill out on us, on me and Richard Lee. A $5,000 reward, shoot-to-kill, and all that shit.

Did you get in any shoot-outs?

No, but I would have shot them sonofabitches if they'd rolled up beside me. I had Richard Lee make me a rack to go up on the side of the car and I had this gun up there. If they pulled up when I put my hands up, I was going to start shooting because I know what I was going to get when they got me—this life sentence.

I knew I was going to get it, so I just was going to go ahead and go crazy.

I just went ahead and stole all I wanted and everything else.

We come back to his mama's in Dallas one afternoon and his mama says, "You all better hook 'em [take off]. A man was here a while ago and Decker's been calling out here."

Now Decker's the kind of sheriff that if he calls out to your house and tells you to come in and talk, you go talk. You won't go to jail if you go talk to him, he'll let you make bond right then. So we got out a little piece to Denton and he called his sister and she said, "Decker wants you to come in and surrender yourself on these bonds. And he'll work something out." So Richard Lee goes for it. He goes to see Decker.

I tell him, "Boy, you're a sucker." I'm a Harris County [Houston] gal and I believe that when them sonofabitches call, trick them, I'm gone.

Anyway, Richard Lee calls the bondsman and he comes out to meet us. We're sitting there out on a country road and this bondsman is with us and I says to Richard Lee, "If you're not at Al's"—that's this bootlegger; he's like Murder Incorporated, he used to be there in Dallas, but he's squaring it now and he's just a bootlegger—"If you're not out at Al's house at six o'clock when I call I'll know that you're in a switch. I'm gonna be there and if you ain't out there I'll know you didn't get out of jail."

The bondsman keeps looking at me kind of funny and Richard Lee says, "Maybe you better not go out to Al's. You go to my sister-in-law's."

I says okay. Then when Herman, the bondsman, leaves, I tell him, "No, I'm going out to Al's. I feel better out there."

I went to Al's. At eight o'clock that night I'm sitting there all on the nod [on narcotics]. Al was saying something about Richard Lee being two hours late and just as he's starting to call somebody I looked up and I seen these flashlights. Now they live way out in the country and I seen these flashlights coming across the field. I had a white Oldsmobile that I had beside the house with a canvas over it. So I ran and hid behind the front door. When I started out they was all around the side and the front.

The bondsman snitched you out.

That's right. There was a venetian blind on the door that was partway open and they seen my pants leg. Mordan opened the door and he said, "Well, goddamn. Come on out of there, girl." I sat down on a chair and he said, "Why don't you get your business straight in Houston?" Then he said, "Man, I wasn't looking for you. I was looking for Peggy Fry."

I said, "You lying sonofabitch, you was looking for me because you knew my goddamned business as soon as you seen me. You knew I was going to be here." He was trying to cover up for the bondsman. I told him, "Herman will make my bond and Herman will pay for this little number."

"What do you mean, pay for it? What are you going to do? Are you going to blow his car up?"

I told him, "No, I ain't going to harm him, he ain't going to be touched. But that motherfucker will lose."

So I went on to jail that Tuesday and everybody in Dallas said I wasn't going to be able to make bond again because I'd jumped bond in Houston. I was one of the worst bond-jumpers in Texas. They know when I hit the ground, that's it, Jack, I'm gone. There was only two people I wouldn't jump bond on, Sam Hoover and Horace Cook. I just respect the hell out of them. Sam, he's doing sixty years now over here and we always had a feeling for each other. Decker and all of them were saying, "Well, you're not getting out of jail anymore, I bet you." On Friday I hit the ground. On Saturday morning I had the bonds in my hand from Cook to get Richard Lee out. I walked into Decker's office.

He said, "You're not getting him out, you're not getting him out." I presented these bonds to him and he said, "Well, I'll be goddamned. You Houston gals can't be beat." And I laughed. And he went ahead and he says, "Well, be here in the morning. But you've got to have $2,500 cash bond."

When I'd hit the ground on Friday I called Herman that had done me around and I told him, "Herman, I'm out."

He said, "You're what?"

And I said, "I'm out. Send me $300 to give Cook."

And he says, "Well, goddamn, Sal . . ."

I said, "Don't give me no bullshit, baby. We've been giving you a world of money every goddamned week." And we had. We'd come in from out of town, burglarizing places up through the States, and we put it on his desk. So I said, "Don't tell me that bullshit. All I have to do is call Ray and he'll come over there and get it one way or the other. Now are you going to send it to me?"

He said, "Goddamnit, I didn't say I wasn't going to send it to you. I just said I'd have to go to the bank."

I told him, "Oh, while you're at the bank, get $2,500 to get Richard Lee out on Federal bond." Boy, he was dying.

He said, "Goddamn, I spent a lot on him on the bond."

I said, "Twenty-five hundred. And $300 to Cook. And $100 for my plane fare."

So he sent it. Hell, there wasn't nothing else he could do about it. Two or three people called him up and told him, "If you don't get him out on bond you're going to find yourself flying through the goddamned air." And he's just square enough to really get uptight. They was real sincere people.

So, anyway, he says, "I'll tell you what. I'll come to Houston and get you."

"All right. Be here at ten o'clock tonight."

Hell, I was so fixed and so knocked out I couldn't even meet him at the airport. I was an hour late and he met me at the Rice Hotel. I had my boys with me and we went down the next morning and he paid Cook and co-signed to get Richard Lee out. Then he come on back and we got Richard Lee.

And so we started out on our spree again.

Something else. The night they busted me out there at Farmer's Field at this bootlegger's house, the Federal was with them. They had searched my car and found a gun. This stud that we was stealing with was supposed to have unloaded all the guns but there was one left in back of the car. They traced it down and put it on us and the Federal filed for transporting stolen arms across state lines. They tried to put it on the boys, but it was my goddamned car and they wasn't there when the gun was found, so how can they say it belonged to them? It didn't hold up. But it come out in the newspapers, this is how fantastic the newspapers can play things up, that we was gun-runners for Cuba. I don't even know a goddamned Cuban!

So the Federal arrested us on that anyhow and I stayed in jail four months and we got out again. It was about three weeks later and he was due in the Federal court in front of the commissioner to change this $2,500 bond into another bond and we was driving down Buckner Boulevard in Dallas and one harness bull is following us about five miles an hour. We'd been out on a party all night and I had one of those cellophane bags full of narcotics that we had got out of these two drugstores upstate. I was about five miles from the stash where we was going to stash it with the other stuff and I was counting these pills. All these dollies [Dolophines] and everything in my hand. I had seven hundred of fives, sevens, and tens. I was telling how much I could get out of them if I didn't want to kick my goddamned habit. This bottle's about the size of two packs of cigarettes. And I had about seven little bottles of morphine and seven bottles of Pantopon. Just oodles. The papers called me the Walking Pharmacy. When the harness bull drove up and stopped us, Richard Lee got out of the car and left the motor running. He meant for me to take off with all the goddamned narcotics. I kept thinking, "Should I throw it in the ditch or should I go ahead and drive off?" He's already in the police car and he's calling in on us. He wouldn't just give Richard Lee a ticket, he had to call in downtown to find out what to do. I knew Richard Lee would get beat to death if I run off and left him there, so I thought, "No, I'm going to do something with this goddamn narcotics. I don't know what I'm gonna do." Anyway we went on down to the police station. I had one of those Alan Ladd jackets with deep pockets. I had that bottle still in my pocket from the party that I'd forgotten about. And I had these toreadors on, but the toreadors were real loose. So I put this bag between my legs and I was making it just fine. I got in the police car and we was telling them we had to go to the commissioner's office. I knew that if I got to the commissioner's office I could ditch it.

So we got in the police car and while they was shaking our car down, Richard Lee says, "Put that goddamned stuff under the seat."

I'm telling him, "No, it's all right."

He says, "Put it under the goddamned seat."

So I unzip my pants and all I could get ahold of was the joints and I pulled that out and got it under the seat and by that time the police turned around and seen me. So I'm cooling it and everything. I'm sitting there looking off and he don't let on that he busted me.

Now Richard Lee never had a habit. He had had yens, but he never had a habit before until he got with me. So we got in the police department and he's on the third floor. These other detectives are trying to find a woman to shake me down. I'm standing there and he says, "What are you going to do?"

I says, "I don't know, but stand in front of me."

I got this bottle, this big one I told you about, and stuck it up my pussy. Bottle and all. Boy, it was the biggest thing I ever had in there. I took two vials and laid them right in the cheeks of my ass.

So I'm in the police station with all this, and Richard Lee's saying, "What're you doing?"

I told him, "I can't get it all up me to carry in jail, but I'll bet you one goddamned thing, I'm going to get caught trying to carry something in there to keep my habit on."

He says, "Oh, my God!"

And he's shaking and everything. Now he's an old-time thief. He got caught sneaking narcotics into the Dallas jail and everything else, all of this, but he's still nervous. So he said, "What are you going to do?"

I said, "Well, goddamnit, I'm fixing to get busted, that's what I'm fixing to do." That's all I could think of to tell the crazy sonofabitch. So we go down there and they couldn't find nobody in the office to shake me. We get down in the jail division and the matron says, "Come on back here, Sal."

There's my sister-in-law in the phone booth, Richard Lee's other wife is what she really was. She's with his brother. They done got in jail. She's trying to get me to give the dope to her and I'm saying, "They're behind me."

I just reached down into my pants and pulled that bag out, turned around, and told the matron, "Here's what you want." I was thinking I'd save my stash.

She says, "I still got to shake you."

I says, "Okay."

So I went on around there and pulled my pants down, dropped them.

And she says, "Bend over."

I told her, "You going to bend me over? You better get that fucking man out there to help you 'cause I'm not bending over. I gave you the goddamned narcotics."

I just bluffed my way out of it. I says, "You got them, fuck it."

And she says, "Okay, but I shook you."

I said, "You goddamned sure did."

And we walked out and I was saved. I got up and went to the commissioner's office.

Isn't this bottle getting kind of lumpy to be walking around with?

Oh, God! I kept telling Richard Lee, I said, "If I didn't have my habit I swear to God I'd bust my kicks [have an orgasm] right here."

He said, "What do you mean?"

I told him, "Goddamn, I got that bottle up me. Don't you think I feel it?" And he was cracking up at me, and here we are, we're going to jail, and we're just cracking up laughing.

That bottle. It was the biggest sonofabitch I ever seen. A square one at that.

Later we went to the commissioner and then I nearly killed my fool self taking too many of those pills over at the jail. I don't know what happened, I just blacked out for about three days on this habit. They couldn't find my stash. They knew I had a stash but they couldn't find it. It was the craziest damn week I ever spent.

What I'm really trying to stay out for was the Dawson boy got out of jail. I wanted to get him on his feet. He's so goddamn helpless. Show you these idiotic things. I was going to get him on his feet. I had this Cadillac and I was going to give it to him. I got this fifteen years from Dallas in the state and I had two years in the Federal. Then I went to Houston and I got this life sentence. There was ten lawyers sitting in back of me trying to get me to fire this court-appointed lawyer they had gave me 'cause he wasn't no good. You could see it.

Why didn't you?

I don't know. It was the damndest thing I ever went through. I was in a stage where I just didn't give a damn. Dawson had got out the day after I got my fifteen years, and he didn't come to see me. He didn't do nothing for me. I stood by him the seventeen months, even when I was on the run, even when I was in jail, I stood by him. And I believed in him. I believed in him more than anything in the world. In the meantime, Leo had the chair, and Carolyn, my friend, she had the chair coming up. Richard Lee was on the run again with a shoot-to-kill on him. I couldn't make bond no more, and so I just didn't give a fuck. I felt just like I had my back against the wall and that was it, Jack, that's where you say, I've got to the bottom. I went in the courtroom and I got that life sentence and the judge asks me did I have anything to say. I told him, "Have I anything to say? I got a lot to say. It won't do no good, but I'll tell you one goddamn thing. I do not accept it. And I won't accept it."

And I still haven't accepted it. Maybe that sounds strange, but I have not accepted it. I have not accepted that I have got a life sentence.

Something else: this old policeman that picked me up, I told him I didn't have a habit. Because you know what, I couldn't admit that I was a dope addict. I couldn't. That was the hardest thing for me to do, to admit that I was a dope addict.

After shooting for fifteen years.

It was the hardest thing. Up until I got this time and then I finally just told myself, "Boy, you are a dope fiend."

Now I've got this fifteen and the life for habitual and the two years on the Federal detainer for robbery.

I noticed that there's another detainer from Houston.

That's two years in the county jail for collision by auto or something. I like killed a little boy. I was all knocked out and I like killed a little boy. And they gave me two years.

When you were working—everything from burglary to boosting to turning tricks—did you buy your way out of many things?

I tricked a judge one time for some boosting cases that I had on me. I got out of some jail time that way. And one old detective that busted me, he wanted the merchandise I had, one of them big tape recorders, the radios, and that power saw, I want to call it a jigsaw but I'm not sure what the name is. Stuff I legged [boosted by hiding it between her legs under her skirt].

You legged a power saw?

I got scars on my leg. I had about $500 worth of merchandise and I kept telling them that this old trick gave it to me, that he had this shop out of town, that he gave it to me and it was legal. He told me, "If it's legal then you won't be getting no goddamn lawyer and trying to get it back, will you?"

I told him, "I really won't."

He said, "Well, I'll break this hold on you in the morning." And that was it. I just lost my merchandise and he didn't file on me.

Sam told me that just about every time he was busted his apartment was cleaned of everything except if there were any drugs there they left enough of that to make a case with.

I know it. That's all it is. That Strickland, the one that busted me with this cap of dope in my purse that wasn't there, he isn't on the police force no more because they found out that he was crooked. The grand jury investigated him and his job.

Until Captain George Severan came in office in the vice squad in Houston and started an investigation and started cleaning up Houston I had a regular payoff man. When Severan came in, I had to close my house down, had to get out of Houston for a while and everything. That's when I started doing time, when they started closing the red-light district and getting real tough on the addicts.

What about lawyers?

This last time is about the only time I had one paid off before. See, we was always in with the bondsmen and lawyers. I've used everyone in Houston almost, because I had a good name with them. Even jumping bond as I did. They knew they was going to get jumped on, that I was going to run on them, but they knew they'd get their money too. But still, they have to hold that bond till I'm caught, and they knew that eventually I'd get caught. I knew it too.

Then I'd have different things, like boosting charges, on me, and I'd call up this payoff man and I'd tell him, "See how much you can get that store not to file on me for."

He'd say, "Are you going back in the store?"

I'd say, "Hell, no." Something like that. And he'd promise them every goddamned thing under the sun.

He was a policeman.

Jack: "The criminal code is bullshit . . ."

To me the criminal code is bullshit. The very guys that promulgate it are the ones that violate it. If you're tough enough, if you're bad enough, whatever the individual does then is right, and that includes snitching. That's the biggest bunch of shit.

You ask the old-timers has the joint changed for ratting and snitching? Almost every one of them says, "Yes, you bet, boy, really changed." But this code is so much shit for the young ones, it just doesn't exist.

It exists to this extent: might makes right. In the convict context.

I like to say I'm not a snitch. I probably have done some snitching, not to my knowledge directly, but I'm sure in the code it would be considered that. No one has ever come to the joint with me, I've always come alone, but you'll notice down here they always have a "fall partner" [partner convicted at the same time]. Some people must be doing some talking if they're always getting convicted together. I don't know, I've never quite understood that, but it occurs.

Now the way the Rangers carry on with you—I've had dealings with them twice, not for prostitution but other areas, robbery—the way they carry on with you you'd probably say your mother is a no good so-and-so and you boys just put her in jail. They are rather strong in their methods.

My first experience with the Rangers was when I was young, real young, I was seventeen, right before I went in the navy. It was in Houston. I used to box then, amateur fights, and I had won quite a few. We had gone out to Playland Park, it's an amusement park, and we got into a few cars. There were four other guys and three of them I knew through the fighting and they were characters.

So we all go to jail. This one guy who was a sergeant in the sheriff's department and two Rangers, they carried me out and took me to a place they called the Windmill. I was handcuffed, I was by myself then and I didn't know where the other guys were and it was at night. They were going to put me over this kind of wall they have there. They take a chain with a weight on it and put it over the wall and it pulls you off the ground. I had heard about this and I was scared to death of it. I don't care who knows that, I was frightened. I'm talking about *afraid!* I'm not talking about that big tough bullshit. I'm telling you, I was afraid. I was young then.

Instead of doing that, they just went through all the motions of doing it. But this one guy, this sergeant—I say sergeant, I don't know that he was, but he acted like one—he had a blackjack in his hand and he kept hitting it into his palm. Instead of putting the weight over, what he did was he hit me up the side of the head with the blackjack. And I fell down, it knocked me down. And the Rangers started kicking me. I don't know if you've ever had boots in your butt or stomach or in your nuts, but *man!* It's very painful, I was still chained, and as I say I was extremely frightened.

But that's not all they did. A very good friend of mine, he's doing life now, they put a wire to the battery of a car and they put the other wire to his testicles.

How long did they have you there?

It seemed to me like forever, but I guess it was a couple of hours.

Did they bring you [make you say what they wanted you to say]?

Oh, yes, I admitted stealing it. You know: "Yes, sir!"

Sam told me, "I'm always a half-nut and I always used to say I can't be brought, but they brought me."

There isn't anybody that can't be brought, and that's what I mean about the inmate code: the bravado, the facade, call it what you want. It's so much shit.

The only thing I do say is that we're put in prison for violating laws, they are behind the shield and can do the very same things we are behind bars for. To criminals they can. I know they're not going to go up to *you* and hit you over the head or put a wire to your testicles, you know they just won't do it, but to people like *me* they will, to people in my element.

Nick McMurphy: "They liked to beat me to death . . ."

The first time I ever thought of cracking a safe I was a little boy around Root Square Park and I heard older men talking about it. How they did it. And I guess I was about thirteen and I went out and tried it and it worked. That first time, I just went and got me a Model T valve from a junkyard and I went to a service station, stole me a sledgehammer, and broke in a place, knocked the knob off the safe and drove the spindle back, and it come open.

Root Square Park. It's a city park in Houston. I can remember Clyde Barrow, Raymond Hamilton. I know you know of them. People would come by that park. Of course they are from Dallas, but they made their connections at Root Square Park. I don't know—I was raised up around there and that was a park that every character that I know hung out at. Just seems like they were raised up around there and congregated there, would meet there and go steal them a car or something. Everything I got introduced to, that's where I got introduced to it, right there at Root Square Park.

Model T Ford valve and tire-changing hammer, about a six-pound hammer that I got from a service station. That's just "driving spindle." And when you use a punch and a hammer, that's called punching a safe. When you blow it that's called "blowing a safe." When you rip one, that's just destroying it and ripping it.

Is that the same as peeling?

That's peeling, yes, sir.

Which do you prefer?

I prefer blowing one. I blowed quite a few.

How did you learn how to use explosives?

Practicing on tree stumps. I never did use any nitro. I've had some around, but I never used it. I used nitro gelatin. It's safer. If somebody wants to get after you, you can throw it out of your car or something, it's not going to go off. If you have to ditch it and some-body finds it, they're not going to hurt themselves with it because it's going to take a forty-pound jar plus fire to set it off. You have to use a cap. But nitro, you can just stand back and swing a sledgehammer at it and knock it off. Have a wreck or something, somebody get after you and you have a wreck, you're liable to blow yourself up.

How long were you a burglar?

I'm forty-five years old now and I turned out when I was thirteen. That's a long time.

How much time since you were thirteen did you spend in jail?

Almost all of it. I did three hitches in Leavenworth and I did a ten-year bit here, and now I've got life here.

The Federal: I fell out of Houston on a narcotic charge. I wasn't dealing, I was using, and I was filed on for possession. I was burglariz-ing drugstores and hospitals and things like that.

Were you burglarizing drugstores for money and drugs?

Just for drugs. Naturally you're going to take the money too, but I was after the narcotics.

I love to work Sundays in the daytime: supermarkets, drugstores, anything like that in the daytime. Because you can put on a suit of clothes, a topcoat, and you can have your tools around your waist and walk up to it like you're using a key on the front door and walk right on in. It just looks like you're dressed nice and everything. And if you go in a country town, put on a pair of khakis and cowboy boots and a big hat, and if you're in a city, well, you dress like you're going to church.

And I've never been caught in a place but one time in my life, and that was in a professional football joint in Houston. I run into that silent alarm, that ADT, and it was hid. I knocked it off but I couldn't get out of there in time because I had already locked up be-hind myself when I went in. See, when I go in the front door I lock it back.

What I do is, I've got a short jimmy [small crowbar with a bent bill] up each sleeve and I put one over the lock and one under the lock and across, then open the glass door or anything else. You've got so much give and you put your knee against it and the one that swings, if it's a double door, you just push it in and then when you step inside you throw your jimmys over and under it and lock her back. That's for anybody who's shaking the door or anything. Make sure that you're careful and don't leave marks, don't do any damage. If you damage the door you know you're going to have to get in there and get it done and get on out of there. If you don't do any damage you know you've got as long as you want in there.

I've spent all night in buildings. I'd a lot rather come in than go out. It's not as scary going in as it is coming out because you never know, there's always that chance that maybe somebody saw you go in. And around Houston you know that those police won't come in after you. They lay and wait for you to come out and then they try to kill you. That's Houston police.

They're not going to come in after you. They're going to let you come out and then they're going to shoot you. If they can see you when they drive up, if they can see you inside the building, they're liable to shoot you or maybe come in after you. But if they can't see you they're not going to come in after you. I've been in there and knew I rumbled, had them come in shining lights all over the place, and I just had to run out.

Don't you ever carry a gun when you work?

No. It's a bad thing to get the reputation of carrying a gun. You know you've got your death certificate signed then.

My wife, I'd rather have her than a man working with me. But I won't let her go in a joint with me. I have in a case of emergency, but that's all.

I was surrounded once in a little old country town. I looked out the front and there's shotguns and everything else at the windows. And I hear the horn on my car—beep, beep, beep—and here she comes down that alley, there's that car jumping in the air. She come right through them, picked me up, and drove on out. You won't find any men that'd do that, they'd run off and leave you. They'd say, "Man, I didn't see any way to get in there to you." She just drove down that alley and picked me up. She's got a lot of nerve, more nerve than I've got, I guarantee you.

There's been a lot of stories about her. She was Texas' bad girl for a long time. She killed a matron in the Dallas county jail and escaped about eleven times from Gainesville and from the woman's Tennessee joint. All the old-time bad boys know her. She turned out when she was eleven years old. I've got a picture up there that she just sent me, it come out of a detective magazine. Her mother sent her it out of her scrapbook and she looks like a little baby. And she was already in a detective magazine. Boy, if that isn't awful.

Like she told me, "Hell, just drive the car. Get me a pistol."

I says, "You dummy up. I'll do the stealing and there ain't gonna be any pistols."

I've been with her since 1951. We've actually been lawfully married since April 4, 1960.

She was seventeen years old and had just got out of Gainesville for two weeks. She was down there on murdering that matron in the Dallas county jail and they finally turned her loose on account of she was a bad influence on the other girls and everything. They couldn't hold her and they finally give her Christmas clemency and told her not to come back. She's thirty-three now but she still looks like a twenty-four-year-old. But she's done all of her life in the penitentiary. All of it. From the time she was eleven years old on up to now.

She's in for Western Union money orders this time. You get a book of those money orders and sit in front of the place and type them out, whatever you think they go for—$100, $200, or whatever it is. They'll cash it. She was in the Federal for that. And she's got a $200-and-something fine for three assaults on matrons on Houston. She's got jail time on it and everything.

She keeps hitting matrons.

She'd rather whip a matron than eat. I don't know why.

Once when I was on parole from the Federal they had the joint I was in surrounded. In Lufkin, Texas. I ran out through them and got far enough away to where I could fight the case—half a block or something. That gives you enough room to fight your case, anyway.

I stayed out three months that time and went back, was out four months, and went back on a C.R. violation. That's conditional release. The Federal has parole and also C.R. The good time you earn when you're in the Federal, you still have to answer to them when you get out on it. In Texas, the good time you earn, when you're discharged, you're discharged.

So then I was out and I still had that Lufkin case on me. I was out for months and they tried me on it and I got ten years. I made an appeal bond on it, and while I was on appeal bond I accumulated quite a few cases and then I lost my appeal. Then I appealed to the Supreme Court of the United States and they refused it and I come on in.

I did the ten, then I was out and I didn't do anything for a year. Didn't do any wrong at all. Matter of fact, I didn't even steal a bobby pin. I was going real good and bought me a home in Mesquite, that's at Dallas. I opened me up a little cleaners and had another laundry and cleaners doing my cleaning and laundry for me, until I could get all my presses and everything in. And they kept riding me, kept riding me, kept riding me. My old lady, she couldn't go to the grocery store without they arrested her. Same way with me, and we hadn't done anything. Now that's the truth. You hear people say, "Oh, they rolled me, they did this and they did that." But that's the truth. And they finally busted me.

I had a lot of sickness too. I had a heart attack, and just as soon as I got over that I come down with hepatitis.

I just sold everything I had and went to shooting dope, went to getting me a few safes. That's the way it was.

How long was it after you started with safes again before you were busted?

It wasn't long because they know my work. Even if they're not sure, I mean if somebody don't tell them I done it, they still can pretty well tell. It's like everybody has a pattern—and I don't care how hard you try to mess it up, but an old-time policeman knows your pattern. I've went in places and they've had a couple of safes and I'd hurry up and get the money out of the one I knew the money was in, then I'd jump on the other safe even though I knew there wasn't nothing in it because I wanted to throw them off the track. I'd just damage it up and make it look like an amateur had done it and taken off. And I've had them tell me, "I knew you made it."

What is there about your method of operation that they can recognize so well?

Say I walk in and there's a safe there. First thing I do is I try it for daylock. If it's not on daylock, then I'll knock the knob real quick. Punching is your fastest way if it'll punch real quick.

You mean the pin behind the knob?

You knock your combination off and then there's a spindle. Most people will just haul it loose and hit that spindle and drive it all the way out. Well, on a safe that messes you up sometimes. You can move a spindle a quarter of an inch lots of times, just barely move it, and she'll go ahead and come open. These new turnouts this day and time, first thing they're gonna do is hit that spindle and drive it all the way out. Say it will come open when it's only moved one-quarter of an inch, inch, say it comes open. Well, that's it, I'm in there, I get the money, and I'm gone. The minute they look at it and see it's only been just barely tapped they say, "Nick McMurphy."

And say if I ripped one. If it's a solid steel box and I'm in there and I don't have any explosives, I hit to the left top corner and that'll blow the corner out. Then I take my hatchet, jimmy, or whatever I got, and lay it right there on that seam and it'll come down. And if it's not a solid steel box, if it's just fireproof, I just cut a windowpane right in the front and reach in and cut the locking-bar strap, turn the handle, and it opens. They got that new-style fireproofing out there in these safes now that is more like a gum. It's as hard as this table, but when you try to chisel it out, it gums. You rip one and then you've got a half a day's work to get through the fireproofing. The old-style fireproofing, you just hit it and it just crumbles all out, just like old concrete or something. And if I work on a gum they know it's me because I'm not going to do all that work on it. I'm just gonna cut me one little hole there and cut my locking-bar strap and get out of there quick.

And aren't there enough burglars who are that experienced to know that's the way to do it?

No. Burglars out there today, they'll make two or three safes, get busted, and then they'll know that they made those two or three and when they get out they don't go back to it. I don't know how it is, but they can just tell if it's a professional job or an amateur. And that's why when I was out this time I tried to mess up everything I did. If I done something real fast, then after I got my money I'd go ahead and do a little more to it, to try to throw them off.

Don't the safe companies weld a steel plate behind the door to keep people from punching it?

They do. They weld steel blocks behind them and put soft lead spindles on them and everything else. But when they do, they just get their safe tore completely up. If I see that he's got it rigged where it won't punch, I'll bring me some gelatin and I'll lift his door off there for him real quick. When you make one burglarproof it's just more expense on you because you're going to buy a new one.

Those keysters, nigger-heads [round wall safes], they're punch-proof. You're not going to punch them or anything. On a keyster, the majority of them, you've got a round door, and then you've got a chromium plate over it to make it look nice. Well, that's just sweated on with solder. You knock your knob off and knock your handle off, then you take your chisel and you just hit that chromium plate in front on that door and it flies off, and there's the old rough steel. Then there's a little quarter-inch plug in there, you just take your punch and hit it once and it falls out. And if you're good about lining things up you could line up, with your wires, line it up and work your combination. But me, I'm not going to take that kind of time. I'm going to flip her right up on her back and either fill it with sand or fill it with water, either one, then take my cutting torch and cut me a hole big enough to get my hand in, reach in there and bring everything out [the water or sand is so he won't burn the contents].

You're not going to cut that door. You cut around it. Take either one of your front corners or your back corners.

I've heard people say they're just about impossible to open.

No, no. You can drill them quick and take a star drill and drill them and they open. Now those big old cannonballs, something like that as big as that box over there and all in concrete, I wouldn't fool with one of them. Not for anything in the world, because I know I'm not going to get in. One of them that got a big old steering wheel on it about that big around, a big old crank you have to crank the door out and all that kind of stuff. I wouldn't fool with one in a minute, not at all.

You catch a lot of wall safes in homes. A lot of them got a cast-iron door on them and people think, whenever they see that it is a keyster, "I can't get in there." But if they take their ten- or twelve-pound sledgehammer and hit that door three or four times it'll crumble all to pieces. They put those cast-iron doors on and ride along on their reputations.

How would you pick the places you hit?

A supermarket's good anytime. I'd always get a look at the safe or get somebody to go look at it for me. I'd want the name of it and if it was a square door or a round door, if it was a drop handle or a T-knob. That's about all the information I'd need. To know what kind of tools to bring.

I'd usually carry about a ten- or twelve-pound sledgehammer with a short handle, three or four punches, a pair of vice grips, and I'd have me two jimmys that I'd worked down a sharp edge on both sides of and made them thin where they'd go in the crack of a door without having to do any damage to the door when it's getting in there. And that's all I'd carry unless I'd take some explosives with me. And if I took some explosives I'd usually have a little old one-horse drill and an extension cord. I'd carry it all on me and you wouldn't even know I had it. I'd stick the sledgehammer in my pants.

What is the burglary-tool law in Texas? Do they have one?

You could call it a burglary-tool law. If they catch you with them they're gonna beat you half to death.

That's a little different. Have the Supreme Court decisions in the last few years been cutting down on beatings?

Not when I was out, it hadn't done anything or changed a thing then. I'll tell you what changes it: if everybody that got whipped would file on the police. The reason I say this, I filed on them in the Federal when they whipped me at Lufkin so bad. They whipped me for three days down there. It was Beaumont, and Port Arthur and Nacogdoches.

Were they taking turns?

No, they all come down and met at the same time. And they carried me up to the jury room up there and they whipped me and whipped me and whipped me, and then they carried me to the river and put handcuffs on me and held my head under the water. And then they told me they were going to bust my spleen and my kidneys and everything. A big old sonofagun would jump up and down on my stomach. Stuff like that, you know? They whipped me for about three days. When the Houston police came to get me—and some of them are still at the Harris county jail in Houston and can verify this—they wouldn't accept me. Because I was beat up so bad. They made them carry me to Jeff Davis Hospital first and then they accepted me afterwards.

My Federal probation officer came up and saw me the next morning, and he called the FBI and the FBI come down to where they had me in jail and wanted to know what they could do about it and what I wanted to do about it. They said I could file on them, and I said, "I don't know any of them's names."

They said, "Well, we'll find the names, you don't have to worry about that."

I said, "I just know what towns they're from."

He said, "We'll find the names."

So I filed on all the counties. Then, when I got out of Federal, they wanted to know what I wanted to do about it. I told them, "As long as they leave me alone I don't want to do anything about it."

That case of mine, they never even made me make bond on. Then the statute of limitations was up on my Federal case in three years, and the day after the statute of limitations was up, Lufkin came and got me, made me make bond, and three or four months later they tried me. That was in 1950.

Court rulings that are coming down now, I believe it's going to help everybody. Not only the criminal, there's a lot of people who get locked up and get slapped around.

Have you ever had any experience with the Rangers?

A long time ago.

Are they as bad as everybody says?

They're worse. You can't describe Texas Rangers when they take you out.

And not only them. There's others. Like ———— from Houston. He's pulled up now, he's high-up in the police down there. Inspector ————. He used to be the hired killer for the Houston police department. He's pulled up now, but then, he'd see you in a drugstore, he'd just walk up to the glass and shoot you. Just ask any Houston thief or Dallas thief about ————. He just believes in killing you. I don't know if he knew who was in the place or not, but there's one boy in here that he shot three times through the window of a place. He was bent over the safe and he walked up to the window and shot him two or three times. The boy laid in front of the safe and played dead until some more people came in there. The police were in there and they thought he was dead. But then when some more people came in the store, then he started moaning, "Get me to the hospital." He got twenty years, just got out a while back.

I've never heard of Rangers getting caught up for beating.

I've heard of that but I've never heard of one of them getting any time yet. But I have heard of them getting filed on. There's a boy right here now, he just went back on a writ. He said the Rangers whipped him and whipped a confession out of him. When he got through, the Rangers told them that he's lying on the stand, so the court turns around and files perjury on him, habitual criminal, and gives him another life sentence. But the Court of Criminal Appeals took it off him, said, No, you can't give him a life sentence for perjury on the habitual criminal. But he's still stuck with the same life sentence he went down to court on. And because he said the Rangers whipped him and because they said they didn't they filed perjury on him.

They used to be bad, but in the last twelve years I haven't heard too much about the Rangers.

But they still do it. If an old-time character is in trouble someplace and they think he's been messing with several different counties and towns, they'll go get him. They'll hide him out, they'll carry him to this jail, and as soon as they've stayed there a couple of days or a day, they'll carry him to another. They might take him to some ranch house out in West Texas. They used to have a favorite spot close to Houston called "the Windmill." If you've heard anybody talking you've heard about the Windmill. They used to take you out there and whip you. Your lawyer would look for you, he'd get on your trail, he'd trail you over here to Richmond or Rosenburg, and the minute he called they'd grab you and take you to another jail, and they couldn't catch up to you with a writ that way. And that way they'd just whip you and whip you and whip you—and finally get a confession.

You can take so much. I used to say, "Well, they couldn't whip one out of me." But I've had it whipped out of me so I'm not going to say that any more. You just get to the point where you don't care. You'd rather do some time than take any more of their whipping.

I'm telling you. Now I can't see them slapping somebody and "Yes, sir, I'll sign anything." But I mean when you're *really* whipped. When your eyes are shut and your ears are perforated. Man, in Lufkin they made a believer out of me down there. They like to beat me to death. They perforated my left eardrum, my groin was swelled up where I couldn't walk, my fingers was swelled. They'd take my fingers and bend them, twist them, stomp on them. And these muscles here [just above the clavicle], they'd work on these muscles. Did you ever have anybody to work on that muscle there? I mean squeeze it and just see how it hurts. They had my neck where I couldn't even move it and my nuts were all swelled up too. They kicked me in my nuts. All messed up. That was three days and nights of it. Knocked me out and as soon as I come to, they'd start again.

The lawyers you used, did they specialize in characters like you?

Well, Sam Hoover—he's here in the penitentiary now—he was one of my lawyers. He engineered some thieves to go out and rob somewhere, and he got sixty years out of it himself. He was a heck of a criminal attorney. I think he had a ninety-something average over the years he'd been practicing. They hated to see him come in the courtroom. Like Percy Foreman, you know. But he just couldn't keep from being in a little crime. I don't know what's the matter with old Sam Hoover. He's worth a million dollars and that wasn't enough for him.

Did you ever buy your way out of a charge?

Yes. One time I put $3,000 in escrow to a district attorney and he got ten years off my sentence. He did get impeached. Not on my deal but because he was operating whorehouses in Houston. And another time, I sat right across a table and gave him $400 in San Antonio for a no bill. See, if you've got a reputation outside with police officers as being tight-mouthed and tending to your own business and not putting your business on the streets, they'll talk to you pretty much.

Like now, it's no secret, they know that I had a payoff with the man who finally done time from Houston. They know that every time I was raided I was tipped off first, and everything else. Matter of fact, it's no secret no longer, it used to be years ago, he sat with the police car radio and jiggered [acted as lookout] while I made joints. He finally got arrested for narcotics. Heck, I've gone to the border and scored and had him come, call him that I was on my way in, and he'd come and take my stuff off because he knew they were going to try to raid me as soon as I hit the city limits. And I've had policemen catch me dead and right, not in the joint but dead to right with the stuff out of the joint, and I'd give them the stuff and we'd forget about it. You know that stuff never went back where it came from.

I always had me a lawyer who had as much larceny in his heart as I did, one who was always expecting me to be in some trouble and was always ready to come and get me wherever I was.

Did you pay him when you weren't in trouble, just for being ready to come?

I'm going to tell you the truth. Like if you've got a narcotic habit you're not going to be giving a lawyer any retainer fee because you're going every day, every day. I was in a joint every day or every night.

Margie and I, it would cost us $100 a day for our narcotics. If we had more than $100 a day to spend, that's what we spent. Whenever you found it, you'd spend everything in your pocket then because you didn't know how much trouble you was going to have scoring again. Say a pusher is pushing a hundred to two hundred caps a day. It isn't hard for him to run out real quick because there's fifty dope fiends coming by buying two or three caps off him or ten caps, or twenty caps at a time.

I've had a two-cap habit at a fix, and that's about every four hours. And I've had three caps and four caps and five caps at a time.

That was at $7 a cap. And of course every time I fixed, Margie fixed. We had a little agreement that we'd never fix without the other. If it come time for her to go to work, and I'd go case something to steal and then I'd go make a safe. It might be a water haul, I might make the safe and there wouldn't be anything in it. Maybe there's $50 in it and maybe there's $3,000 or $4,000 in it. Then we didn't work anymore until that was gone. She didn't work and I didn't either. I'd have me two or three things lined up. I'd ride around and spot something, have it lined up where I could get it later.

That's the main problem, the finding the narcotics, because it takes up all your time looking for it. They wouldn't have a narcotic problem if a character could run in a drugstore and hand him a dollar and take care of his habit that way. Wouldn't have all of the thievery problem either, you could go home and go to work. If you could go to work, if you had a job and could just go to the drugstore in the morning and buy your dope, go to your job and come home at night—they wouldn't have all that trouble.

You know, you can't tell I'm a dope fiend. You can with Margie or the majority of dope fiends I know. But nobody ever knows that I shoot stuff when I'm outside. Unless they know me. I don't act any different than I am right now. I went around Margie's people and just as often as if I wasn't on, because I know you've got to eat and you've got to take medicine to keep your system clean and eat regular to keep from getting all run-down and everything. And her people accused her of getting me on stuff when they found out I was on because they didn't believe I ever shot anything.

Now there's a lot of people, square john people, who won't steal with a drug addict, and a drug addict won't steal with a square john. What you call a square john thief, maybe he's got an old lady hustling or something like that. He steals but he don't shoot no dope. Maybe he'll smoke a little weed or eat a pill or two. Now they figure a dope fiend will get in jail and a policeman will offer him a shot of dope and he's gonna tell him anything. But it's born in you. If you're gonna snitch on somebody, you're gonna do it without a shot of dope. Some people it will bring around quicker, but there are others who just get sick. I know, they laid it in front of me and I was tempted myself, the police will do that. They'll pull it out and say, "Well, are you sick enough to want some of this now?"

I can remember the time they carried it around in cigar boxes under the police car seat. The police did, the detectives in Houston did. They used it to get tips. I know several hustling girls that would fill dates with policemen who would give them a few grains of stuff. And I know of thieves the policemen would keep up their habit and they would take some safecracker and put him in a building for the police to put him in a trap, to kill him, or build a case against him. I know lots of cases.

From 1944 to 1946 I didn't do anything but drugstores and I didn't have to spend any money to buy drugs with then. But I quit making drugstores because they kept drugstores staked out for me, especially to get me.

They used to try to get other thieves to get old Nick to go to a drugstore and I just wouldn't go for it. You can ask Margie.

She used to have to haul me around because I'd have a tail on me. She'd haul me around and turn the corner and I'd bail out of the car and go get in another car. I used to keep one car that I didn't do nothing but steal in. The police didn't even know it. If I got in that car

I had my tools and I was going to steal something. Then I'd drive back and lock that car back up.

My worst problem after I'd stole was to get back home with it. They knew me and if they saw me I was automatically stopped and searched, no matter where I was.

Why didn't you pull out to another state?

I don't know. It's just that Texas was my home and I knew everything here. Every time I got on my feet real good—I've been on my feet two or three times—I'd lay down to kick the dope habit and then I'd find myself broke again and that's the way it would go. I've checked in hospitals and paid them $125 a week and bought the medicine that they used for withdrawal and I had to kick the door off to get out. Paid to get locked up and then had to kick the door down to get out.

I've taken heroin, I've taken morphine, I've taken Dilaudid, I've taken Pantopon, I've taken tincture of opium, and I have used just a little bit of paregoric. I couldn't drink it, I never could drink it, I shot it. I never did try to keep up any habit on paregoric. When a panic hit Houston or something I have went and bought me a pint of paregoric and cooked it down and taken a sick off with it.

Heroin is the strongest. It don't hold me as long as doctor's medicine does, but it makes me feel better and takes the sick off easier.

And all the world that heroin does for me, or any shot of narcotic, when I have a habit, is to make me feel normal. Natural. I don't know why I ever get hooked because I hate it. I do. There's nothing about narcotics that I like. I'll tell you what traps me. Say we're sitting around and we take a shot of narcotics. Well, naturally, the first one after a long time, that feels good. You just sit around and coast and then I'll take another. And I'll take three. Then I'm going to start looking for a connection because I'm hooked.

When I got out last time I went to Chicago and waited for Margie to get out and I didn't touch anything for a year. I had a heart attack and the first thing the doctor did was hit me in each shoulder. They tried to check me in the hospital and my sister-in-law was a nurse at that hospital and she agreed to check me every day if they'd let me go home. So they let me go home and they gave me my medicine and they gave me a synthetic narcotic and in two weeks I was up chasing the connection around. And that's the way I get trapped every time. If I just wouldn't get around I never would use it.

Margie McMurphy: "Everybody seems to think that I'm the fastest gun in Texas . . ."

When I first started out, I started using a little grass and then, naturally, a few of the kids had pills. And I was taking those and drinking a little vodka. Just anything for a kick.

How old were you then?

About eleven.

That's when I met my first husband at City Park. He was in the service and he was AWOL at the time. And he was also a junkie. Of course I was curious enough at that time after smoking grass and taking pills, so I was ready to graduate a little bit. I had heard quite a bit about heroin. I thought that sounded like the ideal kick. In fact, at that age, I thought that anybody that was anybody was a dope fiend. So I had my first fix and I was like everybody else, just wanted to see what it was like. And that just called for another one.

It didn't make me sick or anything, like it does the average dope fiend. The party that fixed me, I guess he knew what he was doing. He was also a big connection in Dallas. He gave me just the right amount. He was a big connection. He's dead now; they machine-gunned him.

His two daughters ran around with me and they was smoking a little grass too, but they wasn't using stuff. So I just continued going over there and scoring myself, and the next thing I knew, I was cashing these checks. This boy that had introduced me to the connection to begin with, I started seeing him a little more frequently and we got into this check deal. And to keep him from getting in any trouble— like them filing on him for contributing to the delinquency of a minor —I decided I would marry him. Then, too, my people was hounding me and everything, so I thought that would be a good opportunity to get away from home.

And how old were you when you got married?

I was still eleven.

I looked a little older than eleven. I matured quite early. In fact, I looked then just like I do now, other than I didn't have the gray hairs and wrinkles.

That lasted six days. After we was married and I had been going with him for two weeks and living with him. With the exception of having intercourse with the boy—we never did that. In my childish mind it was a business arrangement and that's the way I kept it. We got busted cashing these checks and he got eighteen months in the brig and the probation department agreed to putting me with my family with the understanding that they get an annulment from this boy. Of course my mother was more than willing to do that.

Of course I had to kick that little yen that I'd already got. The probation wanted to run it down to my mother that I was hooked on narcotics and all that. And that scared her to death, 'cause you know back then the squares didn't even know anything about narcotics. Well, she proceeded to keep me in the house. She went to the bathroom with me, she got my water, she brought it to the bed. Oh, she stayed right with me. But this friend of mine would come over and we'd go to the bathroom and I'd cop a little old fix and be straight for a few days.

My mother was taking nerve medicine herself and she was so determined to get me off dope, she seen what a struggle I was having on my own, that she would give me two yellowjackets [Nembutol] a night to try to make me sleep. Course that didn't even faze me. Finally, after I got halfway on my feet, she let up a little bit and I started running around again. I got hooked and run into these dope fiends out of Houston, one of which later became my second husband.

He was a dope fiend and a thief, a pretty good one. You probably know him, Johnny B———. Him and I got married after a long courtship, if that's what you want to call it. That didn't last too long because I was busted boosting and sent to Gainesville.

That's where my crime really started was right there.

Before I went there I wasn't too hip to things, and what I didn't know I was taught there. And I was very rebellious because I didn't feel that I had been given any chance whatsoever. The girl that I was busted with had a long criminal record and had been in the life for years, but she got cut completely loose and I got sent to Gainesville. So I went in there with a heck of an attitude.

I made up my mind before I ever got there: they put me here, now let's hope they can keep me.

So I was there I guess three or four months and I played out [escaped]. I went to Dallas and stayed about nine months, got busted and sent back. At that time they was putting chains and bald-shaving your head for escape. And that really made me that much more rebellious. So I run off again with my chains and my little bald head and my long dress. I was a pretty little sight out there on that highway hitchhiking a ride.

Then I met this other boy and he was I guess noted as one of the best thieves in Dallas. Everything he did was planned to the hilt. He didn't mess with Texas business at all; everything he did was out-of-state.

And it was comical how I got with him. By this time I had gained me a pretty good little reputation running around with characters, and he needed a girl to go on these out-of-state trips with him to kind of keep the heat off of him. And so this other character told me all this, and told me that he also had a box full of dope. So I went out to this tennis court and met him. He had dope's mammy! We had a little party, a speedball party with cocaine and heroin and drugstore stuff— Dilaudid and morphine. So he propositioned me. He told me, said that I would get my cut out of everything that was made, so I ended up marrying him for the same reason I married the first one.

These are legal marriages?

Oh, yeah, they're all legal marriages.

And we started making trips. The one we finally got busted on was the Tampa Municipal Hospital. I flew the dope back to Dallas. They busted us with machine guns surrounding the Skyline Motel— we had been snitched on, you know. Like I say, I flew the stuff in and the two boys drove in; we was there three days and somebody put us on the spot and the police run in and kicked all the doors down and found the dope, then found the receipt for the dope that I had mailed back from another drugstore. So they filed on me for interstate transportation of narcotics. And of course I couldn't make bond. When they took us before the commissioner the next morning these other people got to make bond, and I was returned to the county as an escapee.

Two weeks later they told me that I was going to the Federal penitentiary, as it was apparent that they couldn't keep me at Gainesville. So they filed on me as an adult.

I must have been thirteen or fourteen, something like that. And the head of the narcotic bureau at that time, he told the probation department that since I was going to be tried as an adult, I should be allowed to make bond like an adult. Which I did, and then I went to Houston.

I had another husband in between there, by the way, a stone square. I had run off from Gainesville and had met this boy over in

Fort Worth. We was out partying this particular night—I'm the world's worst for jumping up and marrying people—so I wake up the next morning and my aunt tells me I'm married to this boy. And that I'm no good. So I called my mother and I go back to Dallas. And that's the last I ever saw of that boy.

So I go back to Houston to stay with my sister, thinking maybe they'd kind of forget me in Dallas. Well, that wasn't any good. So then I met Nick. In the meantime, though, I met this pharmacist that I married. It's hard to keep it all together.

Were you getting divorces from these people too?

No, I wasn't. In fact, I didn't get my divorces till I got out of here in '59. I got a divorce and an annulment. This boy, this square that I married, he got the divorce himself. Then after I married this pharmacist he got a divorce from me. And I married him and we was together three or four weeks, and his daddy filed on him, put lunacy charges against him. 'Cause he had spent about $9,000 in two weeks' time.

So I get busted, sent back to Gainesville as an escapee, and they tried to get him to file on me for bigamy. Well now, he doesn't know anything about my past record or anything like that. And he didn't know I had been accused of killing this matron in the county jail or anything. But he come up like a champ. He flew me a lawyer and his lawyer was supposed to get me out in July, and I run off again in June.

So I went to Houston and met Nick, and him and I's been together ever since.

Nick told me that if you'd been a man you would have been an old-time badman.

He's about right.

When did you start working with a gun?

When he got his ten years. His appeal had come back affirmed and I was left with a dope habit and, though I did a little hustling during my time, that's never been my shot. I'd rather just take what I want than to have to give my body up.

That's a slower way to accumulate money, too. When you were working with a gun did you usually work alone or with other people?

There was another boy with me. We heisted a drugstore in Dallas and stole a car, got on the highway and was making drugstores between Dallas and Tennessee, where I eventually got busted. I got ten years out of that, and Missouri had a detainer on me and Texas put a detainer on me. I did fifty-one months in Tennessee and was paroled to my Texas detainer. And only got seven years out of Dallas.

Were you ever working by yourself regularly or did you always work with somebody?

I've always worked with somebody.

When you were working like that, did you have a lawyer you paid all the time, or did you just go to one when you got in trouble?

I had one. In fact, we had several of them, so if one wasn't there we could always call on the other.

And would you pay them even when you weren't using them?

When I was working in Houston I think it was $200 a week, regardless of how many times I made jail. If I made it ten times that week it was still $200, and if I didn't make it any time it was $200.

Nick told me about one time you drove right up when the police had him trapped.

Oh, that. I was sitting about a half a block away on the main drag. I had acted like the car had stalled. And I saw the police drive up there and I beeped the horn, you know, and I didn't see any action going on. By that time, they was already at the door fixing to go inside the place. Well, I snapped: they're going in. There's supposed to be somebody in there spotting, surely they see them as well as I do. So I give them a few minutes to make it out the back door and whipped down this side road. It wasn't an alley, it was a side road, and I was driving real slow. I was looking all around and didn't see him coming out, so I was fixing to make it myself. 'Cause if I'm busted at a place like that, I'm gone, too, you know. So I'm about a half a block from the place and I heard somebody holler, "Baby!" I slowed down. Nick and this other boy jumped in the back seat and we took off. There was three of them the job and one, when he was trying to run out, he run in the closet. He stayed, and how the police missed him I'll never know, but they shook the place down and didn't find him, and after they left he slipped on out himself.

This last time when I got out in '59, Nick and I both made a joint effort not to go back on stuff. He got out in March and I didn't get out until October, and he was offered dope on every corner and wouldn't touch it. He didn't touch it until after I got out there. We was out about three months before we just said to hell with it.

The police was riding us night and day. They put us to bed and they got us up. We paid down on a little home just outside Dallas, we tried to open a dry cleaners, and we was doing real well. But you can't live square paying a lawyer $50 to throw a writ—that's $100 for both of us. And there's no possible way you can make it. I've got thirteen vagrancy cases pending on me right now that I just refused to pay. I was going to fight them in court because they didn't have any case on me.

See, if they haven't anything else to file, and they see you walking down the street, they pick up you, put you in jail, and file vagrancy on you. If you've got a pocketful of money, that makes no difference.

Tell me about the girls' reformatory.

I could talk all day and couldn't tell you how it was there. They did everything they could to degrade you. And on a kid, that makes a hell of an impression, you know? Like beating you, and shaving your head, and putting you in chains. That's no way to train anybody.

Gainesville was a pretty good-size place. It looks like a college. It's got about twelve different cottages. I hear now it's more like what it's supposed to be, a training school. About the last year I was there a new superintendent took over, she recently died, and she really made a big effort to make it a training school. I know that on one of my escapes, Dallas had written it up that I had been busted and was being returned to the Gainesville reformatory, and she called the *Dallas Morning News* and made them retract that statement and put it in the paper that it was a training school, not a reform school. And she took the girls out of chains and stopped shaving their heads.

When I was on parole I went on a TV program called *Confession.* Mr. Decker [Dallas D.A.] told them that they would like for me to go on it, that it was more or less to help the younger generation. It was supposed to be nationwide, and I was the first series that was going to be nationwide. It was filmed, took us three days to film it.

I told them about the matron, 'cause I was kind of bugged about that, ever since that deal went down, 'cause the newspapers played it up so bad. I wanted everybody to know that I just didn't deliberately kill that woman, you know, that all I was trying to do was escape, and so I went on that program for that specific reason.

All it was, actually, was a planned escape. But they played it as the most brutal murder Texas has ever had. Premeditated first-degree murder is what they filed on me.

I got five years with no clemency, thanks to Sarah Hughes; she's a Federal judge now. The D.A. wanted to hold me until I was an adult—I was sixteen years old at this time and he wanted to hold me until I became twenty-one and try me as an adult and give me the chair and ninety-nine years. And she had just taken over as juvenile judge. She had been sentencing the men and women before. And she told him I did it when I was a juvenile and I would be tried as a juvenile, and so that's what they did, and she gave me the max, which was five years with no clemency.

The most you can get in Texas as a juvenile for murder is five years?

Until you're twenty-one. See, I was sixteen, so I didn't have but five years to go.

The escape wasn't even mentioned in the paper. They just played it up like we just had a grudge against the woman and we just killed her for no reason at all, except that we hated matrons or something like that.

And why did she get killed? Instead of—

Instead of what?

Instead of just getting hit on the head or something?

What she died from was a concussion. See, we had sent her to get some syrup. I had planned this deal once before and even went as far as tearing up the blanket to make strips to go down on. The window is on the fourth floor. And I had gotten out of jail that time, so I just left the blankets and everything up there. That was four or five months before it actually went down. So I had gotten busted on another one of my escapes and they were sending me back to Gainesville. In my little childish mind I didn't think they had enough to send me back to Gainesville. Of course I was just on an escape and had been busted in this hotel. So I told my probation woman, "Well, if you send me back, you'll have a reason to send me for."

So I tore up the little blankets and there was a little girl in there for running away from home and they were fixing to send her back to Georgia as soon as her people got the money to her. I started talking to her and she agreed to help me. And I had an oil-burning dope habit then—I don't know if you know how you connive and scheme when you're that sick. You just do anything to get it.

Miss Chandler was one of the best matrons up there. There's no way in the world that I would have hurt her intentionally. All I meant to do was get the keys and unlock that window which swings out and get on that landing and go on down. Her shift came on at twelve o'clock, so about twelve thirty we told her we was hungry and sent her to get us some syrup.

Well, she brought the syrup and I don't know if she was hankty [suspicious] or what, because she handed the syrup in, in a cup, and kept her hand on the grill. This girl was supposed to pull her on into our tank and I was supposed to grab the telephone and hit her on top of the head. But she was scuffling too much for all that, so finally I had to just pull her on in too, and the syrup went every which way, and she slipped on the syrup and hit her head on the concrete.

I had this Kotex to go in her mouth and this string to tie it around. It was supposed to be a big deal, you know. But in our anxiousness I had forgot to put the rag close enough so I could reach it. 'Cause I figured that when I knocked her out that would be all of it, there wouldn't be any hurry to get the thing to tie around her mouth. But she was steady screaming all this time and I'd just get the Kotex in her mouth and when I'd reach to get this rag to tie it around her head, well she'd spit that out. By this time the elevator operator heard her screaming. We heard the elevator stop and we got up and left her laying there and went to the kitchen.

So they throwed us in the hole. About one or two o'clock the whole homicide squad was up there and had all the newspaper reporters wanting to take pictures, and I wouldn't come out of the hole. I told them no, they wouldn't take any pictures of me. He told me they was going to take pictures of me and he didn't want it to hit the front page with me laying on the concrete in that hole, and if I come out in front of the cell I could cover my face. Which I did. I come out and had a picture taken with both my hands in front of my face.

They filed premeditated first-degree murder on us. This other little girl got a year with clemency and I got five with no clemency.

Since your first bust, how much time have you actually spent out?

Four years since I was thirteen. And in that time, those first two years from '51 to '53, I was steady ducking and dodging. They kicked me out of Gainesville. I might as well tell you that because they made a big stink over it in the papers and everything.

Miss Birmingham told them that she was in her legal rights to furlough me. That I was a bad influence on the other girls, that she knew that I was leaving, and every time I left I took three or four of the girls with me and got them on narcotics. So she gave me a furlough to get me out of her institution.

She really got in my corner there for a while and she tried every way to get me paroled to Dallas, Fort Worth, Houston. Nobody would accept me. They said the public hadn't forgotten my brutal murder.

So they started this furlough program. And I did 139 days in the hole in Gainesville at that time. She said that Austin had agreed that anybody that made three months' perfect record would get to go home on a two-week furlough. I was determined to make these three months, even though everybody was telling me—screws on down to inmates—that if I made my three months I wouldn't get to go home because of my bits.

And I told them, "Yeah, I'm going. Either they're going to let me go or I'm going. 'Cause if I make my three records it doesn't make any difference what I'm here for. I think I'm entitled to go."

So it was real cute the way it went down. I made my records and the day that she was going to call everybody's name out that was going to get to go home, she had us all in the auditorium. She went all the way through the alphabet and she didn't call my name. Went ahead and made this spiel. So at the end of that she says, "Oh, my goodness, I believe that I've forgotten someone, and I believe it's Margie . . ." And everybody just got hysterical in there and started crying, jumping up and down.

Now I'm a funny person. If somebody puts a little confidence and trust in me, there's no way in the world that I'd betray it. Now I had already escaped five or six times from there at this time. And I had spread it on the reservation that if I got to go home I would come back. I wouldn't guarantee them how long I would stay after I got back, but I would be back. So sure enough I got to go home, and I stayed my two weeks, and I come back on time.

And I went to Miss Birmingham and told her, "Now I'm giving you two weeks to get me out of here. If you don't I'm going the best way I know how."

So she steady went to work for me, and that's when she got these letters, wrote all these letters in my behalf, trying to get me paroled.

So on Tuesday before the two weeks would have been up on Wednesday, I went to the administration building and told her, "I guess you know what tomorrow is: M-Day."

She said, "Yes, I do, Margie. I want you to come in my office. I've got something that I want you to read. This is very unusual. I don't ordinarily let the girls read letters from the probation department." She called me in there and she let me read this from Dallas, where it said that they didn't believe that the public had forgotten my brutal murder.

I told her, "That don't leave me much choice then, does it?"

She said, "Yes, it does. I want you to go over to the cottage and pack your clothes. I'm taking you to Dallas right now."

And that's what she did. And that night I go out partying and my sister-in-law and I are riding down the highway and the vice squad sees us and I guess they think I'm on the lam. They take me to jail. And my sister-in-law's never been in any trouble at all. They file an investigation on the Harrison narcotic act on us.

The newspapers find out I'm on the streets and they're going to investigate the rights of Gainesville for paroling me without the permission of the district judges and the probation department. So that's when they called Miss Birmingham in Gainesville and she run this story to them that I was a bad influence on the girls, she knew that I was going to leave, and every time I left I took three or four of the girls with me and turned them out on narcotics.

That wasn't true, by the way.

She came by my house the next day and told me, "Margie, don't worry. I was in my legal rights by furloughing you. I was the only one that had that legal authority." And she run it to me to try to be good and live it down. Well, I knew I couldn't live it down in Dallas, they was going to hound me to death. So I got to Houston.

You know what goes on with studs and queens in county jails. Is it the same in the women's section?

Usually when a butch comes in jail they more or less want to be by themselves and they will try to hide the fact that they are homosexual. I mean, if they're not masculine or dressed in drag or something like that. If you're not hip to gay life, then you wouldn't knock them off for being a butch or anything. Some of the most feminine women I have seen are homosexual. But an average person wouldn't know this if they just haven't been around this type of life.

So in the county jail, who was more likely to get things going?

The fluff. 'Cause, like I say, the butch usually has their business on the street and they're concerned with that—wondering what she's out there doing. They're not interested in getting one of those little fly-by-night deals going. But now the fluff, maybe she's been in there three or four days and her habits just coming down on her and she wants to get a little something on. Usually it just might be for a chuckle, or maybe just a release. They'll just force the butch down at times.

I believe a lot of them here get a little curious behind that stuff and they're deprived of it or rode shotgun so much in here behind it that they might want to get out and see just what it would be on the streets.

Has this been different in different institutions you've been in?

Oh, lord, yes.

How?

One of the differences is that they sanction it in the Federal. They have begun to accept homosexuality. Like if you're like married to a woman there and they know that you're making it and they feel that you're good for each other or one of you would be a good influence on the other, they move you to the same cottage and you're put on what they call the "Pay no mind list." Here, for anything, you're subject to blow every day you hope to earn [lose your good time for petty infractions].

And it varies, depending on where you are. In different parts of the country it's run different. Now like for here, if you got with a real stud broad that was gay from the streets, she feels like she should support you. If she could she would do your laundry, she would see that you didn't want for anything, and supply your other needs as well. But up north, they feel that if they are taking care of the business for you, you should play the wife's part by doing all the laundry and whatever else is to be done. Then you find those cases where they feel that if they're good enough to go down on you, you're good enough to go down on them. But that's not the way it's supposed to go.

It's more that way for the penitentiary turnouts, they're the ones that figure turnabout is fair play. The ones that's really that way wouldn't think of letting you do anything to them in return. Because they are the aggressor and that's the way it's supposed to be.

Any other differences between the ones who become penitentiary turnouts and the other inmates?

Well, they're more hard-walking, because to them it's just a front and they got to prove that they are daddy. And your regular homosexuals know what they are and they don't have to prove it to anybody. And they're a very sensitive bunch anyway and they don't believe in putting their business on the street.

Talking about putting business on the streets, are women as hard on snitches as men are?

I think they're a little more understanding toward them. They may blow them off and not have anything to do with them, but women are a gutless bunch. I mean as far as laying in the chili for one of them, they don't do it like the men do.

Does what you've done outside have anything to do with your status inside?

Oh, lord, yes. Like if you're a child-killer or something like that, well that's about the lowest you could be. And nobody socializes with you.

*Does it stay that way throughout your sentence or is it just that way
   at the beginning?*

I'll use one girl as an example here. She's here for killing three of
her babies and she's been here for about ten years and the girls are
finally beginning to melt toward her because she has gotten one put-
off after another. Like I say, women are kind of tender-hearted, I
guess, and they're beginning to feel that regardless of what she's done
she's paid her debt to society.

Who's got good status coming in?

Being in the life, being a character.

How is she treated differently?

If she's good people and everything and they know she's right-
eous or boss, then all of your friends, even if they don't know you—
you might be from out-of-state and a character broad, and it don't
take but a few minutes to knock you off as being people, you know—
anything you want that they have you're welcome to it. They say,
Here's toothpaste, cigarettes, deodorant—all the necessary things that
you may be hung up a while getting otherwise, if somebody isn't in
your corner to send you a few of those things.

*What about women who aren't anybody and don't have any money,
   how do they get things?*

They do other people's washing, they roll cigarettes, they crochet,
they knit, they do different little things like that. Or some of them
might turn out to scarf and rim [cunnilingus and analingus] to make
it.

People learn some things in here. Certainly some square subjects
come in here that's never heard of boosting or scallybipping—that's
where you go in people's houses when they're not at home or maybe
when they are at home if they're in the backyard hanging up clothes
or something—you go in there and ransack their house and get their
money, they're known as "bippers," "scallybippers." And they learn
everything that's connected with crime. If they're in here for forgery
they think, "Well, I'll be a lot better off if I can learn a little boosting,
how to leg and so forth."

Do women make better boosters than men?

Oh, yes. 'Cause men can't very well leg out radios and drills and
things like that, where a woman can.

Are women more likely to be cool about it than men?

I think of pretty frantic women boosters that just go in and hog
'em rather than using any kind of finesse about it.

Did you boost too?

Some.

You said before you turned tricks for a while. How long?

Just when I got destitute and maybe needed to score for money, or maybe my old man needed some money to go out of town to score something, I would make expense money.

How did you turn out as that?

I turned out when I was a youngster, but I mostly worked more on my own than when I'm with a man. Because I've never been with a pimp, I detest a pimp. I've always been with a thief. And the men that I've been with have never wanted me to do that, but I've always felt, I'm a very independent person and I believe in carrying my own weight, and I'll get out there and turn a trick or maybe I've got some personals or something. I don't have to hurt too much.

Did you ever deal?

I never could be a dealer, I'm too free-hearted. I'd give it away. I can't stand to see anybody sick. I'm a stone trick and always have been.

I've never been sinister as far as *I'm* concerned. But I got that reputation and everybody seems to think that I'm the fastest gun in Texas, but actually I think I'm a pretty kind, considerate, understanding person.

You know, what I used to think was glamorous and exciting no longer affects me that way. I used to kind of get a kick out of doing the things that I did even though it was a means of survival for me. It was still a kick to do it. But now, as I look back on some of the things that I've done, it seems that it wasn't even me that done them. A lot of the things I did was pretty gutty and I'm not a gutty person. Like taking that pistol and running in there [robbing a store]—I was in one of those places for thirty minutes, I paid off the iceman and throwed candy to the children and everything else. I don't think I would have the heart to do things like that now. Or sawing out the bars and escaping or going out the window naked and all that stuff.

Why did you go out the window naked?

I didn't have time to saw but one bar off and that took two weeks and I was scared it was going to get knocked off and I was too fat to get out of it, so I stripped and put morline [grease] all over my body. And even then I wore stripes from that bar for a good month.

Doesn't being in joints like this so much of the time get to bugging you?

I am bored stiff, believe me. I am at my wits' end.

I'm pretty interested in school this time. It's the first time that I've ever taken any interest in anything while I was doing time. Usually I just lay down with my time and that's it. But now I'm trying to better myself as best I can. I think Lex [Lexington—the Federal narcotics hospital/prison] did that for me. Like I said a while ago, I gained a little better insight into myself while I was there and I feel like now I need a little training and education and working and everything they got to offer me. I participate in everything they got going around here.

What's the worst part of doing time?

Being away from my family.

What place has been the roughest on you?

This one right here. I've been in five different institutions and out of all of them this is granddaddy. It's not the institution itself, it's this pettiness around here, they put so much strain on the brain in this penitentiary. And I've been in some rough ones. Now this place is nothing as compared to Gainesville. The brutality that went on there —there's no physical brutality that goes on here, it's all mental.

At Gainesville, in addition to the haircuts and chainings, what did they do to you?

Beatings and things like that.

For what?

The one I had put on me, it was a minor thing. I was accused of instigating, I don't know if you'd call it a riot or what. A bunch of the girls was supposed to have put cold cream jars in their socks and knocked out the matron and locked up all the girls that didn't want to go and hook 'em, you know. And I was singled out of about fifteen girls and they proceeded to get one of those switches off a tree and held me down across the bed and whipped me. What they was trying to do was make me cry, but I was very stubborn at that age and I wouldn't a shedded a tear if they'd a killed me.

So you came away not liking matrons particularly?

I have no grudges against matrons. Some of the finest people I have met was matrons. One of the best friends I believe I have ever had, in the character life or any life, was the warden of the Tennessee joint. That's right.

How was the Tennessee joint?

It was jam-up. Jelly-tight. It was, it was really a kick joint. 'Cause you did your time there and nobody wasn't constantly riding shotgun on you.

Do you prefer cells or dormitories?

Personally I prefer cells because I like a little solitary now and then. Most girls prefer dormitories, especially the first offenders, be-

cause they don't much like being by theirselves and they feel smoth-
ered in one of those little cells. But I'm so institutionalized I guess that
nothing don't faze me.

Bob: "I worked as a shill . . ."

I worked for a while as a shill at the Bowler Club. A shill is a man who
works for the house. He works eight hours a day. You gather around a
table and there'll be six—if the table's empty—six or seven shills will
gather around. And each bets the same, they bet a dollar at a time, all
on the pass line. If they pass they pick up their dollar, leave the one
down there; if they lose, they put down another dollar. The reason
they all bet the same is they all get the same amount of money to start
and that way the table boss can look around and make sure nobody's
making any money off the house because they've each got the same
amount of money in front of them.

I worked as a shill for about four months and I finally got a job
after going through a short training period as a dealer on a regular
draw poker table. At our poker table there were eight seats—the
dealer don't play, all he does is deal, make change, cut the pot—normally 10 percent. But of the eight seats, only three are open. The five
other seats are filled by house men. And most people don't realize
this. The house men have certain rules they must play by. The house
man can't open on draw poker if he's got anything less than two pair.
If one house man opens and if I haven't got two pair beat and I'm
working for the house, then I can't call. In other words, the only time I
can call is if I have something better than two pair. And we never
draw to a straight and we never draw to a flush. I've got to have three
of a kind or two pair of face cards in order to call the bet. And if I call,
the next house man in turn has to have something better than that. In
other words, if he has had one house man open and another call, the
third one has to have three of a kind in the face cards in order to call
that bet, otherwise he drops. So you can probably see how much
chance a sucker's got if he's playing it.

If the sucker opens, hardly anyone will call. If a sucker opens, the
house has to have better than two pair to call. In other words, he's got

to have at least three of a kind even to call the sucker's bet. We call *suckers* the three men sitting down there. The house figures they take an average of $200 an hour out of the poker game. Since they're only paying the five shills sitting there a dollar or two an hour, they're making pretty good money.

When I worked there, which was a few years ago now, you made $22.50 a shift for dealing. That's an eight-hour shift with work forty minutes and off twenty every hour. Which amounted to $132.50 a week on a six-day week. Now there are ways to subsidize your income down there which we were taught. Everybody wears French cuffs and the shirts are supplied by the house. They give you one new shirt each week because you wear the bottoms of your cuffs out on the green top of the table doing the dealing and dragging your cutter's percentage in. But the French cuffs are fake French cuffs, they're sewed on so there's no place you can stick anything in the cuffs.

But at novelty stores there they sell what they call "snap-backs." They advertise these things and sell them in those stores. A snap-back is nothing more than an alligator clamp-type affair on a long rubber band that you pin one end of the rubber band underneath the armpit of your shirt and the alligator band comes down to your watchband. There's a little unit that you put on your watchband and hook this little alligator clamp on. The alligator clamp is open and it's got a device like a mousetrap in it; when you touch that with a chip the clamp will automatically close and will loosen itself in the watchband and in turn the rubber band will snap it right back up under your arm again.

Chips in Las Vegas are as negotiable as green money. You can take them into any club and cash them in for money, for $5 or $10 or whatever it is. So all you've got to do is put a chip in the end of your fingers, turn your hand down like you're trying to touch your wrist, and you can comshaw—or steal—comshaw is a much better word—a $25 chip from a table.

They also got what they call false trousers. They call them "falsies" for short, but not falsies like you wear in a brassiere. They're a unit made in Las Vegas and they fit under your trousers, under the belt. The top part of them is made of metal and they're about six inches long. You strap them around you like a money belt. Only they're a sack about fifteen inches long that goes down your pants leg. The top of the unit is held open a quarter of an inch. The metal is stiff for that quarter inch, but it's got joints in it which are flexible and concur with your waist. When you're standing at a table or when you're getting up from a table, if you palm a chip and stand up and rub your trousertop, rub your hand across your belt like you were checking your belt, the chip will automatically go into this open slot, which is held open by the metal, drop down into the sack in your leg. And that's the way you can steal some more from the club.

Usually, if you're careful, you can make anywhere from $20 to $50 a day with a few chips. At night or whenever it is you're off, you cash them in at a club.

I got caught and was fired. There's no penalty for it. They don't take you to court for stealing, they just fire you and put out what they call a blacklist, and that blacklist is sent out every month to every club in Nevada. Come hell or high water, if you get on it once you won't get a job there again. Of course, if you figure the price is worth it you do it anyway. I know people there that's gotten away with it for years and never been caught.

There are other devices, but those are the only two I'm familiar with because they are the only two that I tried, but they do work and they are very effective.

I'll tell you about a little scheme that was, to my knowledge, used to defraud one of the big hotels in Las Vegas out of some money on a false arrest suit.

The way it all started was two gentlemen got together—we'll call them Number One and Number Two for clarity. Number Two goes to the bank in Los Angeles and opens a checking account for $10,000 there in the name of Number One. After opening this checking account, Number One goes to this hotel in Las Vegas and registers in his own name and goes to the cashier's window and requests that his checking account be approved so he can cash checks in Las Vegas.

The setup there was they fill out a card on you. You don't fill it out yourself—they fill it out with information on your bank, the amount of money you have in your account, how much you want to cash, and how many checks you want to cash, things like that.

Number One man in Vegas, he tells them that he would like to cash checks for no more than $500 each and no more than ten checks in the time he's going to be there. That's $5,000. He goes on up to his room and the hotel checks on his account and finds out he's clear for that amount of money and approves his checking account. Next morning, Number One comes downstairs with a checkbook.

This checkbook has been made out by Number Two in Los Angeles—only not every check. The first check is left blank, the second check is filled out, the third check is left blank, the fourth check is filled out, etc., all the way through the book. They know the dates they're going to cash the checks and that's all filled in prior to coming to Las Vegas. The only thing left blank is the "Pay to" line, that's because all the hotels in Las Vegas use a stamp rather than making you write in on the "Pay to" line.

Number One takes this checkbook to the cashier's window on that second morning and requests to cash a check. They ask him to fill out a check. He takes out his checkbook in front of the man and when he comes to "Pay to" he asks the man, "Who do I make it out to?" They tell him to leave it blank, they have a stamp for it. He continues filling out the rest of the check with the amount—$500—the date, and he signs his name and he picks up the $500. *But* instead of tearing out the check he's just filled out, he takes out Number Two's check, he tears that one out—remember, that one has been filled out prior to this by Number Two in Los Angeles—and hands that one to the cashier. The cashier will stamp his check in the "Pay to" column and stamp the back of the check and give him his $500. Which he, in turn, either keeps with him or sends back to the man still in Los Angeles.

In the meantime, in the first day, the man in Los Angeles goes to his bank and closes out his checking account, he takes out the $10,000. Then he leaves the city, going to some predesignated spot. But the man in Las Vegas continues cashing a check every morning for $500 until the first check bounces from Los Angeles.

When this check bounces in Los Angeles, the bank in Los Angeles will automatically phone the hotel in Las Vegas to tell them they have a check for $500 in a certain name drawn on an account closed. That used to take approximately nine days—it's probably somewhat less now that they're computerized. The man in Las Vegas, Number One, on the eighth day gets rid of his checkbook and all evidence of a checkbook. He tears it up, flushes it down the commode or whatever he wants to do to get rid of it. Even the pen he writes with he gets rid of. So they can't identify a pen. The hotel will come and arrest him for cashing checks on an account that's been closed. They figure that he must have flown back to Los Angeles and pulled the money out. It's only a short flight from Las Vegas.

The man that's arrested makes no statement. He does not deny it, he does not admit it, he makes no statement of any kind. He submits to arrest and goes to jail. He gets himself a lawyer. Usually, of course, the lawyer has been arranged beforehand. Within fifteen days, normally, in Las Vegas, they'll take you to court. They're not slow about that whatsoever.

In court they try the man for cashing checks on an account that's closed, which is fraud, or robbery, stealing, whatever you want to call it. And he pleads not guilty. The evidence they have is the checks, plus the cashier's positive identification that he watched the man write out the check. In examination and cross-examination it is brought out that the cashier witnessed the man writing out the check, watched the man tear the check out of the book, hand the check to him, that he stamped it and he will identify the check by his initials and stamp on the back. The defense calls a handwriting expert. They take the man's driver's license out of his wallet, his registration card from the hotel, and check the handwriting: they're not even similar. With it being proved that the checks weren't made out by this man they've got no evidence. The only thing they have is the man's statement that he witnessed Number One making out the checks and that has to be a mistaken identity, somebody that looked like you, because then it's his word against yours. The evidence is thrown out of court and they will throw the case out too for nonsufficient evidence.

At which time the lawyer for the defense jumps and says he does not want the case thrown out for nonsufficient evidence, he wants an acquittal. That's legal. So the court will have to acquit the man because of insufficient evidence.

The lawyer then sues the hotel for false arrest.

I think you'll find that 99 percent of the people in Las Vegas, the hotels and gambling houses, they will settle out of court. This particular scheme worked for about $20,000 that time. That's in addition to the $5,000 for the checks.

What if the clerk asks for sufficient identification and checks the signature?

Ah. I think if you'll ever cash a check in Las Vegas, after you get the check card made out and approved, you'll find that the formality of asking for additional information, especially if you are registered in the hotel as a guest, is something they consider embarrassing and they don't do it. For a one-stop item they might. But I think you'll find that at your better hotels, where you check in and pay when you leave, that if they see you come up there and your account is approved and you're living at the hotel, there really is no need for any more identification because they've got you right there. They won't ask you for any more identification. And to forestall that, if necessary a duplicate set of identification with the signatures of the man still in Los Angeles could be brought along and that could cover any such problem.

But as far as I know they never asked the people involved in this deal for any identification, and it worked fine.

Red: "I like credit cards . . ."

I like credit cards.

I could take one of your cards and go down the street with it here and make $400 or $500 in a couple of hours. As long as it don't have a picture on it. You know, something like an Enco card. You just go around buying tires and stuff like that and reselling them. You resell them at the next station.

Diner's Cards and American Express, they're no good because they've got the owner's signature on them, but a lot of cards don't. I got one guy's wallet once and it had about forty-five of those cards in it and a lot of them were unsigned even though there was a space, so I just signed there so the signatures matched.

I used that batch for about sixty days and it was worth—for my part of it—about $18,000. The FBI brought the cards in for me to identify and those onionskin papers measured about 12 ¾ inches high. That's a lot of those papers.

I got everything from watches to a girl. I was in the Hilton in Los Angeles and spent $75 on a girl there and got $4.25 change off of her. That's the way they operate there. They'll come up to your room with a voucher—they check to see if you've checked in on a credit card— and they just bring the voucher up there and write the card number in the space and fill out some money and you sign it.

This guy had good cards, all of them. One had an airplane rental thing, and he had a gas card for every kind of gas company I ever heard of. Even those little old DX cards. He had a Sohio card too and that's one of the best cards you can get. It covers lots of stations and you can travel with it.

I had a girl with me and I'd drive up to a service station and I'd put a story on these service station men. I'd say, "I just picked up this broad and she's on the make and I need a little cash. I can't write a check, so how about putting me down for four or five tires and giving me $70 or $80 and you just keep the tires." They do that. And we'd do it for eight hours a day.

You buy a lot of tires. I've bought a lot.

When did they finally catch you on that?

After I left Mississippi.

Did you do Federal time on that?

No.

State time?

No. They dropped it.

Why?

Damned if I know. They dropped every bit of it. Everything went off me. I got some state time for a burglary, but on the cards I didn't get anything. They filed on me for a Hertz deal. I got a new car with an R.A. on it. A rental agreement deal. Police stopped me but I had a rental agreement on it. Brand-new Ford without a mile on it. It sure had more than that when I got through with it.

How much time have you spent in jail?

Altogether?

Yes.

Well, I've been in Mississippi, Alabama, Louisiana, and the Federal. Six times. Spent seventeen calendar years in prison out of forty. I'm forty years old now.

I've done almost everything on the books, everything from those credit cards on up.

Did you like working with a gun?

Yeah. I kind of like working with a gun. It's quicker and easier. It wasn't a thrill or nothing. I was after the money, that's all I wanted. The most money I ever made with a gun was $9,000 and that was three of us splitting that up, that was a supermarket, but I've made more than that off those cards than with that gun. With the cards you got to play the part, and as far as playing the part goes I'm a pretty fair actor. You pull up and put some story on a young kid and he's going to go for it real quick.

But I've never wrote a hot check in my life. That's the only things I've missed out on I believe: checks, murder, and rape, those three are the only things I've missed out on.

I can understand the other two, but how come you never wrote checks?

I don't know. I just never worked myself up to walk in there with a piece of blank paper in my hand. I don't think I can stand up under it. I can take a credit card and walk in there in front of a man and I don't get upset, but I don't believe it would pay to give me a good check and send me in there. I'm so scared, even knowing it's good. I'm just leery about those checks.

Webster: "The American
Services Association . . ."

There's an old game called the American Services Association. Generally, the way it is, you get you a lot of pamphlets and things made up. Say you got an insurance policy and you have a pamphlet showing a lot of stores and businesses and things. You go, you knock on a door, a lady comes to the door and you say, "Good evening, madam." You start conning them. "Good evening, madam, is the lady of the house here?"

And she say, "Well, *I'm* the lady of the house here."

So first thing you did, you paid her a compliment, so she's all ready, at ease almost. You give her some, you know, "Well, you sure look young to be the lady of the house," and so forth. And then you tell her, "Well, I'm with the American Services Association. We are in connection with the American Automobile Association and the NAACP, and I'd like to interest you in a project which will enable you to benefit yourself. I'm going to give you—" then you stop and say, "I'm not going to *give* you anything. I'm going to put you in the position to grab some of the goodness this organization has to offer." And you proceed to tell her how you get a discount on everything from a shoeshine to a hairdo. And you show her your pamphlets showing her all the stores and if she's a member of this club all the things she can get. And you show her all the benefits that you can get from it and it only costs $37.50 a year. She can either pay all of it or half of it. Anything you get is a gift, you know, so you accept it. So now most of the time if you actually get them in this mood and show them all the facts that are connected with it, they'll pay the whole thing. So if they pay the whole thing you tell them, "If you pay the whole thing, the whole $37.50, you don't have to worry about any additional cost that comes in. You get a $500 bail bond certificate. You know, in most states if you have a wreck you can't be moved until the police officers arrive, but if you happen to be a member of this club and have a bail bond certification, then you can be moved right away."

You explain to them that if you're a member of this organization, then if you happen to have a wreck any bond that you would have to pay up to $500 you can get out without having to pay one penny. And then you explain to them that your lawyer for your organization is an ex-judge and he'll fight a traffic ticket if necessary. And if they have a gas war on, you get a percentage still for your gas. Anything, anything you can think of that there could be a percentage for it, you tell them they get a percentage if they're a member of this organization. And usually they pay the whole thing.

I'll tell you, most any game that's played, there's more than one way to play it. That's with the Drag Game—there's several different branches to it, and the Pigeon Drop, they're all different, and even the O'Grady. It all depends on who's got the game, who knows it, and how they play it. But mostly any game used can be used on white or colored, except that one I was just telling you about, the American Services Association thing. Mostly that is used only on colored because now there's this integrational crisis and you make sure you tell 'em, say, "Most white people already have this benefit, they been having it for years. But now, with the NAACP's official okay, the Automobile Association has banded together with several other millionaire businessmen to give the colored people the same benefit." Now this automatically gives a little boost.

How many of these can you make in a day?

Usually we go to a project area. Like there's middle class people, they all live in these government projects. They automatically looking for some help. You know this from the neighborhood. You make a door-to-door call. Sometimes I've seen in the run of a day where I've made as much as $600. All depends on how hard you're willing to work, if you're willing to go make these calls, just go from door to door. Some doors you might not make it, then next two houses you might make it. And you'd be surprised how those $37.50's run up.

At one time there were a couple of young ladies under my guidance we'll say, but actually as for the term "pimp," I've never actually been a pimp. But I've had a couple young ladies and we'd boost. We had a little setup—we'd go downtown and steal in various shopping villages and then we'd go around to different beauty parlors and sell our merchandise. Mostly I hung around in the same center with the dope fiends and weed-heads and thieves, and this was just a major part of my environment. We'd sit around, plan out what we gonna do, and enjoy it after we do it, and this is it.

A character, as I believe, is someone who lives outside the law, who doesn't give any regards to society's right, we violate every society right. But most characters like myself have a moral standard we live by, certain things we do and certain things we won't do. For instance, rape or maybe murder, something of that nature. This isn't part of my game.

Why not murder?

I just don't believe I have a right to take another man's life unless, you know, it's a necessity, unless it's a case of self-preservation where mine is endangered. Other than that, like say in a robbery. Take a man's life, this to me is an animal form of act. And I try to keep myself in the category where I'm not considered as actually an animal. But I understand that it might be in my field of work, in any field of work in the criminal field, where we violate the rights of other people, this *is* an animal act. But now we try to use a little discretion, you know, to keep from actually being what we are. This is a false pride, I guess, a false pride we give ourselves. This certain thing we won't do, these certain things we will do.

You seem pretty conscious of this business of violating other people's rights. How do you feel about that while you're working? Is this something you just forget?

This is, I guess, like a district attorney. Take a district attorney, he realizes the fact that this is another human being he's trying for his life. But he disregards this altogether because of his job, because he knows it has to be done and he feels somebody has to do it. So since he's been appointed to do it, he does his best. The same thing applies to a character. He doesn't necessarily want to take what he don't have, but in order to have, in order to get, he just supplies the means to get it, disregarding the fact that it is wrong. Just blocks it out of his mind, it is just something he feels he has to do, so he does it.

Larry Kent: "Mrs. Hyler says she still likes her Tucker . . ."

That deputy warden, I've gone round and round with him. He had the audacity to have the mail room put a censor stamp on a patent application that came back from the Department of Commerce. I told him, "Don't you never do that again, Warden, don't you never do that again."

He said, "You know, you're pretty sarcastic for an inmate."

I said, "You were in the Pentagon? You know *I* was. You know what my military record is."

He said, "You've got a good one."

I said, "You're damn right I have. And how did I get it? A two-time loser and an officer in the United States Army. How do you like that for apples?"

He said, "Oh, you're a cocky somebody."

I said, "No, I'm not a cocky somebody." I said, "How many battle stars do you have?"

That done it. That froze him. Hey: I don't have any. But he doesn't know that.

Forty-six months overseas and a two-time loser and right from there into Oak Ridge as superintendent of power. He saw that on my record and he don't know how *that* happened. "How did you do that?" the FBI men asked me. They said, "How did you stay at Oak Ridge for thirteen months before they caught up with you?"

How did you?

Well, nobody knows. I sit there in my office, took care of my duties, and I was fourteen months at Oak Ridge. Not quite fourteen months. I expected it any day. So one morning my secretary told me, "Mr. Kent, there's three FBI men."

Well, we used to rub shoulders with them all the time, there was all kinds of them there. I'm smart enough to know some of them when I see them—some of the boys are not. She said, "They want to talk to you."

I said, "Bring them on in, I'm always glad to meet the law." I said, "Greetings." Here they come, three of them, with my chief engineer, Paul ———, a small boy.

"Mr. Kent?"

"Good morning," I said, "good morning, gentlemen. Your identification, please. Let me see if it's a forgery." They laughed. "Yours is in order, yours is too, Mr. Merrick. And you were an accountant or a lawyer?"

"I was an accountant."

"Fine. It's all in order, gentlemen. What can I do for you?"

He said, "We're going to have to ask you to resign."

"Oh, wonderful," I said, "I've toughed it up quite a while, haven't I?"

He said, "We've been working on this for quite some time, Mr. Kent."

I said, "Well, that's remarkable. I'm sorry; I enjoyed working here."

And Paul, he said, "Larry, we hate this."

And you know, they had a man working there that was wanted for murder, but I wasn't wanted no place, I was in the clear. Hell, I just came back from overseas. This man, they were looking for him for a murder in Birmingham, Alabama, and *he* was there seventeen months before they caught him. It's just a slip in the records.

I've been in five different institutions, Federal and state.

In 1926 I was sent here and then was pardoned by the Governor. I was only here nine months. First time I was ever in any kind of trouble in my life, any sort of trouble.

What was that for?

They had me charged with burglary.

That's a bit out of your line, isn't it?

Bit . . . it *is,* that's what I say. But you couldn't do anything with them. The Rangers grabbed me on the street. I was engaged to a young lady then. I hadn't been out of school long, I had my first job, one of my first jobs, at the Texas Power and Light Company, and I was going with a young lady in Bay City and just because I left at three thirty in the morning to come to Laredo, Texas, and was going to meet her at San Antonio and there was some things missing out of the home—later, they found that it was the Mexican servant that took them and they pardoned me. Well, when I come on down here, I surrendered, what they term a voluntary surrender. The sheriff, he'd beat my head in and everything else, then he come on down and said, "They need you down there. Here's your papers. Do you want to go to the Walls yourself? You'll be full trusty when you go down."

Well, I was scared to death anyway 'cause I never had had no brushes with the law, and the Rangers scared the hell out of me by whipping me in Houston and everything else, so I said, "Yes, I'll go down there." They gave me five years and I said, "I'll go down and do it—for nothing." Which I knew it was, for nothing.

So he says, "Here's your papers." I got on the Greyhound bus and come on down here and walked into the warden's office. Wearing civilian clothes. That was back in the days when the inmates were really running the institutions. Very few civilians. Today they've got two hundred and some up front, but back in that day we had five civilians. Inmates run the whole setup practically. Run nice and smooth. They had no trouble, no riots, no nothing.

I was there for nine months. If I wanted to go to Dallas, I just ordered my driver; I had a driver. They had Buick touring cars with "Texas Prison System" in gold on the side. We all wore our civilian clothes. There was just four of us in the system that had our own drivers.

Why did you have a driver?

I had charge of the electrical equipment. Not only in this institution. I had charge of the electrical equipment in the capitol building and at Rusk—their insane asylum—and all of the state buildings with that electrical equipment. That was my job. I overseen it. I could call trusties in, I could call electricians in if I knew they were good electricians, talk to them, examine them, if they were good, appoint them trusty. "Warden, I want this man made trusty. Give him a button." They were out then. We run all over the state. Never lost a man, never.

After serving this nine months the pardon came in one morning. They all called me up at the office and said, "We got good news for you." I didn't hardly know I was in the penitentiary anyway. I was making some extra money. I'd contracted some house wiring here and everything else. Warden, he says, "I don't care what you do, Lawrence, just keep my electrical system going." And back in that day we had two powerhouses. We had a DC plant and an AC plant.

I was at the Walls, but I'd go all over. I'd sometimes come and sleep uptown at the hotel nights, it didn't make any difference. I was on what they call "off-count," I wasn't even recorded hardly. I'm just off-count.

So I was pardoned. Well, things were so rosy and I opened up an office in Kennedy, Texas. Contract engineers. And done very well. I was the only electrical man in the city outside of the power and light company and I got in good with the power and light man right away. He was an E.E. too, of course, the manager. He said, "I'm going to start recommending you because you people do nice work." So I hired electricians. I got going real good, making a lot of money.

I got in business with a fellow by the name of Croutch. He was an alcoholic. He was a likable fellow. I took him in because he was a plumbing man, and a good one. He was a good plumbing engineer, so I figured electrical and plumbing go good and there's a lot of building, so we got a contract from the local banker to put up twenty-six homes. That was pretty nice right away. But from bad to worse, from good to bad. He wasn't sober half the time. I was getting aggravated because I don't drink to that extent. So I got aggravated one day and I said, "Look, Charley, we've got to quit." So we sold out. I put my money in my pocket. I still got a little money, I think, in that bank at Kennedy. I think I had $60 or $70 that I just left there.

I got to running around. I wanted to go abroad. Went to Shanghai, China, and stayed seven months in Shanghai and come back in the latter part of 1929.

What did you get in prison for the second time?

It appeared to me, after I came back from Shanghai, that things were so easy that I would tour the country a little bit, and I went down to North Carolina and I came through the little town of Rocky Mount and I saw a bank building right on the corner. It kind of attracted my attention. I had a little money of my own, $6,000 or $7,000 in cash, which is a little money to me, and I looked at that bank and I parked my car, an old Packard touring car, and I walked up there and it had this big marble front, a beautiful bank building in Rocky Mount, right in the center of the tobacco belt where all the big money is from the tobacco people. There were newspapers blown up in the doorway and everything. And it was for lease.

I looked it over and what's left of my little brain started clicking and I went to the hotel where I was staying and paced the floor a little bit and decided there should be a bank for the people, a people's bank for the people. So I called up the leasing agent and put an ad in the paper the next day for tellers, bookkeepers, secretaries, general office administrative help. And I opened up a bank. Called up calciminers, plasterers, plumbers, and the whole works, and rolled up my sleeves and took off my coat and started driving, and told them I had to get this thing open on a certain day and went to work to open the bank.

Splashed it up: the people's bank for the people. I lined them up for two blocks long throwing their money in that bank. I got $184,000 in about four days' time. Put myself in as president. Didn't ask the state banking commission nothing, it was before Roosevelt's bank moratorium, but you were supposed to apply to the state, the state had bank rules.

What year was this?

This was 1930. You were supposed to apply to the state for permission to license, an incorporation charter, this and that, but I ignored all that and figured hell, I know what I'm doing.

I opened a bank and it's going nice and smooth. So there are deposits and I'm the big president of the bank and I'm only a young punk kid and I'm just walking around, living off the fat of the land, got me two secretaries, and they're bringing me my dinner in at night and I'm in there with my secretary and we're having a Scotch and soda during a dry era, and a rap came on the door and I said, "See who it is."

Constable, big chew a tobacco in his mouth. "Your name Kent?"

I said, "That's what they call me. What have you got there?"

"I'm the constable."

"Wonderful," I said, "I see by the big star there."

My secretary said, "I know him, he's mean."

I said, "He don't look mean." Big pistol hanging on him.

He said, "I want to let you read this to me."

I said, "*You* read it."

Ah, there it was: fraud and everything else. Five warrants. Just five.

So the chief of police had me down in that little cell and I'm telling you, he worked me over, he took all my clothes off and everything.

But I had a little chauffeur that was loyal to me and I told him, I said, "Go right down before they close that bank"—he had come to the jail—I wrote him a check and I said, "Take this in to Evans right away." Evans was my cashier. It was for $150,000. I said, "Give it to him right away and take that money"—he was an orphan boy, a good boy, honest—"and put it in that little black satchel that I've got in my office and take it, take it to your home. Tell nobody nothing, Henry."

He said, "Mr. Kent, I sure won't. I'll do anything you tell me to."

I said, "You do that and I'll see that you're well looked after."

The boy went over there and he had just handed the check in and got out when the sheriff slapped the thing on the doors. Cashier just handed it out. Hell, it's an order from the president. He gave it to him. They didn't know what was happening yet, the sheriff was on his way, the boy was just lucky. Just got it and got out. Left $117,000 on deposit the way the books were at that time.

So he took the money home. In the meantime I was making arrangements to get on bond. I got three smart Jewish lawyers and they really went to town and they batted and batted, but I got fifteen years and fifteen years consecutively. Thirty cold years.

And I got kind of shook up, as these boys would say in their slang vernacular.

How much time did you do on that?

I did eleven months and got a full pardon . . .

What did you go in for the next time?

The time I went to Georgia on a pretty fast real estate transaction to a man in Savannah. I went to the county assessor's office and took the pages out of a certain section that had nice property in it and I got those big ledger pages out from the assessor's books and I went out and matched the paper in a stationary store in Atlanta. They didn't have any in Savannah, so I went to Atlanta and I found the identical ledger sheets. Then I arranged the ledger sheets and put this property in my name there and then I went back with that sheet, those ledger sheets. They let you go into the tax assessor's office there, you know, you go in there and you're checking for property. So I watched them and I watched them and I pulled those little things out, lifted them off and put them back in where they belonged, put them in there and then run an ad in the paper. And here come my clients to the hotel. General Oglethorpe Hotel. And this one Jewish fellow come to the hotel and he went crazy about the property right away, and I said, "I've got everything fixed up." I had title papers, fixed them all up, typed them up, fixed the name on them and everything else. "Meet you at the bank tomorrow at ten o'clock." He met me at the bank and I had the titles and abstracts all fixed up, a big bundle of them and everything all fixed up for him.

He was so anxious to get that, he said, "Are you sure you're going to let *me* have it, are you sure you're not going to give it to anybody else?"

I said, "I got it right here. Write your check." Wrote his check, $64,500, cash check. I said, "All right now, come on downstairs." We went down in the elevator to the safe deposit vault.

"When do I get my titles?" he said.

I said, "When this check is okayed."

"Oh, you don't trust me."

I said, "I don't trust anybody. I don't trust anybody."

"Ah," he says, "you're a hard businessman."

Downstairs I open the safe deposit vault and show him the papers. I says, "See this safe deposit vault? This key, when I get the money, is yours."

I go right upstairs with him, wait till he goes up, the vice-president okays the check, and he says, "How do you want this, Mr. Kent?"

"Let me have it in five hundreds and thousands."

He hands me $64,500. I said, "Thank you very much, Mr. Goldberg. Here's your key."

Sam Goldberg. He himself had gone to the Federal prison with what they call the Big Five, the liquor men during prohibition. He had gone and served two years in Atlanta. I didn't know that until later, when they got me and tried me and sent me up there in the Georgia prison.

I told him, I said, "You sorry thing," I says, "I heard about you too. Now you're going to get me."

They didn't get me on that, though, for two years. I run around the country and they grabbed me and took me and gave me two years. For $64,500 I get *two* years.

What did you go in for the next time?

Next time I went back for a check, which I shouldn't have gone for, no more than I should have this one now. For a measly check. *Insufficient* funds, mind you, not a worthless check, just an insufficient funds check. Now Percy Foreman and some of our outstanding lawyers have spelled it out many times that an insufficient funds check definitely is *not* a worthless check [i.e., it's not the same as not having an account at all or using a phony signature]. Now many times my bank account in Houston, when I was in business in Houston, would be $1,800 overdrawn and I wasn't even aware of it. Even my bookkeeper wasn't aware of it until the bank would call and say, "Well, you were a little over, but you had some big deposits come in this morning." I'm traveling around the country, big deposits are coming in, I'm getting the checks, putting them in the mail and mailing them in, and we're sending out a lot of money buying things, you know, and the bank account goes and comes, you know. Anyway, *that* was the way they caught me that time.

Where was that?

In Georgia again.

And the next time?

It happened twice in Georgia. Next time was Illinois for a check that was an insufficient funds check for $50. Give me two years. Charge of electrical equipment.

How much time did you do on that one?

Eleven months.

What was after Illinois?

Next time was Federal mail fraud. That involved machines.

I went in and signed up with a company with the understanding that I would take their machines. I would hit the road with their machines, they would supply the machines and I would send the orders in for them. I sent many orders in, but they weren't supplying machines. The next thing I know, the postal inspectors are trailing me. I see them and I don't know who they are or anything and I told my wife, "Those strange men there, they're not FBI men by a long ways, they're not acting like them. But that's the same man who was in the dining room at the Statler in St. Louis the other day and here he is at the Mule Box in Kansas City." Next thing, another one joined him. Next thing I know, I make a talk before the American Legion on a machine, sign a contract with the American Legion and agree to get the machines to the American Legion and everything else and leave Kansas City to go to Topeka and they broadcast it in Topeka, give my description and everything else. "Pick up this confidence man" and this, that, and the other thing. They don't arrest me in Topeka. I get out of Topeka and go to Pittsburgh and I hear the broadcast. A postal inspector and the Treasury agent came to the hotel looking for me. . . . A porter told me about it. So I told my wife, I said, "You sit tight. They haven't anything on me. If Arnold and his partner have broke up and the company is defunct, I should have been notified. After all, a registered letter should have been sent to me."

There was some argument in the courtroom about that, too. I almost won the thing. But they finally decided, "Yeah, you'd better send him down for a couple of years." And the judge told me later that he was sorry that he sentenced me. He said, "Now I find that the company that you were selling machines for *was* defunct. It was a defunct company. You had no knowledge of it, you weren't advised."

I just kept on selling it. Hell, I just kept on selling. I kept sending the orders in to them. And then I find out that the company that's way out in Seattle and I'm way up in Kansas City around the state of Kansas is defunct. They don't say nothing to anybody and I just keep taking orders.

How much time did you do on that?

I only done nine months.

Next time?

Here. The other one, I was here twice. Once five years ago. Nine months. That was for a check. A check in Houston which was really a case of an insufficient funds proposition again.

And the next time?

That's this one.

And how much of a sentence are you on?

Seven years. I've got five more months.

Weren't you mixed up in some car deal once?

Oh, right after the war, I went with Tucker. Tucker Automobile. And we sold a lot of stock in Chicago and it was a good proposition. We were cleared by a Federal court. We were tried in Chicago by a

Federal court on twenty-eight indictments of stock fraud. We sold $16 million worth of this stock. I was assistant sales manager.

It come about by living in Ypsilanti, Michigan, where Tucker had his plant. His mother had the plant, Aviation Accessories, he gave it to his mother. His mother was rather old. And he was a great fellow to build things as a hobby, little automobiles and things like that.

I knew a man by the name of Fenjerk who was a mechanical engineer, graduated from Michigan State, was a very good friend of mine, and Fenjerk and I used to go to each other's home and play bridge. Fenjerk said to me one night, "Say, Lawrence, you aren't really doing anything now?"

I said, "Well, I've got a little coal burner I'm developing." I was developing a burner. Instead of burning oil, I was going to burn powdered coal and blast it through a burner similar to an oil burner. I was developing that and getting ready to float a stock issue on that.

He said, "I've got a man I want you to meet. I want you to see something."

I said, "What is it?"

He said, "This man is building an automobile. And," he said, "it's amazing. I think it is. I believe this thing has possibilities, Lawrence."

So I said, "I'd be glad to meet him. Who is he?"

He said, "His name is Tucker."

"Oh, that's the Aviation Access——"

"That's right."

We all had lunch the next day. Preston, Ralph Fenjerk, and myself. His home, the way their house is built, they have an incline and it goes down under or below the house. The house is over and their garage is like underground, below the ground level. We go in there and he's got this damned automobile. And his basement connects with that setup. And he's got this big long chassis of a car and it's got a lot of chrome trim and I look at it and I said, "Gee, this is something. What are you going to do with it? Will it run?"

He jumps on it and whoop! right away it starts up, an air-cooled airplane engine, a rear engine. Perfect. My brain starts to work right away. Stop, stop, this is a terrific thing, this thing should be promoted, this man is an idea man and a mechanic but he's not a promoter. I said, "Mr. Tucker, why don't you put it on the market?"

"Market? What with?"

He's just a hobby man.

I said, "What with? Do you want to put that on the market?"

I looked at it some more. I said, "Will it run out on the road?"
He said, "Tomorrow we'll take a ride on it."

And it was just a chassis. We put a seat on it the next day and he
and I drove all the way up to Ypsilanti. I said, "We'll put this on the
market."

He said, "Where will we get the money?"

"We'll get the money. We'll get it."

So a friend of mine had just come out of Illinois prison, he was
involved with the insurance swindle there in the state of Illinois, the Illinois insurance exchange, and he'd got in tight with the actuary of the
state, and they all got mixed up, five or six of them. He went down
and got five years. He wasn't doing anything then. He was in kind of
bad shape there in Chicago. I got ahold of him. I said, "Listen, I got
something that's natural. We can get it going right away. The Lupscomb Corporation is renting the Dodge plant that they had during
the war building the R-3400 engines." I knew about that, too. I said,
"I'll contact my friend Capehart in Washington, D.C., and we'll get a
lease on that building and Lupscomb's getting ready to be kicked
out."

And we did, we leased that whole damn building. That's the largest factory in the war, you know. Building those R-3400's, that Dodge
plant. We got the lease on that. Lupscomb was folding up, that mobile
housing outfit, they folded up, they weren't making anything. So we
got in there and got an office. Hired stock salesmen and we started.
We got models, we set up a nice office, we floated a stock issue, we got
the okay of the Michigan SEC and we went 300,000 Regulation A,
what's called Regulation A, and we went to the SEC, the United
States Security Exchange Commission and got an okay, and we had
salesmen out, we were ordering steel, we were building automobiles.
We built twenty-two of them.

All of a sudden, jealousy. Two or three magazines—*Reader's Di-
gest* and *Changing Times*, I think—hurt us more than anything else.
They started blasting us—ex-convicts organized an automobile company, and this, that, and the other thing. We had people out in sixteen
cities.

If everything was going so well, how did you get busted on it?

All right. The rule, the law is that when you're selling stock that
way you're allowed, the corporation itself is allowed to withdraw 15
percent of the total for their expenses and whatnot as long as they
make a record of it, and we made a record. We paid ourselves salaries
and one thing or another. And we had sold, up to that time when we

were arrested, $16,760,000 worth of it and had agencies appointed already and was taking the money from people for franchises for the agencies. And along comes a warrant claiming that we were living high off the hog and this and that and the other thing, and all of us ex-convicts. So they charged us with stock fraud. We went to trial in Chicago and was acquitted. After a thirty-one day trial we were acquitted on twenty-eight counts of stock fraud with the money in the bank. That's what acquitted us: the money was in the bank. We had piles of books in the courtroom. The trial lasted thirty-one days.

When was that?

1947. It began in 1946 and extended on into '47. Tucker got sick over the thing. They had five of us. Tucker got sick of it and the poor guy was so upset over it and everything else that he went to South America and he died there a few years ago. But he did build a car in South America and got it on the market.

Did they file on him too?

Oh, sure. Everybody. Yeah. But here was the bad part. After we were acquitted by the Federal government on twenty-eight counts, five days later we were all at the Abe Lincoln Hotel in Springfield celebrating it and we're talking to our lawyer in Detroit. He said, "Full steam ahead. Go ahead and sell. You boys are in the clear."

There's a rap on the door. I had a glass of Scotch in my hand. I walked over to the door and opened it. Huh! A captain of the Illinois State Police with all his gold on, lieutenant of the Illinois State Police, two gentlemen in plainclothes from the Illinois attorney-general's office. "Mr. Kent?"

"Come in."

All my partners and their wives are there. I said, "Gentlemen, presenting the law." In all their regalia they come in.

"Sorry, Mr. Kent, we got warrants for you. All of you."

"Warrants for what?"

"Fraud. Stock fraud."

"Oh," I said. "Use the telephone?"

"Yes."

Called Walsh in Detroit. Let me talk to him, the attorney-general. I put the captain on.

"Oh, yes. I see. Uh uh. Yes, $25,000 apiece. Ya. Oh, yes, we can. No, no. No double jeopardy. All right there. We'll have them on recognizance. Sure, these boys with the money they've got! Yeah, yeah, yeah. I'll release them." That's the conversation.

"All right, let me talk to him." I say, "Yeah, George."

He said, "Larry, sit tight. You all got $25,000 bond. We'll bust that case and," he says, "if they send you down we'll have you pardoned."

So I said, "When are you going to get down here?"

He said, "I'm flying tomorrow."

I said, "All right."

He was down the next day. We all went out on a date. He just let us loose there on our own recognizance. We went down the next day and made a bond of $25,000 apiece.

Gave all five of us five years apiece in Illinois prison. I mean, we got acquitted by the Federal government! And we got that.

We were only in the Illinois prison about seven months. We all had key jobs around the place. Civilian clothes. One of them in the dental lab and another one of them up in the hospital, worked with Leopold up there in the hospital. And I was in charge of electrical equipment under the civilian engineer there. But they just give me charge of it and he just sat on his fanny. He liked that.

After seven months they called us all to the warden's office one morning. We go over there and he's just smiling. Hell of a nice fellow. Smart. A penologist. Oh, smart. (This one here wouldn't hold a candle alongside him. This one should travel around and see how prisons are run. I know how they're run. Five of them I've been in. Always been in key jobs in them.) Anyway, he said, "Well, boys, I'm glad to see this." He said, "I'm sincere in telling you that I'm really happy to see this. The governor says that he always thought there was more to this thing." Here's who was fighting us: Henry Ford, Chrysler, and General Motors. And I had some of the big men from General Motors tell me themselves that they would get up on the witness stand and tell, "When you ordered that two hundred tons of steel from Cleveland, from Bethlehem Steel," he said, "I can prove that they went underhand to kill it so that car wouldn't hit the road."

If that automobile would of ever went on the market, oh, believe me—

It's a good car?

Oh, it was terrific. I can show you one yet. I just got a letter the other day from my sister. She said, "Mrs. Hyler says she still likes her Tucker." She's still driving it. She's still driving it in Ypsilanti. They were our grocer there. Old-time independent grocery. Real nice fine foods, you know. And she had one of them.

Slim: "I follow the dice . . ."

I follow the dice. When I hit a hot streak I follow them. I may start to gamble in a joint in East St. Louis—gambling in St. Louis is illegal, there are no open betting places, but across the river in East St. Louis it was wide open—now I go over there with $200, $300 in my pocket and hit a hot streak and I may wind up in Oklahoma City, I may wind up in Des Moines.

What gets you to Oklahoma City?

Well, I hit a hot streak and when the game break up someone say, "Let's go to Oklahoma, they raising hell there." Or somebody come in from Oklahoma—gamblers move around, you know—and say, "Ole So-and-So cooned out the other night and he went to Tulsa." Man, if I had me a roll I'd follow that sonofabitch 'cause he's gonna drop it sooner or later, and everybody shoots for him. I don't know, it's a dog-eat-dog world.

Is this gambling world you move in, is this integrated or all Negro?

Anywhere you're handling money like that, it's integrated. It's been that way since I can remember. I made some of my best money in southeast Missouri off a white boys. I shot a man out of five bales of cotton once, with his dice.

And what did you do with it?

It was cash. After he sold the cotton, I took the receipts and got my money. That's one of those times that my wife didn't see me but seven days out of a month.

Like that, when I make a pile, I usually send it home, you know. It's a true saying, Bruce, "If luck lasts, dice pass." And you can't just keep shooting and shooting because eventually, if you got a roll as big as this one in your pocket, boy, it goes. So ain't no sense pinching it off and pinching it away. Send the biggest portion of it home, so you know where that's at. You can afford to lose what you got in your pocket and still not be hurting. That's a gambler's way of looking at it, you know.

They say, "All is velvet." That's shit; it's not velvet. It's harder to stand up at a dice table all night than to get a decent job and work a week. That's square business.

Then why do you do it?

Why do I do it? Hm.

Well, I don't like for nobody to tell me what time to get up or what time to lay down, or blow a bell or ring a bell for me to eat, make my check out, I got a certain amount I got to get and all of that. I just don't go for it. So I find some other way.

It's not that I'm lazy. Hell, I have worked, I've worked hard. I've skinned mules, goddamnit, I've pulled logs, worked in sawmills for a timber company, I've unloaded whole cars of coal by myself. I don't give a damn about working, but I just don't want no sonofabitch standing over me telling me, "Well, you've got to do this and you've got to do that."

That's why I can't be a backyard soldier (noncombat soldier). Now in combat it's a little bit different. Orders come out, you do 'em and that's that. Do 'em to the best of your ability and that's that. But you get one of these jobs, you get a bunch of cocksuckers bucking everybody, jockeying for position. And actually nobody's going to make anything until the company decides, you know, and nine times out of ten the cocksucker that's doing all the jockeying for position is not going to get it anyway and he's there breathing down your back, running to the Man, you know. That's shit.

Christ. I take me a pair of dice and beat that shit, or a deck of cards, or if it comes down to the nutcut, I'll sell a sonofabitch the Brooklyn Bridge.

Nutcut: that's a southern expression. When they line the hogs up to casterate them, it's what they call "coming up to the nutcut." You getting down to brass tacks.

When all is said and done, when I get out of here this time, I think I'm going to have to settle for that, 'cause I'm too old to spend nights standing up over a dice table. My eyes are getting bad, my hearing is gone, nerves are shot. I tried to palm some dice the other day and I dropped three out of seven. That's no good—get killed that way. At one time I could carry a seven-dice combination. Seven different dice, not counting the two in your hand. But now I can't do it. I could even palm those big drugstore dice. I had dice to match every illegal house and legal house from Memphis, Tennessee, to Detroit. I could walk in there and look at their dice and go out to my car and get a set just like them.

You were living dangerously.

Well, no. Look at it like this, Bruce, life itself is a gambling jack, you know. Now I step out that door, I ain't got no guarantee I'm going to make it to the hall. Some fool may be out there, some other fool may throw a brick at him and miss him and hit me and knock my cocksucking brain out. So I'm living dangerously anyway. Or I may try to cross the street and here come some drunken cocksucker and run all up the sidewalk and kill me, you know. So if I'm going to live dangerously anyway, I might as well make some money out of it.

But now you speak of living dangerously like that. Actually, it's not dangerous. Not to no extreme, you know. Because when the house man throw you the dice you catch them, shoot yours out, you got his, you just put 'em in your pocket. Shoot yours till you get tired and take 'em out and put his back in, go on about your goddamned business.

I've did all of that. Your big houses, like out in Las Vegas and what have you, well, I've never been in them. But I understand they hire men like myself to stand around and make sure you don't put your shit in the game.

And actually, I have got my stuff caught, but *I've* never got caught with it. Some square around the table will get caught with it. And I'll bitch louder than anybody in the house: "No wonder I ain't making any goddamn money. This sonofabitch here he boy boy boy . . ."

And then, too, the art of gambling, especially with dice, it's more of a talking game than anything else. You have to first convince the cocksucker that he can't beat you. Or you get him vexed. That's my way of doing it. In the game of cooncan, I get a man vexed and he's mine.

Cooncan is a two-man game, you find very few white men that play it. It's really what they call a coon's game. An old expression.

It's a ten-card deal and an eleven-card spread. You start off with ten and wind up with eleven. You take out all the eights, nines, and tens. I could show you with a deck a hellofalot better than I could explain it to you.

That's one of our games. It boils down to this: you think you slick with cards and I think I'm slick with cards, so let's get it on. You have to have a good remembrance to play it, you have to know what's gone by. And after three pulls, if you a good player, you should know what's in his hand. And if he gets down once you sure enough should know what he's got in his hand. Approximately, I mean, you can never be positive.

There are tricks to the game. If you pull a card and throw it in the dead face up, I can't touch it, but if you turn it down and it's my card you can't do a damn thing with it, you can't go back and get it, you know.

Now a lot of guys will "smack the dead." They take the card and

bam! you know, and make you break for it. Well, if you break for it
he know you want that card and he can put it back in his hand (because he hasn't let go of it yet). Ha!

You can do that once.

You'll go for it if you're not a gambler. Now a lot of gamblers like
myself will break for anything that you smack on the dead. You say,
"Well, you want that one," and you put it back. Well, I don't want
that goddamned card.

But you load him up with cards he doesn't want either.

Right. And now I know where the seven of clubs is at because he
smacked the dead with it and I'll get pat to the seven of clubs because
I know eventually he's got to throw it away, he ain't got a goddamned
thing to do with it, if he had a had he wouldn't a been smacking the
dead with it. And when he throw it away, that's my card. "Well,
buddy, that's the way it goes."

Oh, life's a motherfucker, Bruce.

Cooncan is a serious game. It's just about as serious as chess.
And chess is sure enough serious. Because it's really wits, a game of
wits, battle of nerves. Sonofabitch play cooncan all night, next day he
can't hold a cup of coffee. 'Cause he's shot to hell.

But really, Bruce, I'm no gambler. I'm a cheat.

Cheat?

A cheat, yeah. I'm no gambler because if I tried to gamble, fuck,
I'd lose my goddamned drawers. Everything I go at, I look at it from
being a way of making money, I'm looking to cheat. Yeah, I cheat. I
ain't gonna lie. No sense in lying about it.

Remind me not to hire you.

Well, it's not like that. In work I do an honest day's work. But in
cooncan, in gambling, I cheat. Just remind me not to gamble with
you.

I have did some honest work, Bruce, I don't mind working. I just
can't stand that no one standing up over me.

I was in the first invasion of Africa. I fought all the way. In '45
I'm down here in Gordon, Georgia, doing some training. I was train-
ing commander there. I'm walking along with a .45 on my hip and a
BAR on my shoulder, and you know what a farmer asked me?

"When did they start letting you niggers carry guns."

And there was Patton. George S. Patton. After all of that fucking
fighting we done. Now there was times in Oran when I've seen studs
dash out in the streets and get it. When the war was over, you know
what he told us? We were six miles from Berlin, we parted and let the

Russians go through. He got up on top of a Sherman tank. He said, "Ah'm a Southerner, my daddy was a Southerner, his daddy before him was a Southerner. If they knew I had you niggers over here shooting at white folks they'd turn over in their graves."

Why didn't he get shot?

Why didn't he get shot? Why don't a lot of people get shot? Why ain't Faubus dead? What about the man that gave the order to drop the bomb on Hiroshima and Nagasaki—Truman—why ain't he dead? There's a lot of whys that's gotta be answered.

You go through life, you stumble along, you pick up bits here and bits there and I don't know, you try to get it all together. Here's one thing my father told me:

Life's a funny old proposition, from the cradle to the grave,
And it matters not your calling, be you rich man, beggar, or slave.
A man comes to birth on this funny old earth with not a chance in a million to win,
To find that he's through and his funeral is due before he can even begin.
He gets one fleeting look at life's mystery book and the curtain rings down the show,
Before he gets set he finds he's all wet, washed up, and ready to go.
He'll stumble and strive with this thing called life, but a man at his best is a slave
Stumbling at a grind like the rest of his kind till at last he pulls up in the grave.
The thing never stands, the tightly drawn strands seem to fall apart like sand-woven rope,
And all you get is a record of debts you fail to cash in if you're broke.
Nine-tenths of the times you're not worth a dime, and the whole damned thing was a joke.

That's the only way I find that you can actually accept life and live it. It's true. If you stop and think, experience is the most brutal teacher there is, but yet she's the best. What you learn through knots and hickies make a ass out of what you learn out of books. I trained there down in Camp Gordon, Georgia, for eighteen solid weeks. Okefenokee swamps with seven rounds of ammunition for fourteen days.

But you know where I got my lesson at? In the Libyan desert, that's where I learned it. 'Cause there I had to face it: "Slim: if you want Hattie's boy back over there you got to face the music."

You can take all the books you want, man, there's no such thing as a man being an educated man out of a book. You can be a widely read man. And there's no such thing as an educated fool: once a man is educated he takes in all aspects of life. He has to travel, he has to get practical experience, and then he has to read. He has to be able to see what he want, mean what he say, and say what he mean.

There's not very many educated men.

No, there's not.

My old man was a scoundrel and a old roustabout and what-have-you, a gandy-dancer, a poet, a soldier, and so forth, so it's hard to tell. I'm just a chip off the old block, I guess. He taught me quite a few intellectual poems. Well, they're not what you would call classics, but they're classics as far as a man of my father's standards would be calling them because usually his stems around a bunch of "Mother-fuckers," you know. And when he would run down a clean one I would marvel at it. Like that "Life's a funny old proposition"—that's a beautiful piece of poetry. Like "Sam McGhee," that's one of them. I think he got that out of a handbook. And "The Lure of the Tropics," he got that and all those out of a handbook, I believe. But they were nice and clean. Usually his were something like "The Blue Velvet Band" or "Lady Liberty." That's one he taught me:

> Gather round me, fellas, I have a story to tell,
> I want you to listen carefully so you can learn this lesson well.
> You see I fell in love with a brown-skin girl that carried my heart
>   for a whirl,
> But the bitch was like a timberwolf all year round.
> She was on my side when I was on my feet and on my ass when I
>   got down.
> So you see, fellas, I've traveled this wide world over now, and I
>   know there's only one bitch for me,
> She has her face on a silver dollar and her name is Liberty.
> She feeds me when I'm hungry, keeps my clothes outta soak,
> And as long as I got this fabulous old broad I can't be broke.

He taught me that, he ran that one down to me. What led up to that, I was in high school and I got strung out behind some old cottontail, you know. I come home and run the spiel down to the old man, and he run that down to me.

He said, "Boy, you just can't make it like that."

Tell me how you got two lives and a 160.

This cocksucking judge gave me life for robbery, then he gave me life for assault with intent to kill. The cocksucker asked me did I have any objection to him sentencing me to twenty years addition to this for a sawed-off shotgun. "Man, you kiss my ass."

He said, "Twenty more."

I said, "Man, you crazy!"

He said, "Twenty more." Every time I opened my cocksucking mouth he said, "Twenty more."

I get to the courtroom door when the sheriff's taking me out and he's sitting up there shaking his fingers or something. I said, "Aw, man, fuck you."

He said, "Twenty years!"

That's how it goes. Yes, sir, that was the case.

I come here, I see on my commitment papers, I had a stack of armed robberies against me and the judge was really pretty lenient, I guess, after he cooled off. Just gave me twenty for the robberies. Just went through the stack and picked some out and gave me twenty on each one. I guess that sort of helped out, because if he had put all that on the record, man, I would have been in a world of trouble.

I had the two lives already and he was going to give me twenty additional years for the shotgun, because they're illegal when they're sawed-off like the one that I had. The guy was pretty lenient, I guess. If you boil it down, he could a put that shit on the record the way it was and aw, man, I'd a been in a world a trouble. There wouldn't a been no sense in me even talking to these people here about parole.

That was St. Louis where I fell out. I'm originally from Arkansas.

I don't have enough flaws in my case to get a pardon. I don't have enough errors on the part of the court to get me a pardon, in fact I don't even have enough to get me a time-out. I've tried it all to no avail.

I've had a lot of guys ask me how can I go around laughing and joking at it the way I do. Hell, I don't see nothing else to do. Why worry about it? It isn't going to solve anything. All I'm gonna do is make myself sick, go around with my head down, and eventually all the people that I know, when they see me, they'll start to running from me 'cause they don't want to hear my troubles, they got troubles of their own. So I keep friends that way.

Sometimes, I'm gonna tell you, Bruce, sometimes it gets heavy. But it don't last long. When it get heavy I make me a batch of brew and get drunk and forget it. Wake up too sick to worry about it.

How old are you now?

Thirty. [He was thirty-seven.]

I thought last time you told me you were older?

I might have. [When he first was convicted he claimed he was twenty-five so he could get in the reformatory which was easier time and offered a better Parole slot. It didn't work.]

Actually—now I'm not trying to make any allowances for what I did and I'm not trying to make any allowances for the time, you know—but under the circumstances I think that I got a little bit more than I should have gotten. My rap partner wound up with eight, one of them, and one of them wound up with five. I got it all.

Were you the one with the shotgun?

Well, yeah, on a couple of occasions, yeah, I was.

But I didn't ever shoot anyone with it that I can recall. I might a sprinkled a couple. Nothing serious. Except that one time . . .

But just like everything else, life's handed to you in two buckets —"I ain't tried that yet" and "I ain't going to do that no more." Let's put this in that "I ain't going to do that no more" bucket and leave it there, 'cause it just didn't pan out. Like Louis Jordan say, "Fortune and fame just ain't for me."

What were you robbing?

Loan companies, mostly.

How many?

I had thirty.

The last one, I walked in and threw down on [pointed his gun at] the guy. It was a big liquor exchange and warehouse. This was in St. Louis.

He had a nice ring on his hand. He's a young boy. I say, "Off the ice, buddy."

He said, "Look, Jack, I just got married a couple a weeks ago and my wife gimme this thing. Gimme a play. I just work here, man. Take the money but, fuck, man, gimme a play. The money I got in my pocket, man, is my check, I gotta take it home to my wife."

I said, "Well, I can dig it, buddy, 'cause I'm hooked up myself, I got a dough-roll [wife] and two crumb-catchers [children], you know."

So I left him. I said, "Rack up the company's money," and he did, "and set it on the counter," and he did that. When I gets the money, my rap partner—he was nervous because he had killed a guy previously before this happened and he was a little shook up—he turned to the door and made a lot of noise. I turned around to see what was happening, thinking it was the police. Instinctively I turned and crouched. The guy behind the counter shot me in the back. The one that I had left the ring and check with.

When he shot me he turned me around. He was shooting a light weapon, but oh, man, that sonofabitch packed a wallop. A little .32 Mauser. It turned me around. That was it.

Did you shoot him?

Yeah.

Kill him?

No.

Did you hit him?

Yeah.

Where?

Just over the heart.

Very fortunate.

Yeah, for both of us. He cut two of my main arteries. [He shows me the entry and exit scars.] It cracked a rib, cut a artery to my kidney and one to one of my lungs, and they were two hours getting me after that. Wouldn't a got me then if I hadn't passed out.

Because I had already made arrangements for that sort of thing before it happened. A man out there doing stuff like that, he's gotta put protection on himself. Just like a man who's got a bunch a whores out there, he's gotta put protection to keep them on the streets. I made all those arrangements, but having a young rap partner, it was to no avail.

I got a lot of regrets, you know.

But do you know, Bruce, laying all bullshit aside, I went practically around the world. I been in Africa, I been in Europe, I been in South America, I been in Latin America, been in Canada, I been in Greenland, I been in Alaska. But I never saw it fail, every time I return to St. Louis I get fucked up. That's square business.

First time I came back my whore tried to kill me. Yeah. She did that to me. [Shows me a thin scar across his throat.] Cocksucking razor.

That's what it looks like.

That's what it was.

How deep did it go?

I don't know. I was *so* scared. I think they took four stitches on the inside and five on the outside. It was gushing blood. This deal here was cut—

The tendon?

Yeah. It wasn't cut in two, but it was cut. Man, if I hadn't a been full a that alcohol I guess I'd a died. I looked down, my shirt was turning red. "What the goddamned hell is going on? Aw, Lord!"

It was so quick, you know. I didn't even know I was cut. It got to stinging. The weather was hot, it was in the summertime. At that time they didn't have too many air-conditioned taverns. That's where it happened, in a tavern. I'm sitting up there chin-musicking with another broad and she just walked up there, threw her arm around me, you know, and when she fall back she says, "Well, I'll see you, honey."

I said, "Yeah." I sit there and then, "What the hell is this!"

She just swatted you with the razor?

Yeah.

How come?

This other broad I was talking to. See, oh, it's a long story. The girl that cut me, she was doing everything that was humanly possible for her to do for me. I had a car and nice clothes and all that, thanks to her. And I'm sitting up here jawjacking with this other tramp. See, I'd bullshitted her: "Well, we go through this for a few years and then we'll buy a home and then we'll get a business," but every time she'd give me the money, right across the dice table it would go, whap! So she tried to cut my cocksucking throat.

Man oh man.

Then I had another one that tried to shoot my arm off. Went in there and came out here. Caught bone and all. And I ran like something hot. "Goddamn! You going kill me yet!"

Life has been a running comedy skit with me—for the other fella. It wasn't funny when they were fucking me.

Aw, man, I've had some good women though.

I had a good woman when I got busted. Least she was good long as I was out there. You know the old saying, out of sight, and out of mind. You know, it's one of those things. She's married now and doing damn good, my mom tells me.

You expected that.

Sure. It would be the same if she was in here. I damned sure wouldn't be wasting *my* youth out there. I'd do for her what I could. I mean, she does the same, she writes me a line every now and then, if I need something I write to her and she sends it to me, you know. That's the best she could do if she was waiting. Plus she's got those two crumb-catchers, she's gotta do something.

On top of your head—is that a part or a scar?

That's a scar, man. Got one there and one there. That one's a bullet. I got that in Korea. Went in there and came out there. Went in between the head and the helmet and sounded like a bunch a bees in that motherfucker. I didn't know what the hell was coming off. And that one is a fight I got in here. I got drunk—that's the last one—I got drunk and decided I could whup two motherfuckers and they whupped me. This happened two months ago, it's a new tattoo. That's a new ooo-eee notch I got here. Ooo-eee, that's an expression they use here. You know, a motherfucker hits you, pow! You go Ooo-eee.

When they're all through with you they can take your skin and tack it up on the wall for an exhibit.

And no one would believe it.

Where are you working now?

I'm in the chair shop—the furniture factory.

Is that where you were when I was last here?

No. When you were here before I was one of the political inmates, I had a political job, was supposed to been boss of the street gang. They clipped my wings. Yeah. They clipped my wings.

What did you get in the hole for?

Fighting and getting drunk.

Getting drunk?

That's how I got into the fight.

On booze or pills?

Booze. I'm a little wary of these pills. I don't even fuck with them in the streets. I'm a booze man, I'm a booze hound. And when I get drunk I feel like I can whup the world, and I usually try. Every time they proves me different, you know, but next time I gets drunk I try again.

And when you get out? If you get out?

I'll tell you, Bruce, knowing that when I get drunk I'm gonna fuck up, it's best I don't get drunk. I figure that I can sacrifice five years drinking for the rest of my life, 'cause the odds are against me. It don't make sense to go out there and fuck up. I got too much to live for. It's hard enough to get out there the first time, let alone go out there and screw off.

If you make this parole, what will you do?

I promised my mother I was gonna buy her a house, so I imagine

I'll have to get a job. And under the circumstances they're letting me out under I *know* I'll have to get a job. In fact, I already have a job with a construction company handling heavy equipment in St. Louis. Like I told her, the first five years I'll be on parole and I'll have to keep my nose clean and my ass at home. But after that, I plan to keep my nose clean, but I doubt if I'll stay at home.

Yeah. I probably won't be with that job too long. I probably will try to get transferred to the Veteran's Hospital. I'm sick, Bruce, I'm sick. It's nothing that these people here can do for me 'cause they don't have the facilities. I've lost fifteen pounds in the last three months. Nothing ain't doing me no good.

Is this the result of various injuries or . . .

I got a pulse-bladder. Like a cyst, but it's choking the artery to my balls and it hurts a lot of the time. Boy, they ache. That's from being shot, kicked, not taking care of myself, catching the claps and the crabs and what-have-you.

Like a bitch gave me the claps in Texas and I told her, I said, "Bitch, you lousy motherfucker, I bought that pussy from you and you gave me the clap!"

She said, "What did you pay for it?"

"Bitch, I paid you ten dollars."

"Aw, fool, I didn't give you no claps. You bought the claps, I gave you the pussy."

Man oh man. Strange things happen. She really run that down to me.

I done got too old to do time, Bruce. Aw, it's gotten where it kills me. Every time them doors rack . . .

See, when you start out to doing time—this is not my first bit, you know, I did a little light taste in Arkansas and I did a little light taste in a prisoner-of-war camp. But this bit here, man, aw, it's a dickhead. Every time they close that door, man, it seems like something's gone.

What did you do time in Arkansas for?

Murder.

How did you get out of that?

I got five years out of it. It was broken down to manslaughter. But it ain't nothing to be bragging about. I don't like to go into that. Something that's gone now. I was young and foolish then, thought I was mean and got all fucked up.

See, just like I told you before, Bruce, life is handed to a man in two buckets. It's a bucket full of "I haven't did that yet," and then

there's an empty bucket marked "I ain't gonna do that no more."
Now you reach into this bucket of "I haven't did that yet" and you
come up with something. You try it. If you like it, you hold that, you
know, you hold it to you. And you get another one of those "I haven't
did this yet." But if it fucks up on you, the first thing you do is drop it
over here in this "I ain't gonna do it no more" bucket. That's the way
I feel about life, you know. That's one of those things that's in that "I
ain't gonna do it no more" bucket—like doing time in Arkansas.
Don't do that no more. I got enough of that, and it didn't work out
right, so I had to put it in that bucket.

Just like when I walked in there. There the system then was a
hellofalot different than it is now. You had four square men [civilian
employees] in the whole penitentiary, in the whole camp. I was on
Cummins Four Camp. There was four square men on the whole camp
and the rest of it was handled by convicts. You had convict guards
and convict cooks and all, everything.

The hard part about it, when I walked in, this deputy warden was
sitting behind his desk. Sitting with a big old ten-gallon hat on, spurs,
and he's got a big old rawhide whip laying on the desk, and he's got a
big old .38-40 on his hip, you know. Well, all the convict guards carry
that shit. He says, "What're you in here for, boy?"

I says, "Manslaughter."

He looks at me and says, "I said, what're you in here for, boy?"

I says, "Manslaughter, Captain, that's what they told me."

That cocksucker hit me right on top of the head with the whip.
He said, "You in here to work, ain't you."

I said, "Yeah!"

He said, "Well, there ain't no damn man in here to slaughter."

And I knew right then I had to put it in the "I ain't gonna do it
no more" bucket.

Man, life is funny. I ain't bullshitting you, life is full of mysteries,
you know. There's a lot of comical things that happen to you. They're
not comical, they're not worth a fuck *then*, but later on, you sit back
and look at 'em and crack up. There's a lot of things that happened to
me that at the time they happened I said, "Oh, man, Jesus Christ, if I
live through this . . ."

Like they used to have a fucking old locomotive on the Texas and
Pacific, a old steam job, a mountainjack job, called the Maw Ferkins
or Maw Perkins.

Out of where?

Out in Oklahoma. A damned old steam engine that ran from

Tulsa, Oklahoma, down into Texarkana, Arkansas, or Texarkana, Texas. And the sonofabitch only made two stops from Tulsa to Texarkana. She got her water on the fly and all of that, you know.

Well, I fucked up in Tulsa and I caught her. She had manifest flags on her, you know, but I had been riding manifest freights before.

What does that mean?

Spoilage, vegetables and things like that. They have to keep moving. She took water on the fly. They took water then, it wasn't like now. Man, I got on that damned thing and I got on a damned oil car 'cause that was the only thing I found that I could get on. I caught it while it was moving, pulling off. And the damned car turned out, as it would, to have a flat wheel on it. That sonofabitch like to shook my intestines off. Man, I couldn't turn it loose. I said, "Lord, if I get off this damned thing . . ." They had a little walk, you know, around the side of the oil car, and I got to hold on with both hands, man, my arms was tired. I said, "Man, if I get off a this damned thing I ain't gonna hobo no more. I'm not catching no more freights if I just get off a this damned thing." That sonofabitch was blowing hot cinders down my neck, it just beared 'em in and I just couldn't turn loose to fight 'em off. Aw, man.

You couldn't get back to another car?

Hell, no! I couldn't get off a that thing. The next cars was all refrigerator cars. I said, "Lord have mercy if I get off a this damned thing." Fucking old flat wheel was aw, man! And that thing was running, man, that thing was going about seventy or eighty miles an hour, running and screaming, and I was about four cars from the coal tender and when she'd take water that damn shit would just swish over me. 'Cause she took water on the fly, you know, steady moving and taking water.

How did they do that, another train alongside?

Hell, no, they just opened the tank. They had a thing come over the track and they open the tank on the train as she go by, hell, you releasing about five hundred gallons in a minute there, shoot it in. They start the stream before the engine get there and she get what she can on the fly. The rest of it come back in the coal tender and all over me. Aw, man.

Up here in Kansas I got screwed around. There's a damned old bridge abutment up there right out of Hutchinson. I caught it this time of the year. I was about as far from the bridge as from here to the capital building. I figured there was plenty of time to get on the car. But I caught the car wrong. Instead of catching it where the cars come together there, I caught it further up. Now when I come up there's this damned old bridge abutment and there ain't nowhere for me to go but just stick there on the side of that car and pray and feel them slats brushing my ass. "Lord, if I get off a this one I ain't coming back thisaway no more."

There's a lot of places you ain't going back to.

Yeah, there's a hell of a lot a places I ain't going back to. Boy, when I once say I'm through with a place, I'm finished. I ain't going back.

Oh man, life is cruel. But it's sweet. I wouldn't trade it for anything.

There isn't too much you can *trade it for.*

No, I wouldn't trade her. Because every day to me, the life that I lead, every day is a book, it's a brand-new book, every day. When I wake up in the morning I'm not like most guys—they wake up with a plan: "Today I'll do so and so." The only plan I have is, "Well, tonight I'll lay down sometime." Other than that, take her as she go. Every day is a book. But it's beautiful. Because someday I'm gonna be too old to do these things. I'm gonna sit back: well, it wasn't no fun when it happened, but I'm glad now.

Matt: "You leave a certain amount of your feelings buried deep . . ."

In this part of the country, I'm known as a torpedo. In other parts, up north, I'd be known as a hood.

This sentence here I'm doing is not a question of guilty to the extent of time I have. Before this I had beat a murder charge, before that I had beat a manslaughter charge. This was something they could get a better angle on me on and hand me the stiffest penalty. I have the papers over there if you'd care to look at them sometime today.

I'm here for subduing a deputy sheriff and taking his pistol. And for that, I received ten and a quarter, that is ten to twenty-five years. Now you know and I know that for taking a man's pistol, no matter damn if he's the president, there's no such reason I should have that time.

But I served seven months on a manslaughter charge, I was lucky enough to beat that. I served a little better than a year on a murder charge, I was lucky enough to beat that because I proved self-defense. So now I jumps up and takes a deputy sheriff's pistol and I do more time than I've done for lives.

I can't ever scream about being bum-rapped. I won't tell a lie. I'll admit that the sentence they gave me was entirely too stiff for the crime. Had I beat him or shot him, which it was at my disposal to do, but I didn't—I merely took his pistol so he couldn't shoot me whiles I left. Ten to twenty-five years is too much for that thing.

But that's one of them things.

You told me you were a farmer?

Yes.

Are you really a farmer?

I'm from a farming family, let's say, in a farming state. I own a farm, but I never worked it. I have a family living on it in order to help my wife and they work it on shares, see. They take care of the farm. She gives them so much for their part. I built the house and everything for them, a real nice house too. That's in Iowa.

When you were out, where did you work out of?

Moline, Muscatine, Rock Island, Galesburg, Ill., Chicago—

Just all over the Middle West?

Memphis, Tennessee, Minnesota, Colorado. I worked the United States.

You traveled around quite a bit.

Well, you have to.

That was one of the things that brought conflict for a while between my wife and I, but after she saw what I was really after—it was a long time before she knew what I was doing, and I never have been what you'd call a hot-nut Louie or Casanova. I mean when I'm working it's strictly business. Every babe I'd see, I'm not interested in an angle. I married my wife, when I get ready for sex life I believe I can go home. So after she did discover it, I was about ready to give that up anyway, it didn't matter a hell of a lot. It's just a chance you take.

With me it's not a calculated act of hating the world in general and so forth. I'm a licensed electrician. I took a test here in '55 at the Bell Telephone Company. I had a choice of California or Alaska because they don't hire colored around here. Even in this prison it's like that: any job you look at around in here—you got the mess hall, they don't used colored for any place but porters. They got this hospital; they don't use you anyplace but for porters. You've got the machine shop; they don't use colored for anything but porters. You got the carpenter shop; they don't use colored for anything but porters. You got the bakery. Oh, you can just name them right in this little few acres here.

With my trade I could work up around my home state, but running into that kind of stuff . . .

You have some intelligent, educated, and broad-minded as you would expect to find Negroes in this place. But you usually find them using a broom or a mop. That is their level. You could search the institution over and, out of all the jobs, I doubt if you would find two Negro clerks anyplace in here.

Because they're just not given that kind of job?

That's out.

I'm a licensed electrician as I told you before. I mentioned a job of working in the electric shop and you would have thought I requested to spend a night with the official's wife. That was the other administration, things may change, but they screamed and hollered: "We don't use 'em here." "Well," I said, "you only have one or two licensed men over there and I do have a license." No deal.

Here's the thing. You can be offered a job. You take it. Me, when I entered this place, I was offered the job as porter. I saw that as a direct insult to my person as well as to my intelligence. Some of the guys they were requesting that I clean up behind were drunkards or bums of the lowest form. I have not the greatest education in the world, but I'm proud of what little I did acquire while I was acquiring it. So why should I be made because of pigmentation of my skin to go around and clean up when he throw a cigarette butt on the floor?

I felt that the officials after checking my record should make some type of effort to give me something I was closely qualified, if not qualified, for. Give me another job beside cleaning up behind someone. I'll admit I realize you lose your rights as far as rights go when you enter this place, but there's no sense once you enter this place to rub a man's nose in the muck when you have the upper hand.

I don't want to give the impression here now—I'll stop and say this—that this is what drove me into crime. I don't want you to get that impression at all, because it isn't. Greed and the desire of something for nothing, in a manner of speaking, is what started me off on that. I once saw how easy the dollar was and I began to enjoy it.

There's no rationalizing. I can't blame the law if they put me in here, because I got caught. I figure when I go into doing wrong if I haven't got enough brains to survive, well, hell, I'm gonna get caught and end up in here.

In order to survive in the life of crime, it's just like anything else. A bat can't go it.

Bat? You mean a dingbat? [fool, incompetent]

Yeah. I mean you got to try as best as you can to keep up with the times. And psychology is the thing, you know. You get a chance to study things from all angles. You hear some of the stories that the guys look at you and expect you to believe, that when they get busted the Cadillac company have to close their doors. Three-Gs and the others are no longer made 'cause they're not there to buy them. Then you get a look at their packets and they've knocked over a filling station.

Then they get in one of these places and they become con-wise. Everybody's a dingbat, a damn fool with them, including the officials. The officials are squares. Yet the officials go home every night and draw monthly salaries for watching their goofy ass. So you decide: who's the dingbat?

He'll bust his wig over here in this hole for a number of years before it dawns on him, say, "Well, *I'm* the dingbat."

By then he's got a penitentiary record that ain't worth a damn.

I remember the last administration here was locking up guys (in solitary) every day. A guy asked me, "How do you stay out of the hole, man?"

I said, "Well, hell, there isn't anything in here to go to the hole *for*. I don't gamble because there's no money in here. I don't chase punks. I don't have anything against it, but hell, they got barbells over there, I go out and make twenty-five or thirty laps around that field, and boy, what sex energy I have at my age is worn out. So I stay out of trouble."

In here, you just sit down as they come up with a rule and figure a way around it and still do what you want to do. I realize they have to have rules in here or this place would be a madhouse, but some of the rules are so small.

They try to rob you, looks l'ke, of your own ability to think. No man needs to be told when it is cold enough to put on a coat. But you'll see signs hanging around.

"Coats on?"

Yes. It's stupid.

My mind is constantly seeking that thing called *why*. I don't know whether it grew up with me, being the youngest of nine kids.

You know, the only thing that arouses a kid's curiosity around the house is his older brothers and sisters whispering and giggling and seeing them stashing books like *Lady Chatterley's Lover* and all those books they read, *Wuthering Heights*, things like that. I'm not old enough to read them because I don't understand what I'm reading, so that makes me want to read them more than anything. Curiosity.

So I just grew up looking.

When you approach me with something, maybe it's that I'm suspicious-minded, I don't know, but I say, "What is the angle?" Because I actually don't believe that there is something for nothing in *any* walk of life. It may not be a financial motive behind it, but it's *some* motive.

One of the reasons I was reluctant to converse with you is because in conversing you can hold back ever so much, but here and there a true part of a person will slip out. And as an observant person probably you'll take this thing and carry it and read it and listen at it and you can peek here and there. And then a part of me *you* have, 'cause unintentionally or intentionally certain parts have been bared to you. And I don't give a damn who it is, any time they converse there's something that can be used against him in some manner. I don't care who it is.

But I gave my word that I'd talk to you, so I will. You give your word and you're a prick if you don't follow through.

See, I observed you around now for a while and I said, Now what the hell is he up to? And after several of the guys said, He's a guy working his way through college or something, we can give him a little help, you know, I said, You can say so much and no more, you know. But what is there to lose—I'm already in the penitentiary. There ain't too much more you can take, no ways.

Bebop said he was trying to figure out if I was an FBI man investigating the prison or a warden's man investigating the prisoners.

I thought along those lines too. But I stopped and thought, after I'd given my word that I'd make a tape with you, I'd a felt rather small going back on my word. You caught me in a good mood, I said, "Well, yeah, I'll make one." You sneaked it in to me. So after saying yes, well, it was hard as hell to say no afterwards.

I'd like to be able to say I cleverly planned to ask you at the right moment, but I didn't.

Well, I don't know whether it was that, or various feelings against hearing so much crap about dope. My boy Bebop, I like him, I think, as well as any inmate in here. But, man, when I heard him make that statement that our officials should be dope fiends—hell, they're not studying dope and the effects of it. The doctors and things maybe should be more familiar with it than they are. Take several of them and use them as guinea pigs and then put the effects down later on, you know. Just imagine, you got enough screwed-up government officials now—half of them can't do their damn job—so what you gonna make dope fiends out of them for?

You know, I used to be a runner. I got to hob-nob with them. Not because I was a musician—I guess I lugged my horn around for better than two years before I ever realized they published books to show you how to blow the damned thing.

Were you blowing it or just lugging it?

It was a front.

Did you ever blow it at all?

No, that wasn't my way of life. But it was good for getting stopped on the highway at three or four o'clock in the morning. Say I've got to make a delivery to St. Louis. It used to be that all your musicians laid over between Springfield, Illinois, to St. Louis going south. Coming back they'd stop at one of those spots. I've gone clean down to Enola, Mississippi, on a run.

For which you'd get—

Normally, a runner makes $250 and he's on his own.

That means you pick up your package and—

That's it.

They don't know you anymore?

That's right.

See, like I'm running for you. I'm furnishing my own car and everything. If it's a long run, say from here to Memphis, Tennessee, here to Minamola, Tennessee, here to Ramsey, Arkansas, Proctal, any small town, I'll get the $250 and a certain amount for mileage and expenses.

So, in doing so, I hobnob, as you might say. Though I'm not interested in that because a dope fiend I've always considered a weak person. I've seen guys that was real regular. I've had some close friends, and no matter what you say, they're for it. But, boy, you get downtown and they lay the tablet up before 'em, that capsule and that needle, and you put a piece of paper and pencil and he'll sign his own life away. Those in my opinion are dope addicts.

They'll do anything to get that stuff, from peddling their sisters, their old ladies, and, if necessary, they'll find a trick for mother. Yeah.

I don't have anything against dope, but there's a Shakespeare saying, "Methinks the lady protests too much." Whenever you start hollering, "This is the best way," you are as fanatical-minded as a reformer who is out and saying that it ain't no good, that ain't good for you. He don't know a damn thing about it. That's the way I see it.

If a man is going to use dope I look at that like anything else: use it, and use as much discretion as possible. But when you get a pop, don't go to screaming about everybody else is a damn fool or they're square because they're persecuting you for using it. Just say, "I done used it, I got caught, it's against the laws of society and conventional-thinking people, so now I got to serve the consequence," go pay 'em. Don't jump up and convert every damn body else into doing something merely because you wants to do it for your benefit.

To them, I'm a square because I don't use dope. I've handled as much, I guess, as any two or three supposed dope fiends in here. I've been in a room where there's five or six of them and they're popping and they're smoking and I've got me a jug. If I want to drink, I'll drink. If I don't, I'll sit there and look at it. So I can't agree with that thing about, "Oh, if you're in contact with it long enough you gonna use it." That's bull.

Did you ever feel a temptation to try it?

No. I've often wondered what makes people use it.

You go to a place like the Rambogee or De Lisa in Chicago, if you go in there say around eleven thirty, after the first show for the night, and you catch the last of the show. Here's a babe up on the stage, oh, boy, Venus had nothing on her. But let her go downstairs in her dressing room and can't get that stuff in thirty minutes, she look like she was in the Korean conflict. I mean, her nose is running, her eyes are running, her mascara, makeup is dropping. What the hell does anybody want to put themselves through this mill for?

I know guys that say, "Oh, it makes me know my horn, I can get over my horn." Well, hell, if he needed all that uplift to blow his horn, he's not a very good musician, in my opinion. That's like taking a horse, or a fighter, and doping him up and putting him out there to fight. He can't feel the blows. He's not a fighter because normally he couldn't take a punch.

Bebop is thirty-eight and I'm thirty-four. We can converse on different outlooks concerning life because in my walk of life it have taken more brute force and to an extent a certain amount of animal cunning—maybe not altogether brainwork—to survive than in his. And he feels it's taken a certain amount of courage and so forth and all in his walk of life.

Well, I admit, I've observed some musicians step out on the stage and blow some music that it really took nerve to get out there before the public that paid to see 'em and blow. I can accept that.

I likes to always try to the best of my ability to analyze a man's pushing point. How far he can be pushed. And have the edge of knowing him a little better than he knows himself. Few people will look down into themselves and actually try and learn themselves. They look all around and they don't say "The fault is with me." No, "It's with Tom, Dick, or Harry."

And I feel that if I understand him a little better than he understands himself, then I have the advantage over him. And also in understanding him to the best of my ability I dig deeper within myself and that's what I really want most—me.

I hear these rationalizings: "Well, I was brought up in such and such a place and such and such a thing started me to doing such and such a thing." Oh bull. Why hell, you've had bums become presidents, haven't you. Environments don't mean a hell of a lot in that respect.

Do you come from a poor family?

No, I can't say I did. I don't know if any of my family have a record but me. One of my brothers, if you ever get around to it, you can look him up in the library, he writes novels. I'll give you the list—he's got nine of them out. There's some over here in the library he sent to me and I donated them because I don't have any more use for them.

So I can't fall back on that.

What caused me to commit crime is the thing I suppose every person that's truthful about it will admit: thinking the next guy got caught, but I won't. I can see his mistake. He shouldn't have done so and so. So I come along and pull a crime and make another mistake. I think within myself, I made that mistake, but when I pull this next trick I will be straight. So I make another mistake.

Each time you go along telling yourself you can't get caught. What the hell. The next guy didn't know what he was doing.

That's out.

I remember my old man used to make us listen to that *Gang Busters* every Saturday night to show that crime didn't pay.

In some respects I disagree with that about crime don't pay.

I think it depends who you are whether it pays.

That's it. I'll tell you, the lawyer loves crime. It pays, for him it pays a nice dividend.

One of the things I do believe that keeps a man going in the life is one out of two. He either sets a certain amount, a goal, and says, "When I get that I'm gonna get away." And those that do that usually end up pretty nice. But then you have a larger group that will set a certain amount of goal to reach and when they get that amount it comes so easy they say, "I'll stay here and get a few more dollars."

And that is the time they're kicking the law of averages right in the face. So they get a bust. Usually it takes all that they have made, or close to it, to beat this bust.

So they gotta go make some more.

They got to then try to recuperate their losses.

On top of that they're hot now.

That's it. So the odds are much higher against them.

What's the biggest load you ever carried?

I drew down a little better than $18,000, but it was a three-man split. That was with a gun. Now there, it's not a question of making money with a gun, it's a question of how you conduct yourself after you get it. That's where the bust usually comes.

I didn't mean a robbery. I mean, what was the biggest load of narcotics you ever hauled when you were a runner?

To be truthful, I couldn't actually answer that. A lot of times I may have been on dummy runs so far as I know.

You mean they may have been testing you from time to time?

Yes. All I know is one thing: that my fee comes to $250. No questions. The less you know, the less you can tell.

They believe and I also believe that if I'm not involved in something, I don't want to know about it. So I couldn't truthfully answer what is the largest amount I carried or how much money was involved in it. It was just one thing of business with me. I wasn't interested in who was getting hold of it to use it or anything like that. I never thought, "Well, they may be giving this to school kids." Around St. Louis you have a guy that hangs around different schools and they catch the school kids during lunch period for their pickup. Now they may have two or three supposed-to-be hip daddies in school. They keep them supplied so they can peddle to the other kids. I'm aware of those goings-on, but I never question them, because to me, I was just one cog in the wheel, as you might say. I've observed the harmfulness that dope can do and actually I'm more against it than I am for it, I suppose. There's no such thing as an open mind or impartial to anything, because once you thinks about it, you're either for it or against it to some extent.

I'm against it in one respect and if there were some other . . . If I could carry some cattle from here across country and it paid the price I requested that would be just the same to me.

I've learned to harden myself to feelings, to certain things that I knew was wrong, but a man has to live with himself. And I never dug too deep on myself. I didn't try to evade 'em and say, "That's the way life is and this is that." I knew they were wrong, I knew I was breaking the law at times when I broke it. I knew if I get caught, well, there's no grumble about a bum rap, see. So it was just a matter of business with me.

You said you knocked off $18,000?

Yes. I've handled up to that amount with a pipe in a robbery for a three-man split.

That is nice money when you put it to good use. I've heard guys mention this $60,000, $70,000 robbery stuff. I've never been able to touch one of those and probably doubt if I ever will, because the way I feel now, my wife and I are getting along pretty nice, she's been pretty regular about these busts of mine. I have a daughter now. I don't have any record in my home state. I'm willing to go out there now and set back. Not, as you might say, off the fat of the land, because I couldn't sit it out if I tried. That's one of the reasons I work so hard now with my horn is to relax with it as well as with the other stuff I do, literature and so forth. If I wish to sit in with some little group playing in some little place, well and good, but if I don't, I don't have to depend on it for a livelihood.

You have enough put away to survive a while?

I believe I do.

I noticed one thing: a lot of guys go out of here with no family and nothing put away. Everything they had before is shot on lawyers. They get what is it, five bucks or ten bucks?

Fifteen.

Fifteen. Then it seems to me that if they don't have something pretty good set up, then they might decide they have to knock off a gas station or something.

To that I can mostly in my opinion say it's the fellow's fault.

I worked with guys that were real regular. I mean as far as making some money, keeping their mouths shut, and not being flashy. They may be living with their mother and father and maybe have two or three younger sisters. And then they make $3,000 or $4,000, or $7,000 or $8,000, and they go every place but home. Scotch is the cheapest liquor they gonna drink. The minute they blow the money on this babe or that one, they go back home, lay up two or three weeks, eating up everything that won't bite them first until someone approaches them with the idea to go out and make some more money. They go out and make that. They stay away from home again until they spend that up. Then, I hear guys bitch in here about me getting mail. If they didn't think enough of their people when they were out there and could help themselves and their people with the life they was living, I don't think they should feel their people owe them anything now, that they should write and send them $25 or $30 every time they write for it. It seems so ass-backwards. No one likes constantly to be kicked, not even mother, and she's capable of going further with you than anyone.

Whenever I made money, wherever I was I always made a point to make a trip to three or four post offices—never all the same spot—and I'd send $700 or $800 here, send $700 or $800 there, send $500 or $600 there.

Say I made some at night. I used to try burglary quite frequently with a few fellows up around Indianapolis there and I've made a couple of thousand dollars in one night. Maybe we finish up and divide at three o'clock that morning. If you met me at noon that day, you'd be lucky to find $200 on me. You could shake my house down. Why I want the money on me? I don't believe too much in parties, I don't drink a hell of a lot, and it seems stupid for me to go out and take a chance on life and limb kicking a safe open—which is harder than construction work, believe me, you try beating on a metal safe and then you liable to open it and there is nothing in there—so I'm going to make me a couple thousand and then I'm going to your crap table? Like hell. That's your hustle, mind you, and me try to beat you at it? I can't think of anything, nothing that I could think of would cost me $200 moving around town. So why do I want it on me? I'm not a good-time Charlie. So what the hell. If I see you, I like you, you buy a drink, I buy a drink, that's the end of it. You ain't my running buddy.

Jerry was telling me about when he and some friends knocked off that criminals' resort in Illinois, and they got $31,000, and—
How many man split was there, did he tell you?
There were two of them and then the owner of the joint found out about it, so then there was a three-man split. But the point is, the money was gone in a week or two.
That's better than $10,000 apiece, mind you.
Yeah.
So what was it for? Aw, he threw parties. Yeah.

I remember a group here, one of the fellows was real outward, real friendly, he had a nice personality. They got lucky on a deal like that here in Naptown [Indianapolis]. I think it was about three or four of them, they knocked off thirty some thousand. And this guy had changed suits once a week, normally on the weekend like any working Joe, had a car leaning sideways, you know. But then he started walking into the crap tables throwing out $500, hollering, "Let 'em roll." He'd throw craps and say, "Hell, there's plenty more where that come from." Changing suits two and three times a day, throwing parties, drinking champagne out of women's slippers and then he'd buy them another pair, you know. So the minute the pop comes, one of the guys that was out in front during all this, he was offered a ten-flat [ten-year sentence], I think it was for $2,000 or $3,000. This guy couldn't afford it. His buddies were able to hand the detectives a few dollars and let them water it down a little bit and they come up with ten-flat. He had nerve to say, "Some dirty rotten sonofabitch must a ratted us out."

I said, "Boy, you are sick."

Now he got a ten-to-twenty-five. His buddies got a ten-flat apiece because they had a little money to pay off.

He never stopped to realize he drawed heat on himself. They didn't even connect colored with the job. They figured it's some white guys out of Chicago or something. But then he screams, "Impartial justice! That's what it is!" How the hell can you expect anything but impartial justice [he means the opposite] when the whole American system is based on the American dollar?

In here it's a noted fact that I don't play the dozens [playfully exchange insults], stuff like that. So if a guy slips every now and then and I've said, "Good morning" two or three times or "Hi," I'll say, "Come here." I won't scream out a bunch of "I don't play that, you do it again and I'm gonna do this and that!" I call him to himself, I'll say, "Now there's no offense meant, but we can get along without that. Perhaps you weren't aware that I don't play the dozens. But I don't. Now there's no hard feelings and we can continue as we were, see."

I'm not going to tell him "I'm gonna do this and I'm gonna do that," because if I do that, he'll know I'm gonna do that whiles I'm doing it.

I always give a guy a break. That's the way I always look at that. That's one of the reasons I'm against capital punishment; I suppose, because some guy makes one mistake and then they end up getting the death penalty. And then eventually it may catch me if I continue, so I'm doubly against it.

But, as I was saying, I don't scream at him amongst a group or try to belittle him and embarrass him where he'll have to come back up to pop. But then after I have told him and he does it again, you have this old statement, "You don't cook but you eat." If he says that, I category him right there. Somebody like me, wishing to avoid conflict in any amount, maybe he'll slip again later on, so I'll say, "Now let's straighten up, you can do without that. Let's break off the association." But if he comes back with, "You don't cook but you eat," I say to myself he's a bulldozer.

A bulldozer. He wants to throw his weight around. So next time he slips I look at him and look for something heavy to drop on him.

I don't go tell him, "Well, I told you." He's aware that I told him before. So when he do it again, well, hell, that's it. You don't have to contend with that anymore. In a place like this you find what is supposed to be the largest and baddest fellow in there and you get things straight with him. Then things are fine.

I've hit towns where they've had kangaroo courts in jail and you get one big brawny buck in there and, boy, he's talking loud and he's ruling the joint. So the first thing you look for is the heaviest loose object that you can use for a weapon. And what he say may not really make you angry—'cause you never fight in anger, which I never have. After the first blow, if I *was* angry, I'm just as collected as if I hadn't been. But the least little thing he push on you—you're not angry over what he says—same as name calling, but you retaliate in that manner with brute force because that is what he expects, see. He means it as an insult, but you're not insulted. But you nevertheless go right into the act of cracking his head. You get along with the hundred people in there—you done killed the big dragon. He may walk around, mumbling around you, but as long as he don't bother you no more you don't care.

In here you have some who play the male in the light and they're actually the girls in the dark. And they would treat their kid as they call it, their better half, or their rib, as they would a woman. I've read several reports including Kinsey's where it's no disgrace to go down on your wife. So they go down on a kid, and in my way of thinking you don't have the kid, the kid have you. And then you start pulling on the rope [masturbating him] or try to throw the bald-headed champ [perform fellatio], boy, you have reached rock bottom in my opinion.

I don't see anything wrong with a man who wishes to give his outside helpmate the satisfaction and experience, and they both enjoy it, of him going down on her. I can't see any act that would be considered unnatural between a man and a woman. But I can sure in hell consider it unnatural when they make those moves with another man.

You take a guy into this place and he have a desire to live high off the hog. He wants his clothes pressed all the time. He wants the best the commissary has to offer and things like that, and he knows there's one way of getting them in here: submit to someone else's acts. You very seldom catch an outside fag enter here. Most of what you have in here are known as candy-bar punks. Every now and then there is one that those guys take advantage of, rape him, but usually he seeks revenge.

He has a lot of ways of getting his revenge without going to the officials. You have gasoline at your disposal twenty-four hours a day. There's acid can be got to in here and there's croton oil. There's various ways you would get revenge without going to the officials.

What do you do with croton oil?

You sit next to him and as you attract his attention by having someone call him and you dump a small bit in his tea or coffee or whatever and let him, as we say, shit hisself to death. Most of his food in here consists of starch without grease, so think what a heavy dose of that croton oil will do. It would tear him up inside.

I don't know why that comes about or how, but you will seldom see a colored guy with a colored kid. You will seldom see, unless he's awful young and you don't have too many young ones up here, an elder white guy with a white kid. There's always a colored guy with his kid which is white, a white guy with his kid which is colored. I don't think it's so much a question of racial thinking there involved. It's hard to say exactly what it is.

So by them putting a clamp on it, as they do, it don't serve any purpose because it's just like a woman in the streets. You can watch all you want to. If she wanna do something, she gonna do it anyway. She'll find the time and the way. In here, it's the same thing. At the same time, I can respect and realize their reasons for having such a heavy rule on it.

So any way you look at it, you can't definitely say—I can't, maybe someone else can—what makes a person in one of these places turn punks. One is through fear. Another one is through a desire of something for nothing. There are others that accept what is being done to them and I suppose that anything that you do after a length of time you begin to get some type of enjoyment out of it. They're not punks, they have no desire maybe to be them, but after enough guys roughshoot 'em, bulldoze 'em, and they submit—well, that's that.

You come in here and every guy will paint you a pretty picture of the thousands to be made in crime, the women that fall at your feet, the beer and whiskey parties. A young guy will go out and, in my opinion, if not a better criminal then one with a broader scope to participate in crime than when he entered.

You don't have impartial justice in this state. If a man with funds commits a murder he'll hire his lawyer with two or three high-priced psychiatrists and they claim temporary insanity and you stay out of circulation for six months or a year and he's back on the bricks [out in the free world]. If a man without funds commits the same act and have an awful good reason for doing so, even in self-defense, he's not nuts, he's just a low-grade person and deserves the worst.

There were several cases during Craig's administration—if I'm not mistaken every one of his administration but four or five, and that's a lot of people, has been indicted for some type of crime against society. Such as one guy padding the books, hiring his buddy to do work he never done. Property that is confiscated and never sold to the people. But do you think that the large men ever get anything out of it? Oh, you had a few come up here to make a showing, then you look up again and they have been secretly paroled.

I knew two cases special: one guy I worked with for a while here and after he come up with a two-to-fourteen or a one-to-ten, he served a month inside, then they put him in an honor camp. He could have his wife down there when he got ready. He could have his family down and live off the state property. So you look up and he's doing a two-to-fourteen and he's made it out in a year. He's not eligible even to go to the board until he's in two years, but he's out.

They had a scandal when this administration took over—the dealings the officials were doing and so forth. They never told of the brute force that was used against the convict. Not one was mentioned. They took some of the convicts that started the ball rolling and they issued them a parole. Most of them are back by now, by the way.

Anyway, they're the boys with the brains, they saw an out and they took it, to their way of thinking. The very ones that done the screaming were the very ones that were walking around with the last administration selling this and that, and splitting the money with them, the officials.

This is one form of human being that I consider his life worth the price of a bullet. If you do something with me, don't turn around afterwards and blow the breeze. If you're strong enough to indulge in it, whatever it is, or commit it, take the consequences.

They won't let them out in the population. They give them a job over here in the A and O or someplace. Next thing you know they get a parole again.

One thing I could never see is catching somebody like you out there. A guy trying to run around trying to make a buck on an honest job, and robbing or using you. You don't have anything. If anything, if I know you, and I'm snatching good, I say, "Well, hell, Bruce, how's the family coming along? How's the bills?" I throw you a few dollars, but I never use you for a running buddy.

I've had times I've had a wanted sticker on me in this state and I knew that they were aware of all my associates in one respect or another. So the only people I could turn to was working Joes, people that's connected with no kind of crime, some of them don't have any records at all. I laid up off of two of them for better than a month and a half. Didn't go out. I never saw outside at that time. Everything I wanted was there. I mean, I lived like a king. Even my family didn't know where I was, they only knew I was on the run.

So I figure that it is cheaper to have you as a passive associate than an active enemy. If I could do you a small favor which cost me nothing, well and good. There's no telling when I may have to call on you for the same return.

I see no sense in walking around with my collar turned up and talking out of the side of my mouth, you know. Yeah, that's backwards. I wants to look like anything but what I actually have lived the life of being: a thug, a bum, a damn fool, or whatever you want to call it, because when you boil it all down, I think that every man that actually after the first bust commits a crime again, he is some way in his mind messed up. As I said, that greed and so forth, it's all involved in it. The days of the broad shoulders and you jump in your car and you roll away with the gat, with pistols popping, that went out with the twenties. That was well and good then. They didn't have two-way radios, roadblocks set up like they got now.

The two-way radios really hurt, don't they?

Yeah, and them walkie-talkies.

You know I once introduced some guys—they was good fellows in my way of thinking, as far as burglary went—to walkie-talkies. I first began to observe it over in Italy. I used to do quite a bit of scout patrolling in my outfit, and after I left the trucking division I went to the communications center as a lineman. And I introduced some fellows in the U.S. to the walkie-talkie system for burglarizing. I said, "You take one man and put him on top of the building. You know the system that the police cruise with their lights on or off after certain time of night. I said one man up there on the tallest building around can wire the others about what's going on. He can talk to the man behind the man working on the safe."

It worked for a while. Then you got a bunch of hip daddies, a few of them with their "Pick up, baby, the stars is *so* bright. Yuk yuk a duck a duck."

So the police tuned in on it. Yeah. They pick up the walkie-talkies and followed that. They bust the walkie-talkie, so that killed that system. Before that, you could walk in any army surplus store in town and get you a walkie-talkie and no questions about it. Then too many asked. Then when they begin to observe burglary men with walkie-talkies they'd lock them up on suspicion.

But I'll tell you. Each thing you come up with to beat the system there are fifty high-paid people figuring to overlap your beating it. So it's just constantly a rat race, you know.

And it usually ends in one of these spots because you're kicking the odds.

In my walk of life, you got to use a certain amount of cold calculation, at times animal cunning and brute force, to survive. And in doing so, you leave a certain amount of your feelings buried deep. You try to keep them that way. It's not like a person doing wrong and don't know they're doing wrong. Or know they're doing wrong and try to laugh it over with someone, someone else.

In my way I can tell when I'm wrong. If I collar a guy in here and knee him in the groin, smack him across his windpipe, take the flat of my hand and smack him between the eyes, I know I'm wrong. I don't need anyone to tell me.

And I can walk by and say, "Good morning" every morning and smile to the guy. I'm good-natured by practice and habit.

I'm not interested in being tough. Every act I have committed to an extent has been on the basis of the buck. 'Cause I've learned— maybe from reading a lot and observation—that the buck is what makes you an American citizen as well as a person to be respected. A broke man is like a dead man. No one wants to hear what he's got to say, 'cause, what the hell, he must not be of any value if he's not using it for his own benefit.

Richie: "You should use some finesse . . ."

I've been a pimp, drug addict, dope peddler, professional crap hustler. I turned out as a crap hustler, card hustler, drag games or bunko games as they are commonly known. I served my apprenticeship as a card mechanic; I was in the Federal penitentiary and practiced diligently for ten or twelve hours a day for about two years. I'm not as much a perfectionist with cards as I am with craps.

I specialize in manipulating legitimate craps, legitimate dice.

I do—and this is a divergence with what I just said—work with what they call a "bust-out" mob. Craps in conventions, picnics, things like that. There you work eight- or ten-handed. Oftentimes you have eight or ten men and they're within the group and all are capable of shifting. And in situations like that, you're working with tops or bust-out craps.

Those are spotted, ace, trey, five, for example. A crap has ace, deuce, trey, four, five, and six on each crap. But on bust-out, there's no possible way to get a seven, so you just pass. You *can* crap, but you can pass anyway. You just keep on passing.

Don't people notice this?

That's where the professionalism comes in. When you switch the dice, there are about five basic moves, and in the event they should spill or there is any kind of mistake on your part the rest of the mob is there to cover up for you and not let the suckers get to you.

In terms of working with legitimate craps, that's where I depend on my skill against other gamblers. My skills to manipulate the craps. The other hustler knows that you may be in that situation, it's an understood thing, and it's a question there of who is the best, who had the most skill.

I should add that the fact that I turned out at a very young age was a great advantage. No one ever suspected I knew as much as I knew. I used to shortchange a lot. That was kind of a daily must because I could go out and make—without too much effort—$40 or $50 a day. There's a minimum of risk and it's a misdemeanor in the states I worked anyway, so there was really no risk at all. I usually did that during the day and gambled at night.

You have to have a place where they have a cashier. There are two systems, one is called "working forwards," and the other "working backwards." Probably what is most common is working with a $1 bill and a $20 bill.

A man will come in and pay with a $20 bill and when he receives his change he'll go to put it back in his pocket and he finds that he has a one and he say, "Gee, you know I had a one all the time. I didn't mean to cash the twenty. Can you use some of this change?" And so he plops out the ten. "Can you give me a $10 bill for this change?" he says.

So they give him a $10 bill. He puts it in with the other money and counts down $9 and hands it to the cashier. Naturally the cashier will recount it before he puts it in the till and he looks at you and says, "You only have $9 here."

You say, "I'm sorry. Let's see: you have got nine and one more is $10. Here, take the $11 and give me my $20 back."

You've got their ten in your pocket, right?

That may be a little crude. There are variations that depend on the individual, how he works.

Sometimes I've worked with other guys. Some of them use no finesse at all. I think, doing that sort of thing, you should use some finesse.

I had my first prostitute at sixteen. At that age, she had me.

That in itself is a profession and when you're young like that, you make all the mistakes. You have to make all the mistakes even though you're advised how to avoid them.

There's a very definite line there. Because a woman gives a man money, that doesn't make him a pimp in the professional sense. If he compels her through a physical threat, a threat of violence, that's not accepted either. I'm talking about the people who are more or less successful at it.

It's a mental thing. A woman usually turns to prostitution because of some inadequacy, some inability to adjust or cope with society. As a result, prostitutes are always strange. Just one step away from a mental institution. A lot of them probably should be in a mental institution. Some of them I had should have been. Naturally I had no qualms about taking money. They want to give it to you.

It's another world. I've read a number of books by people who aren't in prostitution or even in drugs and I know that they're not right. It's not for real in those books, but the average reader doesn't know that. He has to accept it as being valid where it isn't. With all those little discrepancies. I don't know if I can bring the whole philosophy down. Let's see. A prostitute needs a man. Some are termed mustangs, those are the ones that don't need a man. There's a big difference between colored and white prostitutes. The colored prostitutes, honestly, it's almost like they accept their fate, you know. And there's a great deal of homosexuality that exists among prostitutes of both colors.

You ever hear of what they call a "jasper broad"? That is one who is bisexual, she likes both men and women. And since she's a prostitute she can entice other prostitutes to work for you or even turn them out and make them prostitutes for you. If she's your woman you're all set. She can get you a stable and maintain the stable and keep it under control. There is little or no responsibility for you, all you have to do is get the money.

You don't have to worry about putting them to work or when they get sick. All these problems she takes care of. That's the ideal situation. They accept this stable type proposition easier among the Negro than the white prostitutes. White prostitutes have a tendency to be more possessive. They don't like the idea of having to compete with other women.

But you *have* to set up some kind of competitive system. To the average person it must seem incredible that a woman should think that way or be induced to think that way, but she can.

And you have to be supportive. I once thought you have to prove yourself to be real capable sexually, but sex is no problem because a prostitute who's been out working all night is not interested in sex when she comes in. There are those tricks she's had and they've done things you never thought of doing. So it's not a question of that. It's that she needs a support, she needs someone to handle her. She's like a robot and she has to be guided. She has to have support all the time. I think everybody makes that mistake in the beginning. They think that if they lay on her all the time, it's taking care of the business. But if you make yourself too common with one and she's been out there quite a while, she will lose respect for you and eventually you will find somebody is shortsocking some of that money you're supposed to be getting. I tried to tell some of these guys and it was hard for them to understand what I mean.

I had one girl. She was about your shade. She was colored and Mexican, a very exotic-looking girl. She was a jasper and very intellectual, very smart, a chic person. She was fabulous in bed, but rather than lose respect and lose the discipline and control of the situation, I avoided her. I wanted her and I would a lot of times be aroused and I'd get up out of bed and leave rather than touch her because I knew that as soon as she became conscious of the fact that I had weakened in that respect, as soon as I had what they call "got my dick tender"—that means you've got to be with a woman all the time—they figure they're out working and you're out chipping someplace. So what good are you? If that's the kind of person you are, they don't need you. You know what I mean. Consequently the respect is not there.

I've had a beaucoup of them, some for just a short time, and I've taken money off some I didn't know if it was a man or a woman because I was never in bed with them. That sounds strange, but it's true.

Now a prostitute takes pride in a man she wants. You'll find in the world of pimps and prostitutes that certain pimps gain a certain amount of prestige. A prostitute will be going to him just because she can say later that she had him. She'll stay with him a while and give him her money and then she'll say, "Well, I had him."

So it's an important thing how a man carries himself in this element, in this environment. His conduct, the way he dresses, the way he carries himself, the way he conducts himself around people, around his own people. It's an important thing. He gains a certain amount of prestige. His woman wants to see him in a nice automobile, she wants to see him dressed nice. She wants to see him go into a place and pull out a roll of money and look good, because that makes *her* look good. It's her man, she represents him, that's *her*.

Before I got into this metaphysics thing I didn't understand a lot of things, but now I do. Now I hear a religious sect and I hear their creed and I can respect them all, where before I didn't because I didn't understand. I now think that things must make sense, since we are living in an orderly universe. Things *must* be purposeful, otherwise they wouldn't exist. Even the experiences I had in war must be purposeful, otherwise they wouldn't exist. Even the experiences I had in war must be the effect of cause-and-effect situations; it's just that I don't know what they are yet.

Some things are tangible situations, situations and things we can equate with ourselves in a finite sense. And there are other things, other laws and things of that infinite nature that the mind cannot perceive. I don't worry about the future anymore because I know that concept isn't real.

I used to. I never was confident before.

I would fool with stuff a little bit and I'd see a Chinaman coming

—that is, I'd see a habit coming on—and I would back away and smoke reefers for a while, then I'd juice a while. I drink, you know, and then I'd smoke reefer, then I'd drink, then I'd use a little stuff. I never got the habit.

But the principle was the same: I always needed something. I don't need anything now.

The last time I went to prison, it was drugs, and I did a thing I don't usually do, something that wasn't *me*. I held up a finance company. Drugs will do that to you, they will make you lose sight of certain things. When you're using drugs there is a certain complacency and you do things and take risks that on the natural you wouldn't do. You put yourself into situations and the situation compels you to do certain things that normally you wouldn't do.

When I robbed that finance company, I didn't even need the money. I had been to Chicago where I bought some stuff. When I came back to Indianapolis, a friend, a very good friend of mine, had a habit and his wife was sick and he had some stuff and I stayed there with them. Next thing you know—it's difficult to be around somebody when they're using stuff every day without you using it—he started and I started and he suggested the robbery thing and I told him, "No, that's not me." Eventually, though, I consented, and we robbed a few finance companies around Indianapolis.

I don't want you to take what I say as fatalistic, but I believe it was meant that I should go to the penitentiary. I needed it then. It had to happen. I had two books in prison about Zen and thought for a while I should go to a Buddhist monastery when I got out. One book was a compendium of Oriental philosophy, it had parables and things of Buddha. The other was a group of sutras.

Wilbur: "Pay, fuck, or just get out . . ."

You were pimping at sixteen?

I had my own house. Yes. I had my own women. They busted me in a house of prostitution but they couldn't prove that it was my house, but I went to the reformatory on a lesser charge. That was in

Galveston and that's when it was really going wild there. At one time you could get anything on the streets that you wanted—dope, have somebody killed, women, anything.

Run down the economics for me.

All right. You had to have a permit, you had to get that from the police officers on the beat. It wasn't legal to run the house, of course, but as long as you gave them their cut—which was 25 percent—plus they get all the free pussy they want plus they can drink there also, they don't ever bother you. That would go to the detectives on the beat, two on the daytime shift and two on the nighttime. The 25 percent protected you from them. We didn't have to worry about the foot patrolmen because they were nothing. They were there. If somebody got drunk and we kicked them out, they made their money off those guys to keep them from going to jail. And we got a cut of that.

Now when you buy your permit—that's what it's called, buying a permit—it's just partial protection. When the Rangers are coming and the local cops know about it, they give you a phone call beforehand. When the Texas Rangers come in, then you're on your own.

What you make depends on the girls and the operation. There are two kinds of girls in a house, "dirty legs" and "racehorses." A dirty leg is the $5 or $10 trick. The racehorse is strictly for $40, $75, and $100.

Why does the racehorse get so much money?

Because the racehorse is something that's kind of hard to find just walking on the street. A racehorse goes four ways. She gets tricked two ways. She eats the person up and also—actually, she does anything a man wants, that's what she does, she's all the way around. The racehorse is a champ. And a racehorse is better looking than the dirty legs, your racehorse is just a little bit more smart than your dirty legs, and your racehorses have more class and better vocabularies than your dirty legs.

A dirty leg is just for a guy that comes in, a drunk maybe, and wants a $5 or $10 piece of ass, well, you just turn him over to one of them dirty legs. But you can't make it unless you've got them all: dirty legs and racehorses. If I had my choice I'd just take plain dirty legs 'cause I know when a man gets a racehorse he may not get a big trick all the time, but with the dirty legs you always got those $5 and $10 tricks coming in.

At the time I was busted I had ten girls working in the place and four of them were racehorses, what I'd call racehorses. During splash days in the summers, when kids would come in from out of town, you could make anywhere from $1,500 to $2,500 a night. That's just on the women. That's not counting the liquor, beer, and jukebox. I had my own jukebox; my mother had several joints, and I got the jukebox from her.

Now the girls that didn't turn any tricks didn't make any money. The ones who turned the most tricks in the part of town I was in was the two colored girls. They turned the most tricks because it was in the colored district of town. They would get 25 percent and I would get 75 percent of what they made. That's because if they go to jail you're there to get them out. And if there's a lot of heat comes down you're the one that has to ride that heat, things like that.

Actually they think you're doing all this, but actually you're doing nothing. You're doing nothing at all. You're just there. You're in the clear. Like the girl that was with me the night I got busted in the house. They pinned the house on her and convicted her for running a house of prostitution and she got two years in jail. I done ten months in the reformatory.

The police officers come every Friday and Sunday. That's to pick up their money. They come those nights so they can tell what's happened, judge how much money you've got. And you just tell them, "I made $1,500." I got to pay the girls off and pay for my beer and booze, and so you give the cops $100. That's for those two at night, they split that; then you've got to have another $100 to give the two that come by in the morning. You've got to have that—if you don't, they'll close you up.

I didn't have to pay for beer. That was because I had a bunch of kids breaking into trucks, mostly kids who would do that, and you'd give them $5 and a free piece of ass and you get fifteen or twenty cases of beer for that. That was mighty cheap.

And wine cost me fifty cents a fifth and I'd sell it for $1.50. Whiskey, I got whiskey wholesale. I'd go down to a Thrifty store and get it. After 10 P.M. in my place a little half-pint costs you $5, a pint costs you $10, and a fifth costs you $15.

Why after ten o'clock?

All the liquor stores close at ten, so if they want it they have to buy it at your price.

There's one other deduction, in addition to the operating costs of the place like the towels and rent and things, and that's for cabdrivers. A taxicab driver, you have a lot of them pimping for your house, and you give them 25 percent of the dollar-take for what they send in, but that's worth it.

How do you decide how much a trick is going to be worth?

When he comes in, he sits at the bar and your girls would walk up to him and ask him, "Do you want a date?" Whatever he says, they'll say, "How about buying me a drink?"

The guy pays $1 for a glass of champagne, and that's not champagne. All it is Seven-Up and grapefruit juice. You know. Welch's grapefruit juice, and that's $1; it don't cost much to make it. The girls get fifty cents off this. Now she asks him, "What kind of a date do you want?"

"Well, I don't have too much money . . ." Blah, blah, blah.

"Well, you don't want to talk to me."

She done made a few dollars off the drinks and so goes off and then another girl goes up there. She talks to him too. If he's one of them guys that says, "Well, I already spent my money on drinks" or something like that, that's where I come in.

I walks up to him and says, "Look, mister, we don't want no trouble and we ain't gonna have no trouble. Either you want pussy or you don't want pussy. There's the front door. One of two things. Pay, fuck, or just get out."

And if he gives me any hard static he's looking down the barrel of a .32 or .45, and he's gonna leave.

Of course if he comes up that he's a $5 trick, then he and one of the girls go upstairs. A $5 trick lasts about that long—snap, snap, snap. And I go knock on the door and she's got to come out.

You knock on the door?

That's right. She's gonna come out or either I'm gonna come in. One of them.

How long is a $10 trick?

That varies. See, a gal knows just about how much money a man's holding. If she goes into a room when he's paid for a $10 trick, she maybe tricks him for five minutes or so, and if he hasn't had his climax by that time she tells him, "Now wait a minute, buddy. Your time's up." While he's getting out his $10 and giving it to her some time passes, and then it's going to take him just a little bit longer to stop and go through that, and I've seen it run up to $100 or $150 on what was supposed to have been a $10 trick.

And for a blowjob?

We call that French, a French trick. That's both ways. It's up to your girl. The girl that's making the living. You're just sitting back and taking in the money. The girl can go for what she wants to go for. If the man tells her, "I'll give you $25 for a French," and she wants to go for it, that's good 'cause she's getting paid for the tricks she's turning and that's the only thing she's getting paid for. Other than that she don't get paid. If she don't make much she don't get much and she's going to make what she can.

Are many of the girls in a place like that dykes?

I can't answer that because I really wouldn't know. I've wondered, but there's no way to really know. I had a girlfriend once that was a dyke.

You mean she went both ways or she was a dyke?

She was a dyke. I made love to her twice in the six months that I went with her, and she'd shake me off for a girl in a minute.

Making love to them—that didn't matter anyway. If you've got one whore, she's got to be hung on you, but if you've got two or three hung up on you or more, then you can't make love to one of them because this other one over here is jealous and she's going to do something to you and that other one is going to do the same. First thing you know is you're gonna get something done to you all the way around.

So you don't make love to any of them?

That's right. You don't make love to any of them. It has to be that way, it has to be. You just tell them, "I don't feel like it right now." Something like that.

That's a weird world. I tell you, I met one of the finest girls in my life that I would have liked to have had and she was a prostitute and she gave me these words: "Why should I have you? And support you and take care of you when I can get out and hustle myself for the money I make myself." *That's* what you call a prostitute. That's what you call a woman who knows what she's doing. That is what you call strictly hustling.

That's the kind that's the best to make love to. That won't have nobody else, a pimp or anything. Like she said, "What do I need you for when I can find my own tricks? I can do better than you can. All I've got to do is just shake it." Which is true. So when she goes for a guy—well!

Jack: "I am a nickel-and-dime pimp . . ."

I've never had a joint. I am a nickel-and-dime pimp who has been built up in the papers to be more than what I was. The only thing I've ever had was an apartment where I had three girls at one time. And that was a very short time. I mostly had one girl and that's it and I became strictly a pimp. I didn't write checks, I didn't rob. A lot of pimps are like burglars and they'll have an old lady, they'll send her to work only when they need bond money in the event they get busted trying to make a joint.

I've been called the vice lord of Harris County, I've been called the Lucky Luciano of South-Central Texas, and I've *never* had over three girls in my life. That really annoys me.

The only time I made good money is when a perfect square turned out and while I was with her she would make anywhere from $500 to $1,500 a week. We were only together for about a month because I was doing a jail sentence in Houston there for a while. I have had some girls who could make close to that for short periods, but most of them, it was between $300 and $450 a week, that's all.

Everybody thinks being a pimp is easy; it's not easy.

There is more headache in pimping and prostitution than you'd have if you were working on a space problem over at NASA. Probably you'd have less headaches at NASA because with the whores you've got their emotions to contend with.

And I've never had a dope fiend whore and never will, this is just regular whores I'm talking about. (Though they all eventually get on pills, on Nembutal or barbiturates of some kind, most of them that I've seen.)

I've had call girls and this is the best area. And I've had what I call "joint girls," and I'm one of the kind of pimps that over the years I've felt if a girl will be a good whore she will work in a joint. It's a test for me. If she's there working in one of those places when I come by, fine, and if she's not, fine. But I would, when I could, put a girl in a joint first. If I got a girl to start with, when I first got with her, that's my test.

In a joint you meet every kind of situation, perversion, and what-have-you, and if a girl's going to be a good whore, then before I put her on a phone or a trick book this is what I do. I don't know what others do.

I think a lot of people think that a pimp goes out and says, "Mister, would you like to screw this good-looking cunt?" They don't do that, not in Texas. Now I don't know how they do it in New York or Michigan, I'm talking about Texas, the things that I observed.

So what does a pimp like you do?

He really takes care of the girl. He takes care of her sexually [most pimps disagree with this], and in this area allegedly they're both in love and she wouldn't be working if it wasn't her love for him. In turning out a girl the same thing occurs as when you get involved with a girl.

A pimp in Texas, in my school of discipline, if you want to call it that, doesn't do *anything*. He just takes care of her in the sense of maintaining whatever needs to be maintained in the apartment, he makes sure that they have that. If you're working on the phone he makes all the necessary business arrangements. He does make contacts, say, if you're on the phone, to different porters, hotel porters, key people that generally have use for that business.

When you got into it, was it easy for you to connect with porters in the big hotels? Was that ever a problem?

Never, never. Even after I'd been in some trouble and had become a little notorious, it was no trouble at all.

My trouble, trouble in Houston, was staying out of the police station. Especially after I got so much publicity.

See, there's one of those things that I am hostile about, that when I first began—this sounds like self-pity and maybe it is—but when I first began I used to go to jail for nothing. And in order to pay $25 bail bond, the lawyer would handle it for $10, but I had to have the $25 cash and I'd always get the $15 back, but it would still cost me $10 on the bond no matter. It cost me for him to make a $25 bail bond every time. I never got convicted.

The reason was that at this one time I was with a girl and she was a whore and I was not her pimp, but we were out and the police officers who arrested me knew me and I told them a lie. He says, "Is that a whore?" And I says, "Oh, no, sir. Square, she doesn't even really know me." Which was true, the girl didn't really know me, but I knew that she was a whore and I told him no. So he says, "Well, you lying sonofabitch, I'm gonna see to it that you go to jail from now on, every time I see you." And I went one time three times in one day.

This $25 bail bond business got expensive. I was working then, I was not pimping, and over a period of six weeks I went to jail something like eighteen or twenty times. I went one time three times in one full twenty-four-hour period. So I said, "Fuck it, I can't afford it."

Maybe that's my excuse, because I did enjoy the role, the life. I can't say that I didn't. I did.

You said a few minutes ago that part of the pimp's job was to keep the girl sexually satisfied. What happens if a guy is running three or four girls? Doesn't that kind of exhaust him?

Very. Actually, if you have over three whores you'd better have a job—it's that much trouble. I never had more than three at any one time, and I only had the three approximately four weeks, and I may even be stretching that. I don't know. Two whores is about all I can handle, and it's best to keep them separated.

I'll give you an instance.

The girl that I was married to worked eleven years before I ever married her, worked for me for two years and I pulled her up for two. (Presently, I understand, I was just told by a guy that knew her and knew me, that she's pulled up and is now married to a farmer. I don't know.) But anyway, she was sick, she had had a miscarriage and was in very bad physical condition at the time. So she was laying up in the roost in a motel at that time. She was laying up in bed, so I'd been out and I scored for this other little girl, about eighteen or nineteen, maybe twenty years old. And I brought her home, brought her to where we were staying. And she was a swinger.

See, ordinarily I don't mess with dirty legs, or scaly legs, or whatever you want to call them. Tramps. There is this type of thing even in the rackets. So I brought her home and I remember it vividly: my old lady was laying in bed—and this had never occurred to me before, never; it may have been in my mind, but it never entered—she's laying in bed and she says, "You're gonna kill me if I ask you something."

I says, "What do you mean?"

She says, "No."

And it pissed me off. I said, "What, goddamnit? Don't bring it up if you're not going to finish and tell me."

She wanted to make it with this gal.

It didn't make me mad, but it kinda stunned me. Actually, Terry probably saw in me what was in me that I didn't see, but I dig that, you know.

What, watching?

No, no. Participating. So there's three, you see: two gals and myself. And from that point on, like I say, it's no problem. It's no problem if you have the right kind of old lady.

Now the young girl in this case would be what we term a sister-in-law. And that's it, that's all you do.

Point: when Terry got well, she and Debbie went to work at Dot's in Beaumont. That's an old, old-time whorehouse. Been there for years. On Crockett. I understand it isn't there now, but it's been there for thirty years that I know of. Very plush, posh place. Various rumors always has been that the ex-governor used to do a little partying down there. He's from nearby.

Nevertheless, they went down there and I collected about $1,200. Then I had a rumble—I think it was in Galveston—and they'd been there maybe ten days, and they got me that $1,200. Which is not bad during this time. So I go on up to Oklahoma City. I think the girl stayed with us maybe two months, possibly three. Well, she left and that's it.

What I'm driving at is, I personally have never had a stable of four, five, or six, I wouldn't know what in the hell to do. I'm just going to tell you like this: I wouldn't have the slightest idea and don't know how a guy—and I know a lot of pimps—keeps that many. I've never known anybody's had that large a string of girls.

Did you ever turn out any square girls?

No, and this is one of my pet peeves. I've been accused of that. Every girl I've ever been with was a hustler, and that includes this most recent beef. I didn't know that at first, I thought she'd never been turned out, but I found out during the course of a year and a few months, fourteen months it was, I found out she had turned a few, had a few dates down in Corpus. But I didn't know that at first. So I would have to answer your question yes, to begin with, but yet it never turned out that any of them were square. Never.

Now I'd like to make one thing perfectly clear: there's a difference between what I would call and what the police would call and what you would call a whore and a square. A girl that is what I call Saturday-night hustling, she would be a square to the police and very possibly to you. She's a whore to me. If she sells pussy at *any* time, she's a whore. And this is a big definition problem there. You see, when I say a "square," I mean or equate that with a girl who has never gone to bed for some sort of money or something you can turn into money—like a $5,000 mink coat.

Part of a pimp's job is protecting the girl from men who are giving her trouble. Did you ever have any?

Rumbles? Yes. This is what a pimp does, Texas-style. And I'm sure that this style does not just stay here. I know some pimps in California: same thing. Many times, over a period of ten, fifteen years, many times I've had this type situation.

One time in particular I got busted for. I was with Terry, she was in this hotel in Houston and it couldn't be worse. It was a skid-row area, but the hotel spot is not bad. Money-wise the spot is not bad, but the location of the hotel is terrible. And there was a rumble there and it happened to be a pimp.

He was just passing through and what he did is one I've played myself. A lot of times you'll go to a hotel or spot where you know you can make out with the gal, and you might even trick her and play the role of the square with the intent of stealing the whore. In other words, winning her affections, trying to get her to join up with you.

So Terry had the trouble with this dude in the room and she came back up to the room where I was at. I wasn't staying there but I was there that evening for a few hours. And she told me about it, so I go down there. I had my pistol and she had told me that it was a character, although she didn't know who it was, nor did I.

I go into this room and he's about half-juiced. And he opens the door. When he sees me—he's in his shorts, his undershirt or pants, and he had a bottle of beer I think in his hand—he tried to shut that door shut. Well, I took that pistol and, believe it or not, I just went like that, pointed it at him and pulled the trigger.

I don't know whether the bullet wasn't in the chamber or it didn't fire for some reason, but it did not fire. And after that, oh, man, about a week later, it shook the shit out of me. I actually got afraid, scared. I could have shot that guy.

Anyway, we tussled and I ended up whipping him over the head with the pistol and he took the bottle and he tried to hit me over the head—and may have. I don't remember. We all ended up in jail eventually because the manager—not the porter, the porter tried to cool it—he called the police while I'm up there cursing and carrying on and whipping on his head and all.

This is a trick of whores, you know. They'll rib you into these kind of positions. Many a pimp and many a character has been killed, shot and killed, because of some whore playing a trick like that.

It seems to me that some women thrive on that sort of thing.

Some whores are nymphos, they say, I don't know. Some say they're frigid, some say they hate their father, I don't know. But some, I think, thrive on thrills, and they get some sort of bang out of getting their old man and another man feuding and they become the center.

So when I look back on this one particular case, I think maybe that's what she did. Anyway, we all went to jail and I got filed on. As I told you, there's a popular misconception—not that anyone is particularly interested, but it is a misconception—about pimps going and saying, "Say, buddy, you fuckee my sister two pesos," or "How about spending the night with my old lady for a hundred." They don't do that. What they do is they make the contacts with porters and madams, people like that, they make contacts with people who set things up. They do not themselves call up the customers.

You may work a trick book. You may work that up yourself or you may buy it. In the trick book there are alphabetically listed different tricks, or customers, and these vary from $20 to $50, or there's one in Oklahoma that's $5,000. I know a girl who made a dude in Amarillo for $55,000 over one week's time. That man, the trick, is from Canyon, there's no sense mentioning his name, what matters is that tricks like that are rare.

You buy a trick book. You buy one in Chicago or you buy one in Dallas or you buy one in Hollywood. And these say who goes for what. Like the Hollywood trick book says that —— —— goes for three girls, freaks, you know.

That's one of my kicks too. I'm sure there's a deep Oedipal complex involved, or some terrible side of me, but I became freaky in this sense myself. I just can't dig a kick with one girl.

In fact, that's what got me into trouble this last time. This girl made a pass at my woman, my old lady, which I don't mind, but the point was she didn't know it was my old lady. Secondly she wanted to get this stripper and they were going to some stag party and they would each make a hundred or so after the party. I know what that means and one thing led to another and I guess I got kind of brutal. I told her, "You want to play pimp, I'm gonna help you," and we got into a beef and that was it. I didn't want to let her go because of what would have happened when I let her go, but I couldn't keep her either. A real switch.

I used to teach dancing at Arthur Murray's. We taught rhumba and other Latin American dances. I was fairly proficient, not necessarily as a teacher, but as a dancer. After work a lot of times we would go over to these Mexican or Latin American clubs and it was there I met this girl, Juanita, I never will forget her, she was the first whore I knew or ever was with in my life. We would dance from when the studio closed at ten until twelve or one in the morning.

We spoke and we danced and she invited me out a couple of times. I was just going out for fun. I didn't even know what she was. And then one night that we went over there she mashed a little money on me and though I didn't even know what she was doing, I'm not a fool, I've known characters in Houston intermittently all my life. So I took it.

Next thing I knew I went over to see her at the place where she worked and it was a dimly lit place, you'd probably call it a denizen, a place where there were a lot of very tough Mexicans sitting at tables drinking beer and a bunch of whores and the lights were real low and there was a big flaming jukebox blaring out things and they were doing gyrations and so on.

I was with her about a month or two at the most and that's how I started. As a pimp, I mean.

I was in school at the time, I was going to the University of Houston. I was going with a girl whose father was an executive with Socony-Vacuum and she was from California and we started going together just prior to me meeting Juanita. We had intentions of getting married and everything. Anyway, her father had apparently heard something about me—at that time it wasn't bad, but it was a question of social status I'm sure—so he sent her to Syracuse University for a year. When she came back we still went out a few times and then sometime in the spring semester she came back down and she showed me a big diamond ring and I thought, "Wowie!" She had become engaged to another guy that lived in Houston. I knew him and it pissed me off. I guess I was about twenty-one then, and you know how those things are.

I was working part-time and going to school, like I said, and that thing affected me, I admit it. But I went with Juanita anyway to this whorehouse over on Canal and there wasn't anything necessarily exciting about it. Funny thing about it was, though, she gave me the clap. I had to get that taken care of, which I did, but I was in school and it was something of a burden, but this other girl that I knew that I used to go with, she gave me some money to take care of it with, and it just got to my head.

"Well, this is strange," I thought, "that you can get money from women."

All this time I had known of pimps and certain type clubs I could go to dance at where there were whores and there were men there all the time, and I was aware of it, but I didn't know anything about the business, how you become or how you *are* a pimp. I even knew some. But at that time I thought they were the lowest crumbs on earth. I really did.

Next, I met a girl who had been hustling for a dude named Charlie and she had left him for some reason. I met her down in Galveston at another club. It was called the Rocket Club and the counterpart today would be a hippie joint or a rock music joint.

See, I used to go to rock and roll music places when it was against the law to go there. In Houston I went to the Club El Dorado and the Club Madelee. It was against the law for whites to be in that kind of a joint, it was a Negro joint and if the vice squad or the police caught you there you were in worlds of trouble. This was a while back, of course.

Anyway, I met her at the Rocket in Galveston and I said, "Why don't you leave that sissy you're with and come with me."

So we left and I tricked her and the next thing I know she's madly in love with me and I told her "The only way that I associate with you is if you sell pussy." Just like that. And sure enough, she did. Fantastic as that may sound.

This may be a square question, but how did it feel having a girl you knew other guys were fucking all day?

I've been asked that before and I've gone over that in my mind a lot. I once talked to a doctor about that and he told me you can be around something so long you're just part of that. I don't know if I can explain it the way he meant it, but the way I interpreted is, you just don't pay it that much mind. And I found this to be true, Bruce, really. The more I was in it, the longer I was in it, the less qualms I had. And if there was conscience or guilt, it became more repressed.

At that time, I just didn't have any feelings about that. I didn't think of it in that sense because I don't think I really cared for the girl in the sense that society accepts for the word "love." When I was with Betty, it just didn't bother me one way or another.

I'll tell you what I did feel bad about then. At this time I was also going with another girl who was a debutante in Houston, they lived in the Row. Betty was now working out on South Main in the motels. I felt rotten, not about the other guys having sex with her, but because I was taking her money and using it on that other girl. That didn't seem right, for some reason.

There are types. I've never worked with any girls on the street, so I can't say anything about them, but that's a type. A call girl is a type. Call girls, by and large, are very bitchy.

When I first got out of the joint I was going to try to be a square. It was the Federal, I just got out after doing forty-four months on a conviction for white slavery, the Mann Act. Pimping. I opened up a little art shop and what I was doing was going to different photographers and trying to get them to let me do a pastel or painting of photographs they have taken. They would sell it and I would do the work and it would be a package deal. I didn't make a go of it, needless to say, and four months later I got with this call girl that had run away from her old man. I didn't know it at the time but she did that regularly.

I carried her down to Corpus along with this other girl who belonged to a friend of mine, Margie was her name. We went to Corpus. As a rib I told them I was going to put them in a joint until Bob joined us, and they had a fit. "My goodness," all that, and told me that both of them went to the best of the better residential schools in Houston. I was only kidding, but they got all bitching. They're just difficult to get along with.

Another instance: a friend of mine in Houston had four of those Hollywood starlets but they were hustling girls and they had him what we call "washing their panties." He's got him a pistol and he's out there robbing the supermarkets. For a pimp this doesn't make sense, and I told him that. They're very haughty, those call girls.

I've been running whores quite a long time, but a lot of the time I'm what they call a "would-be" or a "mo-gimp." That's a pimp without a whore. I've worked at periodic jobs a lot of my life, six months here and then I'd quit and run into a whore and be with her a while, then I'd work some more. Then I married one and I pulled her up and she didn't work and I didn't pimp for almost two years.

She divorced me about twelve months before the end of that forty-four month sentence. That made me kind of bitter. In the joint, I'm around a lot of people, but I don't associate with many. There were two guys I associated with, I became friendly with, and I let this one guy go by and see her because he got out before I did and she had been sick, and he ends up getting her to use dope and then he sells her to another dope fiend.

Even among the criminal element you have your own connotation of what's sorrier-than-thou and a guy like that is one of mine.

What do you mean, "sells her"?

In the business of prostitution, a lot of times a guy will sell a girl to another dude. In this case I don't know the exact transaction, but the guy who bought her is in prison now. The one who sold her, I don't know where he is. They were both using narcotics and he probably needed some money and so he sold her for $400 or $500 or so.

How does the girl feel or what does she have to say about transactions like that?

Let me say that when you equate feelings in the racket, depending on the length of time you've participated, they're quite a bit different from the socially legitimate society. I don't know if that makes sense. What I'm trying to say is "right" and "wrong" or "good" and "bad" or just feelings per se, depending on how long you've been in the racket, change. The girl doesn't, to my knowledge, *some* don't, have any feelings; if she's a new turnout she might feel terrible.

Most girls I know who turn out do it for their old man, because of love. I know that to the legitimate this sounds perverted for her to do that. Norman Mailer, he says someplace that a woman would never forgive you if you did not want possession of her. Well, a whore will not forgive her pimp if he does not want possession of her. *Not* with the tricks, but with other pimps. And this selling back and forth would just bother her, I guess.

Another point that I'd like to stress: most pimps do not force their old ladies to go to work. This is a common misconception, maybe it's done for law and purposes of social control, I don't know, but I do know that the implication of it is that the girl would say, "Oh, I only did it because I was afraid of him." That is so much bullshit in most cases.

Does she always turn over all her money?

In the school—I never went to school for pimping, but the area I've worked in—yes, she does.

Now if a girl would turn her money over to someone she did not know just on the first or second time around, then she's probably an outlaw whore. An outlaw whore is one that has turned herself out.

A good example is that call girl in New York, the teacher that went to work selling pussy. She worked by herself. She worked with other girls and maybe she sometimes worked through a man in New York City. They busted her after she'd been working maybe two years. She was a high school teacher, but she did not have an old man, she probably had a boyfriend. There's a distinction.

How many guys a girl tricks a day varies. I've had girls trick one dude a day per yard, you know, $100. This is what I try to work it up to. I try to get it even better than that.

There are some steel men out of New York they sometimes have conventions in Dallas. If you can get in on this particular group, they're down just once every two or three months, but the girl doesn't have to do anything after that, they're paid all the time.

The girls that I've had, on the average, well, it varies. Some days they may trick five or six dudes. Working in a joint is different, of course. In a joint I've had a girl trick as many as twenty a night.

A lot of them are not penetrations. A lot of them are sitting on their face or pissing on them or you know maybe he'd be going down and giving head to the girl. They got one down in Beaumont, they call him Cold Cream and he puts a little cold cream on it.

How many I can't really say exactly. It's not as many as you would think, and yet it's not as few as you would think either. It depends on the girl.

In a joint most of them are straight tricks, but on call about half of them are straight and the other half a little other than straight.

In Dot's establishment they do have $5 dates, but very rarely do the girls ever trick for $5. It just doesn't occur. A guy *could* go to bed with them for $5, but it just doesn't happen. The point being this: that if the man will not go for any more and complains to Dot the madam, she in turn will tell the girl either to trick him for $5 or pack him and hook him [get rid of him]. It's a spot where you can't get into these spots just at random. You have to know someone. In turn, the girl that works there has to know someone that knows her, because most madams, most good madams, won't take a girl just out of the clear blue. Won't do it.

In a house like that, what portion of the take does the madam get?

Forty percent. And they charge them, I think, $6 a day for rent, room and board. So your gross, in other words, for $300 is close to $600.

Weird tricks pay more money. The reason they pay more money is that they can't go for what they want to someone they pick up at a bar, and they can't just go out with their secretary. With them it's not just a matter of going to bed with somebody you pick up or somebody you know.

They come up with stuff like, "Well, baby, how about pissing in the cup and let me drink some?" There was a merchant mariner that was in Corpus and he wanted to take some scissors and just cut off some of the hairs, the girl's pubic hair, and he rubs them in his chest and this is the way he freaks off and he gives her a whole check, which may be anywhere from $400 to $1,200, depending how long he's been out. Or they have an anal thing.

I had a girl who was a hell of a trick girl, a freak girl. She could take a freak and make him into more money. In Opaloosa, Louisiana, she met this dude, this man, this trick, the customer, he was spending $150 and when she met him one time she turned him right then and there for $250, and before she had left this place she had worked him up to $500 one time.

This girl, I think the important thing in her background was that her family was carnies. She'd been raised and was around this type of life. If you've ever been to a carnival you'll find most people there are "rounders," so to speak. Not that they're all pimps and whores, I'm not saying that, but I am saying that they hustle. They don't necessarily violate the law per se, but they have shell games, they bullshit the public. She grew up around there and she had an uncanny knack of digging a dude and knowing that there was something strange about his sex habits even though she had never tricked him or anything.

Once I pointed out this guy and he wanted something stuck in his anal passage. She snapped and so she ribbed him, "Well, let me stick the candle up it." I'm assuming that this really excited the guy, and he probably had an extra large charge, and from that she worked him up into other things.

Another one of hers, it was in Amarillo, a truck driver who looked just like Rock Hudson, at least according to the girl, he was a shit freak, he wanted the girl to shit all over him.

I was ribbing this other pimp and I said, "Man, your ole lady's up there and she's shitting around." I was just playing. So he got mad and he started raising cain. He really thought that she'd been messing around on him, but that wasn't what I meant. So we went up to the room in the hotel and man, shit everywhere. That guy said he's watched Mamie Eisenhower shit. Not only a voyeur, but a shit freak himself.

Another guy, this taxi driver, knows his thing, his hangup if you will, so he goes over to him and the first thing he does is he hits him right straight in the mouth. He doesn't hit him hard but he hits him enough to where the guy will fall down. When he falls down, the guy goes over and just barely nicks him. He's got one of those things you use for cutting open a bundle of newspapers, it's made out of metal. He just barely nicks him on the lip and it'll just kind of trickle. He throws him into his cab, curses him, says, "You dirty sonofabitch," you know, and all that jazz, carries him to the motel, and then he does his thing. This guy has to be hung, so the cabdriver and the porter tie him up by his thumbs and they got screws in this particular room in the ceiling and they hang him by his thumbs. And he's naked, of course, and the girl's naked and they leave. She, of course, plays with his situation and tortures it.

This is what's fantastic. She sticks a pin, something that's kind of sharp, she doesn't cut him or anything, but she sticks it on his penis. And this is what happened: the goddam room caught on fire some way and I'm just waiting out there for my old lady, and this old boy, the porter, called up to me, "Come on out here," and I thought, man, I thought it was the police or some kind of rumble or something. I went out there and there was smoke pouring out of the room, lordy me, so we run back and here's this old dude hanging up by his thumbs, and the whore, my old lady, she's just going, "Aaaaahh!" hollering and screaming, trying to get her clothes on, knowing that the firemen or policemen or probably both are coming. Maaan! this actually happened.

There are three judges I know, each one of them is a weird trick, and I sometimes wonder about that. It's like you're sitting looking out into space and you wonder what in the world is all this shit about. This one particular judge, I guess he's sent about a thousand guys down to prison, I understand that he is socially a prominent figure and that community-wise he stands for the old church bit, he's a good guy, but he has this sexual aberration and that's just one of those things I know, and yet that is some of what he's sent guys down here for.

It's very strange that this—what—hypocrisy, ambiguity, something, that it can occur in this so-called society. It doesn't make good sense. You've heard it, "It takes a thief to catch one." To me, this judge certainly ought to be able to catch me because I've got a whore and I'm sending him to her, and he knows and he knows I know.

I don't go with church girls. I don't go with girls that are in coming-out parties. When I went with Brenda, who was one of them, she knew about me, she wanted to go to all the dive joints, and I asked her one time, "Why? You really want to let your hair down, but you just haven't got the cods [balls]."

And she said, "I can't. There's my social position."

I said, "Well, I'm just the opposite. I don't like this area."

I was not pimping at that point but I was going to those clubs. It was the *zeitgeist,* or whatever you call it, but that was *verboten* then. You ran the risk of going to jail if you went to clubs like the El Dorado or the Whispering Pines or the Bronze Peacock. If the white police were there, they toted your ass to jail. It was the same kind of music that nowadays everybody likes. It's very weird.

One of the big troubles in Texas was the colored bellhops trying to trick the old ladies. Midland was very rampant with that, a lot of trouble down there. It's a very weird thing. The police whip the shit out of the pimp, but they don't touch the colored porters who are setting things up.

I had to pistol-whip one colored kid one time because of that thing. Not because he was colored and he hit on a white girl, but because he was demanding, he kept on insisting that he get some. He acted almost as if he didn't give a shit.

It's the same with a white dude you see. If a white pimp is screwing on your old lady and you don't get your business straight with him, you don't have an old lady. It's kind of like in the square world where you protect your wife if someone went up and slapped her or did something that would hurt her in some way. It might not physically hurt her, but . . . you know what I mean. You got to keep your business straight.

I think I was at school and I'll tell you one of the incidents that happened to the very first whore that I ever knew or was with. She was in Galveston and I had just come back from Las Vegas. Now that may sound high-sounding, but it wasn't. We just made a trip there and I was going up actually to make a score, which allegedly was $20,000 to $25,000. I won't say it was a holdup, but a kind of mugging-type thing. Anyway, it didn't pan out.

This other guy I know, a pimp, and I ran out of money, so I called her. She gave me a bunch of shit and I'd been eating pills, so I went down there and I knocked on the front door. One of the maids—I don't recall her name—she said, "Jack, you know the Mr. T.J. doesn't allow people to come by during working hours."

And, like I said, I was a little goofy. And I said, "Yeah, I understand." So I went around the back, and in this particular joint there is a connecting room-type hallway situation where two houses are together. They're two-story white wood houses, and so, as I went around to the back in the alley, these two particular whorehouses, there was the trick going in the other one. As he went in, the maid didn't notice me so I went with him. And I went upstairs. I went right straight upstairs 'cause I, like I say, I knew the joint. And so I opened a window in one of the trick rooms and went over to the other house across the way on the roof.

Now the reason that I did that is because in this hallway, this room, I would have had to pass these people that I knew. And so this other maid apparently didn't know me, and then of course all whore-houses are dark, you can't hardly see in them. So I went. It's about twelve maybe, or one, and I went across there, and I was, like I say, pilled up, and I was mad, mad because of the conversation that this Betty gave me over the phone.

So I went over there and she was in a trick room with a trick, up-stairs, and I just so happened to hear a voice and I recognized it. So I'm banging on the door and I've got my pistol in my shirt and this trick's all upset and he comes out with his shirttail flapping, and half-dressed, you know. And she comes running out buck naked and she splits and hits this corner room.

I turned and was running after her. I grabbed for her and missed her, and as I did, well she ran in the room and locked the door. Well, I had to kick the door down, which I did, and in the room—she wasn't in there. There was just a bed and a closet and a sink—typical joint room—and anyway she had gone out on the roof.

And there she is naked out on the roof and it's, like I say, late at night, past twelve. So I go out on the roof and I'm brandishing this pistol, you know, and raising hell. Anyway, I chase her, and she's jumping from roof to roof and I'm jumping from roof to roof. And in the meantime, naturally, they heard the ruckus downstairs that I was having upstairs and they called the police.

The whorehouse called the police?

Yes. This is one of my pet peeves about the rackets and about the character world and still is. It's all a big façade, you know, we're prob-ably the biggest hams in the world. (I'm being discursive.) Anyways, you know, it's all appearance, everything has this appearance. It's an illusion-type thing, like a dope fiend would have, and this is not his natural self. It's not my natural self to be violent, running around strumming whores, it really isn't, but under this particular situation I was pilled up. That maybe helped some too, but I'm saying that sober, without any type of stimulant of any sort, we still, I still, use different masks. Anyway, especially in the criminal world, or let me say I notice it more there.

So I ran in, up and down the roof, and the police are on both ends of the alley and they've got these spotlights, and if you can imag-ine the scene: there she is, she's blond, buck-naked, and the moon's out and it's a really wild scene. I finally snapped: boy, these sons-ofbitches get me they're gonna do me under.

I split. And apparently she got back into the joint where she was working.

I went to this friend of mine who's a square. I had a lot of square friends from college before I got involved in the rackets. So I went. He lives in Galveston, so I went over there. And in Galveston, these homes are on stilts because of the 1900 flood, I suppose. You know, they have a fear of being right on the ground. So most of the homes there have a third story or an attic. I stayed there three days, and I happen to know that they pulled [set up a roadblock on] the Causeway Bridge, which is a big event down there if they're looking for someone like an escaped convict or any type of bad situation. This is a way to seal you off on the island, and that first night, if I'd tried to a gotten away I would been busted. It's not a dragnet, it's just four or five policemen. But then it became where everybody was looking for me, so I stayed over there and they pulled the bridge, and in the third day I just caught a bus and left. It was that simple.

I think one of the things that has lured me and fascinated me or I've been perverted behind it is the fact that I see whores as a Whore. An attorney asked me one time, "If you had a wife would you let her run around half-clad all the time?"

I said, "Well, it's not the same with a whore. It's not the question of her screwing another man but it's the question that she *is* sex, that her sex is uninhibited, it seems that way, or even enormously less inhibited than a square girl."

As I told you before, I was engaged at one time, a square girl, went to the university, and I had every intention of getting married. But ever since I've been involved in prostitution I can't seem to get by with this moralistic or acceptable context of sex.

I dig the shit out of having two whores and watching each of them giving the other head [cunnilingus]. That represents to me the epitome of sex. That's not a bourgeois thing but an upper class entertainment.

You know Beaumont used to have lots more whores and joints than Houston and I broke it down by population once and you know what? They got less sex crimes in Beaumont than in Houston. How about that?

My wife, she's the one who really turned me out. She was the one that *really* showed me what's happening, so to speak. She was meticulously clean and she went to work like it was a business.

The FBI guy in L.A. who busted me for carrying a girl over the state line, he said, "Your woman, she's amoral." And I said "Why do you say that?" And he says, "She just is."

Amoral. Neither moral nor immoral. And since then—that was in 1956—I've looked back on it and it's true. That's what a lot of us are. Just amoral.

Doc: "I did my undergraduate work at Texas A & M and at Yale . . ."

It started in 1952. How it came about is not truly clear to me, the mechanism surrounding it. I can tell you a little bit about the physical part of it.

I started on codeine. I was in an automobile accident and had some broken ribs. In this small town I was doing general practice in, I was doing some difficult extractions—by difficult I mean they were hard to remove without using some force—and in this process I put a strain on my side and it affected those broken ribs injured in the automobile accident. And I was having some pain—whether it was enough at the time to justify a drug as strong as codeine I won't say—but in any event, I did take the drug, orally, and I found that it gave me a lift. At the time, not knowing I had an addictive personality and was ripe for such things, it didn't mean much to me other than as help along the way. It soothed things out for me, it helped me to do my work daily without the pain in my side. And subconsciously it eliminated some of the fears I had at that time in everyday living. It seemed—although you don't get much euphoria from codeine—it did give me enough to allay certain feelings and tensions that I had.

I was having domestic problems. My father was a physician, and mother and dad separated after some thirty-seven years of marriage, and all this came about in a period of two or three years there, and the immediate family was in a turmoil. And my brother-in-law had gotten out of the army and had gone and borrowed a quite sizable figure from the R.F.C. and the family was in debt a little. Along with problems such as these, the codeine helped.

From there I graduated to Dilaudid, taking it IM, intramuscularly. Taking it small doses at a time. This went on for several months.
What's the biggest habit you had?
The first one. Dilaudid, fifty sixteenths a day. That's approximately 200 mg. of Dilaudid a day for about a year. There was a morphine habit I had, I ran that up to about eight grains a day—that's over 120 mg. of morphine a day, along with other drugs too that I was taking at the time, along with some Demerol, in erratic amounts along with the morphine.

And of course Dilaudid is one of the drugs you can increase the tolerance to more rapidly—at least it seems that way to me and in talking with individuals these last few years—you can accumulate a terrific tolerance for this drug in a shorter amount of time than you can the others. You can build an astronomical habit on this thing and the first thing you know . . .

I was unable to account for the prescriptions. I had exhausted all my friends, doctors, and had become enmeshed in Federal charges over improper use of wholesale forms that we use to get these drugs, and I was about to go in the army at the time—called back in the reserves for the Korean War. This uncertainty along with the other problems were so big for me at this time that I know I felt I must have had the need for the drug. And I didn't stop using it. I was addicted for a year and a half and during this time I went to John Sealy [hospital in Galveston] voluntarily to withdraw myself.

But never really made any headway with it. I was an ambulatory patient and was permitted outside privileges. I had a wife who I had married in 1949 who was a registered nurse and she was with me at this time. Now to show you how you can delude yourself—or how *I* can—I was receiving these withdrawal doses. They were cutting my dosage down. So when I began to feel just a little twinge of discomfort I would go out and supplement what they had given me, and that's while I'm paying $300 a week to try to withdraw. This doesn't make much sense, I know that, but this is the rationale that sometimes one uses while on drugs.

Well, it so happened these cures proved unsuccessful down there at John Sealy and I was given a two-year sentence. I did that sentence at the U.S. Public Health Service Hospital in Fort Worth, I think it took nineteen months and six days. I wasn't granted parole.

I had never been arrested before, I had never been charged with anything until I was twenty-seven years old. I had never been arrested until this time. And I didn't make too good an adjustment.

It was a hospital, but you can call it a prison: it was compulsory, I didn't have a key, I didn't choose to go there, I couldn't leave. I was sentenced by a Federal court, by Judge Ben Rice, Jr., who made the comment at the time—I remember the words still ringing in my ear— he said, "I'm not trying to punish you. I understand it takes two years to cure addiction. I sentence you to two years."

Well, I did the two years.

I came out. I made a stab at trying to stay off drugs, which lasted three weeks before I started taking something. I didn't start injecting things then, but I did take some oral preparations of drugs of lesser magnitude than what you think of with addiction nowadays: some codeine again and some oral Dolophine tablets and things like that, and I became dependent upon these.

I started teaching, instructing at Baylor University in Dallas. My license to practice had not been revoked that first time. Why I don't know, but the state board members, whom I had known for quite some time, came out to see me. They said, "We're going to give you your license to practice. We feel that you can make it. We feel that you have some ability, we want to see you make it." I'd say they were very magnanimous in their efforts. On the other side, I was very insincere about it, not truthful with them or myself. I got my license— rather I had it, they never did actually revoke it, I just paid my dues up and started in general practice with a man in Dallas and teaching at the university part-time.

It wasn't long before I fouled that up.

I became addicted to Dolophine this time and had a course of about four or five months on it. I became involved with state laws. I knew this was going to lead to some kind of demise like I'd been through in the past, so I flew the coop. I took off to California. At the time I had some money and I did know some unsavory characters where I could obtain these drugs and I did take half a suitcase full and make the West Coast. I was in Boston, too, for a while, visiting some friends. I was addicted all this time and I guess they all knew it. I thought I was pretty slick in keeping it from them, as an addict will, but they could easily tell because I was taking massive doses of the stuff.

Finally I ran out. The Texas authorities and Federal authorities were looking for me all this time, they'd missed me several times. I finally came back to Texas and was arrested and convicted and given a two-year sentence.

It was a possession charge, but it was a deal. I took the two years on it. They had some forged prescriptions I'd written. I'm morally guilty of a whole lot more than the possession of the things, but they chose not to file those forgeries on me and let me go ahead and plead to the possession rather than file the forgeries on me, and they gave me two years and I came to the Texas Department of Corrections for the first time. And served a two-year sentence and got out and did fairly well for a while.

This time my license was revoked. I did pretty good for a few months, four or five. After that I was again on these drugs, ones that are fairly easy to obtain, and if you don't become too involved with them you can sustain them without too much fear of discovery. Codeine, and there were some new drugs out at the time like Leritine [a synthetic narcotic analgesic, manufactured by Merck, Sharp & Dohme], and some other drugs. I got on these drugs and while on them I applied for my license back.

In 1958 at the Shamrock, which is now the Statler-Hilton, I met the state board with a friend of mine. I was actively addicted to codeine; I don't remember if I was taking Dolophine or not, but I was taking some massive doses of codeine and Hydocan, which is dihydrocodeinone bitartrate, a synthetic drug, it's a class A narcotic. It's strong. I was taking it orally, for the most part I was. Occasionally I injected it. You can't hardly inject codeine in the vein. It will give you phlebitis, a little inflammation of the veins. If you're going to take it any way but orally IM is the only way to take it. It will swell your eyes shut and everything else if you take it IV—I've had that experience too.

While actively addicted to this stuff I met the board, as I said. And I convinced all members and got a unanimous decision from them. They called me three days later at my home in South Texas. The secretary of the board, Dr. Weber from Austin, called me and he told me, "We're happy to tell you that we're going to give you your license back."

Mr. Gentry, he's the narcotic agent in charge of this region, headquartered in Dallas, also went along with it and he let my narcotic tag come back through. I had lost my stamp before, you know what I mean, but when the board gave me my license he didn't make any to-do about it. I had done a lot of oral surgery in the past and I was going to be doing some again with some men that I had worked with before in the oral surgery field. If properly used, I actually had a legitimate use for a narcotic license. So I applied for it and he didn't see any objection, or if he did he went ahead and granted it anyway.

Now I didn't abuse this license like I did before, but I did abuse it some. This was 1958. In 1960 I was in a mess again, addicted this time to morphine. I had quit practicing, I didn't think about even using my narcotic license to write drugs. I went to Dallas to go to the Federal hospital there at Fort Worth, to check in voluntarily. I went, but they wouldn't take me at the gate. I had just enough narcotics to get into the hospital.

What I'm going to tell you now, this is something I have strong feelings about. I had to wait, they wouldn't take me, it was because I had been there before they said. I had run out of my supply and I was taking morphine. I had been getting it in devious manners, in devious ways.

When they wouldn't take me at the gate I went over to my sister's in Dallas and waited for the papers to come back to give me my admission acceptance. I started getting withdrawal symptoms. I couldn't go to a practitioner—they shun you like the plague in Texas, there is no such thing as going to a physician's and saying, "I'm addicted, help me," because Texas at that time had a law that said it is a crime to be an addict. This discouraged even the most helpful physicians, the most conscientious ones frowned upon giving you anything. I was having withdrawal symptoms, so I went to a drugstore about eight blocks from my home. I still had my narcotic license and I wrote a prescription for my sister for just a maintenance dose, two maintenance doses of Dolophine. I had the papers of acceptance in my coat pocket, I was to be at Forth Worth the next day.

When I came out of the drugstore the Federal agents arrested me.

They wouldn't let me go to Fort Worth. They threw me in the Dallas county jail. I got so darned sick . . . I had a pretty large morphine habit. I got sick, I got pretty despondent, I had some emotional things happen. Instead of filing these prescriptions on me they filed addiction. At the time, my thinking was such that I was wanting to get off of it so bad that I believe I would have accepted anything. I didn't want any more of the drug, I hated what had happened, I just wanted off.

And I took a two-year sentence for addiction. Got down here in the last of 1960. Was on the Ramsey One and went over to the Ellis to help with the hospital there and discharged out in the fall of 1961. Three days before I was to get out—I was in the Walls waiting for discharge—one of my friends came over and said, "They're looking all over for you. They've been calling over the loudspeakers. Mr. Heard and Father O'Brien want to see you."

Well, just like in the past, every little crisis that would come along, I would be tripped for it. Set up for it. Everything seemed a stumbling block to me. My emotional threshold was such to where any of these situations would arise, I just couldn't cope with it. This happened on a Friday: they notified me that my mother had a stroke and she was in very serious condition, critical condition. They were standing by to release me. My discharge date was Monday and they were going to release me on Saturday, but they called back and they said that they thought she would be all right, that she wouldn't die before I got there.

Well, they let me out Monday and I think it took me thirty minutes or forty minutes after I got my clothes to go down to the drugstore and get a bottle of something with codeine in it, I've forgotten what it was. Thirty or forty minutes after I'd gotten my clothes and discharged! I put on the clothes that I'd bought—I threw away the prison clothes—I went down to the drugstore and bought something with codeine and went to San Antonio.

My mother and I had had some gross misunderstanding in the past, that's putting it mildly. I never did very much accept her as a mother. For some reason she had a compulsion to push me faster. I graduated from high school when I was fifteen and was in college when I was fifteen, I had to get a waiver to get into Texas A & M. It seemed to me she was more interested in me because of what I could do, because I was her child, than my welfare. And we weren't ever very close.

I got home and I was very distraught. I felt guilty about the stroke. I feel that part of the stroke was attributable to her anticipation of me being released from prison. And she didn't take her medicine. She had been prescribed some stuff for hypertension, which she had had for a number of years. And I suffered guilt like I had caused her all the worry and part of the stroke was directly attributable to my release. I felt this way, I kind of still feel this way, but I don't know how much guilt I carry now in comparison to the guilt I carried in the past.

In order to secure drugs—to defer to this habit and perpetuate it —for the first time I started burglarizing places that contained narcotics, such as clinics and doctors' bags at first and culminating with a couple of drugstore burglaries. During this time I tried to rationalize things as I did before, but it didn't last very long. Me being a very amateur burglar and all, and living in a community of approximately 8,000 people and everybody in town knowing my history—I had some prominence there before I became addicted to drugs. Everybody knew what had happened, and in the surrounding counties people knew too, and everybody there was well acquainted with my whole family for years.

I was arrested and taken to jail in Hallettsville, about thirty-five miles away, it's the county seat of Lavaca County. I was treated very, very good. This doctor that I had stolen from came over to the jail— the people there had him come twice a day. That afternoon I was sick again. I had broken into his clinic now, and still he came over and gave me a grain of morphine and 200 mg. of Demerol in the morning and one in the evening. The next day they sent me to Fort Worth. This was early in 1962. When I got to Fort Worth it was on a commitment this time, and with a hold on me. All these burglaries I had pulled and everything.

I made a fair stab. I believe I made a better adjustment at Fort Worth than I ever had. I learned some things about myself that I hadn't previously. That ego had prevented me from learning before. I began to learn just a little bit and that was the start of a new process for me. I feel like it was, anyway.

I stayed there and I thought at one time that the detainers would be taken off of me and I could make restitution for what I had taken, but this was not so. I was taken to Victoria, where one of the burglaries had occurred, and given eight years for the burglaries, and subsequently I was taken to Hallettsville and given concurrently a seven-year sentence. And back to the Texas prison system once again. And this time I went to Ramsey and to the field picking cotton.

A very dubious distinction, Bruce, but I guess I'm the first college graduate, much less one with a professional degree, that's ever been to the field.

I did my undergraduate work at Texas A & M and at Yale—the Yale part was about sixteen hours on an army training program—and then I got my D.D.S. at the University of Missouri, Kansas City. At the time I went to dental school there were no class A dental schools in Texas, which was my home, and the one closest to home was Kansas City.

Most college men who come in, they come in just once. I happen to have the unfortunate experience of darn near wearing the place out, it looks like. Well, I stayed in the field close to six months, and now, as you know, I've been in here for close to three years.

I'm in the dental department at Ramsey. At first they were skittish about putting me down here where some types of drugs are accessible. They're not narcotic drugs but other drugs and tranquilizer types of drugs, and after a talk with the warden I assured him I had never used these drugs, had never used barbiturates, that they depressed me, which is true. I have used them but just in a medicinal way, only when they were prescribed for me. I never had any habit pattern on them or anything like that.

The judge that sentenced me is a lifelong friend of the family. He lives across the street from me, I used to play poker with him, drank with him. The district attorney that sentenced me ran track with me in high school, we were on the same track team. I had previously, in my early college days, dated his wife—she wasn't his wife then, of course. So this eight-year sentence came as a little shock to me. After knowing these people and having them knowing me and us being from the same social circumstances, it was a little bit of a shock when they said eight years. I had reconciled myself to something, but not eight years.

Why did they hit you so hard?

This is Victoria County. There was a great amount of publicity on this thing. I don't know if Wiley—the district attorney I'm speaking of—felt like that politically he might be jeopardized if he gave me less time or if he felt this was just. I can't condemn him. I have sort of mixed emotions. I feel like I should have gotten something, but the amount . . . of course, a man who gets sentenced, he generally thinks he should have had less. In this case, I think I should have had less. I don't know about it. He's the one that prosecuted this veterans' land scandal down there, this big thing that the man who wrote about it won a Pulitzer Prize about, and I think he maybe has some political aspirations. I just would like to think I'm not part of the springboard on this type of thing. Being that we had been friends.

There's a feeling that is hard to explain. Before I got into jail, even when I was on drugs, I had no guilt feeling. I mean about being a criminal. I know that morally this was wrong, that I shouldn't be taking these drugs, but that didn't make me feel like a criminal. It wasn't until I was thrown into jail and headlined in the San Antonio *Light* and papers of that ilk that I really began to feel I was something like John Dillinger. I couldn't understand this.

It's so often that doctors get into trouble, but it seemed to me that they had prior warnings from the bureau or something about this. I didn't have any. I'm talking way back, the first time before I became addicted. The guy who is now retired from the Bureau of Narcotics, I've talked to several other physicians that had a problem on narcotics and he had sent special people to see them and had talked to them himself. Mine was boom! The first time I wasn't given any warning. This is back at the very onset of addiction, in 1952.

I wondered why it was just boom. I was arrested and charged with violation of these Internal Revenue forms. In order to secure drugs for your office or anything, you can't write a prescription legally. You must take the triplicate forms and mail them or give them to the druggist and have him send them to the wholesale house and they in turn send your narcotics back by registered mail. Now you can write a prescription for somebody and they can go over and pick it up. But legally, a physician or a dentist, an osteopath or veterinarian cannot write a prescription for his family or himself and go over and pick the drugs up, nor can he write a prescription for a patient and pick it up himself. Of course it is done quite frequently, but it isn't legal. And I did this for a year and a half from time to time, and finally, of course, I was arrested.

How do you think the narcotics agents knew to wait for you outside the drugstore that day?

I don't know. I had written a prescription the day before for my sister for a maintenance dosage. I want to tell you how much it was so you'll know it was just a maintenance dosage: it was 20 mg., that was all it was. This was a dose that I took three times as much in one shot four or five times a day at other times. Their story is that they had just by chance been in there the day before and had seen this other prescription. I was to go on the third day, and on the second day I went to pick up that prescription, I had written it the day before and went back the next day to get it. Something was wrong, I couldn't get it or it didn't look right, I felt something. Anyway, I didn't have it. I came out and was arrested. They said it was just a perchance deal.

The hospital sent word over that they would take me, but the Dallas authorities would not release me to them. I had the acceptance papers and was to go, but of course they wouldn't release me to Fort Worth. They saw fit to keep me in jail and to withdraw me cold turkey.

No, wait a minute, that's not true. Joe ——— of the Dallas police force gave me some Dolophine tablets for withdrawal symptoms while I was in the city, and he kept me there just a little bit longer just so he could give them to me. This is sort of off-the-record, but nevertheless he just gave me some and he knew that it would do some good and keep me from getting so violently ill. I felt Joe was kind of pressured on this deal because the Federal had arrested me and were tired of messing with me. I think Joe really didn't want to prosecute me, but he felt like if he could get me two years or something like that in the state it would be a hell of a lot better than what the Federal was going to have to give me. That would have been ten at a minimum. I feel to this day that Joe of the Dallas police department did me that favor and he went overboard in order to help me on this deal and keep me from getting more time.

Bebop: "Dope hasn't changed me . . ."

I was born in Detroit in 1924 and right now I'm in prison on a grand larceny charge that carries a sentence of one to ten years. That's an indeterminate sentence and it means that any time after one year and any time before ten years I can be released. And I have been released on parole, but I was brought back for a parole violation.

I got a traffic ticket for driving a car for pleasure and then they found out that I owned the car, and then I drank a little bit while out. Not a little bit, I drank. Period.

I'm going to talk about dope, narcotics. Having been an addict I know something about it, one of the narcotics especially: heroin. Some people call it "the Big Boss: Horse." "Horse is Boss."

I've had several bands, been in several bands. I'm called a pretty good musician. I'm a horn player. And I have known some of the greats. Some of them were junkies, they used dope. I've seen a lot of pictures, movies, and I've read a lot of books, but I haven't read one yet that actually told about dope like dope is. I don't know, I think that all of the people that are doing the research, they never put themselves in the position that a junkie or a dope user is usually in when he is using dope, so they really don't know.

I feel very strongly about this because I don't feel that dope was the cause of me coming to prison. I don't feel that dope has caused me to do anything that I didn't want to. I don't think that dope is the controlling factor.

I've heard it said that reefer, marijuana, makes people act different or peculiar. Well, so does whiskey. If a person is gonna steal something, if he's gonna rape somebody, if he's gonna take and beat somebody's brains out, he's gonna do that whether he has the reefer, horse, or whatever, because that's his nature. I don't feel that my nature is to kill a person, so I don't think I'd do it if I shot all the dope in the United States.

I've never seen people shoot dope and go completely crazy like they say. (I don't know about teen-agers because I've never been around them.) I know heroin makes you soothed, it gives you a soothed feeling, you want to sit still and relax. I like to get high and listen to my record player, listen to music. There's no violence in it. I enjoy sitting listening to people talk and trying to analyze what they were saying.

I like to listen to music especially. That's my business and my joy. And if I follow one horn down one time through, maybe I'll listen to one record fifty times and listen to each individual instrument. I feel that dope, as you call it, enables me to center my mind, pinpoint it in other words. I could sit up and the whole band would be playing but I could hear any individual instrument that I wanted to hear, and hear it exact without all of the other distortion.

So I'm in complete disagreement with all of these doctors and all these reports. These people don't know what they're talking about, I don't think.

I've met an awful lot of junkies. I know 'em from New York to Mexico, all through Mexico. I know fellows who steal much more and do all the crimes and they don't do nothing. Some of the worst people in the world, the sickest people I've seen in my life, were winos, drinking that fifteen-cent-a-quart wine. I've *never* seen junkies in that shape.

Most of the time a junkie will get up. If he has to go steal something to get that dope, he'll get up and do it. I've seen winos lay around so sick till they couldn't move. In bars in New York or by my home in Detroit, you can see them in every alley, sleeping out there. A junkie can't afford to sleep in the streets—you get chills when you get sick, and as the dope recedes from your body and you need a shot you start having chills and your legs ache, your stomach turns over, you vomit, I don't know the technical term for vomit but you what we call puke your guts out. And your nose runs, your eyes run, and you can't afford to be out there, you would catch double pneumonia or something. A junkie is going to get him some money if there's any money. And there always is money.

I wouldn't sit here and say dope was detrimental to me. I will say this: had I been a millionaire and had I accomplished in life what I wanted to—which is to become a good musician, I'm thirty-eight now and still have a few years left—but if I had had a million dollars and a place to be left alone with it, I would prefer shooting heroin and cocaine than drinking Scotch, Black and White or Black Label, what-have-you, or smoking reefers or any of it. I prefer it to any high there is because it treats me better. I don't wake up in the morning with a hangover, I don't wake up with all the nervousness, all the hassle.

I don't know. Were I saying this to some reformer or something I would talk a whole lot different, but I'm just talking, I'm speaking my mind.

How I started using dope.

At that time I had an all-girl band and was just starting to make some decent money in music. We were booked out of New York, one of the big booking agencies, recording for one of the big recording companies. My first big break. And I wasn't ready for it in my mind, mentally. I'm from a religious family, and $100 to me then was like giving a three- or four-year-old kid $100—he wouldn't know what to do with it. I hadn't been used to that kind of money. So I ran wild with it, as usual, the old story: women, wine, and song.

And then you look up one day and we were leaving Houston, Texas, going up to Tyler, and we had an accident. I was asleep in the car and my valet was driving. Supposed to have been driving. He let one of the girls drive. He was trying to make her, he wanted to go to bed with the girl and was big-shotting. And he let her drive and she, not being used to power steering, I guess, jerked the wheel.

I woke up four days later with my skull fractured, both legs broke. My bass player, the girl I was personally interested in, a youngster, was killed. And they wanted to cut off one of my legs.

I think that's when I started feeling sorry for myself. Came to Detroit. Laying around there in a cast, nothing to do and a lot of pain.

So some of my school friends came by and brought me some pain killer. And I took a nice shot of it. And it did actually kill the pain. It was heroin. There isn't much cocaine around there, but it was heroin. And in the next day or two they came by again and did the same thing. He was giving it to me at that time and I didn't have any idea that I was getting hooked, but that's what happened. And the fellow who it was, he was one of the big dope dealers in Detroit.

But I had seen before this—all through my life as a musician—
dope addicts, and I had always said that it couldn't happen to me. But
it did happen. And when my convalescing period allowed me to get
up and get around on crutches, I decided to go back in the band business because I was broke—doctor bills and hospitals and everything.
And I went back to New York on crutches and started back to
playing. It was a great handicap and it was inconvenient, but it didn't
bother me much as long as I was high.

And in New York the dope is much stronger, closer to pure, it
hasn't been cut or worked as much, so you get an entirely different
type habit. You hear a guy talking about a habit in the Middle West,
it's about a fourth as powerful as a habit would be in New York or
around Juarez or Tijuana in Mexico. At any of these seaport or
coastal towns you get much purer heroin.

And I was using New York dope. Making good money at the
time. I was using about $40 a day.

After I'd gotten my bills paid, I found that the jinx was kind of
on me because of the wreck. It was hard to keep a girl band with one
of them having been killed. Most women are squeamish about those
type things. So I couldn't get the correct musicians again so I started
mixing the group, and it didn't sell as well.

Naturally: women: they don't have to be able to play any music.
All they got to do is stand there and shake a little bit. And that's all
they were doing, actually. It was a strain on me because I had practiced, oh, so many years, just to learn to play well, then all of a sudden
I got in a show group where you don't have to play, all you got to do
is show.

And with these things weighing on my mind I just kept shooting
the dope along, just kept shooting along, because I had nice money.
And the next thing I knew, I was truly hooked. But I had recordings
out and everything. Money coming from practically every angle, and I
decided I would come back to Detroit and finish convalescing.

About that time I broke up my band, the girl band, and I went
with Lionel Hampton, and he's on the same plane as the Count and
the Duke. I played around the country, in and out of the country with
that band, and then came the wreck down in New Mexico, and I
begin to think that the jinx was on me. Still using dope—there was
about thirteen addicts in the band I was with at that time. So I had a
lot of company.

But I never saw one of them go out and steal anything, I never
saw one of them take anything from anybody. We didn't need to. We

got paid every night and I was making $40 a day in the band myself.

And with all the company, it's easy to stay high. The only thing hard about it on the road like that is finding the dealers in small towns, little places down South especially—by down South I mean below St. Louis, Missouri. When you get down there you have to pick your shots and when you order you have to buy in abundance and that makes a bigger junkie out of you because when you've got a whole lot you'll shoot every fifteen or twenty minutes because you like the effect. So with all of us there we bought great quantities, that's thirteen or fourteen fellas pooling their money.

We had connections coming from New York and everywhere. I mean they'd get on planes and bring us—yeah—bring dope to us. In Mississippi, we'd play places down in Mississippi and Alabama, you know, little bitty towns, maybe our stuff would be just about gone, we would shorten up some trying to stretch it, then everybody's half sick, you're half ill. You're nervous, you're shaky, kind of leaky like you've got a fresh cold coming, no energy, no spirit.

Then you look up and through the door comes the dealer.

Everybody brightens up like sunshine after a rain.

And that's the way we made it.

But then I had the wreck in New Mexico and I made the mistake of quitting the band because I didn't get any money out of the wreck. I quit the band and I came to Detroit.

Detroit—on a New York habit.

The dope in Detroit was so weak until it kept me running to the dope man. I'd get up in the morning, first thing I'd have to have a shot. That shot is supposed to carry me at least four hours, but about nine thirty I'm on my way back down to the dope man. And I knew that wasn't going to work because I was spending too much money.

Anyway, it's really a small town. I was raised there, went to school there at an all-Negro school, graduated, everybody on the police force and everybody in business knows my family. My dad is a civic leader there, he's a deacon in one of the biggest Negro churches in Detroit; he's pensioned out of the auto factories and he's a contractor now. My dad is influential there in things like NAACP. And everybody knows us.

So every time I went down to the dope trap, it's known. The law knows where those dope traps are, they know what's going on, nobody's a fool. So they see me running in there four, five times a day, naturally they know what I got to be going there for. So I got branded like that. I had never had a record for anything or been arrested for dope, up to that time I had never been arrested for anything, never even had a traffic ticket. I was born and raised there and had no record there at all.

I decided I would go into Lexington and kick the habit. I went to Lexington. Now they had told me they would give you dope and gradually recede you or gradually weed [wean] you off of it, they didn't tell me they stopped you all of a sudden.

Then, I thought that they were going to be shooting it in the vein like I'd been doing; then I got down there and they were taking everything orally. Just a little thimbleful of something you drink—I don't know the name for it—but it made you sleep at night.

On dope, when you don't have it, you don't sleep, you can't eat, you can't do much of anything, you're a nervous wreck. It won't let you lay still. It's just like butterflies or ants or something crawling around in your stomach. Your stomach turns over and over and over and a green type mucus comes out of your nose, out of your mouth. Your eyes steadily run water. Well, you're just a nervous wreck, especially if you're hooked.

Sometimes you see guys beat their heads on the walls. Well, they're just weak lilies. If you pinch 'em they'd holler. You know, some people put on a show about anything. I've seen grown men out in the street actually hungry—I think little of a man like that. If he's grown and talking and he's asking me for money to go and get him something to eat, why he's no man, he's *nothing*. And that's the way I feel about these fellas—they holler if you stick them with a pin, they hurt.

My wife used to go to bed for a cold and I never could understand it. Weakness in people. I don't know, my dad was so strong. I guess it was the way I was raised that caused me to feel this way. But I don't believe a person is supposed to show all of their emotions to everybody, you know.

Well, a junkie is a junkie. There is a true junkie, a person that just won't do without dope. I've known fellas that would die rather than give up dope, they'd rather be dead. It's a kick and it's pleasurable.

See, it's such a powerful thing until you never actually get completely rid of it. You hear people make these statements about "I'm completely cured, I'm this, that, and the other about dope," but to me it is the greatest high in the world.

If it was just legal, like wine. I think wine is twice as detrimental. I'm no authority, I'm going only by what I have seen. My brother is an alcoholic, the only brother I have, and I've seen him go completely blind at the wheel of his car just because of alcohol. Completely blind, driving his car fifty miles an hour! Now I've never seen a junkie do anything like that in my life, and I've been around all types of junkies —women, men, and whatever.

I know a bunch of women prostitutes, whores I call them, that are junkies. But I've never known one yet that was a junkie when she started or that she started in the business because she wanted to get some dope. They say that. But I know women that will do anything to prove that they love you, I mean women that are old women, middle-aged and on up, that have never used dope, there's nothing that they wouldn't do to prove to me right now . . . There's several women in this county that I could get in touch with and tell them to turn tricks all the way up here from California and bring me whatever they made and they would jump up there if I would promise them we'd be to-gether after that. So it isn't the dope, I don't think, that makes those women get into prostitution. Most of the girls that use dope that I've talked to have used it because it was a kick. And they find that they can turn tricks and center their minds on their man and believe that it's him. You see they make-believe—as I said in the beginning—I'm able to pinpoint things much clearer, even when I smoked marijuana, it enables you to pinpoint.

When I'm playing, I stand on the bandstand, if I'm tired, I've traveled maybe 300 miles that day and I'm tired, it's the same thing over and over every night, you play the same tunes and things, so I'm just beat. It isn't a big town, there isn't a bunch of friends there, bunch a people you don't know is all, so you feel let down, you need some-thing to give you the lift because you've got to put on a good show. And you know if you drink a bunch a that whiskey you're not going to be able to drive on that next 300 or 400 miles that same night. You'll likely have to leave right after the gig, which lets out about two, and drive on through to day or maybe ten or eleven o'clock before you'll get a chance to rest. So I want something to keep me up, to keep me spry. So I get me a couple of benny tablets, I know I'll be woke then. Then I got to get something to lift me, not to get high. Juice [al-cohol] will make me sluggish, I'll go to sleep. I take me a little heroin, mix it with a little cocaine, and it's *such* a lift.

When I hear people—get around reformers, whatever—talking that talk: "That dope really brought me down to this and it brought me down to that," well, then, I think they're just blaming their weak-nesses on something else, they're just passing the buck.

I know too many influential people, people up there in business, big-timers who've been using it for twenty or thirty years, and they don't have no record, never stole nothing, they don't have any type record, and they are still using it and will probably be until they die. If they use it with moderation and discretion.

So I don't go along with all these books and things. *The Man with the Golden Arm* and that type junk. That's nothing but trash. Somebody was around a junkie or hung around a junkie for twenty or thirty minutes and wrote a bunch a stuff down that he was talking and the only reason he was talking that stuff was they were paying him enough money for him to go get some dope. That's the only reason.

They just give you a skimming of it, the part they feel you want to hear: oh, how low it brings you and how much better you feel.

You know, I've been locked up for two and a half years now and I haven't felt as good one day as I have when I was high. Never. And I been sober—well, I was out in the street almost two years before that and I was locked up eighteen months before that, and I been clean all that time, so I know dope is out of me. There's no traces of anything, couldn't be, because my bones has changed and everything in all that time. I've changed. I'm a completely different individual. But yet and still my mind, my memory is the same, and I know deep down inside of me that there is nothing of those old cells left, I'm a completely changed individual.

I've been reading an awful lot of reincarnation and Freud and Menninger and all of the philosophers, Plato and Socrates, and from the things that I gather, they were some sort of addicts, most of them. And yet and still, that didn't keep them from being the great minds of that era, whatever era they were being of. They still had their great minds and they didn't turn into thieves and robbers and prostitutes. I believe that all is up to the individual, like murder.

With my being here and all of my studying, I still feel that if I had a million dollars and a mansion out somewhere, maybe a hundred miles from the next house, and could care for my family in the correct way (if I ever have another, my wife is gone now and the babies, so I'm speaking if I ever have another, I intend to do all the things that any normal human being does), if I had that and I had my rathers in this world, I would create me a place where the law would legalize dope and not make such a big issue out of it.

I don't believe that it is detrimental, I don't believe that there is any books yet that have proven that it is. I read all this stuff but it all

says the same thing, dope makes you rape your mother and steal yourself blind, run yourself crazy, makes prostitutes out of young girls, and
I don't believe it.

I have known a number of young ones and old ones, I have
known and been intimate with girls twelve years old in the South.
That's right. And they were considered girls, women, they did anything they wanted to, they would live their life. Down in the South,
you know, the age for marriage or going to bed with a girl is much
younger than it is here and on further east. And I been up in Maine,
New Hampshire, on out there, in Boston where they used to have a
whipping post up there and if they catch you in a hotel with a girl you
weren't married to they whipped you. And over in Canada. I been all
over there and everywhere and I seen women everywhere. But I don't
see any difference in women. Women are just women and they all
want the same thing. If you make 'em want you bad enough they'll do
what you say, as long as they want you bad enough. And if they don't
want you, nothing you say makes any difference.

I know that wine deteriorates people's mind, their brain cells,
they get so they don't want anything. They don't even want a place to
stay. They sleep in boxcars and under houses. In New York I'd go up
on the roof of my apartment and there'd be fifty winos laying up there
with newspapers.

In my life I've been lucky. I been in music, so anywhere I've gone
I've been accepted. I know a guy in Chicago, ———, he's arrested for
dope practically every six months, and everywhere you go he draws
people—doctors, lawyers, big-timers, deacons from churches—everybody comes to hear his music. Well, that's all he's interested in. I don't
care what people think of me as a *person* because I'm an individual
and I've got to live my life as I see it. Dope hasn't changed me, it
hasn't made me an illiterate, an ignoramus of any kind, so I don't see
what it is everybody is so excited about.

Three Ladies: "Say you peel two layers of your skin off . . ."

JUDY: I've been on stuff and around stuff a long time. In fact, my friends that I got are mostly junkies. I've been in these joints and in these jails and we've talked just like we're talking right now, and I have yet for anybody to say, really describe the feeling that a fix gives you.

Can you?

It's impossible. It's completely impossible.

SAL: Dig: a lot of people, it hits them in the back of their neck, a lot of people it hits them in their head, and a lot of people it hits them in their box, and that's where it hits me. Right in my box.

Now when I've got a habit, then it don't hit me at all, it just takes the sick off and that's it. I'm normal. But when I'm first getting back on: right in the box.

JUDY: But for an accurate description of what it does to you it's impossible, and I'm pretty well gifted to gab.

And neither can you tell anybody what it's like when you're sick. I can tell about all those little creatures when you're sick, you can tell them, "I was nauseous and I had diarrhea and I had cramps . . ."

SAL: But still—

JUDY: Maybe there was convulsions too, but you can't tell it. If you wanted to set a child down, a teen-ager, and tell him about the horrors of it, you couldn't tell him, and God knows, we've been through it a million times. Every one of us have been sick almost as much as we've been fixed, but there's no way you could tell him. There's no way you could make it bad enough to impress them.

Listen, let me tell you something. We go through a lot of physical pain. We hurt—believe me—we hurts down to the marrow. Every bone we got, but still, that physical pain, I could take it from now on if I didn't have to go through this part, the mental part. The mental anguish that you can't show nobody. You can't take a picture of that, you can't even paint a picture of that.

SAL: I'd describe it this way: say you peel two layers of your skin off and there's the last layer of your skin, open, and you just rub it. Well, that's how your nerves are, right out there, and it's like you rub them real hard. That's the kind of feeling, that's the only way I can describe it. I feel like I'm split.

JUDY: One time years ago Mama took me to a psychiatrist—she thought I was crazy. I was, but this psychiatrist described it as the coating on this here wire, like the coating on the wire of the tape recorder you got. All this rubber coating is wrapped around all these little raw naked wires. Well, in our nervous system that coating is drugs, 'cause when we've been on the stuff so long it coats our nerves and makes us able to stand everything, but when we don't have it, then we've just got a bunch of raw jagged nerves there. Just open for everything—open, susceptible to anything.

MARGIE: Just naked.

JUDY: Just naked.

SAL: But still, you know—

JUDY:—but still even all those words, they don't tell you nothing.

SAL: There's one little girl that's here, she ain't but nineteen years old. She's had a few shots of Dilaudid. She's never had a habit, but she thinks she can mess with stuff every day or every other day or so and she'll never get hooked. And I told her, "You just ain't never had no habit yet."

MARGIE: The first one ain't no snapper anyway.

JUDY: Didn't you, when you was a kid, didn't you think, "Well, ain't you a dope for not trying that stuff?"

MARGIE: Uh huh. And you breeze right through the first habit like it was nothing.

SAL: That little girl got up in the A.M. and swore to God that she would get out of here and shoot dope and not have a habit, not get a habit, and I told her, "I don't believe that."

MARGIE: I don't either. You can't do it.

JUDY: I don't see how she can say that, it's not feasible. I know I can't jack with it and not get hooked. But, see, I had the same idea she did. Every time I got out or every time I punched it [escaped] from these joints, I always said, "Well, I'm just going to try it just one time to see if it was as fine as it was when I went away." That one is all it takes.

SAL: When I got out of here the last time I waited three months, and then got a supply of Dilaudid from this druggist in Oklahoma. My old man and I both. We were clean. We wasn't gonna shoot no dope. All right, we was just gonna shoot this little bitty bottle of D. So we shot this bottle of Dilaudid. Okay. We come to Houston, and by this time we both got ourselves a pretty good yen. We don't have a real habit, but we got ourselves a good yen. After we get back in Houston we start shooting paregoric to get the sick off of us. I don't like paregoric: it burns your veins (I can't even fix my arm here anymore), it burns your veins out. I don't like the flash behind it. If I'm gonna shoot dope, I'm gonna shoot dope, and so I started pushing dope.

So here I sit.

And there you are, for an example. I mean, here I am. We were doing real good till I just happened to run into this square druggist with all this Dilaudid.

JUDY: And you know right there I don't think she could have passed that up if she'd been off ten years.

Why?

It's the feeling of "I can beat 'em. Here's a chance to beat 'em." She could have had her home, her family, and everything, but I don't think she could have passed it up. I don't think I could have, or that other one either.

What's the longest you stayed clean outside?

Well, not long. Maybe just long enough to go home and lay down and kick.

SAL: What about when you was working in that joint there when I came over and ran into you. You'd been joy-popping, but you didn't have a habit.

JUDY: I wasn't hooked, but I was constantly waiting for somebody to drive up with my dope. I was off about three weeks that time. That's about the only time I can really remember, because I was gonna say six months when I had the kid, but I wasn't really off, I had a stomach habit, I had a codeine habit. I was squaring. My old man was working, going to work. I packed his lunch every day and put two bottles of Costamil in it. When he come home at night I had his supper ready and I had two bottles of Costamil on the table and a cake in the oven.

And we was squaring it, really.

We'd get up in the morning and drink our two bottles apiece. We would do it just like we were on stuff. We'd have our wake-ups because the drugstores aren't open at five or six in the morning before he went to work. We'd get out in the evening and get our little bottles together. A lot of times me and James would be sitting there at night and he'd say, "Well, I just want one more bottle." We'd save all those bottles because it's a syrupy substance, you know, and it clings to the bottle. After you drink a bottle, after it set there, there'd be a little bit left, and we'd pour that out of each bottle. Can you imagine that? I know it sounds—

SAL:—it's just like when you run out of stuff and you shoot the cotton. It's dry and you gotta wet it and mash it and everything.

JUDY: That Costamil was too much.

What was the most per day a habit ever cost you?

I couldn't really say because it all depends on what I was making. If I made $25, I spent it on that, if I made $150 or $200, I spent it all for stuff. You can never tell what a day's gonna be like.

We were pushing stuff in this little garage apartment which set back from this big house. We'd been pushing about three weeks in this particular spot. I was laying in on the bed and James was sitting on the porch, and I had my little sister over there and they were sitting out there eating ice cream. James looked down the driveway and he said he'd seen the Man coming up the driveway, a couple of men strolling up the driveway, you know. It could have been anybody, but he knew it was the police, and if he got up all of a sudden he was taking a chance on one of them shooting him. So he sent the child in there to tell me that the police were coming.

My sister said, "Get up! Brother said the police are coming." When she said that, I was reading a book and I had some stuff and I kinda just went to my pants with it. I had on some shorty pjs and they busted in right after I put the dope in my pants. They told me to get up and put my clothes on and do it in front of them, so of all things I grabbed a pair of those things that zip up in front. You step in them and you pull them over, kinda like coveralls and look like culottes. Can you imagine why I should grab something like that with dope on me? I don't know, just panic I guess; I'm not real smart. Well, anyway, I put those on. I had to put them on in front of them. And I still got the dope right here between my legs. I know that when the matron at the jail tells me to undress it's going to just fall out.

They let us take my sister to my mother's, then they took us on to jail. When we got to the booking office, as luck would have it, they were booking a couple of winos and they was giving them a lot of shit. They was wrestling, all of them, and they was whupping this wino stud and this gal was trying to whup them for whupping her man. Just a big commotion. They sent one of the uniform cops over to watch these people. "We'll get all this taken care of," he says.

While he was doing it, man, you would have thought I had an advanced case of tuberculosis. Man, I just went to coughing. The whole time I was coughing I was unzipping them all the way down in order to get the dope around to the back and get it stashed. I finally managed it. When I raised back up I was in a cold sweat. But I raised back up and looked at James and told him, "I've got it stashed. If they don't glove [examine the rectum] me, I'm through."

And I did it. I got into jail with it. I think I had twenty or twenty-five caps.

I walked in that jailhouse and there was a batch of sick dope fiends up there and they was, oh, man, sick. Moaning, "I'm so sick."

I told them, "You all better just kinda get yourselfs together. We'll try and get you straightened out . . ."

Dirty Rodriguez was in there: oh, she was just tickled to death.
Have you ever overdosed?

JUDY: God! What dope fiend hasn't.

SAL: You all won't believe this, but I ain't ever been overfixed.

MARGIE: Never?

SAL: Just on coke one time. But then I wasn't overfixed, it got to messing with my heart.

MARGIE: I once had worms and fuzzy things on me.

We just made this town where we hit the hospital; papers estimated it at $20,000. Me and this other girl flew back from Tampa and the two boys drove in. Before we caught the plane they're out there scraping at the bottles, cleaning things up. This girl and I are sitting in the car and by that time I'd done graduated from a teaspoon to a big spoon. We made their big supply. We had eleven of the five-ounce deals of coke, on the twelfth the seal was broken but there was just a little bit out of it. And we had cube morphine, footballs, quarter-grains and sixteenths of Dilaudid. Before the guys came back to the car I took the teaspoon and dipped it down in this coke bottle and put it in a big spoon, then I throwed a grain of morphine in there. I shot half of it and was going to wait a few minutes and shoot the rest.

The other girl sees what I'm doing but she's busy with her own deal. She hit the joint [hypodermic syringe] and knocked it out of the vein and by the time she got herself in, I'm already into a thing. So she starts hollering for Jack and Charley and they come running into the car.

Charley said he threw a grain of morphine into the skin. The third grain he put in there, halfway through, I started coming around. He started to slap me. But I can remember seeing all these worms and bugs and things. And they was trying to get me out of the car to walk me. I was fighting them, I wouldn't get out.

He said later, "The first thing you said, girl, when you opened your eyes, was 'Daddy, let's fix.' "

SAL: The last time I was fixed was when I got out of jail in Dallas. I didn't mean to fix, I meant to kill myself 'cause that was the only reason I wanted out you know. I wanted to overfix 'cause I knew I was coming down here for this number, this life sentence.

Paul cursed me for five or six days afterwards, but I cussed him for saving me.

What happened, I'd been locked up for three months in the Dallas jail and he said, "Sal, don't take too much of this." It was right straight out of Mexico. It was black, they hadn't even cut it, it was his own personal dope. "Just take a little. Won't you just shoot my cotton?"

I said, "I won't shoot no damn cotton. I want a shot of dope."

So he give me just a little bit, just a matchhead. I put it in the spoon and when he wasn't looking I went and got me some more. I thought, "This is just as good a time as any."

When I come to they had torn my clothes off of me and had me in the grub ditch.

Paul was saying, "This silly sonofabitch."

And Raymond said, "Don't be cursing her, goddamn. You'd be trying to kill yourself too if you was facing what she is now."

And they was cursing each other and cursing me, and I waked up and said, "Won't you both leave me alone, goddamnit."

I looked down and saw I had no clothes on, and Paul said, "The bitch is gonna live." They threw me in the back of the Lincoln and brought me back to Houston. I didn't know nothing for two days. But I didn't want no dope. I didn't want no dope for the next three or four days.

Always, always you're thinking: I've been unlucky, so luck's gonna be with me this time. And I'll just try and get me one fix, and then you say that again a day or two later. And then I'll just get me another one and later, even if I'm going to face facts, I'm hooked. But I keep telling myself, if I'll just be a little bit cool I'll beat 'em. Especially when I'm high, then I *know* I can beat 'em.

MARGIE: In AA the other day the question was raised about what made us return to the penitentiary, and I told them, "Because I love dope."

They said, "Do you think that you'll ever get over all this?"

I said, "No. I'll never quit loving dope, but I hope that I have matured enough to know that I have got to find some other way to dig a kick other than through dope because I can't do any more time. And then also I went ahead to tell them that maybe the reason that we continue to return to the joint is hoping that we eventually will show the laws don't make any difference and that they'll go ahead and find this out and legalize it.

> *You said you love dope. But didn't you say before that after you're hooked again you're taking it mostly just to be normal?*

That's right, it's true.

> *How do you put those two together?*

I don't really know. It's a heck of a thing. I guess you love up all that goes with it. All the excitement. Maybe we're even a little geared. And maybe we're masochists and love to be punished . . .

SAL: I love when I face reality, that's what I love the best.

MARGIE: See, I like sleeping till twelve and one o'clock in the day. Jumping out there and making me a little money and running to the connections. It's all a big kick to me, I guess.

SAL: You know, this reality bit, facing reality: I don't know, but it seems like that most junkies, it seems like we see reality in its harshest. And it's not like the bills are coming due Friday, the rent's got to be paid where a square, they say, it seems like they just say, "The Lord will provide," or "Something will happen" or "I can go over to Peter to pay Paul." But we don't do that. We say if *we* don't get it, there we are. We see it just like it is.

MARGIE: And we jump out there and get it.

SAL: And so there's all that responsibility on us that none of us were mature enough to accept to begin with.

> *That's kind of ironic, isn't it? You've told me you don't like to face reality and here you are dealing with a reality that is so much harder than the one you're getting away from.*

I don't know. I just know that if I'm on stuff I make more money, I'm more on my feet, I'm myself more. I like myself when I'm on a natural.

> *You're more acceptable to yourself?*

Uh huh.

MARGIE: You mean when you're on the natural or when you're on a fix?

SAL: Yeah, when I'm fixed.

> *You mean when you're natural with a fix?*

That's it. When I first start out, well, I don't care what happens because I know everything's going to be all right anyway. You know, 'cause I'm fixed right then. But when I get a hook, then I worry. I do face reality when I've got a habit, but still I don't call it facing reality. In other words, I don't like the natural.

MARGIE: You're like me: you love that dope and that's the only thing to it.

SAL: But I never—you can ask Judy—I never did like dope as much as Mona. Like a lot of dope fiends do. And like they'll get out and scuffle, a lot of times, and I'll sit there and I'll think. I knew if I'd be by myself I'd stay home. Now if somebody else is around with me, that's different. Judy can be around me and she'd be my drive, you know. Her old man and my old man might be laying in bed and they're gonna kick their habit, but she and I, we get up and go find some dope.

Judy doesn't look too happy about what you just said.

JUDY: Listen: I am searching. Believe me, I don't *want* it, but I *can't* get away from it, you know.

SAL: That's it right there.

JUDY: I want help, I am open for anything.

SAL: A dope fiend is a searcher.

JUDY: Well, baby, have you ever licked the dope habit on the street? Of your own volition?

SAL: I have. One time, baby, in my life.

JUDY: See, I'm like a different kind. I'd run home to Mommy all the time and lay down because I got tired of scuffling. And when I'm scuffling, believe me, there ain't no harder scuffler on the streets. Believe me. I will get it together. When I get tired I may wake up one morning out of the clear blue and I am tired and I'll go home and just sit down.

SAL: Well, Judy, that's the same as with me, only it's different. It's just getting to you asking what's it all about, what's it for. What is life? Why was I born and where am I going? To a grave, man. That's all there is to it.

JUDY: But, shit, even though I feel that way about it, I can't see no end. 'Cause all them times, I went home and laid down for them two or three weeks and got clean and got to eating good and gained my weight back and everything, and Mommy was ready all them times to put me through any kind of schooling, anything I wanted. It didn't do no good. It seemed like what I wanted was another shot of dope. So where is the answer? Is it here? Am I mentally sick?

SAL: Yes.

JUDY: I got to be. And yet I pride myself as being a fairly intelligent person, you know. And I know that that's real.

SAL: Life is a rib.

JUDY: And every time that we try and talk about this, it shakes me because it makes me see more. Here we are, just going round and around in a vicious circle.

SAL: It's a big waste. That's all it is, you know. Because really and truly, like if we were out and got with this woman that's got this thing going in New York [Marie Nyswander and the methadone maintenance project], that's our out. If we could go and get this legally. We could work even.

JUDY: You know what? Let's just get down to the nitty-gritty.

SAL: What?

JUDY: If we make this woman and she's willing to do this for us, we would figure some way to fuck her out of her stuff.

SAL: Well, if she's giving us everything we need, what do we want to fuck her for?

JUDY: She'd give us methadone and we'd want Dilaudid. If we had it *all* we'd be needing more. We'd go down to the corner and get some stuff. Bruce, does she run into this with the experiment she's going through?

No. It seems the way she gives them such a large dose of methadone that it just carries them.

JUDY: Maybe there *is* enough somewhere.

MARGIE: There is. Because that's what I was using when I jumped out last time. That's why I feel that methadone is one of the most ferocious habits that I ever fixed. We couldn't get Dilaudid or any other kind of drugstore stuff to take the sick off because the methadone was so much stronger. We had got this habit on us and nothing else would fix.

Maybe that's why they're not interested in heroin: it's too puny in comparison.

SAL: Yeah. The heroin you get, that stuff, it's been cut and so messed up with you're really not getting anything.

The point is, if we get say a pill for five cents and we're staying sensible enough upstairs here to work and take care of our home and our family and everything like that, what need would there be for anything else as long as we were satisfied. Like you and your Costamil, you know that was cheap.

JUDY: I wonder. Can those things, like the light and gas and rent, can they become important enough to be important to you, an old dope fiend? Can anything be important enough to you, except stuff?

SAL: If you've got stuff you don't have to scuffle.

JUDY: That's the whole thing, that's what I keep saying. Somewhere there has got to be something that is more important. You know what? I lost a son, I lost a daughter, and my mother is gray. That's what I've lost. That is what I've lost behind the stuff. That ain't been enough. That ain't been enough to bring me. That has not been enough to bring me. Can you imagine that not being enough to bring somebody?

I hear a lot of people say, "Well, I've got my kids. My kid'll help, I'm gonna depend on my kids. My kid'll help me kinda straighten out and stay off the stuff." That's the biggest bunch of bullshit that I've ever hear. Now listen: that's it.

MARGIE: They didn't keep you off when you was out there.

SAL: One of mine used to stash my dope for me, the one that's a Federal agent now.

JUDY: To me, that's lying to yourself. I've been lying to myself for thirty-one years and I'm sick of it. I'm thirty-one years old and I don't have anything to show for it but three penitentiary numbers. Some recommendation. Nothing.

SAL: You've reached the point, you are searching. Before, you could say, "Fuck it, man, I'm going to go out and shoot me some more dope." But now you've started asking, "Why do I want to shoot dope."

JUDY: I know it sometimes. But I do nothing.

SAL: Then you are really searching.

JUDY: I can't. I had cancer; I had a complete hysterectomy from it. I can't have no more kids and I can't get my own kids back. The boy is dead and girl is the same as dead. She don't know me. When I lose my mother—time will take care of that because I darn near drove her to her grave—well, then, that's all else I have to lose. Self-respect, pride, that went with all them tricks. So I've got to come up, I can't go no further down.

SAL: You can go to the grave. That's the only way.

JUDY: Down, down, I've been there.

3. Prison

Prison is the only garbage dump we have so repulsive we encircle it with barbed wire and a wall of stone.

You get there in a closed van, and the doors of the van don't open until the big iron gates have clanged shut behind you. You aren't released until a group of old men, like no old men you ever knew, decide you are a nice, tractable person now, or, if not that, that they have detained you the maximum number of years the law permits. For years you do not touch the hand of a woman or child, wear clothing of your own choice, go somewhere on the spur of the moment; you don't eat what you feel like eating, talk to whomever you'd like to talk, read a magazine you happen to see on the stand and find interesting. That is because there are no women and children in prison (save those beyond the wire grills of visiting rooms), and all clothing is the same in prison, and there are those walls and barbed wire and bars to keep you from going anywhere at all; it is because the only food you get is what the mess hall manages to set out that day or what you can hustle on the side; it is because conversations in prison are guarded or tight or secret, and there are no telephones with which you may have casual chats with casual friends, and there are no magazine stands on which to find that potentially interesting magazine.

Prison is a place where all sorts of things are not there.

What is there hurts: sameness, bars, guards on towers with guns, guards walking the halls with clubs who find you strange and alien and perhaps even hateful and evil because you've been judged a criminal by a group the state insists represents your peers. They look at you with fear or hate or contempt, perhaps only because you're a nigger or spic, or perhaps just because they don't know what is going on in your head, and that alone is frightening enough to make them hate you or fear you. And you them—hate and fear are always bilateral affairs. In addition to the guards are the people with whom you must live—other convicts: suspicious, mean, guarded, treacherous, and perhaps as frightened as you, surely as mistrusting as you.

The days are short, the nights interminable. In most prisons in this country there is little for inmates to do, so men spend up to eighteen hours each day locked in small cells, waiting to be tired enough to sleep, waiting for sleep to descend long enough to break up the boring run of days in which almost nothing happens, save an occasional letter from home, a fight to watch, an argument to have, a hustle to make.

Prison work is usually demeaning and boring: inmates are paid humiliating wages (in New York, 30 cents a day; in California, up to a dollar for a very few; in Texas, nothing at all) for tedious and often exhausting and usually uninstructive work (picking cotton, stamping out license plates on an ancient machine in extreme heat, pushing a mop, and—yes—even breaking rocks). Some idealistic prison officials say prison labor teaches some men work habits they never learned outside, they say what is important is the pattern of work and not the character of it. That may sometimes be true, but surely not very often.

A good inmate is one who makes no trouble for the institution. In some places he may do whatever he wants within the walls—have homosexual affairs, run gambling concessions, deal dope, brutalize his fellows, peddle soft jobs—but as long as he is tactful about it, as long as he is quiet and makes no trouble the administration cannot ignore, he will not be bothered by guards and will be paroled relatively early in his sentence. A bad inmate is one who makes ripples, someone who complains about treatment or food or lack of educational opportunity or humiliation by guards; a very bad inmate is one who talks such things up among his fellows; an outrageously bad inmate is one who suggests to his fellows that they do not have to submit to such treatment, who tells them the courts may have sentenced them to incarceration but that does not mean the prison authorities have any duty or right to capriciously punish them further. Such inmates do the maximum amount of time the law permits; authorities—parole boards and such— feel they are not fit to be released in society, for they have not learned how to get along.

To operate most smoothly and efficiently, prisons, like nunneries, require the destruction or suspension of the private self. All such institutions, as Erving Goffman has pointed out (*Asylums*, New York, 1961), have a variety of devices which have ostensible functions in the community but really serve to establish power and identify impotence: hair is shaved, mail is censored, private effects are open to inspection by officials who are never required to justify their inquisitiveness; there is no appeal from punishment, no challenge of official truth. Elaborate official rationales justify all those policies and procedures, but the real purpose is to say who can talk and who must listen, who is boss and who is not, who can order and who must submit. In all such institutions qualities and options necessary for survival in the outside world—independence of mind and spirit, privacy, choice-making—are specifically repressed, regularly punished. The institution cannot survive those things, and one significant effect of that is that inmates who learn to get on well in the institution often unlearn how to survive in the outside world.

Prison is perhaps necessary to protect society from the violent, but no more than 10 percent of any prison's population is really violent, and most of those people should be receiving psychiatric help (if that can be made to work) rather than simple lockup anyway. Prison is supposed to reform, but who—after all the evidence to the contrary —can suppose men are reformed by being locked for years on end in six-by-nine-foot cages in communities where homosexuality is a norm, mistrust a necessity, and hate a social commodity? What kind of foolishness informs a parole board which assumes a person who adjusts well to *that* sort of community is fit to come back outside, and that someone who challenges it should be welded away forever?

"I know of no institution," Texas Department of Corrections Director George Beto said, "unless it be organized Christianity, which has shown a greater reluctance to measure the effectiveness of its varied programs than has corrections." Almost everyone—observers, honest prison administrators, convicts—feels American corrections are a dismal failure. We have the longest prison sentences of any more-or-less civilized country, and we have the greatest problems with our prisoners and ex-prisoners. Surely something is screwed up.

The problem is one well known in public policy: the lawmakers say they want the institution to do one thing, the people who run the institutions know that isn't what the lawmakers mean at all. The lawmakers say they want reform or progress, but there is money only for hardware and guards; the lawmakers say the prisons should make better people, but only take notice of what goes on when someone escapes or goes berserk. No warden has ever been fired because no inmate was helped in any noticeable way while under his care, but quite a few have been fired because some inmates in their care chose to go over the wall or burn down buildings.

There are many books you can read to discover theories of how prison society structures itself. For our purposes here, we need only recognize that prison *does* generate a society, a culture, there are norms and violations of those norms, some of them inmates' and some of them authorities'. Violation is sanctioned just as violation in the free world is sanctioned.

In theory, a prison is supposed to simultaneously serve several functions. It is supposed to deter (its presence is supposed to keep those among us of weak moral strength from actions we might otherwise commit); it is supposed to rehabilitate (within its walls those who have, for whatever reason, transgressed society's norms are presumably shown the error of their ways and retooled so they can live outside in more acceptable and satisfactory fashion); it is supposed to punish.

Only the last—punish, the function that requires no parenthetical clarification—is clearly fulfilled. Imprisonment itself is a terrible punishment—one is denied most normal human intercourse, most normal human options—but in most states there are further punishments within the walls.

No one in the section that follows talks about rehabilitation. Some of the speakers talk of being tired of lockup and perhaps quitting crime because of that, but for most it is punishment and punishment only, punishment in the time served, exacerbated by punishment within the prison itself. Few people *inside* the walls take seriously the notion of rehabilitation; for most, prison is to punish, restrain, scare. Most other efforts are distant ideals, nice to talk about and consider, but impossible to effect.

The people who go to prison are those who didn't have enough money or luck or style or social status to stay out. Professional criminals are rarely caught; when they are, they tend to have good lawyers and they don't go to prison for very long. Middle class criminals tend to get brief or suspended sentences. "Last year in Federal court in Manhattan," wrote Glynn Mapes in the *Wall Street Journal* (September 9, 1970), "a partner in a stock brokerage firm pleaded guilty to an indictment charging him with $20 million illegal trading with Swiss banks. He hired himself a prestigious lawyer, who described the offense in court as comparable to breaking a traffic law. Judge Irving Cooper gave the stockbroker a tongue-lashing, a $30,000 fine, and a suspended sentence. A few days later the same judge heard the case of an unemployed Negro shipping clerk who pleaded guilty to stealing a television set worth $100 from an interstate shipment in a bus terminal. Judge Cooper sentenced him to a year in jail."

One might argue that the above says many who should go to prison don't, but it doesn't say that the ones who do go shouldn't. There is no way to argue that, because we don't know what prison really does, what its effects really are, and without that information we cannot evaluate its performance, not if we subscribe to the usual list of functions prison is supposed to serve. Prison makes sense only if we regard it as a place to punish losers, a place to punish fuckups.

Prison population reflects only that portion of the criminal world that isn't smart, rich, dishonest, or lucky enough to stay out of jail. If it were possible to make it criminal to be poor, dumb, black, or anything like that, such things would be on the books. As it is, there are alternative laws and options in the way the law enforcement mechanism works that manage to collar those who are not in the mainstream of American life.

Largely, a state prison is populated by people who are not too bright (and who, therefore, do not steal very well); impulse criminals (whose offending act reflects not a life pattern but a set of extreme circumstances—most murderers are in this category); chronic convicts (a large group of people who stay out for short periods only because they don't know how to get along anywhere *but* in prison, and who seem to spend their criminal hours out of prison not seeking profit so much as unembarrassing reincarceration); some habitual offenders (those who can't manage to stay out of trouble but who still base their value systems in the world outside); and a rather small number of competent working criminals who had a run of bad luck or moment of carelessness.

Prison is like any other community, and every community has its losers, its bums, its second-raters; every community has its in and out crowds, those who, though clearly part of the community, aren't nearly as much a part as other people might be. This of course does not get one very far along the way toward ontological definition, but it does have the deceptive quality of doing just that. One of the easiest ways of knowing who you are is to know who (and what) you are not.

In the free world I suspect Midwest farmers know exactly who the bad guys of this world are; whenever they have doubts they have only to tune in Paul Harvey or Spiro Agnew to get current battle-line positions and uniform standards in clear and unambiguous detail. Hippies know too—watch them when a stranger in a suit and necktie starts walking around the scene. The rich have the poor, the white have the black, the fast have the slow, the smart the dumb. Everybody has his less-than-me somewhere. I guess somewhere you get to the end of the line, the place where there is no one upon whom you may conceptually shit, and at that point you either dive into the bottle or needle—or you redefine the roles so you have one too.

Anyway: prison has that also. There are good guys and bad guys, hip guys and square guys, "in" guys and "out" guys, winners and losers, high and low, all those ephemeral and trivial and absolutely essential dichotomies.

The most obvious we/they in prison—the guards and the convicts—is so basic it isn't enough to structure relationships upon, and it is so bichromatic it would make for a very boring society indeed were there not other forms of discrimination. It is, however, an imperfect we/they. Prison, like any other totalitarian political structure, requires a certain amount of consent from the governed if it is to operate smoothly. When accommodation fails, the system stops functioning, and we have either the bloody suppression which occurred at Attica, or the changes in the system which occurred in New Jersey prisons late in 1971.

Ideally, the guards are guards, the convicts are convicts, the treatment people are treatment people, and each has his job and fulfills his role. I know of no place—except death rows—where that is the actual condition. There are usually too few treatment people to make much difference. Accommodations are made—sometimes to the entire population, sometimes to special prisoners who, in return for power over their fellow prisoners, agree to help the custodians do the custodying.

A very small number of inmates manage to have some status because of things they did outside or because of who they were outside. This works not so much because an outside reputation generates respect of a great order, but because anyone good at the business or noteworthy outside got to meet a lot of people, some of whom are helpful inside; one is a member of the "in" crowd before he arrives simply because a portion of his crowd is always there, albeit on a rotating basis.

In prison a person may for the first time find himself in a social and ecological construct where his personal dimensions are not isolating, debilitating, humiliating, or disqualifying. So many others in prison are subliterate and underskilled that such things hardly matter. Many men adjust to the prison environment much *too* well—no matter how bad or brutal the prison—and do whatever they can, after release, to get themselves back in. Prison may be the first environment such a person has experienced where he is assured of three more-or-less decent meals a day, a bed to sleep in at night, in a heated room when it is cold outside, clothes adequate to confront the weather should he have to go outside, and an occasional visit to a doctor who may even be competent. The only thing obviously missing is women, and there are ways of compensating for that. For such inmates, and I suspect there are quite a few of them, the comforts are too much to miss and they will do whatever they can do or have to do to get themselves back inside.

The inmates who talk in this section articulate none of the political awareness that resulted in the atrocities at institutions like Attica and San Quentin during the past two years. That awareness is new; at least, the articulation of it is new. For most of these speakers, the concern is not how to challenge the system or attack the system, but how to find a comfortable slot within the system, how to do time as easily and pleasantly and briefly as possible. Some talk about inside hustles, some about escapes, some about learning to live the life inside. For all, the problem is how to get along or how to get out, and the focus is the prison itself.

Harry: "A penitentiary is like a prisoner-of-war camp . . ."

I didn't like living in a cell at first. But now, I think it's the only place to live because you can get away from everything.

When I first came down here I was seventeen years old. My philosophy then was that every police character needed to come to the penitentiary as a necessary part of his education, just to see what it was like. And I thought that a person who shot dope was a good guy, or if they was a hijacker they was a big-time crook. I've changed my ideas about this. My ideas have changed considerably in the last thirteen years since I've been in the penitentiary. I'm thirty years old now, by the way.

I used to like to be surrounded by groups of people and laugh and play and giggle. It didn't bother me being in a dormitory. I thought that's where I was happy. If you wanted to do something you wasn't supposed to, if you didn't want the boss to see you, you hung blankets along the sides of your bed and just crawled inside those blankets where they couldn't see you and you did it.

It's not that way anymore. You don't have to worry that the boss will see you. You have to worry about what the convicts see.

In a cell they close the doors on everybody and you've got some privacy. And that's what I like. I like to get in and think about things. Meditate you might say, or just lay there and listen to the jazz on the radio. In fact, in my cell I'd rather have the door locked than the door open. I guess maybe I feel secure like that. I don't really know what the deal is on it.

If you ever look out a window in this place and can't see a bar, you're hurting.

Hurting. Do many guys get like that?

Numerous people get like that. In fact I'd say 90 percent of the people down here are like that. They look like they're in their element, like they're fish swimming in the sea, like they wouldn't have it any other way.

Me, I don't like it down here.

When I look out the window I can see a bar there and beyond the bar I can see a fence out there and I know that there's something better out there than there is in here.

Now I have tried to make the best of what I have in here. I enjoy an education. I may not ever do anything with an education, but I enjoy knowing things when I can talk to people about them. People that I think are my peers. I don't enjoy talking to people that I don't believe are my peers. But I do enjoy just chopping it up, kicking it around and seeing what other people seem to think. And you can't do much of that down here.

What bugs you most about the place?

The incompetent administration around the place.

I like things to be orderly. You might say I'm a conservative, I like the status quo. If something's going smooth I like that.

There was a sociologist down here one time and he said that I was a professional convict. He said I came down and did things as easily as I could and tried to stay out of all the wrecks I could so I could get out quicker without having been in any trouble in the penitentiary. So I could get out and do my messing up outside. Well, he's got a point there, you know, 'cause I don't like it down here. If I protest too much down here I'm going to be here a lot longer than I should be. So I try to get out.

He was weird. He gave me the impression that he thought a man, especially a man with a rather long sentence, should come down here and mess up quite a bit the first year he's here. Then he should straighten up and become a model prisoner so the admission people could say, "Well, lookie here, we have reformed this man. We have made him fit for society again." Whether they have or haven't.

Some people don't just make it, they kind of like it. Get institutionalized. You know, there's a lot of security in a place like this for a person. If a person is insecure in the first place, there's a lot of security in here for him. They'll tell you when to get up, they'll tell you when to go to bed, when to eat, when to work. They'll do your laundry for you. You don't have to worry about anything else. It's all taken care of for you. And there's lots of jobs for a man down here with power and authority. It's well known that power will corrupt and absolute power will corrupt absolutely. There's convicts get into positions of power down here and they get to where they like it and it corrupts them.

Then all of a sudden the institution throws them out in the hard, cruel world out there. I know it's not a bed of roses out there. But the institution will throw these people that have been running things out and they will get out there and they can't run it anymore. And it hurts them. So they come back where they can run it.

These people are institutionalized. These are the kind of people that can't see the bars right here. They don't know that that's a bar.

But *I* know that that's a bar.

A penitentiary is like a prisoner-of-war camp. The officials are the enemy and the inmates are captured. They're on one side and we're on the other.

They're not necessarily *always* the enemy. Here lately they've been making a lot of attempts to help us. Some of them have, but some of the older ones that have been here, they resent it and they think it ought to be like it used to be. They say you're coddling convicts. Mainly, though, the people running it now have more interest in the inmate than they used to have. They still are very security-conscious but they are thinking a little bit more along the lines of rehabilitation.

I believe that the hardest thing about being in this penitentiary and doing time is not being able to trust your fellow inmates. And it makes it hard, you know. Everybody has to have somebody they can talk to, discuss their problems with. This is human nature and down here you can't do it because a person that you think is your friend might not be your friend, they liable to tell someone else about it and you can say some things that'll get you in lots of trouble, and not really mean anything bad. You just saying it just to get it off your chest.

That's been a hassle, I think, in every prison I've ever been in. This thing that most of the time you just never know who you're talking to.

That's right. I came down here in 1955 and it wasn't as bad then as it is now. Seems like they indoctrinate these new people somehow. Snitches has something done to them. Anybody that'll, you know, tell secrets, they'd do something to 'em, convicts would. And you had a lot of people stuck together. It was kind of like in the war, you know. You'd get caught by the enemy, well, you had, the convicts made believe the inmates were prisoners and the administration was the enemy and you had to tell the enemy nothing. But it's changed now.

Why has it changed?

Well, things are changing all over. I believe it has a lot to do with the younger people that are coming to the penitentiary. They're changing a lot, and then, the older a man gets, too, the more he's got to lose. The young ones, they teaching them in Gatesville and places like that. So different standards than they had when I grew up. And the older ones, they have put too much pressure on them. They say, "We'll take your good time [time off for good behavior]"—one of 'em doing maybe twenty-five years, got ten years up on it—"if you don't tell me this, I'm going to take your good time and you'll do all your twenty-five years." And a man forty or forty-five years old, you know, he says, "My gosh. I got fifteen more years: that'll make me sixty. When I get out I won't be good for anything." And that's a lot of pressure to put on a man, and he succumbs to it. The young ones, they've just been taught different. It's just like outside, the people outside. Society's mores are changing. Even now, things are a lot looser than they used to be outside, a lot easier. People my age and a little bit older, things weren't too easy when we were born, you know. Not many people in labor made the upper lower class and the lower middle class you might call 'em, and things were hard and people kind of stuck together. Since then, things have got easier, as I said, and people just don't have loyalties like they used to, or stick together, outside or inside.

This place is like a fishbowl.

I don't accept anybody here at face value until I've known them for a while. After four or five months in this atmosphere you see every move they make. They can't make a move that you can't see, and if they're doing anything that is questionable to your mores, you know that you'd better not fool with them. And that's the way I usually tell.

You wanted to know why I trusted you. Well, it's because Jimmy said you were all right. There are a few people I've known for a long time, like him. There's not over five on this whole farm that I would take anybody's word for about somebody else, though. When they say somebody's a good guy I still have to see for myself unless one of

these four or five people told me he was all right. And even then I'd be
kinda careful around him till I got to know him.

Ray: "The hole.
Oh, the hole . . ."

The camps at Angola [Louisiana state prison farm] are separated and
of course they're completely segregated, black from white. They also
segregate the first-timers from the second-, third-, fourth-timers, and
lifers. I was in the first-offenders' camp.

I still can't figure out why they call it a penitentiary. It's nothing
but a huge farm as I recall it, some 13,000 acres. The biggest part of it
is planted in sugarcane. There's a sugarcane refinery there where they
do their own refining. The place is really pretty much self-contained.
They grow all their own vegetables, they have a large dairy farm, do
their own butchering. I understand that the yearly cane crop is quite a
big thing, money-wise, for the state.

Things have changed a great deal since I was there, they're supposed to be better now. I heard when I was there that they were better
than they'd been before that, so that must have been quite some place
in the old days.

When I was there they had convict guards. I mean that the men
that guarded the convicts, the men who carried the shotguns and
rifles, were convicts the same as we were. I believe Arkansas has the
same arrangement and a few other southern states did too. I guess
they found it a lot cheaper than hiring guards.

Most of the men who did that were men with a great deal of time.
It always seemed odd to me, but there was little instance of any of
them running off although they had plenty of chance to. But when we
went out in the field to work they set up what was called a guard line
with anywhere from four to ten guards, all armed with rifles and shotguns and all of them convicts as we were. They had their own living
facilities, their own dining room and all. They never mixed with us at
all.

Occasionally, to use the slang that was used down there, when
one of them did "fall"—in other words, he broke a rule of some sort

while a guard—he'd very seldom be put in the same camp where he'd been guarding. I know of one or two instances where it did happen, and in one instance the man was dead within less than a week after he came back on a regular job.

I know that even in other penitentiaries today, even up North, when an ex-convict does come in and they find out that he has been a guard in one of these southern penitentiaries he's told not to say anything about it to the other men, they try to keep it under cover as much as possible because of the circumstances.

Were those convict guards harder on the men than free-world guards?

I would say very much so. I guess it's probably a mental thing in our society, they are pretty sure that what they are doing is wrong. The only reason they're doing it is, well, it's not for money because if I remember correctly they only paid the convict guards there $10 a month. Of course their food was better and their living conditions were quite a bit better. The quarters were better. The only other distinction was in clothing. When I was there we still wore big stripes, the kind you see in the cartoons; the guards got to wear khaki uniforms.

But I believe the so-called square guard or the free-man guard is much more lenient, is much more inclined to go along with you than the convict guard ever would be.

Out of the 250 men in the particular camp I was in, there was only two free people working there. Sometimes there was three, but usually just the two: the captain of the camp and the particular free man who was in charge of the field work. Everything else was taken care of by convicts. Even the clerical work.

The camp I was on had two square men, they were brothers. One of them was in charge of what we call the main line, which is the line that works out in the fields in our camp, the other one was in charge of a similar line at the second-offenders' camp. They had both worked at the farm for some forty years. One of them, it was the only job he had ever had; the older brother had worked a little while in Texas at one of the farms out at Huntsville. All that time they had worked colored camps until just a year before I got there and they had been called "Mas," Big and Little Mas, which I found out later was a shortening for "master."

We were told, all of us as we came in, that that was what they wanted to be called. We were told when we entered the field, "Don't call me 'mister,' you sonofabitch. I'm Mas. It's short for master and that's the way I want it to be." Consequently, that's the way it was.

We would be marching down the road going to work while it was still dark. When we brought in our tools at night it was dark. During the summer months we worked six days a week. When it came time to cut the cane we worked seven days a week in rain or shine. Cane has to be in when it's ready or it will sour in the ground, so it's work just as long as you can go.

The physical work is hard, but like anything physical, it's not anything you can't get used to. I think really the worst part about it is the change, the attitude, the mental change that comes over a person in a situation like that. From the beginning you're not treated in any way like a human being, and you're continuously cursed. The first two or three weeks the object seems to be whether or not they can break you. If they can, they proceed to do so just as fast as they can. If not, they finally reach the point to where they finally let up on you and they find that you can take it and you can make it.

Sometimes they're pretty easy to get along with, and after a year or so I got to where I could more or less pick my job as far as the Man, the boss, was concerned. I did just as much as I pleased. There were several of us that way.

But for a lot of guys it's not. You've heard of cutting the heel strings, things of that nature. I've seen it done time and time again. There's one man that's in here now that I did time with in Louisiana who is slightly crippled now as a result of cutting his own heel tendon.

I guess it reaches the point, the work, where you finally feel, what the hell. And the food! I could go on for days about the conditions of the food.

The main diet consisted of rice and gravy or rice and red beans or hominy grits and gravy and I never in the thirty months there saw any beef, and I remember chicken about twice. Although they had a huge dairy we never saw any milk in the dining room. I'm a pretty good-sized man, I'm over six foot one and I weigh about 170; when I left there, I came out weighing 147 pounds.

There was food to be purchased in the commissary. There wasn't any limit to the amount of money you could have, but of course, as in any penitentiary, the money always seemed to be limited to a certain few.

I know of instances where arms and legs were broken in an afternoon's work—anything to be able to get into the hospital. You couldn't just check into the sick line and say, "I'm sick, I want to go to the hospital." You had to have something very definitely wrong with you, and you had to be able to prove that you were running a high fever, you had to be able to prove in some manner that you were too weak to be able to stand up and do the work. Or else it had to be something you could go right to the Man and show him, such as a cut heel-string or a broken arm or leg, something of that nature.

I remember one time, we went out across the levee right down into the Mississippi with the object of bringing whole trees and logs floating in the river to land, let them dry, cut them up, and use them for that winter as firewood. All the boilers were wood-burning boilers at that time. I don't know if you've ever seen the levee of the Mississippi that far south, but it's quite a thing, quite a construction by itself. If you can imagine it in rainy weather, trying to carry whole trees and huge logs on your shoulders and back to the top of the levee to be loaded into buggies and taken back into camp with the men not even being able to stand up under the weight, maybe reaching halfway up or further, one of them stumbling and two or three of them rolling all the way down to the river, only to be told to get up again and start again.

There were two or three of us at the time. We were trimming dead limbs and all off the trees before they were loaded. We were somewhere a way off from the main work gang and one of the boys happened to wander over and say, "Boy, the last time I fell, I sure wish I'd broken a leg. I wouldn't have to put up with this. Get into the hospital."

We were joking about it and one of us said, "Well, you want your leg broken?"

"Yeah."

"Well, we can take care of it for you."

And he thought for a minute, then he said, "I'm serious. Can you break it?"

We laid the lower part of his leg from the knee down over two logs and then dropped another one in the middle.

Word got around. Before the day was over, we'd done away with something like a half dozen arms and even more legs.

Finally the Man decided to take the whole bunch of us in before we crippled the whole field. The Man knew what was going on, but there really wasn't anything he could do about it.

I told you about how it was dark when we went to work and dark when we came back in at night. I remember time and time again when I'd eat and flop down on my bed and be covered with mud from my knees down, after working at cleaning and digging out draining ditches or even just hoeing after a particularly rainy day. Well, I'd say to myself, "I'll just lay here a minute and then I'll get down and take that shower and clean up." And next thing I'd know they'd be ringing that big bell the next morning and I'd still be laying there with the muddy pants and the muddy shoes and muddy socks still on. I'd have to pick it up and go out to work the same way. All you could do at times like that was grab your sleep when you could and try to keep going.

Of course there were what they'd call the political jobs, working in the laundry and the hospital, clerk or some particular little job on the yard, like maybe in the tailor shop or maybe something like that. But these were so few. The penitentiary's main income was derived from the cane, and therefore that's where the biggest work went into. And there was a lot of it. I've walked all over that 13,000 acres from one end to the other, going to and from work.

I couldn't tell you much about the colored camp because we were completely segregated. We were—of course—also completely segregated from the women's camp. The women's penitentiary was right on the same grounds as the men's. The women made all of our uniforms, mattress covers, and things of that nature. But I can remember one particular colored incident that might tell you something how they were there.

Any time a man tried to escape we'd be brought in immediately from the field and locked in the dormitory so that the extra guards could be sent out with the dogs. And this particular day we heard the dogs circling back. A bunch of us ran to the end of the building and looked out the windows. We could see the figure of a man, still in his stripes—you could spot those black and white stripes for twenty miles—and we couldn't see the dogs or horses yet. He ran into a patch of cane maybe four or five hundred yards from camp. One of the guard towers spotted him, and when the other guards did come in sight he yelled to them and motioned to where he'd gone into the cane and they threw a guard line around the patch of cane.

And I cannot recall, honestly, hearing anyone call in to him, asking him or telling him to come out, saying they had him surrounded and knew where he was. But I saw four get off their horses, go into the cane patch, heard the shots, and then I saw the four men drag his body out. And, as I say, I cannot recall, and couldn't at the time, hearing them tell him to come out, they were going to come in after him and . . . they just went in and shot him.

About the worst incident I can recall: I happened to be out in the yard, not working this particular day because I had blood poisoning in my left hand. I was laying around the yard when they brought a group of men over from Camp E, the second- and third-offenders' camp, to the hospital. The hospital was right next to the camp I was in. They were lined up at the gate waiting for the guard to unlock the gate and let them in. Just to the left of the line was a guard tower, it stood immediately above the line of men. And about a city block or so away, in the corner of the building, was the other guard tower.

The guard tower nearest them, the one right behind the gate, was harassing two or three men in the line. What they said I don't know, I was just laying in the grass in front of the building. I could hear the voices and I heard a commotion, and when I looked up one fellow had already started up the steps to the guard tower. When he got about halfway up the steps, the guard got out. Now the guards at the point, the ones in the corner of the square, had 30-30 rifles, and the guards in the gate tower carried twin double-barreled shotguns.

Well, he stepped down when the fellow started up the stairs and shot him in the face and chest with both barrels of that double-barreled shotgun.

He made his mistake when he emptied *both* barrels before the other guard could get to him and summon help. Even though he was shooting right into the middle of the whole bunch of them, there were some twenty-five or thirty of them, the whole bunch charged right up the stairs, drove the guard down the stairs and beat him to death right in front of the hospital.

He made his mistake, as I said, when he emptied both barrels, because then he didn't have anything to hold the others off with.

There was one old-timer there, I'll call him Charlie but that's not his real name. He came from what I understand was a pretty good old Louisiana family and got in for bank robbery and had escaped six different times and each time he was eventually brought back. When I met him, whenever he went anywhere—to the hospital or to the administration building or somewhere else—he never went with any of the other convicts, just himself and four guards. They were a little bit worried about Charlie.

He told me about the time when he was working in the fields and one of the convicts jumped a pusher. Now a pusher was a convict too, although he wore a guard's uniform. The object of his job was to go up and down the line and make sure that everybody was continually working as fast as he could. Anyway, one of the convicts jumped this pusher and gave him a pretty good beating and then he ran into the cane field.

The free man didn't want to have the guards go in after him, so he gave the pusher a cane knife and said, "Go in and get him yourself. Bring him out." He took all the other workers out and had them standing out on the row and Charlie said he heard a couple of shots fired, heard some yelling, and then they went back. He looked down into the drainage ditch and the convict who had attacked the pusher had the pusher down in the ditch and was drowning him. Putting his head under water and drowning him. And the guards were shooting at him and had evidently hit him a couple of times because the water was bloody. But it wasn't doing any good, he was hanging on pretty well.

So the man came over and got off his horse and drug him back up. And he had been hit twice. Instead of doing anything for him or sending him to the hospital and then trying him in a court as they do these days—I think most penitentiaries now have some sort of a disciplinary court—he just proceeded to beat hell out of him right there in the field, then put him up under a water wagon and let him lay there. And the man just died. He just bled to death from the two wounds.

The thing of cutting heel strings goes back years and years. I was back in the Los Angeles county jail two or three years back and I ran into an old friend and he'd been in there again and he'd also been in Texas at one of the farms out in Huntsville, on some cotton farm. And we got to talking and he mentioned a few people and did he know them, did I happen to know them, that sort of thing.

He was sitting on the top bunk and when he got down from the bunk—you've never seen such a sight in your life! One foot went one way and one foot went the other. He'd cut either his left three times and his right five times, or vice versa. Each time they caught it—it seems that if they catch him in time they can pull the tendon back down, but if not, if they wait too long and the tendon jumps back up past to the muscular part of the leg, then the man's gonna be a cripple for the rest of his life. But they had caught him, although he still had the bad scars, and he was only slightly crippled. I mean, he could get around by himself. He had done something like twelve years in Texas and six or eight in Louisiana and, as he said, this time he was going to try the West Coast joints, he'd had enough of those down South.

Remember I was mentioning Mas, the squareman we had running our field gang down there? Now he worked down there for forty years. It was the only job he'd ever had and to my knowledge the only schooling he'd had was very little, very little.

When I first went to work for him he comes on with this kick one day, asking where I was from. I consider California my home, but my father's living in New Mexico and I'd come directly out from New Mexico, so I said, "New Mexico."

"One of them goddamned greasy Mexicans," he said.

I said, "No, New Mexico's in the States."

"I know where New Mexico is, you sonofabitch. Don't tell me where goddamned Mexicans come from."

And you know, in thirty months I could not convince that man that New Mexico is in the United States, part of the continental U.S.A. He had me below that river and I was going to stay there.

Talk about stubborn. I had a nickname while I was down there, the whole time, it was "Senator." It all happened with Mas again. He kept asking me my name which I would tell him, but he couldn't pronounce it and it's not that difficult to pronounce. But he kept calling me "Bilbo." There was a senator in Mississippi, a very well-known senator, named Bilbo. One day after all this I just got sick and tired of correcting him over and over again. We were cleaning out shit ditches and I laid down my shovel and I crawled out up on top and I said, "Now, Mas, my name is not Bilbo. It's spelled—" And I spelled it out for him.

"You get your ass back in that goddamned shit ditch!" he said. "Don't you tell me what your name is. You know it: Bilbo it is. If it's good enough for a United States senator, you sonofabitch, it's good enough for you!"

So from there on, man, it was Senator. That's all you could hear across the field: "Hey, old Senator, get your ass over here."

He was, I guess, completely illiterate. They'd give him his work orders for the day written on a sheet of paper. You know, what cuts we were supposed to take care of, things like that. He'd either call me, or Whitey the waterboy, or somebody, over and say, "I forgot my goddamned glasses. Here, read this off for me." So off we'd go and we'd read his orders for him.

He had false teeth, Mas did. Both uppers and lowers. And to give you an idea of the kind of gentleman I was working under, that was supposed to be my superior: Mas chewed a little tobacco, snuff, stud, anything he could get ahold of. Just as long as it would chew, Mas chewed. But when he got through with his cud and threw it out, he'd just walk over to the nearest ditch, draining ditch or anything else, and he'd take out his false teeth, swish them around the water a little bit, wipe 'em off with his old handkerchief he had tied around—yeah, we were very festive down there—with the old handkerchief he had tied around his neck. Why he'd just plop them back in his mouth and go on his merry way.

He had a new Buick at this time, it was in good condition anyway. The driver's side of that car was just mottled, just spotted. It looked like it came from a paint job that way, and it was from him chewing all the time and spitting out the window. He never washed the car and the whole one side of it was completely covered with tobacco juice. It was the damnedest-looking thing you ever saw. He was something else.

I never will forget that car and him taking those teeth out and washing them in that canal. He was *clean.*

We had a camp captain at one time. He stood about six foot four, I guess. Must have weighed 260 or 270 pounds if he weighed an ounce. And he was a pill head. He was constantly on pills, usually Benzedrine. Occasionally when he got a feeling too much up in the air why he'd bust loose with a barbiturate of some kind to kind of bring him down. I saw him high every night.

We had mail call right after chow, after evening chow. We'd gather round before we went up to the dormitories and they'd call out the mail. And Captain Naba is standing there and he is so high he's rocking back and forth from toe to heel. He's so high he's trying to put his hands in his pockets and he can't find his pockets, and I tell you, he broke up the whole congregation. Everybody stopped what they were doing to watch him just try to get his hands in his pockets. Big old belly sticking out, and he just can't make it.

Another time this fool, he gets all high on pills and I think he'd been drinking too, he smelled like it. At this time I was on the yard with a bad hand. So he called down—there wasn't any trusty on the yard—and tells me, "You S.O.B., go down to the barn and get my goddamned horse. And you'd better not get on him, you walk him back up here."

So they let me out the gate. I wandered down to the barn and I got his horse for him. I got it all saddled, brought it back up. He was going to ride out to the field and inspect the field. And he couldn't get on that horse and he got mad at me because he couldn't get on the horse. He took a couple of swipes at me. I ducked out of the way. I let him get a couple of easy swipes in, you know, but nothing to bother me, and he's just giving me hell.

"You S.O.B., come over here and hold this horse." So I held the horse for him. And for about fifteen minutes this goes on. Finally he just gives up in despair and tells me to take the goddamned horse back down, and he stomps back into the office.

Pretty soon he comes out again. I'm standing over in the yard watching him. He comes out and he's got this Stetson pulled over his eyes. He looked around. Just higher than a kite, boy, I wish I'd a been as high as that man was that day. He was feeling no pain, just having himself a ball. So he looks over at me and sees me standing there and says, "You S.O.B., where's that goddamned horse?"

So I had to go back down and get it for him and this time he made it.

At the time they had done away with the old whipping post. They hadn't done away with the post, they'd done away with the whipping. So they would tie you to the post and leave you there for a day or two while they constantly fed you mineral oil, epsom salts, and stuff like that. And left you there.

But actual floggings and beatings, no. Just the occasional bump on the head or thump across the shoulders. The guards and freemen still carried long sticks when I was there, and they never hesitated to use them. But the day of the really brutal beating is gone.

A group of fellows hit the yard one day when everybody was on the yard and they had some Molotov cocktails all made up. Gasoline in the bottles, stuffed with rags at the top, you know. They came down under the tower in the left-hand corner of the yard down there and they cut loose with their cocktails and they set the guard tower on fire.

The guard was so excited that instead of jumping out on the outside of the wall he jumped in with the convicts, and he took off across the field and headed for the guard shack.

They had a rope all fixed up. They throw the rope over and one of them goes up, and then the next one. If they'd gone over one by one, as they were supposed to, they would have made it because way down at the end where the other guard tower was, there was one guy who was completely dumbfounded as to what was going on, and he probably couldn't hit the broad side of a barn if he had one to shoot at with what was happening there.

But as one guy almost reached the top another one jumped on the rope and in the anxiety to get over, a third one grabbed on.

And blooey, the whole thing gave and they all dropped back on the inside.

There wasn't much else happened after that. They completely gave up and said the hell with it.

It was pretty funny, especially to see that guard jump down in the middle of the yard and take off running.

Talking about breaks. In Angola we lived in dormitory type places, all upstairs. Two-story buildings. The downstairs had a kitchen, a couple of lobbies, a library, a barber shop, whatnot, a little dispensary. And the whole thing was surrounded by a twelve-foot fence, a Cyclone fence with three strands of barbed wire facing in. And guard towers on each of the four corners, and along the length of the fence there were two towers in-between.

Some of the fellows decided that they were going to go. I don't know why they were going to go over the fence. I mean, what the hell, everyday you're outside the fence working, all you got to do is sneak across the cane cut, take a chance on getting past one guard, and hit it. If there *was* any place to go. There wasn't any place to go.

But they decided they were going to be very spectacular about the whole thing and go over the fence in broad daylight. So half a dozen or so got down to the very corner underneath the guard tower, which is no-man's-land. You just aren't supposed to get under there where the guard can't see you.

They proceeded to have a little fight, a little sham battle. The guard jumped down and he's standing over or leaning over them, trying to break all this up. One of these characters, a pretty good-sized boy from Houston, he runs up and grabs a hold of the barbed wire with his bare hands and three of them go up over him, they just use him as a scaling ladder. He drops back on the inside.

This so confused the guards in the four towers that could see them that they just stood there and they looked, and they looked, and we kept waiting. And the suspense got so bad that all of us felt like shouting, "Shoot at them, you silly sonofabitch," but they just set there and they looked. And finally, when those three guys are almost down to the barn, a good quarter of a mile or so away, they finally decided to cut loose on them.

They get to the levee. The only thing left is what they call "running the levee." You try to make it to Baton Rouge along the Mississippi levee. It's been done about two or three times. I couldn't get you the exact distance. I'd say something like about sixty miles. But it has to be done ahead of the dogs, and only a couple of them have made it. Both of them colored guys. It's quite a little jaunt.

Each camp had its own dog house, its own group of bloodhounds. The real bad bunch was up at the administration building and the only thing you could call them is killer dogs. When they brought them out you knew they were really hot after somebody. They decided they were going to use those dogs.

Those guys decided to run the levee and they made the mistake of taking the long way around the levee. I think they thought that if they could get around to the back gate—that was nothing but a ferry landing for a ferry to cross the Mississippi—they could make it that way. For the men in that part of the state who had to bring prisoners into the joint, they came across the ferry instead of going all the way around. It was big enough for one car or a pickup truck. And these guys decided they'd commandeer that ferry and take off.

They got down to the ferry and, of course, there's a couple hundred guards already there. There's no hope for them there. So they swing back and they cut all the way through the farm, they cut right across it. And they bypass the administration building and they head up into the hills. If they can get across the other side of these bluffs in through there and across the river they'd be in Mississippi.

They get up into the hills, and they hunt for them the rest of that day and that night. You could hear the dogs. All of a sudden word came the next day for us to go out to work. We figured they'd caught them. Somebody said, "No, they didn't catch them, they gave up on them." We couldn't figure why in hell they gave up, because the place is surrounded on three sides. It's in a horseshoe bay on the Mississippi River. There's only one way out by land, that's through the main gate.

Well, where in hell are those hoosiers? They gotta be somewhere.

We're walking down the road and we go past the garden gang—they took care of the vegetable garden. Most of them were older men.

We're walking along and I looked down across there by the garden and I looked down there, I look again, I take a third look. I nudge this sonofabitch and I said, "Look at that sonofabitch, that's one of the guys that ran off."

"That couldn't be."

And we looked again and we kept on walking.

You know, those silly S.O.B.'s worked all day out there with the garden crew. And even the guard on the garden crew didn't realize it. They come back in the gate at night, they checked in and ate. The guards didn't find out they were back until they made the bed check that night about eleven o'clock. They thought they'd gotten away and here they just come back in the joint. They gave up and just came back in. And had worked all day with this guard and with this crew. That garden crew didn't have a squareman with them, all they had was this one guard, and he didn't know who he had working for him.

I had told that guy, "I know that's one of them over there," and it was, bigger than hell.

We had a food riot. There was one down there about every month or so that never amounted to anything. But things got really bad down there one summer. Oh, the food was just terrible. We had been living for two or three weeks on nothing but syrup and corn-bread.

We decided we'd had enough of this nonsense, so we called for a little general strike, like Castro. Well, it didn't come off. Everybody said, "Oh yeah, yeah, we're with ya, we're with ya," and the time came and I looked like a fool standing out there by myself. So I sidled off in line with the rest of them.

Finally I decided we're going to have to do something with these fools.

We were on the yard for dinner one day. When we got through eating in the summer they'd let us stay in from noon till about two o'clock, during the hotter part of the day. So everybody's in one of the two lobbies, playing cards or laying on the floor asleep, something like that. Like here right now. So we proceeded to lock the doors and bolt them so they can't get out. They've gotta join us now.

The Man come in. The law claimed that they can't come on the yard with guns, they could come in with sticks or axe handles or things like that, but no guns. Well, the Man wouldn't even come on the yard. He stands in front of the gate and he yells in to us, "What's the trouble in there?"

"We gotta have some food. We can't work the way conditions are."

"Goddamn, we're feeding you sonofabitches good. You're living better than you were outside." All that nonsense.

"That may be, but we can't make it. We can't work every day on this kind of food."

He gets all hot at us and he takes off. We ask to see the warden. The warden wasn't there, or so we were told. A few of the people were getting kind of restless and we had to bang a few heads to calm every-body down. We were in there two hours when the Man comes back out again. He wants to talk to us.

So loudmouth me, I gotta speak up, and he knew there was a Yankee talking somewhere in there. He knew there was a Yankee talking and he could eliminate them on one hand. So finally he said, "Nothing's going to get settled right now. Come on out, have supper, and we'll take care of it tomorrow."

"No, we're going to stay right here till we see the warden and something gets settled."

We stayed there all night long and hadn't anything to eat. Finally, the next morning, the warden comes down and he says, "Well, I know it's been bad, the vegetables are getting ripe, fresh vegetables and everything, food is gonna get better, and I'll give them orders to slaughter a couple of hogs and we'll have some pork chops. Now I won't say it'll get better all the time, but I'll do my best for you right now. So you can come out."

Everybody's getting hungry about this time. Somebody yelled out, "Are we going to get into any trouble over this?"

"No, absolutely no trouble for anybody. We'll just forget about it."

Yeah. So the ones of us that really instigated the thing, there were six of us, we got in among everybody else and filed out. And I'll be damned if they didn't slaughter a couple of hogs. Had some pretty nice pork chops and a pretty decent supper.

The next morning we come down and lined up to go out for work. I'm standing there waiting, thinking that things will be getting better. All of a sudden they start reading off these names, six of us.

Somebody snitched us out, and we never did find out who it was. Somebody snitched us off because they had just exactly the right people. Not even one over or one less or anything, just exactly the right people. They talked about taking us outside to try us, and then they decided not to because there might be a bit too much publicity, the New Orleans *Times-Picayune* was looking for a reason to come on the joint anyway at the time. The food did get better, but the Man, almost any time anything happened, I don't care what it was, whether it was a fight in the showers when the six of us were still out working in the field, we six got rapped for it. He found himself six fall guys, and every time something happened there that he couldn't account for, he knew all he had to do was tell the warden it was the six of us. So every time we turned around we were headed for the sweatbox or solitary. It made it easy for him.

The hole. Oh, the hole.

Each camp had its own sweatbox, usually three sweatboxes. Our particular camp had three. They were about four by four by four, and sitting right in the middle of the whole thing was a toilet stool. You couldn't stand up, you couldn't curl up on the floor because of the toilet stool, and what you could do was sit there on that toilet, that's all. But the law allowed them to keep you there only three days, no longer than seventy-two hours. Of course, they could let you out for six, then put you back in for another seventy-two. So they never actually broke the law in any way.

The main form of punishment for infraction of the rules was what they called the "red hats." The name still held, although the way of running it had changed a lot over the years. In years before, the disciplinary crews had been forced to work at the worst type of work on the farms, such as cleaning drainage ditches behind the hospital and things like that. And to show that they were a strictly disciplinary group they'd been forced to wear red hats and they had a special guard line.

When I was there they didn't work anymore, but they had their own building which is still called the red hat building. If you were sentenced there, it was for no less than thirty days. I was in it twice. The last time was when I was supposed to be one of six who instigated that food riot for lack of food. We weren't out of the cell once in thirty days. We never had a shower, we never shaved in that thirty days. We had a meal every three days. Twice a day we received bread and water.

The last time I was in was during the month of August and part of September which, if you know the South, you know how hot this time of year can be and what the humidity is. When I finally got out, they took us out about ten o'clock in the morning and a truck was waiting for us. None of us could make it to the truck ourselves, they had to help us into the bed of the truck. And when we got there, myself and two or three of the other fellows were completely covered with heat rash. I've never experienced anything like it since or even seen anything like it since. I had heat rash even on my eyelids and on the insides of my ears and my nostrils. From not being able to bathe, from the constant perspiration, the sweating.

I went right back to work that afternoon. These shades I wear, they're prescription lenses, they're not sunglasses alone. But because of that particular incident alone that's why I have to wear them, all during the daylight hours I have to wear sunglasses. That afternoon, when I went out after having been in the hole for thirty days, I went out three separate times with heat prostration and each time I was back on my feet and sent back to work. Right after that, the headaches and all that started and I still have to watch myself in hot days, especially hot sunny days and such, I have to be pretty careful. Make sure I get in someplace out of the sun when I feel I'm getting a little ill.

Pete: "Convict means that you're supposed to be good people . . ."

That was when the guards walked two and two with clubs. They carried dirk knives and so did the inmates. It was a fairly well understood situation amongst the guards that the guards were tough and so were the inmates tough.

We called them convicts, we didn't call them inmates then. Nowadays, in some respects, well, "inmate" is sort of a derogatory word. Convict means that you're supposed to be good people.

To whom?

The inmate body. Wherever you might meet 'em, inside or outside. If they call you *convict* why that means it's what's qualified as you keep your mouth shut and tend to your own business and you're not a snitch or you don't meddle in other people's business or things like that.

In those days you worked from can to can't. You got up early in the morning, at four o'clock perhaps. I have gotten up many a morning myself to start baking bread at twelve thirty to feed the lines so they could go out to work. They turned them out to work from the time they could see the white clothes to shoot at. And at night they brought you in so they could get in the building from the time they couldn't see the white clothes to shoot at. In other words, you worked approximately thirteen to fifteen hours a day.

It was very hard work, farm work, and there wasn't any vocational work of any kind save perhaps a little foundry work or a little cabinet work here in the Walls. But out on the farm the only work they had there was the necessary blacksmith work to keep the tools going. Your tractor was your old heehaw mule, that was your tractor.

And that mule knew just as well when quitting time came as you did. When quitting time came, well, that mule quit too. She slowed down or he slowed down and you couldn't drive that mule, couldn't make it go any faster at all. It waited for the captain to raise his hat and say, "Raise 'em up old bullies, let's go." And that's the way they went.

And when they whipped you they whipped you with a leather

strap approximately five feet long. Pull your trousers down and they'd hit you on one side of the bare cheek of your bucks for a while, then they'd hit you on the other side for a while. Give you twenty licks was what the rule required. And they gradually started progressing, but before it started progressing there was a lot of blood spilled that was unnecessary, of course, but there's a lot of blood spilled in wars that is unnecessary too. In other words, there's a lot of blood spilled for progress. And perhaps that blood was spilled for progress and those poor devils who spilled their blood, why they spilled it for progress. And it has been progressing slowly ever since.

And now I don't know how it's going exactly 'cause I'm here on my back, but I see and observe. When I can, I look out the windows and I look out over there. I keep my ears and eyes open. My body, of course, is deteriorated. My mind, I don't think it's dehydrated any. Of course most crazy men think that, think their mind hasn't dehydrated even though they may be insane.

At one time I was judged to be legally insane when I was under a death sentence. That was done by my friends in San Antonio to avoid my execution. It was the only way it could be avoided. I stayed under that cloak of legal insanity for approximately twelve years and escaped from the death cell in the county jail because I thought I wasn't being treated just exactly right there.

I already had a sentence down here then, when I had escaped from here. I had escaped from here when I got the death penalty out there. And they brought me here for safe-keeping, which in itself was a violation of the law because no insane person was supposed to be incarcerated within the Walls under a gun. But my friends advised me to stay here and I did. And kept trying to make it the best I could and fight the battle out.

Then they got to chopping their heel strings, chopping their arms off under Mr. Lee Simmons. I don't know whether it was the fault of Mr. Lee Simmons or the fault of society, the fault of the prison system or what. I wouldn't be able to know that. But you could combine them all into one and you'd have it, perhaps. But the man was sort of on the brutal side and he didn't employ anyone but brutal men, he didn't want men of intelligence to work these men in the fields. He wanted men to kill them.

He'd say, "Well, son, I've got these men hired to stop you if you try to run. And if he doesn't stop you, I've got his check waiting for him."

So that was the environment you had to labor under then. What little schooling you got was through the unit what we called then preachers, now we call them reverend and ministers and so on. And address them in a different tone of voice. And just called them preachers. They'd take us out of our cells and give us a little extra overtime for attending school and for trying to improve our minds. Of course most men was so tired at the end of that fourteen-hour-day's work on the farm that he didn't attend any school. All he thought about was hitting his bed and going to sleep. And by the time, almost it seemed, by the time his trousers hit the floor before they got through wrinkling good, why he had to grab 'em, put 'em back on, and go back to work again in the morning. That's the way it was when I came here.

You slept on a shuck mattress and moved your elbows around a little bit, tried to get that old hard corner of that shuck out of the way. Filled the mattress up once a week, air it once a week. And here in the Walls, they'd come by with a lantern and hold that lantern to see if you're in your cell. If they wasn't sure you was there they'd take a pole and punch you to see if you were in there, see if you'd move. That was the way they counted you. Counted you every hour. 'Course now all those things has improved and they've passed.

And so has the brutality passed. Insofar as I know, because I don't see it if there is any. Now we have more, whadaya call, psychology. Otherwise known as brainwash. Perhaps that's what you'd call brainwash.

This younger generation, the teen-ager generation of what we have nowadays, they don't seem to realize what it is to be in a prison. And when they come down here, if they had a came in those days, well they wouldn't be anything now except hardened criminals. Or dead.

Nowadays, there's an effort on all fronts to improve their chances of staying out of prison.

I originated in the foot of the Ozark Mountains, down southeast Missouri close to Poplar Bluffs. I have good Christian people out there. One's my niece, she has good education, a good family. Her husband is a 32nd-degree Mason. And I have a brother in Washington who is a retired lieutenant colonel, United States Army. And I have another brother that's in Memphis, Tennessee, or was until a few weeks ago if he hasn't headed for Oklahoma City or tried to come down here. They're gonna try to get together and see if they can't get me loose from this trap here and let me spend the remainder of my days with them outside. Which I hope they can.

I got off death row on a legal subterfuge of legal insanity, Article 921 of the Texas Penal Code. The people in Bexar County, approximately 35,000 people, signed petitions, asking the governor to commute my death sentence to life.

There was a gunfight of three, four plainclothes officers and myself. I wasn't committing any crime, though I was on escape from here. I *was* armed, that's where I was violating the law. But I wasn't committing any crime, I wasn't trying to commit any crime. I was attending to my own business, but the situation developed to such an extent where there was a gunfight and the gunfight put wounds in my legs and I started shooting after I had been shot. Of course the officers say "nay" and I say "yeah." And it stood that way.

Did you get any of them?

A chief of detectives was killed.

There was no bullets removed from his body and the examining physicians, Dr. T. N. Goodson, county health officer, and Dr. H. H. Ogilvy, the police surgeon, made a sworn affidavit and sent it to the governor that, "We, as the examining physicians, could not state whether the wound entered here and came out here or entered here and came out there." If the bullet entered here, perhaps the man that did it was me because I was shooting a Luger and a .38 caliber pistol. And in 1945 there came to light the fact, in Dr. H. H. Ogilvy's memoirs, that a .45 caliber bullet had been extracted from the body of the chief. That was suppressed, of course.

But the people got together when they saw they could save me no other way, and one of them asked me, "Now why are they trying to execute you, Pete?"

I said, "Well, just because they can."

And that person thought that was an insane answer. They used it as an insane answer and a judge granted a sanity trial which required twelve men under Article 921. And the jury judged me to be legally insane at that time. And if at any time I became sane I would be taken back to the same court where the original conviction was had and tried for my sanity again. And if adjudged to be sane a sentence of death to be passed upon me. But W. Lee O'Daniel, as governor, commuted the death penalty assessed against me, which was held in abeyance due to the sanity hearing. And I went right on to work here in the prison in 1939 and worked from then on until I got out in 1957.

I think I had about five or six stays of execution to permit this thing to go along.

[The reason he was commuted was because he refused to go along with an escape with some other men on death row. I asked him about that escape.]

That was the escape of Raymond Hamilton, Joe Palmer, and Blackie Thompson. Historic southwestern individuals. I have regretted that my name has become linked with theirs because I am not a man to shoot a man in the back. There was an officer brought in some .45 automatics and turned them over to the inmates and they came in behind the guards when they come in to feed the men in the death cells and opened the doors and opened mine and I might have taken part in it, but there weren't enough guns to go around. And I didn't want my name linked with Bonnie Parker, Clyde Barrow, and Joe Palmer and Raymond Hamilton.

I try to consider myself as an individualist. I try to stand on my own feet and think in my own way, the way that I think is right, and I've always done that here and I have the respect of all the officers, practically all of them—you may have an enemy or two, but most of them are my friends. And I've stepped on some toes when Uncle Joe Byrd died, 'cause I knew he was the executioner. I'd worked with him for years. Uncle Joe Byrd, he was the executioner at the Walls. I had worked with him here for years and I knew him to be a good man. And, of course, you find some people who think just because a man executes another man that he's got to be a bad man. Well, perhaps there are some reptiles who *need* execution. That's what I call them: reptiles.

Do you believe in the death penalty?

In some cases. Some cases. Atrocious cases I do. I don't believe in mutilating a small child or anything like that. I don't believe in anything like shooting a man down in cold-blooded murder and mutilating him or something like that. I don't believe in that. In other words, if it's even-steven, all right, that's perfectly all right. But I don't believe in any atrocities at all or mutilations.

What were you in for the first time?

Murder.

You were in for murder when you escaped?

That's right.

And then you were convicted of murder again?

That's correct. Circumstantial evidence, both of them. No definite proof any way and whenever I'm laid away there still will not be any definite proof as far as I'm concerned because I do not know. I do know that I killed one man in prison, a tough convict, I killed him. Yes, I did do that.

Were you charged for that?

No. The grand jury exonerated me. Because the man was off base when it had to be done. I done everything I could do to avoid it. Went to the officials to be locked up, they wouldn't lock me up. I said, "Well, I'm gonna have to get me a knife. The man said he's gonna kill me. He thinks because you people turned me out of the death cell after the death cell break occurred that I must a done some snitching." I said, "He doesn't stop to think like a lot of other people, that if I'd a had any snitching to do that death cell break would a never occurred." You see how they operate.

They said, "Well, you been locked in here long enough to know how to take care of yourself."

I said, "Well, I'll do that, sir."

So I did. Took care of myself.

Dutch: "It was men in them days . . ."

When Bonnie Parker and Raymond Hamilton came up there and made their break we was down in what is known as the Weldon Field on the Eastham. I was a trusty and I was fixing the fence about a half a mile from there. And they come by and they just waved their hand like any other motorist does coming by. Well, I didn't think anything of it and they drove up and come on.

Well, I say, I was fixing the fence and I heard this girl, I heard Bonnie holler, "Don't raise that gun." She said, "Come on, Raymond."

And Mr. Crowlson, Major Crowlson, he raised his shotgun and when he did, why she opened fire. I think it was a Browning machine gun, that's what it sounded like to me. I don't know. I know one thing, I got on my horse and went across the brush. And before I got to the brush over yonder, about three miles across the field, the rest of the bosses they was overtaking me. They'd left the squads. I asked one, I told him, "The squabble is over yonder."

And he said, "Yes, and the machine gun is over there too."

They left. They left 296 of them laying down there on the ground, just fell down.

Did anybody else take off?

There was three or four take off after Bonnie and them left. Didn't get very far.

In 1927 there was another big break, one of the worst breaks in the system. It was when they come over yonder after George Dixon on Ferguson Farm. There's a bunch from up north come over there in their big Marmon cars. I had the ferry. I was at the ferry, taking care of the ferry at that time, and I crossed 'em. Well, up between two trees I had a chain where they'd have to stop and then I'd have to collect a dollar for every car that crossed. And I asked 'em, I said, "Is this a grab-bunch or is this for everybody?"

And a fella stepped out a there and he says, "What do you give a damn what it is? Looks to me it's a bunch, don't it? Now drop that chain."

I told him, I said, "Friend, you can't bully me. I don't care. I don't care about dying. I'm a convict, I've got life, I don't care," I said, "death is nothing to me."

And he said, "Listen: we're going up to the Ferguson Farm. We're not going to hurt you. Drop the chain."

And one man stood there and they took and went in the house and they tore the telephone off and took it out there and taken a double-bit axe and cut it up. And they went on up.

It wasn't but a little while till I heard shooting up there.

They went in the picket [guard shack] and asked Mr. Rader, they walked in and they told him, "Don't reach for that gun. We come after George Dixon, Charlie Pryor, and his brother." And he reached for the gun and they killed him.

Well, the other bosses taken the back windows out a the guard shack. Went over the hill.

They come back through there and they wanted me to go with them. I told 'em no. They said, "Well, we oughta kill him," but George Dixon said, "No, he's a friend of ours. He been down here, he looking to go out, to go home."

And I was, I was promised then to let me go home. And they says, "All right," and they lit a shuck [took off].

Well, the captain come down and he said, "Them guys come through here?"

I said, "Yes, sir."

He said, "Why didn't you stop 'em?"

I said, "Why didn't *you* stop 'em?"

He said, "Well, they run up on us with a machine gun."

I said, "Well, they come up on me with a gun too."

He said, "Well, why didn't you phone us," he says, "when they left here to come on up to the building?"

I said, "Can you phone over that phone box that's laying there?" And I said, "You got half your wire taken out from here to the building."

And he says, "No, you're right."

Well, I stayed there on that farm, stayed there on that job a little better than five years. And I was transferred then to the Clemens Farm to go down there to take the stock job over because I'm a stockman and a veterinary. And I was down there when one of the biggest breaks that ever was in the penitentiary happened. That's when all of Number Three Camp but three men left.

Captain W. M. Hickland was captain down there and he had a band. There was fifteen of us in the band. There was eight whites and seven niggers played in the band. And we were over there one Saturday night and we was playing out there and they was all hollering, "Play us the 'Dallas Blues.' Play us 'Fort Worth Spangled-Banner.' Give us the 'St. Louis Blues.' " At the meantime, they had a crosscut saw in the building and was cutting the building. While we was playing.

We played till eleven thirty. Captain Hickman said, "Let's go," he said, "it's eleven thirty." We got out there and we taken the stuff and put it in there and I got in the car. I got Captain Hickman, and the boss and the rest of the men got in the truck, and we went on back. Well, I was sleeping in the office out there and I'd just got my clothes off when the phone rang and I said, "Yes, sir. Number One."

He said, "This is Reeves, Number Three."

And I said, "What's a matter, Captain Reeves?"

He said, "Tell Captain Hickman to bring all his dogs, all of his bosses and the hosses. They've all left us. They've taken the dogs, taken the hosses, and all of the mules and everything."

I went and woke Captain Hickman up, and Captain Hickman says, "Get the car."

I got the car. We went over there. One guy, they asked him, "Why didn't you go?"

He says, "Well, to tell you the truth, Captain, I did." Says, "I went through as far as halfway through and that's as far as I could get through. I was too big to go on through further. The boss went to shooting and I went backwards."

They caught twenty-three of them that night. That was all out a the bunch that they'd caught. 'Course they caught 'em later on. Some of them are still gone.

There was 296 of them that left and that was just before Christmas of 1926.

Out here at the Wynne Farm they had a break out there when they grabbed that boss out yonder. They'd had a gun planted out there on 'em and they picked up a gun and the boss wouldn't give up and the guy snapped a .45 three times at him and it wouldn't go off. And the boss run him down, run him down and knocked him down, he wouldn't kill him. The boss run his horse over him and knocked him down. Wouldn't kill him. Told him, said, "You're crazy." Said, "That gun is planted there, but," said, "it's planted there to kill you. Them shells is blanks."

I was in later on down there on that farm, one a the worst things that ever did happen in the penitentiary. The best steward that ever was in the Texas prison system, Mr. Holman, that was on the Wynne Farm was steward and I was butcher and stockman, trusty out there. He had a guy out there, they called him Red. We all called him Crazy Red. I told Mr. Holman, I said, "Mr. Holman, you better take old Red out a that butcher shop. 'Cause he's gonna kill you."

And he says, "Aw, you're wrong."

I says, "Well," I says, "all right."

I have this scar here from when he killed Mr. Holman. He cut his head slap off.

That scar of yours, looks about a foot long. How did you get it?

I got it trying to stop him from killing Mr. Holman.

You're lucky he didn't kill you too. Looks like he come pretty close.

Well, he did come pretty near there. But God wasn't ready for me to die then like he is now.

On Retrieve Farm in 1935 there was a Mr. Harrison. Mr. Harrison had a bunch a children, and his wife was like a mother to us. You could go down there and tell her to bake a cake or pie or cook a chicken or anything and she would cook it.

There was a bunch figuring on grabbing Mr. Harrison. I was stockman down there and had the lot. I went down there and told him, "Mr. Harrison, you get out of this lot and stay out of this lot.

Your job is outside. I'll handle these mules and see that they're put up."

There was a bunch that was gonna kill me for that. But luck happened. I happened to be a prizefighter, I was champion of the penitentiary, and I could take care of myself. And I'm living today.

I was supposed to been given time [off] for it, but it never did come through. But I didn't do it for no time. I didn't even do it for Mr. Harrison. I done it for his wife and children. Because they was like a mother and like my own brothers and sisters. I thought as much of them as if they'd been my own children. Because they was humans and they was a family that would talk to us, and when they seen us it was "Hello, boys." They wasn't stuck up like the rest a them. She was just a country woman, raised in the country, and all she knew was to be honest and square. And she was as honest and fair as any woman can ever be. And the children was honest and everything.

The boys thought so much of them people that the captain, Rube Connor, that was there then taking I. K. Kelly's place, he let them children bring eggs up in a water bucket to the building and they would sell 'em to us for two bits a dozen. That's the only way you could get a egg to eat in them days. Tell them children, "Tell Mama to make a cake." Well, they'd get it. At times she would tell us, "I haven't got the stuff to make it out of." Well, she would have the stuff before night because we would steal it to take it down there to her. That's just how much we thought of them.

After that happened, Mr. Harrison was moved to the Central Farm and Mr. Mace Thompson that's out here at Midway, Texas, used to be assistant general manager and used to be auditor, he moved me to the Central Number Three as stockman over all the stock over there under Captain Buck Flannagan just on that account. He says, "You stay here and you gonna kill somebody." Which I did have it in my mind. Because if they'd a ever started it I would a done it.

There's a lot a people here . . . I lost one a the best friends not just a little while back here that I thought as much of if he'd a been my own daddy. He fell dead here with heart trouble. That was Captain Joe Byrd. I called him Uncle Joe. There's a man that if a convict would a jumped on in that yard I would a killed him over it, that's how much I thought a him.

I think the meanest man since I've been here was George Dixon. He was just an outlaw, that is all. He just didn't take nothing from nobody. Inside or out. He got killed in 1918 right here at Huntsville.

Right there where that pecan tree is now there used to be the archway. You went through the archway. He went through there one morning and when they got down at the machine shop, why, Georgie was missing. And the master mechanic asked them to get Georgie. When they walked up, they found him laying in the archway with a dirk shoved through his back.

Did they ever find out who did it?

No. You could never in the olden days never find out nothing from anyone about nothing like that. It was men in them days.

It's an old folks' home and a kids' paradise now. There's nothing coming to prison to amount to nothing now but boys that should be taken out behind the barn and leather put to 'em and turned back over to their people. 'Stead a coming down here. They're sending 'em too young.

They have got everything they want to rehabilitate themselves here. I learnt the American language in the penitentiary, in prison. I only spoke Swedish when I came.

Do you still speak Swedish?

Nope. They beat it out a me.

When you first came down here, how were the convicts different from now? What made a good convict?

Keep his mouth shut, tend to his own business, what you done is none a my business, what he done is none a my business, what this man done wasn't none a my business. And they would stick together. You could come up if you want to run off, you could come up in the building and say, "I'm gonna run off tomorrow. I ain't got no money."

They had cash money then. They would go around, everybody would, the men go around and say, "Joe is going to run off tomorrow, you got any money you want to give me?" And they'd make up money and give it to him. And when he got out there in the squad, the squad would hold down or either take out and go like lightning. Boss had to keep up with the majority of them. He got one man he ain't gonna pay no attention to that one man, it's them other eleven men he's gonna watch. Well, then he'd slip off.

But today, now, you take two-thirds a these men and if a man was to run off and they was to tell them, why they'd know it in the office before you got it good out a your mouth.

A snitch in them days didn't live.

What hurts a penitentiary is convicts. It's not the officials, it's not the personnel, what we call guards in the olden days but they call 'em personnels now, call 'em officers. They used to call 'em guards, mulligans. It's not them that hurts the penitentiary. It's the convicts.

Reilly: "In six months they hate guards, it's the natural thing . . ."

I still am antisocial but I can talk to people now, but a few years back I would only talk to my friends, the guys up at the plant with me. I don't want to talk to half the convicts in here, let alone the screws or civilians.

Everybody in a prison for even six months feels, inside of him, feels very hostile toward the screw *qua* screw. Some people can't control the hostility enough, so it never eases itself. Some people can control it enough so they can channel the outlet of it, and some people have no control over it whatsoever. Then every time a screw says, "Get in line" or "Tuck your shirt in" they just get in line or tuck their shirts in, but if they have the opportunity they cut his head off.

And of course there are people there that just have out and out surrendered. They feel the hostility, but their attitude toward it is intrinsically different than a person who had any fiber, what his attitude would be. And this is a perfectly natural thing, you know.

A civilian could come in here, for instance most lifers are unknown criminal types. You know, they killed their wife in a fit of passion. They never done time before in their lives. They think just like citizens, you know. And they'll come in here and they certainly don't hate guards. They think they're being punished justly, you know. Whereas most criminal types are mostly anarchists—they just disagree with all law, so no matter what they've done they're in here unjustly. But this citizen type, they'll come in here with no prejudice or anything and in six months they hate guards. It's the natural thing.

Convicts are very jealous, clannish men. A guy like that who come in—there might be a rare exception here or there, but generally speaking—a guy like that that came in, an old-time convict who's been doing time for twenty years, would never talk to him. He wouldn't be insolent to him or anything. If the guy said, "Hi," he'd say, "Hi," but he'd never tell him anything. He'd never hang around with him and he'd never cut him in on anything that he knew or anything that he was doing.

The average convict or average criminal type convict has been in a correctional institution since he was fifteen years old. He started off in the training schools, then he went to the reformatories, then he came here. And the guy who has never been in prison before he was thirty-five years old, he can never think the same way. He doesn't have the same background of experience that the average convict has. And he never in one hundred years would think the same way he does. And if people don't mean the same thing by the same word they can't communicate.

And the lack of communication, is that maintained even though the civilian has been in for a long time?

Sure.

Then this is permanent stigma?

It isn't so much it's a stigma. It's just that the average convict doesn't feel anything in common with this guy.

And the fact of being in the institution isn't enough?

It's a matter of what you talk about when you're in a bullshit session and things like that. And it's a matter of what your attitudes are. There's a kid working over in the office with me, for example. He's a good kid. He's about twenty-five years old. He's just come in off the street on a life bit. He's never done time before. He did three months in the correctional when he was a kid, but other than that he's never done time before in his life, and some of the things he says just bug you, you know. You just bust out laughing, and in the normal outside society there wouldn't be anything funny about it whatsoever. I remember once he come over there talking and he used the phrase, "Our president," and you know, it just cracked me up. People in here don't think of the president of the U.S. as *our* president. He's part of the enemy force, you know.

About those people who haven't done time before: who is more likely to get mixed up in sex in prison?

Even a guy who's never done time before, there's a certain period of time in, and then he's no more immune to it than anyone who's been in all his life. A guy who's been in prison for—this is arbitrary— for two and a half years. A guy who's been in prison for two and a half years thinks homosexually. I'd say the overwhelming majority of guys, especially guys that only do five or six years; there's a large majority never participate in any overt homosexual activity. But a guy who's doing longer than that, if he doesn't, it's because either he's so afraid of the reality, afraid to be honest with himself that he just keeps on like that, or it's the lack of opportunity. A guy who's been in prison for ten years, if he's never had any sort of homosexual activity either he isn't honest with himself or it's lack of opportunity.

The average guy, the aggressive homosexual, he comes to think after a few years toward, say, an eighteen- or nineteen-year-old boy with the same attitude that you would think of a girl outside. And his object is pederasty. That's what the sexual normal person becomes after a certain number of years in prison. Of course there are abnormal homosexuals [men who were homosexual outside] in here just like there are outside. They're something else. But as far as the normal homosexual [men who are homosexual in prison only], there's no stigma at all.

Those abnormal homosexuals, nobody will assault them or anything. They're just a joke. Once in a great while there will be a guy like that who the cons' opinion of him will be, "He's a faggot but he's all right." That's a rare, rare case.

Before I came here I was in Concord. That was 1954. And the whole atmosphere of the place was not quite diametrically opposite to the atmosphere here but pretty close to it. For one thing everyone who was—I don't really know how to explain it. You were locked up right after the evening meal about four thirty and there was nothing whatsoever to do. You got up in the morning and went to work. You came back to your cell at noontime. You went to the dining room and then you went back to work. You had about twenty minutes out in the yard and then you went to your cell for the evening or night. Because there was nothing to do, and also because a lot of the guys up there are a lot younger and doing small sentences, there was this very palpable atmosphere of solidarity.

There were stool pigeons up there but you know who they were, and there was a very clear line of demarcation between them and yourself. You didn't talk to them. You didn't talk to the screws. If the screw asked you a direct question you gave him a direct answer, but as uncivilly as possible. That was the extent of your intercourse with them. The same thing with the stool pigeons. You had nothing whatsoever to do with them. You stayed by yourself or with your own kind. When somebody got pinched or got into any kind of a beef the other guys were on his side. If anybody got jumped by a couple of screws, which happened every now and then, if there were any of the

cons around, they jumped right in. So that didn't happen too often.
What happened to the cons who jumped in?

They'd all get thrown in segregation, which is a local euphemism for solitary confinement. When I first went there they still had bread and water. You did ten days and got two cups of water a day and five slices of bread, and the cell was pitch black. There was no bed or bedclothes or anything. You slept on the floor and you weren't allowed to talk. In the first place it was physically impossible anyway. Over a regular cell barred door there was a big iron door superimposed. The only difference between the segregation cell, which is known as the plant, and the isolation, or bread-and-water cells, which I know now as isolation, the only difference in Concord is the isolation bread-and-water cells have the windows cemented up. In the regular plant cells you can see out the windows; also in the plant you have a bed. Nowadays in isolation you also have a bed, but when I first went there they still had bread and water. Then they turned over, so bread and water was known as solitary confinement. And they turned over to what they now call isolation, which is one meal a day and you don't have any sheets but you have a blanket and a mattress. And have a sink and toilet facilities.

They used to give you up to ten days on bread and water and then they'd have to let you out for twenty-four hours. What I mean by letting you out is giving you three meals. They didn't let you out of the cell, but they gave you three meals right in the cell and they turned the light on and you were allowed to smoke. And then the next day, if they chose to, they could put you on for ten more days. And I think there was some sort of law that they couldn't give you more than seventy days in any one year. Now they have isolation they could give you fifteen days and there's no limit; I've done as much as ninety-six days. That's on one meal a day. You do fifteen, then they let you off for a day, possibly two days, then you go back on for fifteen more.

You sound like you were particularly—

Yeah. I assume I had more trouble than most had. I just lacked any sense of proportion. Once I got started, that was it.

You were seventeen when you went to Concord?

Yeah. I was charged with armed robbery and I was found not guilty of armed robbery, but I was found guilty of illegal possession of a pistol.

I was in a younger offenders' place in Indiana that had the same kind of age limit Concord did. I think the limit was thirty there. I

found it a pretty rough place, more so than the adult institutions in
the same state.

Concord was like that. For one thing, it's just the youth itself.
Saps are still boiling a lot, more hotly. It's also the attitude of the administration. They figure in a place like this one, or a place like
Charlestown was, that they were dealing with incorrigibles and there
was nothing they could do to straighten them out anyway, so fuck it,
you might as well get on as best you could. Whereas in a place like
Concord you're still young and they still might be able to change the
course you've started on, and therefore they're a bit more gung-ho.
But the way they go about it is, they figure they can beat it into you or
beat it out of you. Whichever way they're talking about it. And it's a
lot stricter. Their attitude is quite different. It doesn't work, but that's
the way they go about it.

You said before there was a lot of solidarity. Were there gangs or did
people operate alone?

There were individual cliques and of course there was always one
clique of guys that ran the other cliques. They could tell the others
what to do, you know. When anything major happened, everyone was
in it. In Concord every year, especially in the springtime, there was always something. One year they burned the furniture shop down and
put a couple of screws out of action. There was always something
going. Not always, but once a year something always happened, and
then everyone was all together.

How did these cliques organize?

They were just social. Guys who were simple acquaintances, people feel included, you know. You just gravitate toward one another.

Do most people coming in there know someone in there already?

Yeah, sure. Most people who go to Concord have already been
through Lyman School, then Shirley. They're state training schools.
Lyman is from seven to sixteen, Shirley from sixteen to eighteen.

Were you at both?

Yeah. I went to Lyman when I was thirteen and stayed there till I
was almost sixteen. I went there the first time, I think it was shoplift-
ing, and I went back for stealing a car. I was there on and off for three
years and I'd say I was physically beaten once a week on the average.
I was nothing unusual—everyone was. In Shirley, you're a bit older
when you go to Shirley, about sixteen, seventeen, or eighteen years
old. I was transferred from Lyman School to Shirley because a guard
—they call them masters up there—a master punched me in the side

of the head and I slid along the floor. I was a bit older then. I was almost sixteen. I said fuck it and I jumped up and I grabbed a chair and I hit him with a chair. So I was transferred to Shirley. In Shirley, although beatings are liberally administered, it's not as frequent in occurrence as it is in Lyman School with the real young kids. I mean it happens every day, sure, but not to *you* every day. In Shirley I had one beating and it was a pretty good one. I wasn't there too long. As I say, I was a lot older then and there was no wall or fence or anything, and I used to take off and they'd catch me and I'd come back and I'd stay a little while and then I'd take off again. I was there from September to August, but I was only there maybe a month and a half out of that eleven months. The rest of the time I was out on the run. And the last time I ran away I stole a cab and cracked up with a New York State Trooper over near Albany and was brought back and give a nine months' House of Corrections' sentence. That was the end of Shirley. They took me out of Shirley and put me in the House of Corrections in Bullerica. I did nine months there. I was out about five months and that's when I went to Concord. I did five years in Concord. I was outside for ten days and I was sent here and I've been here almost four and a half years. This is on assault with a deadly weapon.

Rice: "I've seen them eat plumb up by the dogs . . ."

We had a clown named Slew Davis, he used to clown in the rodeo. He was on the Retrieve the night Ernest Jones cut Redwine's head off. They had an exceptionally good pudding, which is unusual in the penitentiary, we didn't have sweets much in those days. And when Ernest cut Redwine's head off, his head bounced right over that table. Slew Davis was sitting pretty close and he wanted that pudding. But, he said, he just couldn't fade it [handle it], looking at that head. Them eyes was blinking, he said. He wanted to eat that pudding, but he finally had to leave it go.

Why did this happen?

Ernest and Redwine had had a beef. And they fought in the building. Redwine made the mistake of telling Ernest, "Don't come back in the building. If you do, I'm gonna kill you." Ernest worked in the dining room, he was flunkey there. So when he came out there he got old Bill Garrett to sharpen a cane knife. They use them to cut bread in there. Jack Bronson took it back there and got Bill Garrett, a butcher, to sharpen it. And he gave it to Ernest. Ernest went out there and told Redwine, "Redwine, let's talk this over. Hell, I've got to come back in that building, man, I live in there."

And Redwine said, "You come back in that building I'm going to goddamned sure going to kill you."

And so Ernest just stepped back and took that cane knife and whoosh, cut his head off. The head just bounced over the table and Redwine had a Lucky Strike cigarette standing just like that, it never did leave his finger, just kept burning. His body never did move.

And Slew Davis, he said, "I wanted that pudding, goddamnit, but I couldn't fade it."

What happened to Ernest?

Nothing. That gave him five years to run CC [concurrent] with the five he already had. That was in 1948. Redwine already had a pretty bad reputation, you see.

He and I had just got shot off a roof on the Eastham. We cut a hole through the roof and was up there. There was a boss up there that was a dead shot with a rifle, I always swore I'd never give him a shot at me, a name of Gus Morgan, and I didn't know he was up there. He was up on the high part and we were on the low part with the light shining down on us.

We weren't really intending leaving then, but I was showing Redwine how best to knock out the lights when we do leave. Redwine must have saw his hat or something because he started scuttling for that hole. And Gus Morgan shot. He shot right in front of him, right in front of his stomach, and punctured his stomach with all them rocks and everything from the rock and tar roof.

Goddamn, I thought they done stopped up the hole with him. I looked at the hole and there was Redwine laying there and I jumped all around. Course Gus Morgan kept shooting. I told him afterwards I didn't believe he was shooting to kill me 'cause I knew he's a better shot than that. He'd always shoot just where I'd been. Every time. Finally I saw the hole was open and I dove in it. Old Redwine, he was wounded pretty bad. Rocks done went into the hollow of his stomach because of that lead from the .30-30. And he already had some pretty bad escape records against him and everything. So he's paid for it.

Back in those days two or three killings now and then didn't amount to anything. They didn't hardly get any time over it.

Except Clay Whittles. Ankles we'd call him. He got the electric chair for killing old Kelly on the Eastham. Now he didn't have no business killing Kelly. I don't believe Clay would have had the guts to kill him if he'd been sober, but he was drunk.

I was a witness to the killing and everything. But I walked away from there to keep from being a witness. We just had a killing a few days before that and the guy had killed him on my bed. I told 'em I never went back to my bed. Told the district attorney and everything. So when this killing occurred I walked on away.

I knew Ankles was drunk, but I really didn't think he had the courage to kill Kelly. There was a pistol sent in by old Tom Norris sometime before, is what it was about. Any time Ankles got drunk he would jump Kelly out about that. Kelly didn't run in no clique or anything, he was just a man by himself.

When he walked up behind Kelly we was just fixing to go out to go to work. I was sitting up in the barber chair. A boy came up and started playing with me. I said, "Look out, man, old Ankles is fixing to kill old Kelly." I really didn't think he'd kill him because he stood up behind him with that knife a long time. Kelly wasn't paying him no attention, he was just there waiting for the door to open. He finally shoved the knife on in, right in his spleen. Kelly looked around, he didn't say anything, he just looked around right quick and stepped in the corner. By this time the boss throwed a lever on the door and Kelly jerked the door open, and went on out. He died in a few minutes.

Ankles had already done a lot of broadcasting in the building. And just before that, Ankles and I had had a little fight in there. What it was, I had lined some of them up and I was mad because they had run over [beat up] a boy. Him and a couple of other boys. They'd run over another boy in the building and I thought they just done it because he was some old rum [powerless]. I told him, "You'd better not be going down this alley"—I was half drunk myself—"unless you fight me."

They said, "All right, we'll fight you."

I said, "You all fight me one at a time."

They said, "Yeah."

So I said, "All right. Come on back. I'll start fighting Ankles first."

While I'm fighting Ankles, somebody creeps in, cops a sneak on me, and knocks me out.

So Ankles, I figured, didn't have the courage to come right out with anything.

So when he killed Kelly we went on out to work. We just sharpened up a cane knife and figured when we get in we'll just kill old Ankles. He had no business killing Kelly, so we're just going to administer justice ourselves because it really was a killing that wasn't called for.

They had him locked up by the time we got back and they wound up giving him the electric chair.

Of course I wasn't a witness nowhere on the case. They called me up and asked me did I know anything about the killing, and naturally I told them no, I didn't even see it, or I wasn't nowhere around there. They made me say that under oath before a notary public. And therefore Ankles couldn't use me for a witness. I wouldn't be a witness for him, but I wouldn't have been a witness against him either. That's the sort of thing we'd settle ourselves back in those days.

About that gun. We escaped, Gene Paul Norris come and took us off the Ferguson Farm. And Tom Norris had sent the pistol back to a truck driver. This truck driver had sold it to Ankles and a couple of boys. They had showed me the pistol when I came in right after they brought me back off of escape. They captured me pretty quick after escape. I told them I don't want nothing to do with it. I said, "When we want to show a pistol in the building, if we don't use it right then you'd better get away from it. I don't want anything more to do with it." And that's what happened. We wound up fucking around and getting that boy killed. And nobody ever used the pistol either.

Since 1934, I've been on a lot of escapes. I escaped in 1936 off the Darrington. I escaped in 1937 off the Eastham by grabbing a guard. In those days times were different. It was tough then. You'd either escape or get killed in the penitentiary. They put you on the spot [set you up to be killed] in the penitentiary in those days. When you done anything to put any heat on the state of Texas, why you're sure to be put on the spot when you're brought back. So it's either shoot your best stick and get away, or die out in the field. I've seen a lot of men killed in the building, I've seen men killed in the field.

Back in the early thirties the toughest farm was the Retrieve. Warden there was I. K. Kelly, assistant warden was named Benjie Tower. It was brutality plus on that farm then. You see guys at the

Walls with their left hand cut off where they'd cut them off with a cane knife or a hoe or something like that, just to get off that farm, get out of the work. They'd cut their feet, cut their heel string. They wasn't cutting heel strings so bad then, they was cutting their feet plumb off, and cutting their hands plumb off. That's just how bad it was.

I've seen them sit down twenty and twenty-five at a time and cut their heel strings. Course at that time they thought cutting that heel tendon was a pretty bad thing, they thought they couldn't walk or anything. But hell, I've seen 'em cut their heel strings, cut both of them, and in less than thirty days they'd be carrying a row [working in the fields] out there. Just depended on how scared they'd make them. They put a man like Rob Parker—this was a real killer—down here and put him to carrying them and they'd carry that row.

The penitentiary changed a lot from what it used to be. This place used to be wide open. You take a warden on a unit like the Ramsey, he was God. He butchered his own meat and he done as he pleased. If a man got killed, he probably wouldn't notify the Walls or anything for two or three months unless they asked about him. There wasn't no board or anything then. It's just a hell of a lot different now.

Clyde Barrow and Bonnie Parker was well thought of down here, you know, because they was criminals. I knew Clyde, I knew Bonnie. That break they had off the Eastham was just before I got there, but I left right after that. That was when Clyde came down after Raymond Hamilton and Joe Palmer.

Clyde had a BAR sawed off. He drove down this Calhoun Ferry Road when they was clearing that land there. They had already smuggled to .45's in to Joe Palmer and Raymond Hamilton. When he heard the axes falling on these trees where they was clearing land, he just stepped out of his coupe—he knew the squads were at work—and started shooting through the treetops with this BAR. That was the signal for Raymond and Joe that everything was ready, so they came out with their .45's and started shooting. That's when they killed Major Crowlson, one of the guards carrying them. Raymond and Joe and Hilton Bybee all ran, got in the car, and they drove them right on through. Went right into Dallas. Then old Baldy Wallis started hauling them around on various deals. They went on up the country and were squabbling all the time. Old Bybee told me that. We went over the same territory right after that when we escaped. He's telling me they're squabbling all the time. Never making any money or anything.

They finally robbed a little old bank up there and split up. Bybee came down and got busted in Amarillo.

I believe about the toughest man I ever saw down here was old Buddy Barret. I guess he was about half crazy. He's in Rusk; he finally went crazy.

They brought him down from Amarillo along about 1938 or 1939 and put him in the south building. That was on Eastham Farm, which at that time was for incorrigibles. They put Buddy in there. And I believe he is about the toughest damn man I have ever seen. I've seen him whip five or six convicts in there, and still go right out.

I've seen convicts that will fight other convicts, but still go out and take anything from a guard, convicts that will take stuff off of a guard, but still wouldn't take anything off of a convict. Buddy wasn't scared of nobody. Guns or anything.

He was on the lead row [first worker in a squad] and I was on the push row [second worker in the squad] for three or four years down at the south building. Buddy had those epileptic fits. He'd been an amateur fighter sometime or the other, and he had a fever when he was in Kansas City. Maybe it was Chicago. Where they have those Golden Glove fights. And that's when Buddy had that fever, and it made him start having epileptic fits. I don't know what brought them on.

One time a highway patrolman captured me over there close to Round Rock. We'd escaped out of the building down on Eastham and they asked me if I knew Buddy Barret. He's from that area up there, around Amarillo. I told them, "Yeah."

And he asked me, "What makes him have those fits?"

And I remembered Buddy breaking his arm one time, and right after he broke it he had two or three of those epileptic fits. The only thing I could think of was a shock, you know, so I told him, "Well, shock, I guess."

He said, "Hell, I don't know anything that'd ever shock him." Told me he's the toughest man they ever saw up there. I believe he's the toughest man I've ever seen in the penitentiary, and I've been with some tough ones.

Hilton Bybee was about one of the coldest-blooded men I've ever run with. He's the one Clyde Barrow and Bonnie Parker come down here and got in 1934. He left with Joe Palmer and Raymond Hamilton. Right after that, they captured Bybee and brought him back. We happened to be on the same plow squad on Eastham. The high rider had an excuse to bring a man from the hoe squad over to the plow squad, and when he was taking this other man from the plow squad to bring him back to the hoe squad it got him out of our sight for a few minutes. I grabbed this guard. He wasn't very alert, he was what you call a dead head, he's a dead head for the plow squad, he carried a shotgun and a pistol. I grabbed him and held him while Bybee took his shotgun.

Bybee started to kill him and I told him, "Man, don't kill him. We don't want that much heat on us." But Bybee, he wanted to kill him. He's really a cold-blooded killer. And on all our plays after that I believe he's about the cold-bloodest man I have ever been with as far as shooting a man down. He would explain to him what he wanted, but if a man didn't comply he would shoot him down in cold blood. It happened in Oklahoma, it happened in Missouri, it happened in Iowa, and it happened in Arkansas.

He's dead now. He got killed in that last gunfight we had there in Monticello, Arkansas. We just robbed a bank there and we'd come back. We'd cased another bank and one of the boys with us had got picked up. We'd told him to go and take a car out for us. He's supposed to follow us, but he picked up the sheriff, which he shouldn't have done, and we had to turn around and take him away from the sheriff. Then we got in a little gunfight there and got on away.

But we come back. Since we already spent the money casing this bank we was going to go ahead and rob it. We run into the same posse, it was out a week before us, and that's where Bybee got killed.

Old Charley Frazer, I guess he's about one of the coolest men. I believe Harry Roberts is as cool as Charley Frazer. Charley Frazer's escaped from Louisiana penitentiary and killed a captain and a guard down there, and they brought him down here. Then they released him to Louisiana—they figured they'd electrocute him. I believe he is the coolest man in a gunfight outside of Harry Roberts.

Harry Roberts was with us in Arkansas. He killed a deputy sheriff in Brekenridge when the sheriff arrested Hilton Bybee. Harry went down to stop him at the bottom of the stairs. This guy was a crack pistol shot, he was champion of that area. And he was evidently trying to shoot Harry's gun from his hand or something 'cause he shot Harry through his coat sleeve and under his coat sleeve and through his right knee. But Harry shot him between the eyes. And so, that's why I say he's awful cool in a gunfight. We had several gunfights and little escapades after we escaped from down here.

Did you specialize in banks?

No. Anything where there's money. Back in those days it was just wildcat hijacking. The only thing I found that'd really pay off would be bottling works. If they got four trucks you know they've got as much as $400. If four trucks has come in, you can figure $100 to the truck. We specialized in those bottling plants mostly. Banks weren't much good then, you couldn't get over $5,000 or $6,000 out of a bank back in those days. 1936 or '37. Of course they were a lot easier to rob —except in Texas. Texas still had that $5,000 reward for dead bank bandits then. Not live ones, dead ones. Maybe it's still in effect.

We had a building tender on the Retrieve at one time, Lee Smith, an ex-Texas Ranger. What he was sent down here for, he had sent some Mexicans into a bank, and when they're coming out, he killed them, you see? Figuring he'd get the $5,000 reward. And they wound up giving him life in the penitentiary.

Up until recent years they wouldn't dare put a man who had ever been a convict guard in some other penitentiary, like Arkansas, in a line with these convicts. They'd kill him before he'd pass the fourth bunk. I can remember the time on that Eastham over there, on Number One, which was the incorrigible farm, that any man that walked in that door, if he'd been any kind of a convict guard or a snitch ever and anybody knew it—and somebody in there would, because it was all second- and third-timers in there—he wouldn't get past the fourth or fifth bunk. There'd be three or four knives stuck in him.

I've seen killings in that Eastham building and three hundred men could go by that district attorney and the warden one at a time and not a man would know anything about it. It may have taken the guy fifteen or twenty minutes to kill the other one and not a man would know anything about it. That's how close they were at one time.

That's all over with now. For one thing, the overtime [good behavior time] changed it. They had a different commutation law then. And the segregation program [for first offenders].

A young guy comes in the Walls now, they don't indoctrinate him like they used to. An eighteen-year-old boy used to come in the Walls and them old heads would get a hold of him and they'd teach him what to do and what not to do. He'd go on down to the farm and finish his time in the penitentiary under that impression. They'd teach those youngsters to kill all the snitches and everything like that.

What other things would they teach him?

Whatever they could, according to how weak he was or how strong he was.

You know, for my first twelve or fifteen years in here, all I ever thought of was escape. And any man that thought anything else I didn't even want to talk to him. As far as homosexuality and stuff like that is concerned, I wasn't even interested in it. I thought a man that would interest himself in that, I'd think, "Hell, this guy he's institutionalized or something." If a man would order a feather pillow from home—he used to could order stuff like that—I'd think, "Goddamn, he just wants to stay in the rest of his life or something." I never walked out the door expecting to come back that night my first fifteen years down here.

There was a lot more of the homosexuality then. Now the officials let you know you can come to them and get some kind of help. In those days you couldn't. If a boy was lined up on and eighteen or twenty men lined up and fucked him and he goes out there and tells that warden, "There's twenty of them lined . . ." He says, "Hell, there's three hundred of them trying to fuck me every damned day! Get on out of my office!" That's the kind of reception you got, see? But nowadays a boy knows he don't have to do anything like that unless he wants to. You don't see much of it now.

In those days you associated in certain cliques. The hijackers and bank robbers and characters, they'd stay in one bunch, the others would stay in their bunch. They didn't associate with one another at all. That's changed to a certain extent. You never know now. You're liable to be talking to a good friend of yours, you know him and you know he's a hijacker and a character, maybe a safe burglar, but he may have a good friend of his that's sleeping right beside him who's a rape fiend. That's something that used to be strictly out, a rape fiend was never any good down here. Nobody would associate with a rape fiend. Hijackers and bank robbers and first-class safe burglars, they were the elite in the penitentiary, they were the characters. The lowest were the rape fiends, nobody wanted to associate with a rape fiend.

Why do you think that changed?

I don't know, to tell you the truth, I just don't know. It's just a matter of putting everybody on an equal basis around here. I don't know how it came about. Mr. Ellis changed it some way when he took this penitentiary over. He changed so damn many things. I didn't think he could do it, but he changed this penitentiary just opposite to what it was. O. B. Ellis. It didn't take him long. Four or five years it began changing. He took over in '48 and it had changed pretty much by '52. Dr. Beto's the same way. Before them we didn't have educated men in here running this penitentiary. We had Lee Simmons.

I believe he was about the most cold-blooded general manager they've ever had down here. They say he was a good general manager and he might have been, but from the convicts' point of view he wasn't. He had the penitentiary on a paying basis, not only self-sustaining but paying. That's unheard-of for a penitentiary. He done it with pure blood. Many a convict lost his life and many a convict cut his hand or foot off under Lee Simmons. 'Cause he was really bloodthirsty. It's common talk among the convicts that he'd tell a guard—see there'd been a lot of escapes till then—that when a man escapes you go after him and if you don't bring back blood instead of the convict, you're fired. He was really tough.

He sanctioned all. They used to put a lot of people on the spot down here, convicts. I do know that they used to kill a convict on each farm along in the spring and along in the fall. In the field or in the building. Maybe get the building tenders to kill him or shoot him down in the field. That'd tighten the field up, which it will, you know. Bunch of men get to talking—they don't want to be bothered or nothing, so they'll go ahead and work hard.

There were more gangs in the prison in those days. A lot of times if there weren't enough real men on the farm, these kid gangs would form. They can be vicious, these youngsters. A new man will come in, they'll take his shoes and belt away from him and stuff like that. Just flaunt it in front of him and the guy can't do nothing with everybody wearing a big knife. I was always protesting anything like that. Generally on the farms that I was on there was always enough men to stop that kind of stuff because we didn't appreciate it. That just brought heat on the farm. All we had in mind was escaping. We didn't believe in none of those gangs at all.

How many times did you attempt escape?

Tell you the truth, I don't know.

How many did you make?

Three or four times for long periods.

Did you ever get caught by the dogs?

Oh, yeah. But them dogs don't bother me none. I just catch the dogs. One night there was five packs caught up with me. That's about fourteen or fifteen dogs. We'd gone out a window. There was four of us—me and this Ernest Jones that killed old Redwine, Jack Bronson and Carl Hudson. They kept telling me, "You're going back toward camp, you're going back toward camp." When we went out that window they was shooting at us from every angle. It was real dark and you couldn't see anything. I always heard the thick bark and moss on a tree is always on the north side, so I told them, "No, man. Feel of this tree. You know we're going north." And we'd feel of the tree—

you couldn't see a tree, you had to feel it. We kept going and along about midnight the first pack of dogs got on us. We split then, Bronson and Jones went one way and Hudson and I went the other way. First thing I know, we're running in an open field and no trees there to get up on, and I see two dogs running on each side of me. I told Hudson, "Hell, man, you might as well quit. The dogs done passed me."

They were real good bloodhounds. They weren't vicious. So we let that go along for a while and we walked along. The dogs just thought we was dog boys, I guess. I got to thinking about dog boys, how they train dogs. They can't make one-man dogs out of them, it's got to be dogs that any dog boy can handle. So pretty soon we get another pack behind us. They're real fresh, we can tell from the way they bark. And a pretty big pack, and there wasn't no trees to get up then either. There was just one little old sapling and I tried to climb up it. Old Hudson grabbed me by the belt and dragged me down. He wanted me to stay there with him. Finally the dogs caught up with us and we just squatted down. Made the mistake of putting my hand out to pet them. You don't want to do that ever, 'cause them dogs will damn sure eat you up, that's what they're trained to do. I snapped then, they're used to that dog boy fighting them with his hand and a switch. So I just put my hand between my legs. Then they just come in to be petted. Five packs caught us that way that night and we still got away the next morning. We had every dog. We had to lift them over barb-wire fences. The dogs can't get through and if you go ahead they'll start howling and if they do finally find an opening to come through he'll pick up your trail and bark on it again. That noise was tearing me up, I couldn't stand it, so I just picked them up and throwed them over the fence every time. We had fourteen or fifteen dogs.

You don't ever want to try to kill a dog. If you do kill one, them other dogs will go crazy. They'll eat you up. They'll eat the dog up you're trying to kill. So I know better than that. I tried that once before. So we just decided we'd keep them with us. They won't tear you up if they catch you by yourself and you put your hands between your legs. Don't act scared or anything. But if you ever stick your hand out, one dog'll see the other one get a bite and he's going to get a bite. First thing you know they'll tear you all to pieces. I've seen men with their nuts and everything eat up. All this leg muscle torn out. I've seen them eat plumb up by the dogs.

BITS AND PIECES:

"HOG GOT UP AND SLOWLY
WALKED AWAY . . ."

We had a character in Folsom they call Hog. He's a little guy, even smaller than I am. He was an old man when I first met him; he was one of the first people I met when I got in the yard. When they turned us out in the day yard he was sitting out there on a bench all wrapped up in an old coat. And he talked through his nose, that's where he got the name of Hog. These guys would go by and he'd grunt at them.

But he had been a master forger in his day and he was quite a character. He had an old dollar block [watch] and a few picks and he'd lay around the yard and every fish [new convict] that come in, if the fish had anything he'd con him out of it if he could. Those new guards, when they came to work he'd lay for them. He looked so damned innocent and everything. You'd wonder what the hell an old character like him was doing in prison, he looked so harmless. These guards would come in and he'd lay for them. He'd watch them making their circle and he'd lay for them so they'd eventually pass, and him and the guard would get even. He'd speak to him. "How you doing?" Well, naturally the guard's interested just like you are, he'd figure "now what's this old character doing? I'll draw him out."

Anyway, Hog ended up by telling him he's a master watch repairman and that he repaired all the guards' watches and convicts' watches. He'd pull out this old dollar block and ask this guard what time it was. He set this old block every time the whistle blowed. Everybody's watch is usually a minute or two off one way or the other, they don't keep perfect order. He'd tell them regardless that they was off two or three minutes. He'd tell them that he'd clean that watch and adjust it and everything for four or five sacks of tobacco. They would think nothing about it, they'd give him the danged watch. That'd be the last of the watch. They'd come back next day or the day after, when he's supposed to have it ready, ask him about the watch. "I ain't seen no watch. What watch?" There wasn't a damned thing to do about it. He done duped it [sold or traded it] down in the lower yard or someplace where they couldn't never get it back. They couldn't put him in solitary, the old thing would die overnight. So they put up a warning to all these guards.

But the best part of this thing come when I got there. He was due out in about seven months. He used an old broomstick for a cane, hobbling around the yard. So he got out and he went to Sacramento. We gave him a grand sendoff, all these guys were grunting at him and everything.

He goes over there and starts laying this paper [writing checks]. And he buys him a gold-headed cane, a big watch chain, a watch, and fine clothes. They knock him off, thirty miles from the joint. But he was an ingratiating old thing and he had a hell of a line and he looked so damn harmless and pitiful. He told his story to these police in Sacramento and the judge and the D.A. and everybody that'd bend an ear, he'd get to them. He told them he had a brother, they had a ranch with some sheep up in the hills of Utah and if he could just get up there . . . So the judge decided not to even try him and he got the merchants that he beat to drop the charges and they made up a purse to send him back to Utah. Put him on the bus.

He caught the next bus back in the next town. A few days later he's papering the town again.

He was a mean old thing. Ornery as hell. If the guys got close to him when they was kidding he'd knock hell out of them with that cane. Somebody once got hold of a rogue gallery picture of him when he was a young guy. He had one of these handlebar moustaches and a high-roller hat, gold watch and all, he was a dandy. One guy run up behind and grabbed his arms so he couldn't hit him with the cane and another one got that picture and got up in front of Hog and said, "A forger . . . you ain't no forger. You is a pimp! Look at them clothes." Oh, God, he'd go wild.

So this time they sent him back to Folsom. I happened to hear he was coming in and I went down to see him come in. He's sitting in the back of this police car. They drive through the main gate and down in front of the administration building. They get him out and they're supposed to walk up to the captain's office. Well, he's sitting there in the back seat of that car with the two detectives. He's got that gold-headed cane and he's got that gray fedora hat on his head. He looked like a king, as dignified as a guy can be. These detectives open the door to him and said, "Get out."

He said, "Fuck you."

They don't want to mess with the old man and hurt him, so they send after the captain, old Bill Ryan. Him and old Bill Ryan been feuding down through the years. Old Bill comes down there and he said, "Get your old fat ass out of there."

"Fuck you, Bill Ryan. You put me out."

So they sent and got a couple of guys, convicts, and they were as gentle as they could be, but they got him out. Getting their heads cracked. Soon as he got out he set down on the lawn, wouldn't move a peg. So they went and got a wheelbarrow. He sat in that wheelbarrow. A band happened to be practicing out in the yard when they come through the lower gate, and they spied him sitting in that thing and all these cops following, just like a prince with his retinue, and they gave him an entree, a grand entree. They blurred the drums and everything. Get to the captain's office—he won't get out. They pick him up and carry him in; then he won't get out of the captain's office, so they pick him up and carry him. Carry him to the Bertillion room for finger-prints. All through this he maintained this air of dignity. It was something to watch.

Trying to break an old man's will, it amounted to that. He figured he was above all these scenes and everything. Finally they take him over to the barbershop and they shear off his locks, and then they take his clothing. Take his clothes away, his gold-headed cane. He plumb began to sink when he came out of that clothing room. They put him back on the wheelbarrow and wheeled him right out in the middle of the yard and dumped him out.

All the cons was laughing and everything and the guards up in the tower was ribbing him and everything and he sat there, looking like he's sticking to get his temper built up. And he looked from one tower to the other, and he waited until resentment and all that bitterness and everything took complete hold of him. And he started in cussing them guards, one at a time, each tower. And then Hog got up and slowly walked away.

SHOTGUN

There's one guard here, we refer to him if we see him occasionally and feel like we can outrun him, as Shotgun.

When he first came on they put him on guard towers to kind of break the monotony. I think now all they have are .22 rifles and shot-guns in the guard towers, but then they had .30-30's also. They don't want to kill anyone, just slow you down if you're going over the wall.

Anyway, he gets up and there's a sign on the wall of the guard-house, it says, "Guards be sure to check the operation of your rifles and shotguns to make sure they are in proper working order." Something like that.

He picks up his shotgun, looks at it, gives it a pump, pulls the trigger, and blows a hole right through the roof.

It worked.

"THEY PARDONED
RED HALLIDAY . . ."

Four or five guys attempted to go over the wall at Norfolk, and the first thing, Willie the Bungler—who is a story all by himself—forgot the ladder. They finally got that straightened out, but then they hit the wire and they couldn't get over. So they had them up in the plant.

Now Red Halliday hadn't been involved in the attempt because he didn't like the idea, so he's still out in the population.

So Red has a pistol. It's about ten o'clock at night and he goes up to the screw and says, "You know, I always considered you a real fucking jerk, you know that?"

The screw said, "For Christ's sake, Red, what are you doing? Don't say things like that. I don't want to lock you up." Red almost had to beg the guard, but the guard finally said, "Okay, Red, if you feel like that." Red just gave the guard shit for fifteen minutes and the guard said, "Okay, come on, you're going to R.B." [receiving building, where they have the new convicts and also where they had the lockup on Norfolk].

Five or six of them walked him over to R.B. and they brought him upstairs, and the first thing they do in any can when they bring you there is strip you down. So one told him to strip down and he pulled out the pistol and he said, "No. You strip down."

He stripped six of them and he let the five guys out who'd been involved in the attempt the month before. Each took a uniform and they put the screws in their cells. Then they went down to the bottom floor and now it's almost eleven o'clock, which is when the shift changes, when the whole shift changes they have to walk through the lobby of the R.B. So they waited down there for them and they grabbed a knot of about twelve screws going out. They walked up to them and produced the pistol and the six guys mingled in with the screws. They had the screws' uniforms on and they all mingled in with a bunch of them, and Red grabbed one and said, "Look, I'm gonna be frank with you: I don't know what your signal is, I only know that you have one. Now if you don't give him the right signal I'm gonna blow your fucking head off."

See, they have a signal at night when they go out. They have a signal with a flashlight to the guy in the tower to open the first door.

So the guy gave the signal and that door opened and they went in and there's a bulletproof shield between them and the guy that has to open the second door. So there's nothing to do. They can't get at him, but they had all these screws in there with a gun, and Red told them to open the door for them or there'll be a bloodbath out in the corridor. First he told them to open the door where he was because that's where they keep their armory, they wanted to get in there and get their armory.

The screw said, "No, I'm not going to open here, Red. I'll open the front door and you can get the fuck out. I'm not gonna let you in here."

So they settled for that and they made it out.

Red got pinched on a bank robbery a couple of months later down in Baltimore.

They gave him a Federal bit on and after his state prison bit, and when it came to parole eligibility they tried to parole him just to get him out of their hair. They wanted to parole him and then turn him over to the Feds, but he refused to parole. He's doing so much time altogether: he has a state prison bit, he had a twenty-five-year Federal bit, and another state prison bit and state prison bits on and after the intervening Federal bits, so he's wrapped up for life and his only chance of getting out is escape, and he figures as tough as it is here it's gonna be a lot easier than Alcatraz, and he knows as soon as the Federals get ahold of him that's where they're gonna put him, in Alcatraz. So he refused the parole, and finally they hit upon a nice little piece of strategy. The governor's council met secretly one night and they pardoned him.

They pardoned Red Halliday, and they put him in chains the next morning and they carted him down to Alcatraz.

That Red Halliday was an interesting bastard. He was down in Ten Block with me for about a year. He was an easygoing guy, the nicest most personable guy you ever want to talk to. He never swore. He used to say things like, "For crying out loud." He played so many roles that I think he lost track and forgot who the hell *he* was, you know.

There was six of them tried to get out once. Red Halliday, Marty Feenie were transferred to Alcatraz, but when Alcatraz closed they were transferred to Atlanta and then to here. And a few other guys were with them. Three or four of them were working in the kitchen and environs and the others walked up and down the blacktop out in the yard. This was on Saturday morning and a milk truck used to come in every Saturday morning. And it was one of those, one of those closed like a bread truck or a bakery truck. That's the one they were waiting for. When it was parked up at the loading platform they all converged on the door. There's about three instructors and two screws in there and maybe five cons. And they grabbed everybody and walked them in the icebox. They were armed with knives and they put a knife up at the driver's throat. They took one screw with them in the back of the truck. They told the driver to drive out to the trap. So he drove out to the trap. Now they'd been watching this truck when it went through the trap each week and they thought they had the signal down. See, they open the first gate and drive to the second gate and then they close the first gate behind you and you're trapped there until they open the second gate. Now they thought they had the signal worked out, but they didn't. So the screw in the tower didn't get the right signal and so he wouldn't open the second gate. So Red Halliday comes out of the truck and he says, "Okay"—he had this screw standing there with this knife at his throat—"then open the back gate, we're going back in."

The screw said, "All right, I'll do that." So he opened the back gate.

Now, in case of emergency they have this rickety ladder. It's just an alternate plan and it's too bad they didn't make it a bit stronger. When they went back through the second gate they told the driver to drive along the wall. Instead of coming through past the fence they drove up along the wall and they got out and they put the ladder on top of the truck. They climbed up on the top of the truck. They brought the screw with them. Put the ladder on top of the thing, and Red hollered up to the guy in the tower, "Turn the juice off because White"—White is the screw—"is coming off first. And if you don't turn the juice off we're just going over his body. So you'd better turn it off."

They sent White up first and he got three-quarters of the way up and the ladder crumpled and they got trapped, so they retreated to the metal shop. That's when the warden came over and they tied him up. Trussed him up with wire and they dumped gasoline over him.

They were trying to extort their way out. First they had the deputy. A bunch of screws came out before they retreated into the metal shop. When they saw that all was lost they tried to grab a couple of screws, and everyone retreated except the assistant deputy who just retired last year. His name is Thompson and they used to call him "the Alligator." He's an old man and he couldn't make it as fast as the other screws, so George Harrison caught up with him and George grabbed him on the shoulder and he fell down. And George had a knife and he put the knife by his head and told him to get up.

And Alligator Al started telling 'em, "Leave me alone, boys, I'm an old man. My legs: I can't get up."

George said, "Get up on your feet."

He said, "I can't, I'm an old man, boys. My legs, my legs!"

George said, "You're a dirty old mean motherfucking Charlestown headbreaker. Now get up on your feet or I'm gonna stick this through your eardrum."

So he got up on his feet and they brought him to the metal shop and they tied him up.

Then the deputy came over, hollering to them through the door. And they said, "Come on in, Deputy, and we'll talk to you." So he come in and they grabbed him too.

So now the warden came over and he said, "I'm coming in."

They said, "Come ahead." So he comes in.

They told the warden to get on the phone and call the guard in the tower and tell him to open the gate and tell the state police to back off, that they were coming out. By now the state police had the whole place surrounded. Warden said no, he wasn't doing anything like that. Red hit him a shot in the jaw. He picked himself up off the floor and took the telephone and told the guard in the tower to open the gate, but the colonel in the state police countermanded the order. They waited forty-five minutes and then they invaded the metal shop. They come in on both sides. There was about fifty of them; twenty-five come in the front and twenty-five come in the back, armed with Thompsons. They, of course, captured everybody.

Nobody got hurt?

One screw got cut a little bit. Not very much. Most of the physical damage that was done was done to those guys. They brought them down and stripped them down and brought them down to the new man's section. And a goon squad of screws went down with saps and they did a pretty good job on all of them except Red Halliday. Red's a big guy and he's a tough prick. They went into the cells one at a time. One of the guys, Doc Savage, hollered over to Red after they went into the first cell, "See what they're doing?"

Red went over to the door and looked out and caught the play and said, "Well, when they come in here I'm gonna break the first guy's back over my knee." Red was a big prick. And he just didn't know the meaning of the word fear. If that's what he said he was gonna do, that's what he would have done.

So they come to Red's cell and they said, "Oh, Red's all right," and they went by his cell. But five of them got pretty bad jobs done on them.

McCarthy and three in the bunch tried to go one time and they had a setup where they had a pole. And they hooked the pole on one of the stanchions holding up the wires on top of the wall. The pole was higher than the wall, see. So it was about that high above the wires so that if they climbed all the way to the top then you step over the wire.

Were they going to let themselves down the other side with a rope?

No, just jump. What happened was McCarthy was the first one up and the second guy, fucking Feenie, was just too eager. He was supposed to wait till Mac had vaulted over there, but he didn't. He thought Mac was close enough to the top and he grabbed the pole and started for himself. And Mac lost his balance and his ass landed right on the top wire and it shot him over the wall. When the current was shorted, the screw in the tower noticed it and he put the gun out, and there were five of them, but only four were still in the yard. So he covered them with the gun and he didn't notice that somebody else was over the wall.

When Mac's ass hit the wire it shot him over the wall and he laid on his back out there and he was out for a couple of minutes. But it was nighttime and the screw didn't even know he was out there. So when he regained consciousness he just got up and slithered into the grass and he got away.

But he wears those Coke-bottle glasses and he tried to escape once before and he broke them. So this time he brought along an extra pair. But sure as shit, when he landed, both pairs broke and he was groping. He can't see. He's blind as a bat and he was groping around in the woods out there for three days before they got him. And he never got further than the woods.

"MAX CAN TELL YOU
THE SKY IS BLACK . . ."

You know Max who works as a cook in the hospital? He was in the naval prison same time I was. He drove a street sweeper there. He decided he had enough of the naval cuisine out there, I guess. Our prison compound was right inside the base and there's the fence around the prison and of course the fence around the base; he got to the point in two years there where they used to send him out to sweep the streets around the base as well as inside the prison.

So one day he just drove up to the main gate and waved at them real fast and furious and they opened the gate and he drove the street sweeper right out onto the main highway, parked it, and left. You talk about embarrassed!

He was a check writer, by the way. His name, his last name, is the same as a very wealthy family in Buena Park, California, a very well-known wealthy family, and he had the same facial characteristics of that family: pale, pretty good-sized noses, that sort of stuff. Now as I said, he's a check writer, that's all he does when he's outside is write bad checks. So he moved into Buena Park there and got fairly well known in about four or five days as a member of that family. In the next four or five days he dropped $20,000 worth of checks and took off.

One time he was in some little town in Kansas and he went to the bank and picked up some blanks. He was broke, so he went to a small supermarket just across the street from a pretty good-sized service station. The service station had the guy's name on it who ran it. He came over and said he wanted to cash a $50 check and get some groceries. The guy said, "Well, I don't know you, and the bank's already closed. I can't cash a personal check for you because I just don't know you."

"Well, the guy across the street at the service station knows me real well. And he asked me to come over 'cause he didn't have it in the till."

The guy in the supermarket, he says that if the guy in the service station will verify it, he'll cash the check. So Max walks across the street to the service station and told the service station guy the same story, that the guy in the supermarket had sent him over to get the check cashed. He was standing by the door and Max had the supermarket guy waiting for some signal of recognition from the gas station guy and this guy waved and the guy across the street waved and he cashed the check in the gas station and then walked across the street and cashed another one over there.

He said that a couple of nights later he was in a small town in Oklahoma and got picked up for speeding and was taken into night court. He had some checks from that town. He always went to the bank first whenever he got anywhere. That night he got fined $15 in traffic court and he was on his way out of town and wanted to move fairly rapidly since he'd dropped a few checks there that day. He told them the only check he had was already made out for cash for $25 and they took it and gave him the $10 change.

He's quite a character, Max is. Max can tell you the sky is black. He's very convincing.

"I'M NO FREEDOM RIDER,
BUT LET'S FACE IT . . ."

One thing that used to get me. I used to make out the registry there at Nashville when visitors came in. Mr. and Mrs. So-and-So, or Joe and Hattie So-and-So. If they were colored people, you'd better not put down Mr. and Mrs.

I was just out of the county jail then and there wasn't a hell of a lot they could do to me. They could if they could get next to the deputy, you see, but you didn't mess with boys who worked for the deputy unless you happened to be the warden. And I was working for the deputy, much as I hated it, and so they couldn't say much.

I remember one woman who'd come in, she was a big, fat, colored woman, and I'd say, "Well, Mrs. Washington, how are you today? Got anything in your purse?"

"Ah, yes, sir, mister, I've got my toad stick in here."

Her knife, you know. I had to check in the knives. Put them in an envelope. All the old colored ladies there carried knives. This was just to trim fingernails, peel apples, and kill people. Things like that. Protected themselves, you see. But they were pleased to give up their knives to me because I called them Mrs. So-and-So.

This one guy was stationed nearby and he would turn red every time I'd say mister or missus. When I'd write it down he'd scratch it out and put "colored" on the registry.

They were so prejudiced it was childish. They were out of this world. I'm no freedom rider, but let's face it, if a man can do something better than I can, he demands my respect in that particular field, and he gets it. Whether he's white or black or green.

MR. TEAGUE

We had a night deputy warden in Portolla, his name was Mr. Teague. And he wasn't so noticeably illiterate because he had little tricks. He'd wear a pair of overalls, bibbed overalls. This was the night deputy warden's uniform, bibbed overalls. Really. I'd type up the morning wakeups, the men who are to be woken up early in the morning. I'd type them up and on one slip of paper I'd put "upper colored wing," and on another "lower colored wing." And I'd have to take these four slips of paper and I'd say, "Here's the men to call out in upper white wing." And I'd hand it to him, and he'd say it and put it in his upper right pocket. "And here's the men in upper colored." I'd hand him that and he'd put that in the upper left pocket. Then I'd give them the other two and he'd put them in the two lower pockets.

He was so strongly prejudiced that he even resorted to the white on the right and the colored on the left, you know.

And he'd go up to the dormitories and he'd pull this one out of his upper right pocket, this is the upper white. He'd look at it like this, maybe sideways, and he'd look at it real serious, and then he'd say to the guard up there, "Here's the men I want you to wake up in the morning." And he'd proudly hand him this piece of paper.

I thought many times of switching them on him, you know, because he would have no way of knowing, but somebody would have snitched me off. They would. They were terrible there. They'd shoot for you. If you'd a done them a favor they'd try to ruin you, you know.

"WHAT KIND OF THIEF IS THAT?"

We had a fairly decent bit that I had something to do with. I'm proud of it. It's nothing they can bust me for, they can't prove it.

In Nashville, freight cars used to come right inside. They pushed them in with a switch engine. You'd break them on the track manually and they'd push them out with the truck again. The switch engine never came inside. They thought they were pretty safe doing things that way.

One day a car comes in and they found out that it can't be loaded until the next day. A couple of the guys found this out too, a couple of guys that were doing a lot of time. So between five of us we made a false end for the boxcar and five of them got in. I stayed because I was just doing a three-to-seven anyway. Four of them got in and they all got away. They loaded it with furniture and they all got away.

After it was unloaded they just opened the latch and got out. It turned out it was furniture for the capitol building and so here they are, running downtown. Two of them got caught in downtown Nashville, one got away and as far as I know they never caught him. And one came back.

He came back because he was *hungry*.

I mean, what kind of thief is that, he comes back to jail because he's hungry. What kind of thief is that?

"I WAS REAL UPTIGHT . . ."

The roughest joint I was in was Mississippi. I did two years there, then I went back and did four more. I did twenty-one months and nine days on the two, and forty-two months and eighteen days on the four.
They don't give much away, do they?
They sure don't. Almost the only way to draw extra good time down there is to be trusty, you draw sixty-two extra days a year for that, for working on Sundays and stuff like that. So they don't give you too much there at all.
You were a convict guard there, weren't you?
Yes. I did almost eighteen months as a guard down there.
For being a guard I got to go home for Christmas, ten days on Christmas furloughs. And any time there was a special occasion, like going to the coast on a long chase, I'd get to go down there. On Sundays I'd have special visiting privileges.
In Mississippi you can have your old lady in.
Yeah, they have rooms where you can take your wife. On some of the camps it had to be your wife, a real wife, on others it was just like bringing a girl in anyplace. On Camp Five you couldn't have that at all because that was supposed to be the incorrigibles, the hard-asses. I was on Camp Six when I was a guard, then I got sent to Camp Five when I got busted down.
I was on leave and after the ten days I just didn't come back, I just kept going. They got me in Louisiana.
What would have happened if the Texas inmates had found out you were a convict guard?
I've often wondered about that. Some of them knew it. I was busted [someone recognized him] up there on it, but I think I more or less lied my way out of it. I told them, "Man, that dude's crazy, he doesn't even know me." That happened about the first or second day I was there. And there was some talk around, but nothing ever happened. You've heard about policemen going inside jail and being recognized and getting killed or something; I was just wondering if I was lucky enough to beat it in Texas. People knowing I had carried a gun in them overtime bits before. I think I was just one of the fortunate ones, one that got by or slid by, and I guess that's some sort of reprieve, because a lot of them dudes knew me. I knew them when I was

out here stealing with them and they knew I was a good thief and so
they never believed it. They knew what kind of people I was out here
on the streets, and they knew I wouldn't snitch on nobody. And they
still don't believe it.

There was never an opening out there on my record where any
convict could see it. I think they guard those records pretty close, you
know. Things like that never fall in the hands of another convict.

I stayed uptight on it, I was scared the whole time I was up there,
I admit that. I was real uptight about it.

DOING TIME

Roughest part of doing time? Well, I say it's kinda making your mind
up that you're gonna have to do it, and, well, let me say it this way:
some people do it so it can eat you up, and you just become eat up
with hate. If you let it do that, and because you want to take the
blame out on somebody, and you want to resent authority or hate the
people around you, and if you do this, I think that a person can become very sick in his mind if he has to spend a lot of years incarcerated. At one time I thought myself going along these channels. I feel
I'm fortunate I worked it out for myself before it was too late. About
the roughest part of doing time is just making your mind up that you
gotta do it, and going ahead and doing it as easy as you can. Spending
your time while you're in prison doing something to better yourself,
and keeping your mind occupied with something constructive, rather
than just wasting, wasting all these years sitting around here just doing
nothing.

It's very healthy, I know that, but as far as learning a trade in the
fields . . . I knew I'd never be a farmer when I get out of here, I knew
that. Of course, it makes you feel healthy working out there, and you
get plenty of fresh air, plenty of sunshine, and it's not near as hard
now as it used to be. Fact, it's much easier in the field than it was, say,
ten years ago.

It's not really hard; there's tricks you can learn to do the work,
make it easier.

The hardest thing, I believe, about working in the field, is knowing that you've got a man on a horse with a gun behind you, driving you, and most of the time you feel that this person that is making you work and is telling you what to do is an inferior person to you, and you resent it. You resent being driven like an animal, you know, herded like animals down a corn row, or screamed at and hollered at about leaving grass and weeds, when you know that the work that you're doing can be done better and quicker with machines. . . . I believe the only reason they do it is to keep men occupied. I believe they have some kind of theory that if they work they won't feel like getting into trouble in the building, you know, fighting and gambling and playing poker and other things.

NO MORE TENNIS SHOES

I saved that assistant warden from getting hurt. He don't know it. I saved him by talking a psychopath out of it. I actually got him up there and talked him out of it because he knows me from the jail. They were going to throw lighter fluid on the assistant warden and set him afire. He don't even know this; he's wrangled me a couple of times, but I don't say nothing.

I talked to this boy, I said, "No, you're wrong now. You sonofabitch, don't you try that stuff. That's out, that's sadistic."

He said, "Aw, goddamn. We've got a lot of it saved up."

I know what they'd do if that happened: they'd take our lighter fluid away from us, see. Anything like that, they'd take everything.

Like the guy that went over the picket the other day, that young kid, a college boy from Houston. He's all mixed up, though. He jumps the picket and he's got tennis shoes on. He swiped a pair of the guards' khakis and he makes the picket. Because he went over that goddamned picket with tennis shoes on, a bulletin comes out the next day: all tennis shoes will be turned in immediately. And any person found with tennis shoes—and you buy them in the commissary, they sell them to you—they'll be turned in immediately and stored. See, they don't want to involve themselves in outside trouble of a boy paying for it and then taking it away from him. So they'll be stored. Any found hereafter will be classed contraband and confiscated. Just because he goes over the fence.

CHINAMAN

Chinaman, that fella in the garden squad, course he wore down now after twenty-three years in prison, but I've known him to cut in the woods and the boss would holler, tell him—I remember when I first came in the prison, the boss would not let me cut no wood. He asked me, "You ever cut any wood?"

I said, "I've never cut no wood in my life."

"You put that axe down. They cuts wood here. You set right there and I'll show you how they cut wood down."

He hollered over to old Chinaman, said, "Ole Chinaman," said, "sing, son."

Chinaman said, "I ain't got no snuff."

Boss was a chronic snuff-dipper and he generally carried six or seven boxes of snuff in a big jar, a big brown jar. He said that's his social security. Now he knows those six or seven cans he was gonna give to different inmates. He says, "I don't care if you don't sing, I ain't gonna give you my snuff." About five or ten minutes later he says, "Here, Chinaman, here's you a firebox."

Well, in that time cigarette lighters wasn't known in the prison system and everybody made their own cigarette lighters. You made a cigarette lighter out a burnt cotton and a flint rock and a little old piece a file. And that never miss, you could light that in any kind of wind. And he'd tell Chinaman he's throwing him a firebox and he'd throw him a box a snuff. And Chinaman would sing in them bottoms. There'd be three hundred axes dropping with him. When they cut, everybody be cutting. Same thing when they cutting down, he'd be singing lead on "Let Your Hammer Ring," a variety of verses, and everybody be in chorus with him on "Let Your Hammer Ring." All the axes be dropping. When the timber's on the ground there'd be three hundred axes dropping with him. All in harmony. That's something to hear.

I'd never seen nothing like that in my life.

CHOCK

I'll tell you about chock. They used to make it here all the time. Fact of the matter, they had a captain on the Eastham, they called him Dead Easy Hamilton, you know, because he give everybody a break and was easy on everybody. And everybody had him a keg or jar or something he made his chock in. And they'd leave 'em take it to the field with 'em a little bit at a time. Course he had to work, but they didn't care how much you drank as long as you worked. And they had this one steward, he didn't know about this policy, so he went in the building and dumped everybody's beer out. And when they come in at dinner, well, everybody saw his beer was gone. They bucked, wouldn't go to work. So the captain made him roll the barrels back in and give them some more stuff to make some more chock with.

How do you make chock?

Oh you take some cornmeal, sugar, yeast, you get a few potatoes, raisins, put it in there and just let it work till it ferments real good, then you take it off and you put it in bottles. Strain it, you know, and put it in bottles. Then you put it under, if you got warm water, you just let this warm water run over it and add a little more sugar and it makes better alcohol, gives stronger alcohol content. Gets pretty strong. 'Bout 40 percent I imagine.

You can get pretty drunk on it then?

Yeah, you can get pretty drunk.

Some of them on the Retrieve, they had snuck in some copper wire and got some pots out of the kitchen and they set 'em up a real still down there. They was manufacturing the real stuff. Till one of 'em got to making it a little too fast and it blowed up and nearly burned him to death. And that was the end of the whiskey-making. That was back in 1944 when he got hurt. He went out and come back with a life sentence since then. I saw him last June when I went out on a writ.

CONDITIONS THEN

One time was a bunch of us over on the Eastham and had an old camp over there named Two Camp. Well, it burnt down. These convicts set it on fire and burned it down. So after it burnt down and everything, they moved all these fellas over there to one camp where we was at.

We had to go over there and pick off a bunch a peanuts. And the guards, they surrounded the peanut barn, see. Anyways, they got to vying with each other out there and wasn't watching, really, so they pried off the back end of the barn and a bunch of them run off. After they'd been gone two or three hours it got dinnertime and they called us all out and started to counting, you know.

And everybody knew that the one old guard was real bad, so the guys that was in his squad—nobody had gone off out a his squad—so two or three of them jumped out a his squad over into another squad so he'd have some gone so he'd get fired. So they fired him and the rest of them too.

Conditions then was nothing like now. They had just old wooden buildings, you know, wooden floors, there was one layer of wood, one layer of sheet metal, and another layer of wood on the floors. And they just had old iron bars and no windows. But they had building tenders. In every one they'd have four or five building tenders, and that's what kept you from getting out: they wouldn't let you, you know.

And the bunks was just made out a wood. There wasn't no springs or nothing, no steel, just wood, and they had cornsilk mattresses, no sheets, had blankets in the winter. And they had no hot water except a coil that run around and around an old heater that set up in front a the building. And about the first three or four guys that got a bath, they got warm water, rest of 'em got cold. And that's the conditions we lived under up until about 1940. Then they started a building program.

NICKNAMES

The nicknames don't only apply to the inmates. They apply to the officers, too. Practically every officer has a nickname. Course in most cases it's not called to his face. He'll generally be aware of the name, but he never hear of it from the inmates. They speak of the officers' nicknames between themselves. It's Tall in the Saddle, and Two-Gun Peter, or some title of some famous cowboy or the way he act or carry hisself. You take here on this farm, our warden is known throughout the States, not only in the system but throughout the States, as Beartrack. But no inmate would ever have the nerve to walk up and call him Beartrack to his face. The same thing applies to our major, Deep in the Saddle. Some refer to him as the Sidewinder because he strikes when you least expect. Some of the bosses are called Radio Mouth, Tomato Red, Hitler, Mussolini. Sometimes the name fits and sometimes it doesn't.

Generally the name fits the man by the way he acts. In most cases it's perfect. A convict is very shrewd in naming a person. They watch all his actions, gestures, the way he carry hisself, the way he talks, the way he holler when you're working unnecessarily. Radio Poppa was a major on the low farms, on Ramsey. You could hear him holler in the field a mile away. But everybody respected him on his integrity. And they knew him to be a fair and square man, so the only name they could figure out was Radio Poppa because you could hear him all over the farm anywhere he hollered.

I think the funniest part of the nicknames, though, came in the seven and a half years I was building tender over in the maximum security wing that I had all these female impersonators, the young homosexuals, even the young penitentiary turnouts that they couldn't send on the farms because they couldn't protect themselves in the open tank. They had taken up the habit of referring to each other as Miss or Mother. And everyone had a name: Miss Peaches or Miss Chicago, even Caledonia, Belladora. And even those officers that carried them in the field knew 'em by those names that they called themselves. Man, it was something to hear; you'd see the squads working together and they holler back, "C'mon, Sister, and help Mother." We had all a those that they couldn't send in the open tank on the other farms, they was sent into maximum security for their own protection, and it was something to see when you see 'em out in the field working and one holler back at the lead row and say, "Wait, Mother, till I go back here and get Sister." That's men's impersonating women.

When I first came in prison my nickname was Big Four. That was because when I first came in I had four years from Fort Worth and I was weighing approximately 230 pounds and was six foot two. So everybody called me Big Four. How could I be that big with only four years with nothing around but a string of lifetimers. And everybody took it as a joke. I returned to prison with this forty-year sentence and after eight months in the field I was assigned to the building as building tender in the maximum security wing. On one side I had all the female impersonators and the young homosexuals, as I said, and on the other side I had all the potentials, all the deadly convicts that they'd sent out a isolation and I had to keep those from being over at the homosexuals on the other side. So they called me the Keeper of the Sissies because I protected them from all the hard cases, and they began to call me Big Daddy. Big Daddy, the Keeper of the Sissies.

And this has stuck with me throughout the time I've been here. Now, approximately, with good time, I've got about twenty-one years in. It seems like a tag I can't get rid of. I've gotten used to it, it seems like a part of my name now. So when anybody ask me, "What is your name?" I say, "Aw, I'm Big Daddy." Instead of my name.

CAPTAIN COCKLEBURR

One time some boys got out and they came back and they buried some guns on the John Henry ground. I don't know if you know what a John Henry ground is or not, it's a place they spread out the food, you know, for you to eat meals. Used to never go to the building at noontime, you always used to eat every noon, even if it was raining, you eat out in the fields. So these guys got out and they come back and they buried these guns and we took over the whole farm. We locked up everybody in the building, including the captain and his wife and everybody was locked up.

But ole Cockleburr got to thinking about the way they had treated him. His name wasn't Cockleburr then, that's his name now.

He went back over there and he saddled him a horse and got him a bullwhip and went back and got him about ten a those bosses out a the building and he made 'em put cockleburrs in their boots, see. And he went a whupping 'em down the road, you know, made 'em get some hoes and he started 'em hoeing up and down that road, and every time he'd hit 'em with that bullwhip, he'd say, "Call me Captain Cockleburr, you motherfuckers you."

So that's how he got his name.

Later on, this same guy drove a switch engine out through the Walls. Right through that iron gate and he got away. And he went up to Oklahoma and run for sheriff and got elected and was sheriff for three years before this deputy finally snapped as to who he was and arrested him and sent him back.

How did he escape getting beaten to death after he came back from that escape?

Oh, well, he got beat a lot, but they didn't ever kill him or nothing, they just whupped him every time they thought about it.

BUNK GEORGE

On Eastham Farm they had a old man they called Eagle-Eye. That was because he never missed a trick, regardless of where you was in the building or what you was doing, he'd always knock you off. And that's how he got his name. But when he got older, they built some partitions down through the building, he couldn't see everything, so they started calling him old Blind Tom. They changed his name.

And they had a captain up there they called Crying Tom Small. And there were several of these brothers. And he called everybody "Old Butt-fuckers." Everybody was "Old Butt-fucker" to him.

He had a brother named Marble-Eye Small. And he was the meanest one of 'em. He used to whip everybody every morning. He started at Number One Hoe Squad and whip everybody in Number One Hoe, and then he'd whip everybody in Number Two Hoe, and right on down the line till he got to the pull-dos. And he'd whop them. That was on Eastham way back in the thirties, back when Lee Simmons was general manager. They finally fired him and mighty near everybody in the system on account of the brutality. He was the one that hollered "Give 'em more axes" when they was cutting their legs off and arms off and everything, old Lee Simmons.

They had a boss under him, he's still here, he's working on this farm now. His name was Bunk George. And, boy, he was something else when he was young. I mean, he'd whup you in the field and he'd lie on you to the captain, anything in the world to keep you in trouble. And everybody hated him, you know. So one time there was a bunch of us got in solitary because we wouldn't eat some food they had on the John Henry ground. And there was one boy that was named Jerry Lewis that was with us. And you know, there used to be an old saying down here, you'd be told a story and somebody'd doubt and they'd say, "What'll you be?" And you say, "Well, I'll be anything."

So old Jerry Lewis told some old story down in the solitary and somebody said, "What'll you be?" and he said, "I'll be anything." The guy says, "You be old Bunk George?"

He says, "Hell no, I won't be old Bunk George."

So the captain was standing outside listening, see, and he said, "You'll be old Bunk George before you get out a there."

So about the second week we was out there they opened the door and let us on out and old Jerry said, "How about me, Captain?"

He said, "Who is that?"

And he said, "This is old Jerry Lewis."

And he just slammed the door. About two more weeks pass and he went out there and he opened the door and he said, "How 'bout letting me out, Captain?"

He said, "Who is that?"

He says, "This is old Bunk George." So they let him out. Give him some fried eggs.

I never will forget that. They give us all some fried eggs that morning.

KILLER BARRON

Killer Barron, he was just a boss, but he was a bad sonofagun. His name was Boss Barron, you know, but they called him Killer Barron.

He killed guys, you know. There's a squad here and a squad here and a guy came out of his squad over here and in front of his squad and shit. And he told him, "If you shit there I'm gonna kill you," and the guy shit and he killed him.

"THIS IS SCHOOLBOY TIME . . ."

I seen guys get their brains beat out with trace chains, I seen a man be handcuffed and a officer come along and stomp on your wrist with boots. Hang you up there with your toes just barely be touching the floor. Lots of people don't see this. They think it's rough now. It's not rough, this is schoolboy time. Compared with then. There wasn't no rainy days, there wasn't no Sunday. Every day was working day. If it rained, you just worked right on. Boss sitting on his horse with his shotgun pointing down here with his rain slicker on. On the turnrow you had to fish the beans out of the water to eat out of your plate.

"THEN THEY CUT HIS WHOLE LEG OFF . . ."

We had a ole doctor, one guy went up there and asked him for a lay-in [permission to stay in the building during the work day] and he told him, "I'm not gonna lay you in."

So he went back and got him an axe, they put a hood over his face so he couldn't see who done it, you know—they tortured them then to find out who done it—and then they cut his leg off and he went hopping up there with that old leg still in the shoe and throwed it through the picket and said, "Can I lay-in on this?"

See, back in them days, they'd take you out and torture you to make you tell who cut your leg off, so they put a pillowcase over his head so he couldn't say who done it, then they cut his whole leg off.

He just throwed it out through the picket and asked him could he lay-in on that.

"YOU COULD TELL THEM GUYS WHAT GOT WHIPPED . . ."

They used to had to get a order to whip you, you know. The doctor would come down to check your heart to see whether you could stand the whipping or not. And then if you could stand it, well, he'd okay it. And if you couldn't, he wouldn't. A whole lots of times the captain just didn't pay no attention to whether he'd say you could or not. He didn't care whether you lived or died no way. So they'd spread you down. Man would stack up five a them red bricks like them there up on something solid and haul off and hit it with that bat and bust the brick at the bottom. Well, you know about how it'd take on a man's skin. He hit the top brick and bust the one at the bottom. A man had to take all that kind a stuff. Whole lots of them had the whole back of their britches cut out.

You could tell all them guys what got whipped. They couldn't set down. Had to lay on their stomach, and other than that he couldn't lay no other way. All the back part back there would be just raw blood.

But a man went to work after the whipping was over with.

And some would run off. They'd know what day the whipping was coming up and they'd run off to keep from meeting that day set for the whipping.

"HE WAS STABBED SEVEN TIMES . . ."

That clerk, Tony, if he didn't like someone he'll put him where he wants to put him. That killing that happened last time you was down happened because of him.

Now this Spanish boy, he had already killed one inmate on another farm before he came here. Tony didn't like him. He put him in with this boy that the Spanish boy didn't like. He did that for spite. And this boy was epileptic, he had spells. He was awful quiet, but they're all hot-tempered, you know. And I guess they'd had some words in their cell together. You get two people that definitely can't get along, you can't put them in a little cell that's been built for one. All these cells been built for one and now they're crowded because they added another bunk in them. Actually, when one is down making his toilet in the morning the other one has to stay on his bunk out of the way if he's gonna get along, because both of them can't be out at the same time. And I guess they must have had some kind of incident like that because at the show that night he got him just as the lights turned out. Nobody made a move to help him. I'm way on this side and my job in the building was to try to break up something like that before somebody gets seriously hurt, but I'm not gonna run in a bunch of Spanish boys because I've had 'em down on Ramsey in the wing in front of mine and I know what they'll do. If you grab one, seven more will stab you, especially in the dark. Nobody broke that up until the lights come on. And he never made a sound. They didn't know till they saw the blood. He was stabbed seven times.

And that's because of that clerk. That's for power. Some people take a little authority and abuse it. But they going to get him, you'll see.

He made parole before and in no time everybody was shooting at him, everybody was trying to get him. His life was hanging on a thread. They was shooting at him like a clay pigeon. Guys that used to be in his wing. He got a shot through his car, he had his old lady in the car, he got jumped out and he shot back. They sent him back. Now they don't know how many enemies he has. Everybody down at this end, that's all they plan, how to get him. They've set up a thing. There's no way he can get out without them knowing he's going out. Connections all through the Walls, through Identification Unit, they'll know when he goes out.

So he's a dead man when he goes out?

Absolutely. The officers will say that. They won't tell *him* that, but they have told me that and I've heard 'em talking about it, saying, "I wouldn't be in his shoes, he'll be lucky to get out of Huntsville alive."

"THEY DON'T KNOW WHETHER
I'LL KILL ANYBODY . . ."

There is a character I adopt whenever I'm doing time, whether it's regarding sex or anything else. I try to avoid letting anybody know exactly how I stand on anything. Consequently, they don't know whether I'll kill anybody or whether I'll run. You know what I mean?

Johnny Bright: "I escaped
from every place they
ever put me . . ."

Man come to prison in the old days, he had but one thing on his mind and that was escape. That's what they talked about, thought about, twenty-four hours a day. The things that they went through and the things that they did in order to try and accomplish these damn things would amaze you. Some of it was daring, bold, some of it was cunning as hell, some of it was stupid as hell. You contrast those things to the guys coming down here now. Now they've got all these reform systems. Actually the men are doing a lot more time than they were in the old days. In the old days you had a code you lived by. If you stooled, that was it. Today it's accepted as a regular thing.

What was that code you lived by?

They never snitched on you. You never talked to guards in them days. When I first came down here the closest you could get to a guard was thirty, forty foot. You couldn't hire one of them guards to go in the mess hall like they do today. And it was a different attitude between the guards and the personnel. I think the Capone regime changed all that when all them big-shots went to squealing on each other, it broke the code in the prisons. The guys were figuring—of course the politicians helped it—so now there's only a few old individuals in here that you couldn't get to snitch to save your neck.

Like I say, in the old days everybody was obsessed with one idea, and that was going over the wall. Or under it or through it. And some hellacious things materialized in different escapes.

In the old days you were more desperate than now, you had more reasons to escape. The work and the personnel was so different that a man would resort to anything. Men cut their legs off and broke their arms and cut their heel strings and everything. It was a pretty driving condition. That's all been alleviated or erased to where a man, if he wants, can come down and do his time. When you were in the old days, a guard might tell you, "You come back in my squad after dinner and I'm killing you." And he meant just that.

You'd do anything rather than get killed and that motivated a lot of the escapes. In the old days they didn't have the facilities for apprehending you after you did escape. They've got a system now. There's been many guys that got off this farm in the last two years, but very few got away. It's not just beating the walls or the dogs anymore. They've got walkie-talkies and they've got this highway patrol. Everybody has a spot designated and you walk right up to it.

Until they quit looking for you you're as well off one hundred feet in them woods as you are in New York. But these guys don't understand that. You can tell them, "Don't leave. Go out there and as soon as you know you got the dogs beat, sit down. Can't nobody walk up on you. You can tell when they quit looking for you. When they quit, you can walk out there and get on a bus or go downtown and get on a bus." But they're so anxious to get someplace.

But it's harder even in that sense to escape. It's not just getting over the wall or through it or under it, it's after you leave here. And they don't give up like they did before. They used to maybe look for you a few hours and if they didn't find you, the dogs didn't pick up your trail, they just went on back to work. Today they keep looking for you and they keep widening the search.

I escaped from every place they ever put me. I escaped from a place and then got back in before they even knew I was gone. I know that sounds pretty fantastic from San Quentin, but I was in an honor camp. I've been out there where I'd walk off in the day and come in sorry-eyed. Going over that fence with them shooting at me and everything. It was a challenge. And beating down these damned old dogs was something too; it was fun.

Down there on Retrieve, some big officials came down one time for a goose hunt. They was following the squads to the field one morning. Taking us out to work, then they was going to go out to these goose blinds. This old dog sergeant was talking to them and they was talking about hunting. They're right in back of my squad and I'm tinearing on them. They're talking about the joys of hunting, the various thrills of hunting. And this dog sergeant says, "Well, you don't know what a thrill is as far as hunting goes until you hunt a man with dogs. That's a thrill. There's no thrill in the world like it."

I couldn't hold my old Irish mouth. I said, "I know a bigger thrill than that, Sergeant."

He said, "What's that, Old Brains?"

"To be out there in front of them shit-eating sonsofbitches and know you've beaten them and beaten what they brought with them."

He said, "You ought to know."

Down on the Retrieve we built a tunnel one time. Some pretty noted characters were in on it: Gene Paul Norris, Johnny Fox, some of the old Bonnie Parker bunch that were still there. It took us six months. It was about as far as from here to that fence out there. This is fantastic, it's almost unbelievable how it happened.

The guards could see everybody in that tank, every minute of the day and night. Well, back there in the shower bath we had a master bricklayer and he took a drain out of there. He fixed it like a keystone so that you could just set it right back in. See that tower just past the fence? Well, they started digging like toward that tower, they're going to come out in back of it. About every fifteen or twenty foot they dug them a room where they could stand, three by three by six or seven, and they'd throw this dirt back to each other to be taken out of there. Every grain of that dirt—and it was tons and tons of it—went right down a crapper, a handful at a time. They flushed it down this crapper.

We got ratted on three times while we was doing it. We had a warden, I. Killem Kelly. He didn't think much of stool pigeons noway, and the third time he come in, he's standing on this thing and he says, "The next time a guy tells me there's a hole in this building I'm going to make him get up in front of you convicts and show it to me." He was standing right on it.

We had electric lights in that thing and we had fans blowing air to these guys and everything. And we worked months and months and months. Guys that wasn't going, we hired them. At that time you could get Benzedrine—that's these inhalers in here, and you could take a strip of that and it was worth fifty cents. We'd pay them fifty cents an hour to dig on this tunnel. No telling how many man-hours went into that tunnel and under the most dangerous conditions you've ever seen in your life.

If you could go down there and get up in that picket and look, you wouldn't believe that men could actually accomplish a thing like that right in plain sight of this boss.

The way they was guiding these guys underground was with a rod that they'd shove up through the ground. We had a guy up in the schoolroom, a surveyor, and he had a sextant glass up there, a transit. He'd put it on it and he'd tell them which way to go. So we had one of these mulligans—a boss—he's up in this tower and this rod comes up there out of the grass and he spies it. And he's trying to dog-eye that thing. He ain't sure, he can't see too good anyway, and he's not sure what he's seeing. And they'd accused him of being crazy anyway—all the bosses and everybody else several times. He wears a great big gun —and he's shorter than me—and a great big hat; the gun hangs way down to his knee and he looked like a freak. He's dog-eyeing the hell out of this rod. They don't dare pull it down while he's watching. Finally he gets off work and he don't tell nobody about it, he just goes down in the yard and he goes around. In the meantime they've pulled the rod down. He's standing there looking at this thing and this new guard that's relieved him, he's watching him. Finally he gets down on his knees and the other guard's about to fall out of the tower. He thinks the guy is nuts, see? He cussed him out, told him to stop making a fool of himself in front of those convicts. The guy don't dare snitch off what he thought he seen, 'cause if it ain't there he's crazy sure enough.

So, anyway, when we finally come up with this tunnel, instead of being in back of the tower where we're supposed to be, according to our measurements, we're directly to the side of it and even with it, about seven or eight feet to the side. And they'd already broken that hole so we could all come out.

It would have been the biggest prison break in this country with the toughest guys in the system on that farm. It'll show you how fate works against the convict, or wrong-doer, whatever you want to call it, and how it protects some people. We had a couple of guys running the show. One of them was Gene Norris and another named Johnny Moore. They was putting up most of the cash. There was a boss that would come on at nine o'clock that couldn't hear so good. So they decided to wait till this shift came on and they had this hard-of-hearing boss on, so if anybody made any noise maybe he wouldn't hear it. If one guy rumbled we're all rumbled.

The rule is that nobody can go in that tunnel that's got a spot of white showing on him. They showed up in the dadgumdest things. They'd take these old blankets and they'd make hoods out of them with peekholes and everything else, and each guy had to follow the guy ahead of him. And to a given point if anybody ran or got up for anything like that, the guy in back of him is supposed to stab him. If you don't, the guy in back of you is supposed to stab you.

It was a tense thing. It was the end of six or seven months, and most of these guys were strummed up on that Benzedrine too. It was the dangdest thing you've ever seen. If that boss had looked and seen those guys he'd have come right off that picket, they looked like ghouls from the grave. I was with them and it was an eerie thing even to me.

Well, they go down. So many guys in the tunnel and they're waiting for nine o'clock. We're lined up, and as each man leaves the tunnel, another one will come in the other end. It was the damnedest thing you've ever seen in your life. Months and months of work. This fog had come in and you couldn't even see that picket, it was so thick. It was perfect.

And just about ten or fifteen minutes to nine a wind, a slight breeze, and with it just a sort of a sprinkle came in.

This boss had been sitting facing the building and the hole is out here to his side. A thousand guys could have gotten out of that hole and he'd never have seen them. But when this wind came up, it lifted that fog like a curtain on a stage. It was just like a master hand was pulling the strings of puppets. The goddamnedest thing you've ever seen in your life. He gets up and closes the east window and he closes the south window—the wind was out of the southeast—and instead of facing the damned building like he'd been doing, he turns his chair around and he's got his feet in that window and he's looking right in the hole.

He don't see the hole. He don't see it all night long. But no living human being could come out of that hole without the boss seeing him.

Right quick we sent back word and got them to start a fire in the messhall, hoping this guy would change his position and become interested in the fire and a few of us could get away. He just looked a glance over at the fire, then back at the hole, he never changed that position all night long.

There wasn't a damned man got away.

After everybody got out of the thing I went down for myself to see if they was scared or what it was. I've gone over the thing with them shooting at me and everything else and I know that very few guys stick when the chips are down. (Like once there was eight of us left Ramsey at noon on the Fourth of July and there was a hundred waiting to go. They'd planned for months, but they wouldn't crawl out that window. Just the eight of us.) So I went down there and, boy, you couldn't have crawled out that hole without getting murdered. Couldn't keep from attracting that guy's attention.

It's unbelievable how that fog lifted. Just in time to thwart an escape like that.

Everybody gave up about four o'clock in the morning. They had stuff they'd hid in there and they just stripped themselves right where they were of whatever it was they had, they got rid of their knives, just throwed them down. They were just so disgusted. It was like putting a pin in a penny balloon, everything went out of the whole crew at once. They crawled in bed, all wore out, and the next morning they waited for the payoff to come. There was nothing they could do.

So a stock boss came riding by on a horse to go to work and he come by this tower and said something to the boss up there and he happened to look down and he said, "What in the hell is that?" And this guy looked out and seen that hole. He grabbed that shotgun and started to shoot up in the air, calling all the help he could. He figured there wasn't a man in the building.

They took two trucks of stuff out: clothes, shovels, tools. You ought to have seen it. The captain, the warden, didn't do nothing, he didn't say nothing because there wasn't no use. He knew everybody in the joint was in on it. He couldn't punish the whole bunch.

The way it is now, everybody comes down here and they shoot every angle they can to curry favors from the personnel and the parole board and to make all the points they can. Anything to get out. There's no such thing as honor amongst thieves or even a code of real fellowship. There's no such thing. People used to be crime buddies, they used to be prison buddies, but no such thing anymore. Almost everybody's for themselves and everybody's trying every way in the world to get out by crook or turn.

You've got a different element in. Most of these guys are not criminals, they're exhibitionists. Joy-seekers, thrill-seekers, stuff like that. They don't use any of the things that the old-time thief did, such as disguises and stuff like that, to try and get away. They go stick a man up with a gun, without a mask or a pair of gloves on—that's exhibitionism. In the old days a second-story man wouldn't even commit a burglary unless he was masked and had a gun to get away with. Now these characters that are burglars won't even carry a gun.

It's a different element, different type of people that you've got here. And associations and affiliations between the personnel and convicts are altogether different.

There was eight of us left that Ramsey one time. They built what was supposed to be an escapeproof prison down there. Especially the windows. They looked like normal windows, but they had a couple of ribs of beryllium steel in this soft metal. When you hit them with your sawblade, the blade would go into a thousand pieces. I was wiring this building. In them days everything was a challenge to me—a lock or safe or anything I come to, I'm going to open it or fool with it. So they got these windows and I stole one of them, me and another guy, and we got it over in the electric shop. We busted I don't know how many blades on this fucking thing. Finally it dawned on me that there was a couple of pencils of beryllium steel in this stuff, that the outer layer was soft. It'd be sawing soft as heck, cutting like a diamond, and boom, you'd hit that beryllium steel and that blade would go in ten thousand pieces in every direction.

So I finally figured out a way to beat them. I cut out around this soft stuff and was careful, then when I got to the beryllium I just take a wrench and put a little pressure on it and jar it. And just like that steel was glass, it popped, it just popped them windows out just like weeds.

They had the legislature down there, bringing them through, showing them all over this building, and of course I'm following them around and I'm supposed to explain some of the stuff to them. They're stressing this escapeproof stuff and I had already made that out.

We went out that window at twelve o'clock noon. There was a ball game going on out there and two guards with .30-.30 rifles on horses with their backs to us. If they look around they're going to blow our heads off. Hah! If somebody hits a ball over this way we're murdered, that's all there is to it. And in them days they didn't bring you back.

We all get to Oyster Creek and get away. These guys, they took off like quails. I'm the only guy alone. And I'm the only one that got away. They got buddies and everything and they scattered, going just like quail.

I get to Oyster Creek and I turn to watch the building a while. Here comes a colored boy nine hundred miles an hour from the dairy.

He's seen us and he's running to snitch. So I know the dogs are going to be after us in a matter of minutes.

Now, before I'd gone I'd got up on top of the building and took a transit and sighted this little town through the woods. So I led me a rough through them woods and I was in Rosharon in thirty-five minutes from the time I left, just walking. I never ran.

Everybody in escaping down here, they're looking for what we call *dog bait*. Unless you're with a guy personally, you're going to try to feed them to the dogs so you can get away. It's an unvoiced thing, but it's understood. So I've got a little money and I've got a great long knife. In case those old dogs come up on me I'm going to chop them all to pieces. There's two characters that are ahead of me, one of them working here with me right now, and they kept waiting for me to come on. I figured they know I got a little dough and they ain't got no dough and everything's fair in love and war. I figure they're going to try to take my dough or something. So I kept moseying along, and they finally stopped and waited. What they was looking for was dog bait—they wanted to feed me to the dogs.

So we were walking along this creek bank at a pretty good pace, still not running, and all of a sudden they say, "We're going to cross here." And they cut across this Oyster Creek.

Now, when a dog is running, trailing you, even if you turn like that, he'd run way out here a hundred yards, something like that, and look around before it dawns on him he'd lost the trail. But anybody going straight ahead on that trail, he'd go on following him, see? They figured I'd go straight ahead.

I looked up and saw the other guys crossing a foot bridge down there, and I know they don't see me. So I said to myself, "There goes my dog bait." They cross the creek and I kept going. I go down this foot bridge and went up a little rise and there was a crossroad and then a field of cane. I looked into that field of cane, and, sure enough, there's their big footprints. I get in their footprints and keep going straight down about one hundred yards, then come right back up. I know when them dogs come over that hill they're going right in that field.

I get back to this road and jumped off of it.

The dogs got something to trail: they run those guys all night long.

I go back over there and get to this highway. It's broad daylight. High noon. Every other car is a highway patrol or Texas Ranger or prison guard or the Houston sheriff's department or something. I come out of the woods and I crawled up to this fence along this railroad track on my stomach so nobody could see me. I'm looking for one of these little old culverts to go under this highway and this railroad. I've got to get across the highway to lose the dogs if they back up on my trail, see? I went seven different times back into the woods and back to the highway.

Finally I come to this little town, Rosharon. There's no place to go. I've either got to go back to the river and go back around the town or go on ahead. I'm all wore out anyway. And I thought, "How am I going to get across that road without arousing suspicion?" I sat down there and I thought and thought. I could see everybody in this little town. They couldn't see me.

Well, I've got on free world clothes that I stole to go. So I figure, "Well, I'll just make out like I live here." So I got me some rocks, a handful of rocks, and when nobody was looking I ducked out of the woods and I started throwing these rocks, just as nonchalantly as you've seen kids do. Got up on this little path along the railroad. Just as I get to the top here comes the highway patrol. Light going, just lickety-split, siren on. I just don't pay 'em no mind. I'm right up there, just like being right up on a stage. When they go by, I'm going to go down the railroad a little and find another path down to the highway. I'm still throwing these rocks at poles and picket fences and things. I get to the highway and I cross it just as nonchalant as everything. I walk up the highway about fifty foot and there's a boardwalk going over to the school. I'm still throwing them things. They got some trapeze boards and swings out there; I go over and get on them. Front of God and everybody.

Here comes the warden from out the farm with a chauffeur. He's got his wife's car and he's got a boss and two or three dogs in back. I'm sitting there, in front of God and everybody, just swinging to high heaven. They looked right at me. But nobody's going to figure a guy that led a mass break be pulling a thing like that. You just had to do something they wouldn't believe you'd do.

I waited till nobody was looking. There was a water fountain there and I eased up to it and got me a drink. I looked all around: nobody looking. I skidded under that thing and I stayed there three days and nights. I watched them catch two guys right in front of me out there. They come up the river road right into the roadblock. I couldn't holler at them, if I did I'd get the bulls on me. When they took away the dogs and horses from the roadblock, the third morning, I just stepped out there and got on the bus and went to Houston.

We've got some awful guys here on this farm. Real tough, some of them got pretty bad reputations. Guts, see? All these guys wanting to escape. Bunch of them with life sentences and everything. And they have a couple of characters in the queer tank that are not supposed to have no guts or nothing.

Well, I'm up on the roof of this building that I'm wiring and I look up one day and I see a couple of convicts out there picking up papers outside the fence, just walking along picking up cigarette butts and stuff. I snapped just like that. I said, "Good God, looka here!"

They went over and cut that fence right under that boss's picket and they went through both them fences. When they got outside they just started picking up papers around that road and they come on over there. There's a little park out there and they picked them up there and picked them up that side of the road and then went over here and started picking them up in the guards' parking lot in front of God and everybody. All these mulligans watching, but they were so nonchalant about it that the guards didn't snap. They get over there and they try two or three cars and finally they get one started. They just take off, slow and nice. They meet the head major coming up the drive there, but they wasn't speeding nine hundred miles an hour, so he didn't pay no attention to them.

And they got away.

I'm an alcoholic and all my troubles stem from that. I'm an electrician, I've always been able to make good money. I raised two boys, both officers in the armed forces. One of them got killed in a Sabrejet over in Korea a while back and the other's a career officer in the army. Booze has always been my trouble. But I've always liked to challenge things and I've been searching for an answer to this alcoholic problem. I've read everything ever written on it I could get my hands on.

I run into AA in the Walls, and I took to it like a hog took to slop. Now these people wouldn't let me as far as that desk out there from under a machine gun or shotgun at that time. I got two detainers on me, one from the Chicago district attorney's office for several American Express travelers' checks and I owe Folsom eight years and they've got a detainer on me for that. Can't make bond or parole or anything. I joined this AA and these sonsofguns sent me by *myself* up here to Tyler to make a speech to a convention of Alcoholics Anonymous for three days, and then sent me to Fort Worth for five days! A guy that is straining every minute to get out of the damn joint to punch it, and when he can walk off, he won't go a foot. How about that?

I'll tell you how it come about.

We got a prison manager here some years ago named O. B. Ellis. That's his picture right up there. He was quite a character, a shrewd sort of person. I didn't know how much he knew about convicts, but he sure knew people.

He came down on what we called the Bloody Retrieve and he made us a speech. We was going to give him a cool reception. He come in there and he had this cigarette hanging out of his mouth—he used to have a stance in his delivery sort of akin to a thug. He gets in there and he starts telling what he's going to do and what he ain't. He says, "I lead easy but I don't drive easy," and "I just ain't going for this hamstringing and these escapes."

"Well," I thought, "well, we're fifty-fifty. I don't believe in hamstringing and I'm damn sure going to try and escape." So we can meet halfway. Hamstringing is taking a knife and cutting this tendon, and I didn't want to mess up my running gear.

Shortly after he was here I punched one [escaped] and I was gone two or three months. I got caught again drunk on another caper and they brought me back. In them days they put you in stripes when they brought you back from escapes. They had formed this classification board and all these new things and begin to put them in effect and you had to be reclassified and sent to the various farms. I knew this was a formality, I was going right back to that same oil-burning farm. So, he's up in the lobby there, getting a cup of coffee, and I was in the Bull Ring, that brass cage you've seen over there with all these fish in white. They just come in there, all in white, and they're waiting to be classified. Here I am in these stripes—I stuck out like a sore thumb. He had been dog-eyeing me over, but he didn't know me.

I started across that lobby in them stripes and he waited till I got near. "Come here, boy!" Wasn't his nature at all, but that's the tone of voice he used that time. "Where you from?"

I'm from Fort Worth. "Dallas," I said.

"I mean which farm are you off of?"

I said, "The Retrieve."

He said, "Your name Bright?" He knew I was the only one to beat Retrieve in a long time.

I said, "Yup."

"When you come out of that office I want to talk to you," he says. I figure he's going to tell me what he's going to do to me if I don't quit running off. He's going to shoot me if he catches me in the woods, all that old stuff I've heard a thousand times.

So I come out of there and start walking toward him and he starts shaking his head and says, "Bright, when in the hell are you going to straighten up and get this time done and get the hell out of this penitentiary and quit running off?"

I'm standing there right then with a suit of khakis on under the stripes, I'm fixing to beat the joint before they can send me back to the farm. I'm going on out the back gate, see. So I'm wondering what's up—I can't dig this guy. He said, "You know we've just got a large appropriation. We've got a $11 million appropriation and we're going to start a terrific construction program. There's very few men in prison who are qualified tradesmen. You quit this running off, work with me, you could be a lot of help to me." Now I'd already started wiring that Ramsey prison down there and run off right in the middle of it. "Just think about it," he said, "I can be a lot of help to you."

Yak, yak. I'm just trying to figure the guy out, what kind of goon is this, and what's he got on his mind.

He said, "I'd like to keep you in the Walls, make you head of the electric department, but it would look to the other prisoners like I was rewarding a man for running off. Tell you what I'm going to do with you, Bright," he said. "I'm going to send you to Retrieve in the morning. You go down there and think it all over. If you decide to make up your mind to quit running off and go over and wire them buildings, I'll give you two for one, I'll give you all your lost back time, I'll even give you the time you've been out on them three escapes."

Well, I'm flabbergasted. I'm thinking, "What the hell kind of a goon is this? They couldn't find a guy that stupid in Texas, they went all the way to Tennessee to get one." I can't say a word. Usually I'm a voluble talker, you can tell that, but I can't think of a thing to say. I'm looking at this guy and wondering if he's ribbing me or what. He's going to trust *me*.

So I started to cross the lobby and I get about halfway across and he says, "You can write me that letter the next day after you get there, if you want to, Bright."

I got out of there and two or three guys met me at the door. Pretty rugged characters. One of them got killed in the Walls here awhile back and the other one is on the lam now from parole, writes the warden from all over the country and he's on the lam, he's quite a character. Anyway, I go down there and we get together and we're going to grab this picture show man and drive out the front gate. Going to change clothes and one of us get in the thing. It's dangerous, it's suicide if it's wrong, and if it's right, it's a walkaway. We lay this thing for three or four or five weeks, maybe two months. Every time something would happen, right at the psychological moment something would go wrong. It was either, like I say, suicide or a walkaway. It had to be perfect. So they got discouraged and one of them jumped up in the field out there and run and he got shot and they put him in the hospital. A few nights later this other guy I was with kills a guy in bed, so they shipped him into isolation. Now both these two end up on ice and I'm left.

I'm the only one left, so I get to thinking about this character, Ellis. I try to figure whether the guy was ribbing me or what. When I'd got down there I told these guys about Ellis; I said, "This guy's crazy or he's ribbing me or he's sharper than all of us put together. He wants me to write and tell him I won't run off and he's going to send me back over there where I can walk off."

I got a pencil and paper down and figured my good time, and I wouldn't have but about two and a half years to do if I can get it all back. So I wrote him a letter and I told him, "I thought over what you said. What you want's an electrician and I want my good time. Seems to me if I remember right all you wanted was my word that I wouldn't run off. It's a deal." That was on Thursday when I mailed it and on Saturday he answered me with one of these interoffice communications, he didn't even give the classification board a chance to turn me down.

He said, "In spite of the rabbit in this man I want him transferred to Ramsey construction immediately." Saturday they came after me.

Well, I can walk off the first few hours I'm there, any time I want to. So I go over there and I'm not in no big hurry, but if you'd ask me, "When are you leaving, Bright," I'd have said, "I'll be in Dallas by Saturday." I actually meant that. But I wasn't in no hurry. There was a lot of guys I wanted to talk to and see and everything, and I got hung up on this job and the week went by and another week, and then Mr. Ellis come out there. I was in there working on some blueprints one day and I seen his shadow come across the room and I turned around.

He said, "How's things going, Bright?"

"Well, all right. I'm about squared up around here."

He stood on one foot, then on the other, and I knew he wanted to say something. Finally he said, "You know, Bright, Captain Byrd and Warden Moore tell me you're going to leave here." Well, there's no answer to that. It would be the stupidest thing in the world to try to convince him I was or wasn't. So I didn't say nothing. He started over to me, stood there for about a minute and finally walked over toward the door. He got to the door of the shop and turned around and said, "Bright, I want you to promise me something. If you decided to go, you let me know, because I'm going to have to go with you."

Ha! So I done that time.

If you'd asked me, "Bright, when are you going to leave," I'd say, "Tomorrow or the next day," and really meant it. But for some reason I didn't want to let that danged guy down. I don't know what you want to call it. He had something about him, he had the power to lead me. That guy possessed some power.

I seen it in dozens and dozens of other cases. Now he's dead and gone, so this ain't no attempt to feather my nest. The guy was a character out of this world. He had a potential for leading men and changing their lives that he was never aware of. He got lost in brick and stone and steel. He had to *build*, but the guy possessed a thing that was priceless.

He put a trust in me. He sent me to a convention of a bunch of alcoholic drunks up there to talk to them. I thought, "Well, the governor and all of them have gone nuts at the same time." The governor and the parole board and he had to okay it, and when they told me I was going I wouldn't even listen to them, I thought they was ribbing me. The next morning, Mr. Roberts, the head of the record department, he got my record, come by and said, "You gonna be ready to go in the morning, Bright?"

I said, "What they done, roped you in on that rib too?"

The next morning a runner come after me and they took me out there and dressed me out. We're sitting in the Bull Ring and Warden Moore come in and there I am. It was all a rib to me, I couldn't believe it. Here's a guy with two detainers, done escaped three times on this one jolt, and they're fixing to send him on his honor up here to a bunch of drunks to make a speech. It's just fantastic. Well, here comes this character from Austin that's going to drive us up there. His wife's a cousin to the governor. He's an alcoholic. Wonderful, wonderful guy. We get out there and get in the car and he gets going in the wrong direction. He finds he's going wrong and he stops to get some gas. We're about a block from the joint and I'm still looking back at it. He said, "What are you looking at?"

"Man," I said, "when you get this gas, let's go the other way. Them people are going to come to in a minute and we're going to hear more damn caps busting, more dogs barking than you ever heard in your life. They're going to snap that they turned me out of that penitentiary." But off we went.

It's a little insight as to what sort of guy that Ellis was. I finished that ten-year sentence, and the day I went out he come out to shake hands with me and several other people. We was all standing there by that Bull Ring and I said, "I want to tell you something. I've met a lot of con men, some of the sharpest in the country, at Quentin, places like that, masters, but if I was going in the con racket tomorrow and I wanted a shrewd partner, you'd top them all. I never believe that you could con me into doing that ten years."

But he conned a lot of guys into doing stuff that they didn't want to do. Actually, it was against their nature. Not con them, he'd just put you right on the spot.

But he could find the kind of spot you could be put on.

Yeah, he put you in a position where you couldn't let him down.

When I tried to escape this last time this old-timer didn't make it. I hid out on a trusty wing out there on December 25th and freeze was on the ground and everything, there was a torrent of rain, and I was laying in ice water four inches deep. Three days and nights. I turned blue under my fingertips, ran $104\frac{1}{2}$ fever, I had to come out and give up. I went to isolation and I come out and they sent me out here. Warden Sublett didn't know me, but he knew of me. They put us on a box out there and he walked out this door and looked the new crew over and he seen me right back there and he got on the telephone to Ellis and said, "I don't want that sonofabitch on my farm." Man, he didn't want no part of me. What Mr. Ellis wanted me to do was wire this building, see. I went to the field just like everybody, warden put me in the field, give me the toughest stuff. So I'm looking for a chance to escape and a couple of chances, farfetched things, came up. But I was convinced I could beat that field.

Before I could do it I went in to get my glasses fixed and it was the first time I had seen Ellis since I had been in isolation. I was in the Bull Ring up there waiting to see the optometrist, and Mr. Ellis, Mr. Jones, Warden Moore, they came over and started ribbing me. That's the first time I didn't beat them.

Mr. Ellis said, "John, I was pretty disappointed about that deal out there on the Eastham."

I said, "*I'm* the guy that was disappointed. That's the first time I didn't get away."

He said, "I got a lot of electricians. I've got me a dozen white electricians, I've got me a crew of Mexican, I've even got a crew of colored electricians."

I said, "Well, you're lucky."

He waited a few minutes, then he said, "But I ain't got your kind of electrician. When you get back out on that farm why don't you write me a letter."

He had had an accident and he was on a cane at the time. So off he goes on his cane. I think, "Here we go again."

I come out of here and I stayed in the field, I wouldn't write to him. They started pouring that slab and that meant the beginning of the electrical work was coming up. So I sit down and wrote him a letter. I said, "I looked out the window this morning. I see they're ready for a wire twister. You give me a couple of men and you can forget about that electric job."

But I didn't tell him I wouldn't run off, see. Hah!

Being as Warden Sublett was down here, I brought the letter in and at the bottom I wrote, "Now I don't know whether Warden Sublett approves of this or not, but I didn't give him any reason to disapprove since I've been out here." Since I mentioned his name I gave him the letter first. He took it right in to Mr. Ellis. Next morning they put me out there.

I was out there a day and here comes Ellis hobbling on that cane. I hadn't told him I wouldn't run off, as I said, and when he come hobbling across that yard I was trying to make out like I didn't see him. But he knew I did. He waved me to come over there with that cane. I went over and he said, "Give me the business."

I said, "Well, go home and sleep at night. That's what I'm gonna be doing."

That was all there was to it. He just walked off and I stayed. I'm trusted all over the farm, I can go anyplace.

I went out there and I stayed in that AA three years and seven months and I never had no trouble. Finally I had a slip and I got to drinking and went right back. Finally I had these blackouts and everything and I'd been drinking for days. I got drunk, stuck up a finance company there in Fort Worth. It was broad daylight and two guys that had known me all their lives. I stole a red jeep station wagon to go out there in—might as well have had the hook and ladder of the central fire station, it wouldn't have been any more conspicuous. Stuff like that. It's that alcohol. Now I'm doing life on the habitual.

It sounds like you're a better escapee than crook.

Until just a few years ago I never would admit that I was a thief or criminal. Not to myself. I always attributed everything to alcoholism, which in truth it is. I've never been in trouble unless I was drunk. But there was reasons for the drinking, defects of character, and I must have had larceny in me or I wouldn't have done it.

How old are you now?

I'm sixty-two.

How much time have you spent in jail?

In prisons, close to thirty years. It'll be ten years on this sentence in December.

Joey: "I'd rather knock somebody in the head . . ."

Lisa—you know William R———, but everybody calls her Lisa—told me that ever since she can remember she's been wanting boys. First time she ever had sex, that brings it on out. She was raised up around sisters, she didn't like her brothers. She started wanting boys, start hating girls. Girls start making boys and she'd get mad.

And another one, Robert B———, told me that her brother started frigging her, so she believes that's why she turned out.

I like to talk to them because I like to know them little things.

I figured out that the best way to raise a child is let him come up around girls and boys and explain everything to him, let him know something. 'Cause a youngster that don't know, there's no telling what he's liable to do. Liable to start running up on people, you know, fart-sniffers, people that just don't like to be stabbed [fucked], you know, enjoy fucking between the legs, people that likes to look at somebody else and jack off. Anything like that. We got them sick people right there on our wing.

See, I really got there on that wing by being here so long and they had white on this farm, they didn't have no Mexicans and didn't have no niggers here. I came over here on this farm with twenty-five others, we were the first niggers here. There's none of them here now but me, I'm the oneliest one. I been here on this farm longer than all the niggers, because out of the twenty-five that came here I'm the only one's left.

Later on, they started sending all them guys who's messed up, sick. And I been round so long, I been associating with 'em. Man, I'm telling you, for a while I thought I was going crazy, I had to get away from around 'em or something.

You know the way I act right now. I gets around 'em in a way I don't pay 'em much attention, and I stay in my cell a lot and watch TV and just get away from around 'em.

You know recently we had some guys go crazy. We had some hospital, screaming and hollering at night. One guy down there right now, he just liable to wake up tonight. Be hollering about his mama put him in a dark room, bunch a old jive, man. He's really flipped. And I talked to him, too. He told me that his wife was going with another man, that he could feel it. And his mother put him in a dark room when he was young and he never did forget it and every time he think about it it give him chills and set him screaming. Sometimes, it happened last week, week before last. It's gonna happen again. They sent him away from here but they sent him back. They checked him and said there wasn't nothing wrong with him.

C——— was in Number One Hoe Squad. And he wanted me to work with him. I worked with him, you know. He started telling guys I was his wife. Bunch of old shit, you know. Guys told me. I got mad. I said, "Well, that sonofabitch don't know me. I'll knock his brains out." And somebody went and told him and he sit down and started crying.

I know a bunch a crazy incidents C——— did. The reason he not going home is because he cut up a bunch a guys at different times. That's the reason why he stayed here so long. He tried to run off three or four times.

I had all the chances in the world to run off but I never would run off. I know that sooner or later I'd get caught, make it worse.

When I first came here I used to fight. When I first came on this farm I didn't do nothing but fight. I mean, that was every day. 'Cause every time a nigger said something I didn't like I'd knock him in the head or he'd knock me in the head. I got scars.

Well, the penitentiary's changed a whole lot. There used to be a bunch a them in here I always felt they thought they was bad. And if one said something to me I didn't like, I'd get something and knock him in the head. I felt like that was the best thing to do. I felt like that 'cause I seen so much. I was seeing people get knocked in the head. Some of 'em was knocking someone in the head just for a reputation and I figured they'll knock me in the head for the same thing. I said, "If I knock *him* in the head I'll come out a lot better." I'd rather knock somebody in the head than be knocked in the head.

And another thing, when you're around a bunch a crazy niggers like that, if you show 'em you're not scared of 'em you don't have no trouble. I tell you, I haven't had a fight in eight years. With nobody. And that's the reason why. That's one of the reasons. You know what they say? "Old Joey, I remember him with so-and-so. Don't mess with that sonofabitch, he's crazy."

Around people that's got sense all that would never been in the first place, but around a bunch a crazy niggers like that, I knew that's what I had to do. 'Cause the first thing they want to do is try to get a hog in [put pressure] on you. "If you don't want to cooperate with me you're gonna be in trouble with so-and-so and so-and-so." If I had been a chump and tried to coincide with this one and coincide with that one, I'd a been doing what convicts wanted me to do and they would a been my boss and I never would got straight. I said, "I'm gonna stop somebody from fucking with me right quick."

Really, I meant to kill somebody when I first started out. I said, "If I have to fuck my record up behind some of these crazy-assed niggers . . ." We had a gang fight down there one time. Boss ran in with a gas gun, shot it. One of 'em snatched it. Major came in. I got hit with a bat right here, laid me out for three days. I thought I never would get straight.

I'm in for robbery by assault. I haven't never killed nobody. That's something I wouldn't want to do is kill somebody. I don't know how it'd feel. The one thing my mother told me above all other things is taking something from somebody you can't give 'em back and that's their life. And another thing, I don't think I'd feel right if I'd take somebody's life. I don't think I'd ever get over it.

Now I know people that have killed people. It seem like they can be happy and jolly. I don't see how they can be happy and kill somebody.

I know this one guy down here done killed nine people. He was here for murder. They pronounced him insane. His name is John

Henry J————, they call him Johnnie Mae. I imagine you heard about it or read about it. He was a homosexual, he was wearing dresses out there in the free world. He was loving these men, making them think that he was a woman, getting them up in the place, and then he'd put a razor on their neck and he'd switch it around. He'd fuck them. If they wouldn't fuck, he'd kill them. He'd kill 'em if they did fuck after he fucked them. They pronounced him insane. He killed nine men. He killed three white, one Mexican, and five niggers. He killed nine, they pronounced him insane, he went to the insane asylum. Three years later he came to the penitentiary and they gave him thirty-five years.

I ain't killed nobody. I ain't even hit nobody out there. I was the man that held him, took his money, and run. And he identified me. 'Course I could a fixed him where he could never identified me. Now I gets life and John Henry gets thirty-five years.

How come you got life?

I was tried as a second offender. After you been in the penitentiary they can try you for being a second offender. For being an ex-convict already. I had a burglary first time, then robbery by assault as a second offender.

I ain't got no further than the fourth grade. Reason why that was, was my daddy. He was a drunkard, a gambler. He was a good gambler, they say, but his weakness was drinking. He'd win a lot, he'd go off and gamble. He didn't want my mother and the children to know he was gambling. And while he was off gambling he'd get drunk and somebody'd steal his money. Then in the wintertime we'd go barefooted, me and my sisters and brothers. I never will forget it. My mother, she would do the best she could. And we went hungry. We couldn't go to school. We didn't have nothing to go to school with. We mostly had to get down and hustle for ourself when we was twelve or thirteen years old. And I couldn't forget that if I lived fifty thousand more years. And I always hated my daddy for it. He died since I been down here. Week before he died he came down here and he talked with me. Me and him hadn't seen each other for seventeen years when he came down here to see me. And when he came down here to see me he started crying, you know. And he told me he felt like he had misused me. He felt like I wouldn't a been here, he say, if he had a did his duty, if it hadn't been for him.

I told him, naw, it wasn't none a his fault, 'cause when I came to the penitentiary I was old enough to realize and understand everything. And he told me, no, it was his fault. So he sent me $17 and then he send me $10. I got him on my mail list. And Major Duncan, he knows all about it because I had to get his permission to write my daddy 'cause my daddy wasn't on my mail list. And I explained it to him. So he told me the reason why he came down here was that he felt he was going to die. He had had two heart attacks. And sure enough, he died.

And I didn't hear from my mother in about six months after that. Now him and her wasn't together, he was living with another woman and she was living with another man. But him and her had been together twenty some years and she still had a strong desire for him. He didn't have no strong one for her. It was known that she cared more for him than he cared for her.

She was worrying about it, that was the reason she wasn't writing to me. And I thought something had happened to her. And it worried me, she the only person I could lean back on, the only person that looked out for me since I been here. When there's just one person in the world that you can depend on and you think something happened to them, it can worry you. I guess I lost about fifteen pounds worrying about her and one day she came down. Lightened me all up the way.

I lost my grandmother about two months ago. I ain't heard too much from her. That was her mother, you see. I'm thirty-six now. My mother, she's sixty-five, she's going on sixty-six. She hadn't got a gray hair on her head. I was born in Dallas. My mother and daddy quit and parted. Mother ran off and left him and went to Houston. I followed my mother. She went off and left all of us with my daddy.

I couldn't stay with my daddy 'cause he was too mean. He didn't teach none of us nothing, you know. He wanted to take us, put us on a truck, and send us to the cotton patch, you know. And he'd take the money and go gamble it off. He didn't give a damn whether we'd go eat or not.

My mother, she was altogether different. Now some peoples, they like the father better than the mother, but I don't see how.

I caught a freight train, me and my oldest brother, and went where my mother was. I was about fifteen. I thought my daddy was going to kill me, really. He wrote my mother and told her, "That damned boy done run off from me. I doing all I could for him." She read the letter to me.

I say, "Yeah." I told her, "He want us to pick cotton and the white man gonna pay him when we pick cotton and he going to take the money and go drink it up. If he get to the liquor store before he get to the gambling game and it goes there."

Didn't none of the children really like Daddy.

After he died, my mother said didn't nobody hardly weep. I was in the penitentiary. She said she didn't see a tear fall from nobody but her. But she was in love with my daddy. She was thinking about the years they had been together and what he had did. He did a lot, but he didn't do as much as he could have did. As far as she's concerned, he did a lot, because she's been unable to find work, you know. I've told her in letters, "See if you can find somebody to give me a job."

She say, "All right." She wait about three months and she say, "Did you find somebody to get you a job." She just don't know a damn thing in the world about it. She don't like to come in contact with no policemen, no lawyer, no judge, no nothing. She gets scared. She told me one time, "The only time I been in jail is when I had to come see you." And when she first come to see me here, she said, "Well, you had me put in jail and now you drove me in the penitentiary."

Tommy: "If this guy is a creep we set him up . . ."

That was the one that started off a series of riots: 1952. We must have had ten or twelve throughout the country after that. I noticed after that, it seems to be the month of June, for riots. That was 1952 that that one started it and I think we had ten or twelve in a row in the space of a year, all in major prisons. We had ours in Charlestown.

How did the Charlestown riot start?

Foolishly enough. I guess it was building up all the time, but it started over a guard ordering an inmate to press a pair of an officer's pants. Which he didn't have to do. This was on-the-side stuff, you know, the guy doing the other guy a favor. And it just happened that this guard was a real prick, the one who owned the pants. The other guy says, "No." So the guard locked him up that day, he had him pinched.

The next day one of this guy's friends took up a big sword and started running through the yard saying, "Let's go, let's go."

And that did it.

A sword?

Well, it was one of those big things, it was supposed to be a bread knife but the blade must have been twenty-two or twenty-four inches long.

But, of course, this had been building, I think, for a long time. They had a sort of sit-down strike type of riot in '46 that was straightened out without any violence or destruction of property, but they couldn't make it with this one. This was spontaneous more or less.

Course it was a tough joint at that time. Those were the head-busting days. Everyone who got pinched, it was almost automatic: you get pinched, they took you over to the segregation unit, the now famous Cherry Hill section.

Cherry Hill was the segregation unit, the isolation unit. That was a real tough place too. Charlestown was a real tough place. When I went there in '52 they claimed that many reforms had taken place, but by God, it was hard to believe. They still had the old shitbuckets and a pitcher of water and salt. And you were locked in nineteen or twenty hours a day.

I've thought about it. I was in that riot in '52. I went along. It wound up with forty-four guys out of probably nine hundred partici-pating finally who made a stand somewhere with hostages. I think that if I had come in on this sentence—I'm doing a life sentence inciden-tally—if I'd a come in on this sentence to this prison that I never would have participated. Probably.

They'd take all your dignity away, you know. They give you an old oaken bucket and tell you, "Well, you shit and piss in that, and live in it." And you could only wash up a certain amount of times a day because of the water situation. If you could get more water your bucket couldn't hold it. And cockroaches and filth . . . You ate your meals in your room. You picked them up as you came out of the yard, picked them up, them filthy trays. I was never subjected to those kind of conditions. Sanitary conditions I'm used to. . . . I lived in a nice clean home and always had a clean way of life. As far as *that* goes.

That Charlestown riot started in the afternoon and ended around two thirty the next morning. They brought newspaper people in and the commissioner of correction and the chaplain and the warden, and they sat down and talked about what they wanted. The first thing they wanted, of course, was an inmate council, someone to talk these things out so that this wouldn't happen again. And there was only one way to get it. So they gave us the inmate council.

Then we went into punishment. The punishment was very light. The damage was done. We had ten days in the hole, no loss of good time, that was it. Some of us had to wait like six weeks to go in the hole because they only had so many cells there. So we waited six weeks in our cells with all privileges with the exception of being let out. That was pretty good. I didn't care then. I'd only been in six months, so I didn't give a fuck, you know. I was wishing the state troopers would attack. That's what I was wanting and I was dying to get croaked, you know. See, I was crazy.

It's downhill now.

Yeah. After you get by a certain amount of time it is.

I think what has encouraged me is I've seen things get better and better, little bit by little bit, all the time. It gives you a little hope, you know. It gives you a shot. Like, when I come in, there was no twenty years [a lifer in Massachusetts can be paroled after serving twenty years of his sentence], they couldn't release you in twenty years. The parole board could never release you.

Was it flat life?

If you had a life sentence the only way you could get out was with political pressure. You had to have a lot of political friends to swing it with the executive council of the governor. Now at least you know that within twenty years the parole board can let you out. And after you've been around a while and you have a job like I've got, you make a lot of good connections with people on the street that are interested and they write to you and they come to visit with you and you talk with them and after a while you become friends. And these people go to bat for you. And the administration goes to bat for you. You've got it made, usually.

I think that probably I had a good shot at making it last year, my first time up. Two days before I seen the board two guys out of here on parole shot a cop dead in Boston. The parole board was on the fire, so they made no decision, they just let it slide.

And the guys on death row . . .

Yeah, we sweat for them, poor bastards. Every time somebody croaks a cop or somebody outside, we say, "Jeez, there goes so-and-so . . ." Fifteen months ago there was one guy there and he had a good chance of beating this beef, but now his chance is lessened 'cause they say, "Well, for Christ's sake, we got five of them up there now. If we let this one guy go we can't burn none of them. We can't let Kerrigan go because if we do we have to let Detto go. He killed a cop in cold blood . . . blah, blah, blah, blah."

Of course Kerrigan, the one that's in there, got the best chance of all of them 'cause there was no one at the scene. He was never placed at the scene and so there's a lot of doubt in that case. I think that if they could let anybody go [he means commute the death sentence to life] they could let him go, they'd be justified in doing so.

This is a tough state. They blow hot and cold. One year you feel sure that public opinion is such that if there's a referendum that they'd say abolish it, and then just like that it changes again. It's very strange. Politics are very tough.

These two kids that went out and killed that cop—I know both personally very well. We hung round together for a long time. I live in the kitchen block and these guys worked in the kitchen, so we used to have coffee together. I probably spent two hours a day with them, and we discussed everything under the sun and they're a couple of good kids. You know, I mean there was a good chance to do something with these kids if we had that kind of program.

It was just a game with them. Just building up a good piece of casework to make parole. And it's a shame, honestly. That kid I was talking to all year less than a year ago—going out, he wanted to go to a hairdressing school. He couldn't make the adjustment out there. Then he wound up being the guy that killed the cop. And here he is twenty-three years old doing a life sentence. One year you're playing handball with him and he's got a parole, the next year you're playing with him and he's got a life sentence.

The public's thinking is all screwed up: this is the way to cure it, just put him away. They cure that fine, don't they. Put a guy in a hole.

He left a widow and two kids, that cop.

I've always found this strange, because you talk to guys and you know them and there's always this veneer, all the time there's always this façade, you know, they're tough guys, and that's it, you know. But when something like that happens you can tell by what they say that they feel empathy for the survivors, especially if there's kids. They'll say, "Ah, fuck him. He's a cop anyway, he's croaked, good. One less to live with."

I'll always throw this in: "What about his wife and kids?"

"That's the breaks," they'll say. And they get all shook up. You can tell that they do feel about this thing. You would never think so. The public would never think so, they think, "Oh, I'll bet you they're glad. The bastards, a lot they care for a guy's wife and kids." But they do. But you're never going to get them to admit it.

Oh, Jesus, oh, they ain't going to admit *that*. But more than likely, if you weren't around and they're all in their cells and closed in and you tell them, "Now we're going to take up a collection for that cop's wife and kids," they'd pour it right out of their guts. The bastards. They'd just cough up probably half of the money that they've got, every one of them. Or two-thirds of them anyway.

I hear enough of this bullshit. I've heard enough of this bullshit for all these years. When a guy comes on like gangbusters with me and tries to tell me how tough he is: "Fuck this, ah who cares. Church? Why should I go to church with that bunch of punks."

I say, "Your mother a punk?"

"What? Are you playing a game?"

"She goes to church."

"They're all a bunch of punks that go to church here." That's one of the reasons a lot of guys use for not going to church. "Punks and faggots and homosexuals are all up there with their hands like this waiting for Holy Communion and coming out and sucking pricks right afterwards." Shit like that.

"What's that got to do with you? That's that individual. He's going there for his purpose, you go for your purpose. If you want to go to worship, go to worship. What do you care about him."

You get away with it?

Oh, yeah. These are people I know.

I don't know what it is, whether it's sense or what. I don't think I'm that smart. For example, talking to you. Something told me it was all right talking to you after five minutes of talking to you. Maybe I'm absolutely wrong, but yet something told me it was all right. In my mind it's a calculated risk talking to you, and that's the way I operate.

Not right off, usually. Outside here with the guys—after a few weeks I'll watch a guy. I'll talk to him. I'll listen to him and I will make an evaluation. I don't know why, but I'll have a pretty good idea of just what I can say to this guy and how I can needle him and things. And you know, it works out. I've never had any real trouble. Sure, I may throw a few punches now and then, but it's my fault 'cause I get hot, and when somebody gets hot with you, you know, automatically you get hot yourself. And that's always been my fault: I've always thrown the first punch. If I needle you gently you're not supposed to come back with, "Ah, you motherfucker, you prick" or something like that.

You're supposed to come back with another needle.

Yeah, you're supposed to be witty about it. Some guys get very vulgar. And when you tell them, "You're out of line there" and they repeat themselves—I don't anymore, but I used to punch them.

I haven't punched anybody in about five years. My needle must be shortening or something.

Very few of us older guys—I've been in thirteen years, there aren't more than about seventy-five of us that were in the old Charlestown jail left—have anything to do with any new fish coming in. I think guys insist that it's a new type of criminal now, a new type of breed coming. I don't know, really, I have no statistics to say this. The guys that are coming in nowadays, they don't seem to be doing the big bits that they were doing in Charlestown. In Charlestown it seemed everyone was doing twenty to twenty-five, fifteen to twenty, things like that. Now it's more three to five, four to seven, and so forth.

Guys like this, these new ones, they're not getting involved in anything, they won't get heated up over conditions. No matter how good conditions are in a prison there's always a hundred things to beef about. But you can't get these guys involved in anything if you want to get a riot going. If you want to make some kind of demonstration. You can't go very far before you'll get pinched.

Before you could. You could go to a con and say, "Listen, I want to do this. I want to demonstrate. Do you want to get in on it?" And they would say yes or no, and you could go on to the next guy. Nowadays you can't. These guys that got a three to five and are going to see the parole board and they can get out in fourteen months, they don't want to get involved in anything. That's what they call the new breed convict, guys that don't want to get involved.

And part of it is the way the institution is set up. So much freedom now. In the old days you were locked up nineteen hours a day with all that time to think and brood and get bitter about. Now you don't have that kind of mentality because you're locked up just from nine thirty until seven in the morning.

What bugs a new man the most when he first comes in?

I would say that, generally speaking, what bugs him the most is the drastic change from outside to inside. I think that the adjustment is something to make. There's all these restrictions, and all this discipline.

I think he's scared, more scared than anything else to begin with. The first time in, anyway. They're scared shitless, you know. I know that for sure. Because their image of this place—they don't have any idea what state prison is like—all they've seen are these old Jimmy Cagney movies.

A guy like me comes along and I pick them up and take them up to the block. You can see that they're terrified. You start talking to them and it takes a couple of days before they start warming up, and they've got a million questions. All the questions: mail, visiting, that's what comes first. "When can I write a letter? When can I get a visit? Do they allow children to visit?" All that stuff comes first. And discipline, they're very concerned about rules to begin with: "Where can I go? What can I do? What time do I have to do it? What happens if . . . etc." They want to get into the swing of things so they won't get into trouble. Then their immediate thoughts are about the family.

Then they all—I've heard this a thousand times, I guess—"Gee, what a joint. This ain't nothing." I think they're all disappointed, some of them.

There's this kid that lives in my block now. He calls this a reform school for older men. He was in a boy's training school. He thought this was one of those Jimmy Cagney joints, you know. He is terribly disappointed at nineteen years old. "I thought I was coming to the big house to have something to go back to the corner to tell the guys. I go. The big house? Hah."

"Why you punk," I say, "Get out of here." They piss me off. These kids, boy, they burn my ass.

The most nervous place I've been in was a juvenile institution.

The intrigue is something terrific in those places. Them kids are always up to something, you know. Big score: the smoke. "Who's got the butt?" "What time I'm going to meet him? The punk ain't there I'll kill him." "Let's bust this kid's head when he gets a visitor." All that kind of stuff. All that intrigue, that's what makes them like that.

This place used to be like that, about six or seven years ago. It was wide open. Head-busting, all that kind of stuff. Goon squads. It was the old Charlestown style. Everybody was from Charlestown then.

We have two segregation units here. This unit has the departmental segregation unit. A real tough joint. That's Block Ten.

I saw that. That's the one with the stoned-in exercise yard.

Entirely fenced in?

Yes.

That's it, yeah. That's a tough place. It breaks them.

Is that what it's used for?

I don't know if they intend it for that purpose, but that's what usually happens. They keep them there too long. Some guys have been there for two and a half years. They're wacky. Everything's restricted. They don't have open canteen privileges, for example. I think they're allowed cigarette and toilet articles and one newspaper. Magazines and books from the library. Visiting is restricted, and that is only with a guard present which makes for a lousy visit. That's no way to visit anyone. [Massachusetts had, at the time of the interview, abolished the traditional wire-mesh and wide tables separating visitor and inmate and had changed to a room in which people could sit next to one another.] Exercise when they have the security strength to allow it. Wintertime there's no exercise. Twenty-four hours a day in the cell. A system of restricted talking for certain hours. It's a real disciplinary barracks, you know. I don't know if it's intended to break you, but it seems to be the purpose it serves.

You can see them guys come out of there and it takes them months to get reorientated. Jeez, they're jumpy and shaky. They have a tough time getting back on their feet. Some of them don't. Some of them wind up right back there again. They're probably conditioned to it. They become conditioned to the joint and next thing you know they can't stand people around, can't stand to socialize. They don't care. I don't think consciously that they plan to go back, I think that probably unconsciously they do. They seem to follow the path that brings them back there.

A lot of them nuts, they're not nutty, they're foxy. Let me tell you. This is their way of getting their way in this prison. And the personnel ignore them practically. They get away with murder, you know what I mean, all the little infractions. They never bother about them standing at the cell door for counts and all that stuff.

There's an example. You know the size of our cells, seven or eight feet deep, right? Open-faced. A guy comes by taking a count. There's nothing to obscure his view. He can see you just as well if you were sitting at your desk writing a letter or if you're on the toilet or whatever you might be doing. As easily as if you're standing there stupidly at the door waiting for him to get there. In the morning they'll start count and the guy might not show for five minutes and there you are standing at the bars because they say you have to do that. Things like that irritate guys, they can't see it, it seems to be a punishment.

A lot of the guys stand there naked with a hard-on like a rock up there. After a while, they'll tell you you don't have to stand up for the count.

There's one guard, he's an ex-Marine, and he's been here about eight months. He worked in Bridgewater previous to coming here and these fellows from Bridgewater have a very difficult time adjusting. Bridgewater's the nut factory and they wamp them out down there, pull them out when they want to. [When I visited Bridgewater there were three staff psychiatrists for 1,800 inmates; guards and attendants pretty much ran the place.] They're used to having their own way without any questions asked. If an inmate had any questions they'd hit him in the head. Here they can't do that. One day I heard this guard saying to this fellow, "John," he says, "I come by here every morning and you're standing at your door with a hard-on. I mean, for Christ's sake, have some *decency*."

John says, "You were in the fucking Marine Corps, you never saw a guy had a hard-on? You never saw any pricks hanging out in the shower room?" Oh, you should have heard him, this guy is a crude bastard. And he's telling him just like I told you.

This guard says, "Well, you could sleep with shorts on."

"I ain't never slept with anything on in my life and I ain't going to start now. If you want me to be in front of the door in the morning then I'm coming up there the way I am. That's it. I'm not going to knock the shit out of my prick for *you*."

You should have heard it, that guard was acting like a real baby about it, you know. "Well, I could put you on report for indecent exposure."

This guys says, "What indecent exposure? This was the way I was born. I wasn't indecent then, was I?"

So they decide he's nutty, and after a while they just leave him alone.

These people we call nuts: they've got it made. If you go to TV you're not supposed to talk or read the papers. You go to watch TV, they say, and that's all you're supposed to do there. These nuts go to TV and read the paper. The screws ain't going to say anything to them 'cause they're nuts. They're nuts, shit!

Then you sit down and talk to them. They're cagey, you know. Screws think they don't know what they're doing. Hah! It's their defense.

Some guys have different things going for them like that that make it easier. Take a guy who's committed violence at one time or another on an officer, a correctional officer, he's got it made pretty near. At first there are guys that have a little courage and they will give them a bad time, but after a while as new guys come in and hear he was violent and they hear stories and they'll see this guy out of line and they won't bother him.

Another way is just to have a lot of time in. Then you know all the officers and they know you. They're not afraid of you. They know what to expect of you and you've got it made that way. You know all these little things, like standing at the door for counts, and they never bother you for little things.

Are all the cells here one-man?

Yeah.

Were they all one-man in Charlestown too?

This is Massachusetts, man! What do you expect? Perversion? This is Massachusetts, the land of the Quakers or the Puritans.

Are they hard on that sort of thing in here?

They ignore it.

That's Massachusetts too.

I don't mean they ignore it if they *catch* it. So far as the program is concerned they ignore it. They have certain rules that are designed, I suppose, to discourage it. You're certainly punished from court. Some are taken to court, some are not. You can get both punishment here and outside.

You mean outside court?

Yep. Get six months on and after. One guy for sodomy got three-to-five after his original sentence.

They try to make believe this thing doesn't exist 'cause they don't know how to cope with it. And there really is no way to cope with it, I don't think there is in prisons. Probably not outside either. So they just make believe it doesn't exist. And when it does happen everybody is, oh, shocked to hell. "What? Here? Me? In my prison?" I don't know what else they could do that they don't do now, I mean more, because the restrictions that are placed on us because of homosexuality, I resent them.

You're my friend, right? You and I hang together. So I got a cell. You can't come and sit in that cell. You've either got to sit at my doorway while I sit on my bed or lie on my bed, or else we both go out and sit on the floor or something.

It didn't used to be like that, but it is now. And they have a gallery, were you up there? Across from the cells. You can't see in there because it's dark, but you can see out. That's how they catch most of the guys, the ones that do get caught. We haven't had an incident in three or four months now. They'll get three or four years, I guess.

It's weird how that varies with the states. Mississippi has houses for guys who can convince them they're married.

Alaska has it too. They call it conjugal visits. You mention that in Massachusetts and they'll run you right out. "What? Let them convicts get laid on weekends? Are you crazy?"

There's a bill now before the legislature to allow prisoners in the state forestry camps to go home on weekends. We got three forestry camps and they may start it there. That's the way everything's got to start, you know, with the honor prisoners. Everything happens this way. "This man's been a trusty for ten years. We'll allow him to do this." And everybody agrees he should if he's been a good trusty for ten years. These people have proven the worth of forestry camps for several years now, so probably it wouldn't be too much of a stink if they did allow these guys home on weekends. Once they do, we'll start screaming. The state prison prisoners will start screaming. Once the program works, you know.

In Mississippi, they also have twenty-four-hour passes and seventy-two-hour passes. That's a nutty state. On one hand, they whip you for lurking about down at the end of a cotton row, and then they hand you a twenty-four-hour pass to get laid and drunk. That kills me.

As cans go, though, it ain't too bad a can. The screws are okay with me. You know, they're just another guy to me. I treat them with respect, I talk to them like I'm talking to you, like I talk to anybody. If they're friendly, I'm friendly.

They're not afraid to be friendly?

There's a line, there's an invisible line. All the time. It's up to yourself to make your own evaluation of the individual. Guys get bullshit with me sometimes. I tell them I've got more screws that are friends than I've got cons that are friends. These people, the screws, they've got no angle, where half of your convict friends, they want something off you besides conversation and being a buddy. On the whole they're not bad guys.

A lot of the old-timers are retired now and they used to influence the younger screws.

I remember after the riot in '52, they gave us wristwatches. They let us have wristwatches, I mean. One of the things we asked for was wristwatches, and cigarette lighters, radios, little conveniences of that sort. One screw says to me, "I know why you wanted those wristwatches. You ain't bullshitting me. I've been around here a long time. You guys want to sympathize your watches for the next riot."

I says, "You're right, Jake, you're right." Sympathize your watches for the next riot—Jesus.

One difference between here and Charlestown is the freedom-out-of-the-cells bit. We discussed it before. It gives you so little time. You get in your cell at night and you've got to wash, you have to get yourself squared away for the next day's activity. The radio's on. Get all the personals laid out. Ball game is always on—sports on one channel and music on the other. Some guys have classes doing university extension courses. Some guys have a certain type of reading interest. Some guys have German or French, some of the guys are writing novels. They treasure that nine thirty to ten forty-five time. You can talk if you want to, there's no restriction on talking after nine thirty, but in every single block you can hear a pin drop, a toilet flush. A guy slams his drawer and he only slams it once. Somebody will yell at him about his mother: "What are you doing, closing your mother in for the night?" Steel things: chairs scraping and all that. I used to talk to guys about that too when they orientate here. Chairs are steel, the desk is steel—that's stationary on the wall. And that's irritating as hell when you're concentrating and right above you the guy will drag his chair from here to here, he'll be sorry.

I think this joint is safe, you know. They're always saying this joint's sitting on a powder keg, but I think it is safe and that contributes a lot to how the con feels. They feel a little secure. The administration time and time again proved that they'll let a guy do his own time.

People are not going to bother you here. There's no goon squads hitting you in the head and taking your few luxuries and things like that. They make sure of this. That's when this Block Ten came into operation. The first thing that was done was to wipe out the goon squads and gambling and so forth. Guys in here will tell you, "Oh they're petty about gambling. What's wrong with a guy betting a couple of decks?" These things develop into books where a guy becomes a bookmaker and he's got two or three goons to go back and collect the money and guys go overboard. Next thing you know they're in hock for a couple of hundred and they got to put pressure on their family. If they don't come up with the couple of hundred they're going to get their head broken. And after a couple of times the family stops coming through and he does get his head broken.

But still the toughness is here, but it's operated more intelligently. There's still a book here but you're not allowed to go over the limit— $6. After you lose $6 for a week, unless you're in a position to transfer money or send money to a certain place in the street, one of the book-maker's drops, you're shut off. If you don't pay, you might get a slap in the mouth. If you can't pay, you'll get away with it, but if you can pay and don't, you'll get a few whacks, punched out. They're protecting their own investments, actually, they're protecting their own interest by doing it that way. But they're still tough. If they had to stab you, they'd stab you.

We had one guy stabbed to death and another guy killed with a baseball bat during a baseball game. In the middle of the field and not a witness. How do you like that?

Surprise, surprise.

Thought the guy was taking a sunbath. He was croaked. Baseball bat. Terrible weapon. I was fifty feet away and I heard it. You know, it's peculiar: I never heard anyone get hit with a baseball bat, and before I turned around, I thought, "Aw, somebody got hit with a bat." Fifty feet away and I heard that very distinctly.

Must have been quite a thud.

Yeah. I turned around, just took a fast look and saw a few guys leaving the scene and this guy laying there and that's all I wanted to know. Turned around: ball game, outside team vs. Walpole. That's all I saw.

It happened when an outside team was here?

Yeah. The guy on second base, the outside guy, told them, "That guy looks like he's hurt." That's how they discovered him. This is a big yard, guys laying out in the sun, laying around, nobody bothers you. Now if you lay in one spot too long they come along and prod you. It was kind of embarrassing for the administration, especially when you're surrounded by four or five towers and six guards in the yard and somebody walks up in the middle of the thing and hits him in the head. No good. People start wondering and the grand jury starts coming in. They did, too. They made a lot of recommendations. They tightened up the joint a good deal.

There was two guys and one of them cracked and he told them that they did it and that the other guy wielded the bat. They went to trial and the guy denied it, of course, all the way. Then when it came time for his defense he got on the stand and admitted it and told them how the guy had a knife in his hand and was gonna stab him and he struck him with the bat. They found him not guilty.

He beat it?

Yeah. The guy before that, he stabbed a guy down in the gym, on the gym stairs.

They made a mistake of leaving that a blind spot in the corridor. With two stairways, the stairway, the long corridor, and another stairway. And a guy got it there. He croaked. The guy beat that too.

I noticed there's a blind spot by the shops in the basement.

I know where you mean. That's a bad spot. Many guys get wiped out there.

It surprised me when I saw it: it looked ideal for that. There aren't too many of those spots here.

No, they're not. But, you see, it's all in the timing anyway. We know just where a guy is going to be at a certain minute and where the screw will be. That's how it operates. Actually, that's how guys get wiped. There's probably somebody getting slapped or punched every day of the week and probably only one or two complaints a week. Very rarely are they seen. You're regimented and they know where you're supposed to be and you know where they are too, and that's the way it is.

It cuts both ways.

Yeah, that's right. The routine is routine and they keep it routine. Just like people on the street, prisoners are just people on the street. Their routine they follow every day even in their free time. But you know where to find a guy any time, if you want to, if you watch him for a while. I'll bet you there are guys at six seventeen every night you could catch on the stairs. Probably fifty guys you can catch on those stairs. We have this system where you sign out. When I leave my block at six fifteen I've got to tell the officer where I'm going. After supper you go to the block and stay there till six, then you have a count at six or six fifteen and then you're released from the cells until nine thirty. And there's guys that go to avocation every single night of the week. Like I go to gym Monday, Wednesday, and Friday, every one of those nights at the same time, at six sixteen right after the count, immediately after the count. I leave my cell immediately the door opens and I head for the gym so I can grab one of the handball courts. And other guys do the same thing. So if somebody wanted to get me, all they'd have to do is sign out for the gym and get there before me and wait on the first flight of stairs. Those stairs go down like this, then a little platform, then there's a screw at the bottom of the second flight. There's just that one little blind spot there.

Most of the fights are spontaneous, you know. This bit about the administration guaranteeing a guy can do his own time calls for a lot of slaps in the head. Because after a while these mickeymouses and weaklings grow muscles from this, they grow mental muscles. And they'll tell a guy that won't take any shit from people like them, "Go fuck yourself" or "Lay down you creep" or something like that. Some guys wouldn't tolerate that, even if they had to go to the chair. Not from him. That's where most of the slaps in the face come from, most of the whacks.

You get five days for a fight, five days of isolation. Isolation is one meal a day. Regular dinner. You get the whole thing, which isn't bad. You can make a nice mashed potato sandwich. They give you enough bread so you can make a sandwich for the night. Breakfast isn't much anyway, so nobody actually misses that.

You can sleep. You don't have to make any counts or anything like that. If you can go into a stupor you've got it made. Which I find it almost easy to do. I just go into a stupor. If I get five days I just lay down there and go into an actual stupor. I lay there and sleep and I'm half awake sometimes but not conscious of what's going on. Guys will be talking, the guys in segregation will be talking to each other, they'll be passing out meals or something, and there will be a whole bunch of noise and activity and I just blot it out. You go into, what do they call it, a catatonic state. Fine. Five days later the guy opens the door. You go, "Huh? Huh, what?"

"Let's go, time's up."

"Oh, all right."

What's the longest they can put you in there?

Fifteen days at one whack. They can take you out for one day and put you back in for fifteen more. That very rarely happens though.

How did it work at Charlestown?

At Charlestown you got up to ten and you got a loaf of bread a day. Big old homemade loafs. Beautiful pillows. And the cell is bare except for boards two and a half feet wide by seven feet long. They didn't want you to get chilled bones.

Tell me about the gangs in Charlestown. Were there many?

There was always one that ran the joint. There was other gangs, but they were cliques. They weren't gangs in the sense that the big one was. Like the gang that I first got into, which was *the* gang in Charlestown and it ran everything: bookmaking and all the illegal activities, you know. And there were other gangs, but these were more cliques than gangs and guys who were friends and hung out together or found it necessary to hang out together.

I was in a gang of about thirty-five guys. And there were some on the fringe of the gang and you could count on them. And there were several cliques of eight or ten.

Now if I had a beef with you and you belonged to one of the cliques, if the beef couldn't be fixed, well, right away as soon as I had that beef, some of the more powerful guys of my gang would go to the friends of the other guy. They wouldn't go to him directly. And they'd say, "You know what's going to happen if these two guys don't straighten this out. There's going to be bloodshed. He's a good guy and he's a good guy." Now if the other guy wasn't a good guy he'd be uptight. He wouldn't be around with eight or nine guys to begin with.

So they would have a mediator. Whenever there's an argument someone is always probably more wrong than the other guy, whatever started it. The apologies would be like this: "Okay, forget it. Let's forget it." If it's your fault, if they determine it's your fault, you'd have to say to the guy, "Okay, forget it. All right?" And he'd say, "Yeah," and that would be *his* means of apology. Sometimes you both have to say okay and have to shake hands. Sometimes that would end it. But many times these things are not resolved at all and you'd have to go.

So the gang would actually serve to preserve the peace some of the time?

Yeah, because they know that two good guys are going to get hurt.

No point in that.

It's not gonna happen. But if a guy is a creep . . .

If this guy is a creep we set him up and get him and there'll be fifteen to twenty guys that will cover the play. Like one time we had a guy get very close to getting croaked out in the yard and all he was supposed to do was get hit in the head a couple of times. This is in the middle of the yard and there's seven hundred guys out there and probably twenty-five screws. Everyone's in groups talking and this guy's talking with another guy and they just come from all directions. You have four guys here, four guys there, and so forth, and at a signal everyone starts for this point and we're all approximately the same distance away and we just block off the screws and the guy gets whacked out.

There was no concern for him; he's a creep. You know, he deserved it and that's the end of it.

This time—I got very sick at this—this guy had a piece of pipe. The guy didn't do hardly anything to him; I was against this. This is what started me against gangs. I started thinking that gangs were wrong then.

This guy passed a comment to this fellow Duke. Duke grabbed him by the shirt and bam! bam! bam! against the building a couple of times. That was inside. He said, "Don't you ever talk to me like that again." The guy didn't even know what he said that was wrong.

A guy in our gang told me how it happened and I said, "Good grief. Something's wrong with this guy."

Well, the guy who got hit told a friend of his and this friend of his came over to this guy Duke and said, "Jesus Christ, Duke, that wasn't called for, the guy didn't want any trouble with you."

So Duke took umbrage with this guy coming to talk to him. A creep isn't supposed to have anybody go talk for him. It's against the rules. A creep is supposed to take a slap in the mouth and that's it. Be glad that's all he got. So Duke took umbrage at this.

He's just going to hit this guy once with the pipe. That's all he's going to get. Whack him one time.

Is this the guy who came to talk to him?

No, the creep. The creep that he had the words with.

And Duke hit this guy and hit this guy. And a pipe hitting against flesh, boy, it's a horrible sound. I turned one time and I seen this guy —I didn't know at the time he had a plate—spitting all these teeth and all this blood. Started hitting him in the face and over the head. They were really surprised that the guy ever made it. They had to take him from Charlestown out twenty-five or thirty miles to Norfolk to the hospital, and they were amazed that the guy lived.

I knew after that I had to get away from that kind of shit. I couldn't go it. 'Cause if they were going to do that to guys for nothing . . . I could see it if the guy had done something, if he had maybe ratted an escape plot or got someone killed, then it would call for that kind of punishment. But this . . . Well, I started thinking: For Christ's sake, this is all we'll be doing every time someone says anything. If some creep was up there playing handball and one of the guys comes along and says, "All right, break it up. Let's have the court," and the creep says, "Just a minute, one more point," he's liable to get croaked. Things like that started to bother me, you know. I started to think about them: Jesus, this is crazy.

What makes a guy a creep?

Oh, they're stoolies. Usually they're rats to begin with. And they suck around screws if they're not a rat. They suck around screws and are always polishing their desks for them. "Can I do this for you, sir?" and all that kind of shit. Well, it makes them repulsive. It isn't that the screw asks for it, I mean, you might like the screw, but to see someone sucking around somebody all the time . . . There's a guy at the shop that's starting to get to me. I don't even talk to him. Every time I look up, he's washing the screw's ashtray—the screw only smokes about four cigarettes a day—and he's got a rag and he's cleaning his desk. Now the guy's a creep. You ask me *why* he's a creep. What can I tell you?

That's a creep on the outside too.

Yeah, he'll suck around the boss all the time. "Hey, boss, my wife made me two good sandwiches. Do you want one?" Shit like that. He's a creep on the outside. That's right.

It's been a long time, but I wonder if these guys ever say anything about Sacco and Vanzetti here?

They don't say much. I think most prisoners have the feeling—most prisoners in this state, Massachusetts—they're not going to believe these guys went to the chair unjustly. They weren't citizens. I think that they can identify with society and it makes them a part of it. They don't want to have nothing to do with it. You ask a guy about Sacco and Vanzetti and he'll tell you they were communists. "They were communists. Fuck it, if they didn't do the robberies they were commies and they deserved it." You can't tell them they weren't communists, they were anarchists and things like that, that it was a lot of politics involved.

But when they hear things like markings on a bullet after all these years cast some doubt whether the guns that were taken from Sacco and Vanzetti were the guns that were used in the killings, oh, Jesus, they get bullshit. As long as they were commies it's all right, even though they went to the chair for political reasons, but as soon as you bring out some evidence like the bullets didn't match the gun, all of them pricks they go bullshit. "Man, where'd you hear that? What paper did you see it in? What do you make of that? Who's got it?" Then they want to know about it. I think they identify in some way with that thing.

They consider themselves a part of society, a separate part of it. When you talk about Corrigan, they will say, "They are putting him in the chair . . ."

I say, "They? You mean *we*."

"Balls! I don't have nothing to do with it."

"You're part of them."

"No, I'm not part of them."

"Yes, you are part of them."

"Your ass!"

Then we get into all kinds of discussions over something like that, you know.

That's the needle. That's to get them stimulated a little bit. Start them talking about things. You know, it's all right to shoot the shit, but after a while, after you've shot the shit for a few years, you've had it. You've heard just about all there is to hear, you know.

4. Queens, punks, and studs

There are three participating sex roles in prison: the person who plays the active or inserting role (*stud, daddy, jocker, wolf, husband*), the person who plays the insertee role but does not enact that role in the free world (*punk, penitentiary punk, penitentiary turnout, jailhouse turnout, candy-bar punk, kid*), and the person who is an acting-out homosexual on the streets as well as in prison (*queen, free-world punk, original punk, girl*).

Who does what for whom varies with the particular prison and the region of the country. In all stud–punk relationships the stud expects to perform the insertor role, the punk the insertee role, but there are variations. In some institutions the punk is expected to make available for the stud's sexual satisfaction his rectum, his mouth, and his cupped hand; in other prisons it is just one or two of those cavities. In some institutions *flip-flop* (where stud and punk sometimes switch the insertor–insertee role) is heavily tabooed, in other institutions it is common. There are racial differences: in northern institutions a white stud often has a black punk and conversely; in the South, because of outside attitudes and inside segregation, the prison sexual affairs are always white–white and black–black. In North and South the stud is expected to supply his punk with physical protection, especially from other studs who want to fuck him, but he may, on occasion, rent his punk to other men when he needs cigarettes or commissary items. That is, of course, a parody of heterosexual affairs outside: one may pimp one's old lady but one is also expected to protect her from nonpaying assaults. In the free world some men give their women all sorts of goodies, others expect their women to keep them supplied with the necessities and luxuries of life; that, too, is parodied in prison—in some institutions the punk is rewarded with candy and cigarettes, in others the punk is expected not only to keep the stud supplied with material wants but even to keep him in freshly ironed clothes.

Punks have considerably lower status in the inmate hierarchy than queens. When I asked why, one Texas convict said, "Because the penitentiary turnouts aren't man enough to admit what they are," which struck me as a not-inappropriate inversion. A Missouri convict said, "You hate a sonofabitch who tries to act like you do and then turns tricks. But a person who just happens to have a different psychological makeup than you and has brought it in with him, well, hell, we all have psychological problems." This might seem curious, for this comes from a socio-economic group which on the outside is hostile to all homosexuals—they don't like them, they make fun of them, they are afraid of them. Inside, the *queers* become *queens,* and—outside of Massachusetts where everybody is uptight about everything—they seem fairly well accepted by the inmate population. The same discriminations are made as are made outside: outside there are good girls and bad girls, there are girls you love and girls you fuck; inside there are pretty young boys and candy-bar punks and queens. Who has what role depends who you are talking to or about. A man talks about his own punk as if he were talking about his girlfriend; a man talks about other people's punks as if they were scaly legs. Queens are accepted in the social order, but I suspect most convicts would rather have a punk than a queen, for the same reason that outside they would rather have a woman all their own than one who is fucking and sucking all over town.

In so many ways prison is a parody of the free world, and sex is essential to the parody. There are marriages, there are prostitutes, there are studs who get laid a lot and wallflowers who can't make it at all. And there are people who are comfortable with their roles and others so hassled by their guilt feelings they get themselves into all kinds of silly trouble trying to compensate for it. There are three marriages in this book, two of them legal, one of them heterosexual. Nick and Margie McMurphy are a man and woman who have been married for some years. Sugar and Bill were married by a justice of the peace one time when Sugar was in drag; the J. P. didn't think to ask if Sugar was really a female. When I met them they had been married sixteen years and were in adjoining cells in the penitentiary. Roger and Gus are a jailhouse marriage—they have a prison parody of outside marriage and, as they say, expect to continue the relationship when they are released. Because of the various sex roles in prison the female pronouns *she* and *her* often refer to male queens and punks. The only real women in this book are Margie McMurphy, Big Sal, and Judy.

Most studs have the rationale that they are not engaging in homosexual behavior; they say they are simply using a convenient receptacle that is preferable to denial or masturbation; there may be some validity to that argument, but I don't know how much. Often, the prison relationships develop into full-blown love affairs, and they may even be called marriages by the partners. In such cases, violation of the marriage agreement (e.g., screwing around with others) brings down the same kind of anger it would have brought down outside in a heterosexual affair. Several of the speakers here say it is silly to talk of one half of a homosexual couple as being straight and the other half as homosexual, but homosexual activity in prison is different enough from free-world homosexual activity to need other terms. The convicts have their set; sociologists now tend to refer to the roles as *insertor* (the one who gets to ejaculate) and *insertee* (the one who is ejaculated in).

Some inmates insist that anyone dealing with a punk is not himself homosexual but anyone dealing with a queen is; other inmates reverse the equation. Prison authorities are equally divided. This confusing multiplicity of values leads to a variety of logical and emotional differences.

It is easy to make too much of sex in prison. Girlie magazines play it up, prison administrators play it down, and it is difficult to find out just how much activity actually goes on, and impossible to find out who does what to whom. Many queens have told me that they have been surprised at how many presumably straight inmates who visit them want to go both ways. Most informed sources estimate that somewhere between 30 and 50 percent of the inmates regularly participate in prison sexual activity.

Most prison administrators find sex to be a cause of violence (remember, that's what got some of these guys in jail in the first place), and they punish men caught participating. Some prisons have separate cell blocks for queens and punks and others for aggressive studs. Massachusetts actually *adds* time to a man's sentence if he is caught in a homosexual act in prison, treating the problem as if it were a free-world crime, which indicates that society's attitude toward prison homosexuality can be far more barbaric than the inmates'.

I am not convinced that segregated cell blocks for persons defined by prison classification officers as likely sex participants really helps very much (save in the cases of overt queens and very fragile young boys). There are some fish populations—such as swordtails, porgies, and paradise fish—which have the peculiar characteristic of being able to generate new males whenever there are too few to sustain the population. One of the females will go through a complete sex change and will become a male and will service the others. Something like that happens in prison: when the most effeminate members of the society are picked off and hidden away, the definition of "very feminine" shifts a little bit so others may be incorporated into that role. Since much of the impetus for prison sexual relationships has to do with status articulation and affection needs, this is less difficult or complicated than it might seem.

Alfred C. Kinsey (in *Sexual Behavior in the Human Male*, Philadelphia, 1948) said there was far less sexual activity in prisons than most outsiders assumed; he said that the more poorly educated portion of the population is less capable of entertaining extensive erotic fantasies than the imaginative students studying such situations. But there have always been smuggled erotic pictures of women in prisons, and when those are lacking there are inmate artists who will make things to order. I have one letter from one inmate to another, ordering a sex book:

> Say Louis this is Brown on 5 tank man. Look Louis I like the Book Man but I dont have any money at this time. So I cants get the Book. listen man I want you to make me a good Book for christmas. I want about 25 page in it. I want a grey boy fucking his Mother and his Sister. look man make them fat But not fat man. I will pay you good for it as you no that. look man put but ass on them Woman look man I dont want the Book all fuck up man. But make them Woman fat but not to fat. And let me no When you get it fix.

I wonder what Kinsey would have written had he visited a place like the Missouri Penitentiary, an institution where—at the time of my last visit—the only rule was "Don't go over the wall," where an inmate could have transferred to his cell anyone he wanted, where there was a flourishing trade in erotic booklets and pictures.

But many prisons *are* tightly controlled, there are in them many shakedowns and inspections, erotic photographs and drawings are confiscated, nelly inmates are not allowed to do their hair or eyebrows or tailor their uniforms. One might wonder why sexual activity, even on a limited basis, goes on at all in such prisons.

The probable answer is that sexual affairs and adventures are often enlisted in the service of ends not coital in nature. Outside sexual activity doesn't consist of coitus only, but of all sorts of enactments of male and female role options. In prison there is great need for assertion of *maleness*—the punks and queens and the range of available relationships with them are important in a society characterized more than anything else by dependency and impotence. I think

here of a remark in a paper on prison sex shown me by a Massachusetts inmate: "In prison parlance a punk is neither a wise kid nor a
small-time hood: he is a kid that has been made, made many times in
the past, and that can be made now with no difficulty whatsoever. He
is what, if he were a girl, would be known as a pig. Sometimes he is actually a prostitute. That is to say that he sells himself for cigarettes or
for some other economic consideration. But mostly he just uses his
willingness to give himself up to the pleasure of another man to ingra-
tiate himself. Usually with some man that is respected, and perhaps
feared." In a world without women, men are pressed into doing
women's service—to express your machismo you must have people
without it; the mode of expression, as in the free world, is overt sexuality.

Women seem able to move in and out of homosexual contacts
with less psychic turbulence than men. There seem to be more non-
consummated affairs in a women's prison, and, I think, affairs that are
more clearly deeded to the affection needs in which the physical com-
ponent is not dominant. The men seem to have to assert their mascu-
linity by an act of fucking or some parody of it; the women can enact
their affection role without that. I don't mean to imply that there isn't
a great deal of acting-out sexuality in women's prisons when there is
opportunity, but rather that there is more possibility for sustaining
homosexual relationships without as much opportunity, or the need
for such opportunity, as would be required in men's prisons.

There are rapes now and then, but those are rare in the larger
adult institutions. The worst places for sexual abuses are temporary
detention centers, such as the county jails. These are populated by an
uncomfortable and immiscible conglomerate: the innocent too broke
to afford bail before trial, minor offenders serving out short sentences,
inmates awaiting transfer to state prisons, defendants in serious trials.
Much of the population is there for morals or disorderly conduct
charges. The cellblocks are often run by a strong inmate or inmate
gang. Into this mess are thrown first-offenders and often boys who
would not be there at all if they were adults (such as one Ohio youth
incarcerated a couple of years ago because his high school principal
objected to his long hair).

Several of the inmates talk about sexual experiences in the Harris
County jail in Houston, and Sugar talks about being gang-raped in
the Oakland, California, jail at the age of fifteen. There was a scandal
in 1970 about gang rapes in the Philadelphia jail, and even in the wag-

ons going to and from court. There were revelations in Buffalo, New York, of the same sort of thing, but the community didn't even demand an investigation.

One speaker in here says one can't be forced to do anything one doesn't want to do, even in a county jail. Everyone else disagrees with that; so do I. The logic of the speaker is that the victim really wanted to do it, that he subconsciously wanted to be raped. I think that is nonsense.

Of all the changes in perspective one must go through in the process of becoming a convict, I think the change regarding homosexual activity is one of the most crucial. Outsiders worry about prison sex because it is presumably bad or something like that, just as they worry about their sixteen-year-old daughter getting laid on a date. That isn't what I mean.

Acceptance of prison sexual roles is necessary for successful institutionalization; someone who is really well institutionalized—who functions well in those roles and options prison has and the free world does not have—has a greater chance of *not* getting on well in the free world than someone who never really adjusts to prison culture. It is the man who rebels against the prison social structure, who even after years of subjugation to it says, "This is not for me, this is not right," who has the control over his sense of self necessary to make it in the complex world outside. Too fine an adjustment is a death.

One thing more: I think there are a number of inmates who would like to be homosexual on the streets but have never learned how. Being a successful homosexual outside is just like being a successful heterosexual: you have to know the correct gambits if you hope to score without being laughed at. One can gamble with one's seduction techniques with women, but such experimentation is not so easy when one is going queer, especially when one comes from a socio-economic context with no accepted role for homosexuals. Prison gives some men an excuse for being homosexual that they do not have on the street, and prison sex is the reason many of them come back. Instead of treating those men for theft or robbery, we'd do better to learn how to identify them and teach them how to be competent homosexuals. At least that would change them from felony to misdemeanor defendants, and they wouldn't be cluttering up our prisons.

Slim: "We don't laugh about that . . ."

There are two classes of homos in here. You have what they call the "original" or "square" and you have what they call the "candy-bar punk." The original comes in, gets her one man—maybe five or six mates on the side—and fucks it up. Keeps that one man going all the time. Some jokers in here, they refer to that as their kid, some joints they call them queens, gays, whatever, but here they call them kid. A guy'll get him a kid and he'll go to all extremes to treat this cocksucker just as though he was a wife. He will do everything just to get that kid some $4 shoes; the watch that I have on now belongs to my kid. He's in B-Basement for sticking another girl. He cut him. He's in B-Basement, so I took his watch and I'm going to hold it for him till he gets out, you know. Stupid old watch.

Some of the relationships in here are interracial, about 25 percent maybe. The whites say, "Okay, if you wanna haul coal." That's what they call it: "hauling coal." That's the way it is averagely. You have some radicals, you know. Most guys figure, it's your ass, man, if you wanna haul coal, then haul it. Me, I don't do that interracial thing because I don't want anything I can't take back to the cell with me at night.

Out in the streets I'd have no time to be worrying about no kid. I'll have enough trouble trying to keep up with those women, trying to get that money. As I say, educationally I'm handicapped. I have a couple of trades, but most of them nowadays call for college men. I learned them by ear and I wouldn't be able to get the kind of job I think myself qualified to have, so I would still have to rely on my hustling ability. Not dice and cards anymore, but I'd have to use the old noodle, so to speak, you know? Not burglarizing or anything like that either. It would be illegal, but it wouldn't be *very* illegal. There are a lot of things a man can do in hustling, and I just wouldn't have time for a kid. That's all of that. I can do things for him while I'm here, but after that, he's on his own.

Like I say, there's two types here. The candy-bar fag and the original. The original will sometimes fool you by looks. Looks, you know, are deceiving. The boy I have, he's more or less original.

A candy-bar punk is one who comes in and he's a punk out of necessity. He's a young boy and he's good-looking and it boils down to this: you got what I want and I've got what you need; you satisfy me sexually and I'll see to it that you smoke square cigarettes [cigarettes in factory packages rather than hand-rolled ones] and have face soap, square face soap, the necessities. The meals ain't shit so you're going to get hungry at night and I'll figure a way you can eat. That's the candy-bar punk. He had a tendency to want a mate.

The original, he's the type that comes in and says, "I want a man. I'm a punk because I *want* to be a punk." That's it, usually. He has a tendency to stick, too. He doesn't jump from cell to cell, he sticks. The one I've got I've had for four years now.

We had six-man cells here, now they're four-man. How can they stop it? A lot of guys will thump their chest and say, "Well, Jack, I'm a man." But when you pull the curtain, it's a different story. So how you gonna stop it?

Mine told me that he raped men and he has a wife and a family, but every time he has sexual intercourse with his wife he winds up in the nuthouse with a nervous breakdown. So he rapes men . . .

How?

If he can't find one that will go willingly, he'll put his knife on him and take him.

You're confusing me. He plays the wolf?

Female wolf, yeah. He had them screw him.

Now I couldn't say about most of the punks. Some of them are like mine. Some of them in here I knew on the streets. Being a hustler or a roundabout, you know them. Some were married and quite happy. Actually married with the marriage certificates and everything that goes with it: a house, a home, whatever. Some of them are entertainers. Some of them are business ladies, so to speak; you'd be surprised at some of the offices you walk into and you're not looking at a woman at all.

In here, it's just like outside. There's been times in here that I told the one I had, "Look here, girl, bankroll's a little light. The cards ain't falling right. You gotta do something." But that's my life. I did it in the streets so it's got no strings, you know. And he'd go on and do it just like the whore in the streets would do it for me.

Something else about in here that's like outside: it's a good life if you don't weaken. Only, I've gotten weak sometimes.

Daisy: "We're pretty much girls for the girls . . ."

I've had the name of Daisy since New Orleans seven years ago. I'm twenty-five now. I turned out when I was thirteen years old. It was a dirty old man, my former employer.

I've never been in prison before. I'm in for embezzlement. I was city clerk and assistant city secretary until I hit the till once too often with my bookkeeping. I'm on a five-year sentence, been in for two years. After my parole hearing next month I ought to get out, and if not, I'll be discharged next year at this time.

I always dress as a man outside. I have worked drag shows in New Orleans, and as a female mime, and I did a U.S.O. tour for the Air Force for nine months. I was doing drag numbers in that, but it was strictly professional. I'm not oriented along the transvestite lines.

Most of the girls here will act the part, we'll do that. We do that for our own benefit. We go around acting half-nutty, half-calm. Most of us wouldn't act like that on the outside. If we did, it would be to party, that's all. But we carry on that way around here because it's easier for us to make it that way. If we start to get real upset and real nervous and try to watch everything it just sticks out all over that we're nervous then. And there'll be some boss to pick on you every time if they think you're real scared. But if you go right on and say, "Hi, honey," to a boss and just smack and haul like you belong, they don't bother you.

A lot of us have more of an education than we seem. I'm short thirty-two hours of a B.A. And we're probably a little more adult than we seem at times. But it's just easier for us to go and carry on like we haven't got a brain cell that works. Nobody pays any attention to us that way.

Any attention?

We get all sorts of attention, but it's the good kind and not the bad kind.

When you called me out I was talking to two new girls who just got in. They were all scared to death, wrecked and upset and screaming they'd never make it. I said, "You got to grin and bear it and go on. And don't be bothered." The grin-and-bear it type attitude is the best for us girls here, no matter what.

You know, before I came down here I was real down on the characters. But I was surprised at how well versed the men were in all our girl carryings-on. They know our language and get along with us real well and know how to bull with us and all. They come out with their stories to make a hit and get our attention. I didn't expect it. I expected we'd be something like untouchables. I'd never read any books about the penal institutions, so I was surprised. I've done pretty well here.

Most of the girls come and don't feel like they've been picked on just because they're segregated—put in a special wing—they do pretty well and manage to adjust. We depend a lot on each other. The girls and the punks don't get along at all. Someone told me you asked about that when you were in the wing the other day. And I could have kicked Jackie about that. Jackie didn't talk to you much, she could have and—

She just giggled.

Well, you know Jackie. She wanted to make it clear that she was a girl and not a punk, but she was still afraid to talk to you. I don't know why.

She's a free-world gal, you know. No penitentiary could break her.

The punks and queens don't get along. That's our only sore spot: we don't like being locked up with punks. Our wing is about half us and half them because there's not enough of us free-world gay people to have a wing just for us, so they throw all the dirty old men with sex charges on their records, a couple of protection cases and prison turnouts in with us. We kind of resent that.

We used to get down some [manage sexual encounters] before they caught us having a whorehouse in the wing a year ago. But sex is very very limited now and there's practically no opportunity. And you'll find most of the free-world queens, people like Jackie or me, won't have sex with a punk. It's ugh. I don't think any of them would really do it because they have a dislike for the punks. They're not man enough to stand up and admit what they are, so we don't have any respect for them.

We girls are all thrown in there together. We're pretty much girls for the girls, we stick together pretty close. Sometimes there's a little jealousy and feuding between us, but there would be with queens anywhere that run around together in a group. Otherwise we stick pretty close together.

I've never had any trouble. I've gotten a few feuds going, but none of the girls would stoop to physical violence except when they slap each other.

Stories get started, that's how it is in places like this. They're awful bad about jumping to conclusions. And I mean other inmates as well as officials. Three or four of us are real friendly and pretty open with everybody. We'll go through the mess hall and wink at ten people. A wink to me merely is a way of saying "How are you doing today, I'm fine." That's all. I know a lot of these people from having worked out in the hall, and at that time I got to talk to them pretty frequently. So I'll wink at somebody to say hello and a week later up here there's a rumor that's got us all hooked up. The grapevine around this place is tremendous, the only trouble is it's all wrong most of the time. I've had ninety-nine husbands I know about in the two years I've been on this farm, according to rumor anyway.

Once one of them got mad at me—she wasn't a queen, just a dirty old thing—and ran up to the major and told him to take me off my job because I was tricking every day. He didn't even live in the wing that I lived in. Said I was carrying on something awful, having sex every night. Fortunately, they considered the source and nothing came of it, and they just told him to go back to work and leave me alone.

But most of us girls, as I said, stick together. We share things among ourselves and have a pretty good time. In a lot of ways we do have a better go of it than the punks, and we're certainly treated nicer. Those punks—if they see two people getting friendly they'll write a note about it out to the office and they'll say the two had an affair. Most of the times these things are ignored by the officials. I've been running innumerable associations but they've never called me up and talked to me about it. The only time they called me up was when one of the girls got stabbed. Poor girl, her old man's a faggot. She had written a letter to one of her friends and mentioned me. I was a pretty good friend of hers, it wasn't that she had meant to hurt me by it. She'd written that I'd tried to be real understanding with her and that she had told me her problem when we ate together. I had told her I thought she'd better go talk to someone because she was deep in trouble.

She mentioned in one letter the man that I was hooked up with. She said, "So-and-so and Daisy get along so well and I wish we could be like Daisy." All this of course, it got to the major, and so he called me and said, "Is this true? Is this your dream man?"

I said, "Yes, I'm not going to lie."

He said, "I'm not going to do anything to you. Don't lie to me."

I said, "Why yes, we've gone together for years. I'm sure you've heard about it many times before."

"Yes, I have," he said, "but I laughed."

That's all there was to it. Later he made the remark to some people that were in the office that if all did like I did and acted a little discreet about things he'd leave them alone too.

I'll tell you about that major: he hates a lie. I don't care what he'd caught me doing, I'd admit it, I'd cop to him. It's better because you'd have less disciplinary action and you probably won't lose your job. You lie to him and you're dead. You might have to eat paste right then, but later on it's all forgotten.

You know, when it comes to real good jobs, the two-for-one-job, money, secretary jobs, all that stuff, the snitches don't get them. A snitch will get so far and then when it comes to giving out with the goodies the people who have ridden with the tide and kept their mouths shut, they come out ahead.

Where we do get into trouble is with the preacher, the one who works on the farm as sociologist or whatever he is. He's real down on the girls. He preaches a lot about wicked women to us. Four times in a row he did that when we went to church, so we all quit going. He'd tell the story about the woman who couldn't go to the well with the other women to get water, she had to go at night because they'd all stone her because she was an evil woman. And he'd point at us.

The girls can't get a parole recommendation from him. He says, "Are you an overt homosexual?" And it's very obvious that we are. If we say yes, it's an automatic *no* on our recommendation. And if we say we're not and we're sitting there with our plucked eyebrows and everything . . . we can try to come off with some phony story: "Oh, I've learned to control it," but then he suspects we're lying to him, so all we do is pray that they don't ask him for a parole recommendation for us because we know what we're going to get.

We got one girl down here he gave a word association test to and every other word he said was "suck," "dick," or something like that. I mean, what's a poor girl going to say?

He just humiliated her until she was almost in tears when she left the office. Needless to say, she gummed the word association test.

Roger: "What they hate most of all is mothers . . ."

When I went to Ramsey I was recognized as a free-world turnout, a queen, they call them queens. And I was treated with respect, just like a real girl. They name you after a girl if you want to be named after one; call you by that name. And when you walked into the fields people would help you out, whereas they would not help out a jailhouse turnout.

People treated us real nice. There are a lot of free-world queens there that get anything they want: commissary, coffee, furniture, anything, and you get nice clothes if you want them. Your jailhouse turnouts are treated like a machine; when someone wants sex and they haven't got a free-world queen of their own then they go to the jailhouse turnouts. They're in fights. They're always haggling over their men. They might even try to play the man role sometimes.

They had all the homosexual cases in one wing because they didn't want us to communicate with the younger men on the unit, I guess. Even the building tender was homosexual and so was the barber. I remember one night the building tender went to another unit, I went with him, but I heard that while he was gone the whole wing went wild opening cells. It was one-man cells when I was there, and everything just went wild. Now it's two-man cells, they tell me, and it's wilder than ever.

The queens stay mostly to themselves. They mostly look down on punks. They look down on everything actually. The queens seem to be more sophisticated. Most of them are down for a hot check or possibly murder or something like that; from what I've seen, you never see one down for fighting or drunk or narcotics or anything like that. The punks, they're down here for car theft, robbery, burglary. Mostly burglary and car theft, petty larceny, things like that.

It was pretty hard to get a showdown, any kind of privacy, long enough for intercourse anyway. All you usually have a chance for is a quick blowjob. While I was down there, I was punked two or three times. I did have one showdown for intercourse that lasted about four or five minutes. And I had what we call a husband, an old man. I try to be independent myself. Most queens try to be independent. Most of them have their own money.

Since I've been here I've had three old men. One lasted two months while I was down on Ramsey. One lasted six months here, then he went home. I've been married to this last one seven months. [Gus, whose interview follows this one.] These things usually last until you are separated. And then it goes on a while after that, what with correspondence and smuggled letters.

My husband treats me just like a woman. He bought me a wedding ring. At Christmas, my birthday, anniversaries, I get cards and presents. I make presents for him, monograms and things like that. We read each other's mail when we get it. We share our commissary, he draws money and I draw money and it's an equal thing. We have plans for the future; I don't know if they'll work out or not. Right now I'm saving up money to go home. If I were to have trouble among the other inmates he would stand up for me. I try to avoid getting him off into trouble like that, I try to look out for him and he does me. He lives in the next cell.

Most of the guys who become husbands have done that before, most of the ones I've had anyway. The one I had before this had been down here nine years and he had been married several times. The one I have now is a young boy, he's twenty-one. I'm twenty-five. He's been in reformatories and jail a lot, so he's got a lot of experience.

Down here a queen is treated like a woman, if you act like one.
And the punks?

They try to play rough and ready. We don't get on very well. Punks and husbands are often in a swap deal, each partner plays the passive part and one the other role. There's a lot of fighting going on most of the time, and the husbands don't treat punks with very much respect.

Do they protect them?

Very little. They usually look out for themselves. You'll often see a punk fighting it out with somebody. You never see a queen fighting with anyone. Nobody touches you.

There's a difference in the way we're treated on different farms. On Ramsey you're treated like an animal. You're a pig. You're undesirable, un-understandable. You're kind of like a plague. They don't understand you, they don't try to understand you. You're a misfit. Any hell they can give you while you're there they go out of their way to give it to you.

And punks were usually treated a little worse. Usually the queen gets a little better way to go because of the fact of the connections with them and their mothers. They have ties with their mothers, most of them. It's quite something to see some queen's mother down there screaming to the warden at the top of her lungs, "Why did you do this to my baby and why did you do that to my baby?" And the queens have more sense of themselves. They don't take that kind of treatment, whereas your punk is used to it all his life.

It's different here. There's more educated men working in this prison. They don't understand you, but they don't go out of their way to make trouble for you. A lot of the young bosses come to work here and stare at you for a while and then they get used to it. Most of them call us "she" or "her." Most of them call us by our first name, then the nickname. Very nice.

Parole possibilities for homosexuals is zero in the state of Texas. Like I told you before, we're outcasts. Undesirables. You come up for parole and they give you the same old questions, then they go into their lecture.

That you shouldn't be a queen?

Yes. "Why are you one and why haven't you changed and don't you have ambition to change? You'd be so much better off if you changed." You're actually tried and convicted for a felony, it might be anything, but when you sit down in front of that parole board, as far as they're concerned you're down here for sodomy. You're treated like scum most of the time.

Very little privileges for people like us, no job opportunities.

None?

Not unless you're highly skilled and very discreet. With a lot of outside pull.

I used pull just once to get a job in here. I had my mother get on Senator B———'s ass. My uncle was campaign manager for the governor. But my family doesn't want anybody to know I'm here.

Do they think it's a secret?

Actually, it is. The papers never picked it up. My mother agreed to push as long as she could bluff, so long as she didn't have to get my uncle into it. You can get anything done you want, as long as you've got people behind you.

What they hate most of all is mothers. They hate them.

This warden here, some people think he's a homosexual and that's because he's effeminate. His choice of clothes, his mannerisms, things like that. He isn't though, I don't think he is anyway. He's got grace and finesse, that's what it is. Now Warden B———, he's practically a hick, and that's all they'll let him be. But this warden, he'd charm the eyeteeth out of a goat. He could have your son out in the pasture buried with a rifle bullet through him and sneak in smiling from ear to ear. Tell you anything you want to believe and you'll end up believing it. He can charm anyone's mother.

I had my first affair when I was eight years old. Then I was inactive until I was about fourteen and it lasted then for two years. Then I was inactive till I was about eighteen or nineteen. Then I turned out for good.

How'd you first turn out?

A boy tricked me into playing house, something like that. Then he terrorized me. He threatened to tell my mother and father about it if I didn't keep letting him do it. Then we moved away. The one when I was fourteen, that was a normal boyfriend relationship, we just held hands mostly. Some other things.

The place a punk usually gets turned out is the county jail. Or in the reformatory if he's weak. But they usually always get them in the county jail. Especially the Harris County jail, that's in Houston. There's no protection for young kids there at all.

Most of it is open tanks, and the only protection is after it's too late. They don't weed you out or take any pains to try to put you somewhere where they think you'll be safe. Any young kid that goes through that county jail gets turned out. My husband, the one I'm with now, got turned out down there. I don't mean he was turned into a punk or a queen, but they screwed him. He was taken by force both ways.

And the guards gave no protection?

No. After it's been going on a couple of months you've got scars all over. One of the boys from Harris County came up here with scars. He had been burned and starved and beaten. That's by other inmates, not guards, and they do that until they get what they want, until they get a kid to suck them off and let them fuck him, and even then sometimes they beat him up some more if he gave them a hard time about it.

The guards there: do they just not care or are they paid off?

They just don't care, I believe.

And you can't do anything about it, you can't file charges. You can't prove that anything happened because you have no witnesses. You can't drag somebody out of there and give him a lie detector test.

A lot of times, after a kid's been beat up and had it taken from him, after they'd been in there a while and find things hard for them and they haven't got any money coming in, they will revert to being a punk. When they want something then they will trick for it or play the role for it.

How does an affair get started usually?

Well, if the man is discreet or has any brains at all, he will approach you himself. He will write you a note, explain who he is, ask a little about you. Try to meet you somewhere and talk to you. Or, if he's not restrained, he'll write you a note and say, "How 'bout you and me, baby? You want to go down on me?" Something like that. Usually that type strictly stays with punks, but your husband material will talk to you in a nice way. Treats you just like a woman. Would never think of killing you or using you in any way.

A punk will usually approach somebody. Or he'll agree to any old setup, whatever he can get. Or he'll say, "It will cost you so much." Or he'll approach someone with a cash offer and take it. Then they know he's a punk. I've never heard of a queen being punk like that. Doing it for cash—queens in here just don't do it.

Punks are usually a shiftless bunch. They have low morals. Of course, it's hard to say in here who's got the lowest morals, but *them* . . . !

It's hard to get to the queen, you know. It's hard to make steps to the queen usually. Say you have someone working out in the office. Now he is very particular about what type of punk he would mess with because he doesn't want to be busted or lose his job. People tighten up and it's hard to find a queen when you tighten up. I've had several affairs but I've never had anybody give me any trouble behind them. Then there are a lot of queens that trick and talk among the other queens and it gets out. There's a lot of jealousy among the queens. Where I am now there are no queens at all. They've got me all by myself in a place with a lot of punks, perverts, child-molesters, and things like that.

The problem here isn't getting away from the guards, it's getting away from *everybody*. If anybody sees me going down it's going to get back to the warden. I blew a guy once in here and it was snitched off. I did it on the row, up in my own cell. The run is the walkway in front of the cells and somebody saw it and I was turned in the next day. I denied it and the other guy denied it and it couldn't be proved.

I've heard things of some up there with their legs up against the bars and someone standing on the run and fucking them through the bars. But that's not for me. I have had intercourse in the building over there where I could arrange complete privacy. There was no one except myself and the other man and we didn't need a lookout watching or anything.

Ramsey was different. We were in a wing, the cells were in a wing, and there wasn't that run going in front and the Man never comes near a cell except to talk. You can usually make a deal with the building tender. In my jail you had to make a deal with the building tender to get somebody let into your cell or out of it.

The building tender runs the wing himself, he has controls for the cells inside the wing. So if you up a little to the building tender once in a while, a little ass for him, then he'll let you do things.

When I was at Ramsey I did one in the hospital. They kept me in the hospital overnight and there was no guard there. Everybody in the whole thing knew about it and they were playing sleep and it was turned in the next morning. It was denied. Usually, if you get away with it—I mean, if they don't catch you in the act—they don't care. They don't do anything about it unless they catch you. If they get a rumor about it going on constantly, then they have to do something about it then.

Outside the wing it happens sometimes. In the cornfield, when the corn is high, there's a lot going on. A lot of play, usually not with the queens. Your queens are usually more discreet. Your punks really get going out there.

See, you're coming down the row and the corn's about eight feet high and you just work on the row with whoever you want to trick. You get so far ahead of the others. They do it when they're irrigating too. The boss does not come into the field when it's real wet out because it's so muddy. You can lay down in the ditches. Some of them get butt naked and they trick and go on.

Most of the marriages are rings, and "You're mine" and "She's mine" and "He's mine," and everybody knows it. There's no sex, just all talk. A long-distance love affair is what we call them. Most of them are that way because it's hard to get together; there's not many who wouldn't do anything if there was a chance. A marriage helps. You can do your time a lot easier. You've got two people doing your time instead of one. You've got someone to tell your problems to, you're not by yourself.

When I leave here—I get out first—I'll correspond secretly and when I have some money I'll come see him regularly. Send him a little money once in a while. I want to pick him up when he gets out.

The punks come back a lot, get back in. They go out and run in the same old crowd, same old friends. They have no ambition to go. They're just shiftless. I wouldn't say they come back for the homosexual aspect, they come back for a home. They're at home here. They exist. They can tell each other about their hot rods and their motorcycles and the girls they screwed. All this. All the women they've had, and then, later on that night, they shack up with some old man. That's it.

You know, my husband and I have never had sex together. I've had shacks in this place, but not with him. He's in the cell next to me and the only way we can have sex would be when the door was open for us to go to TV, I could go in his cell. But if we were caught we would be separated and we don't want to be separated. So I have sex with other people instead.

In Ramsey I was married to a boy who had been married to Betty Jo, another queen. Betty Jo was married to another boy at the time in another wing, and she made a play for my old man. That ain't good enough, let me try to get it straight for you because it's complicated.

The building tender planted ideas in my husband's head that Betty Jo was out to break us up. And the building tender had been going with Betty Jo and wanted Betty Jo removed from the scene because she was going with someone else now. Follow me?

These ideas were planted in my husband's head. And they got Betty Jo and my husband into a little fight. He kept brooding about it. And one day we went to the mess hall and the building tender kept planting these ideas: "Betty Jo said this," and "Betty Jo's carrying a knife."

Betty Jo was in the barber's and she was laying down in the barber chair and my husband came up and slashed her throat. On this side, with a little cutting knife, an Exacto knife.

Of course the building tender was removed from his job because he let it happen. It was never pinned on my husband, and then Betty Jo's husband heard about it. And then Tommy Jo, that was my husband, got out of solitary and Betty Jo's husband made an attempt to get him. And Betty Jo's husband lost his job and Betty Jo lost his job and the building tender lost his job.

I was scared to death, because I tried to avoid this. I'd gone and talked to Betty Jo. Later Betty Jo and I were transferred. She went to Ellis and I was in the hospital at the Walls for hepatitis. Betty Jo came in and we talked it all over and figured out what had happened. She told me what she knew and I told her what I knew. You know, she still had that little blade stuck in her throat.

So you figured it all out.

Yes, the whole plot.

They sure do get devious, don't they?

Yes, oh, yes. It's very treacherous at times. Especially with someone like Betty Jo who keeps a lot of mess going.

I try, even now, not to get involved in other people's business. I know everything that's going on, nothing gets by me, but I don't get involved in it. I don't try to give anybody advice. If somebody tries to give me advice I'll listen to him, but I won't tell him what I'm going to do. I won't necessarily do what they want, I'll do what I decide to do. And I haven't had any trouble. One could say I've been lucky, but I've just used my head.

Gus: "You can buy you a showdown at breakfast time . . ."

Well, I've played the man most of the time. But when I was in jail I had a hard time and I went through a lot of hell, but I ended up getting turned out. After that happened I didn't say anything. I didn't snitch or anything, but I stayed in the tank. But when they found out about it later and caught me out, I said that I was a homosexual to keep from having to be snitching. That's the only time I've ever been punked.

That county jail is a bad place, isn't it?

Oh, yes, it sure is. It is. I mean, you have a kid come in and it's the first time he's in jail and he's scared. Four or five of them get to whipping on him, well, he's gonna do most anything.

The first time I hit that county jail they put me in the hard-ass tank. That's where they've got the boozers and butchers, killers and everything, all the robbers. They're mostly habitual criminals. I was nineteen years old. I fought, but it didn't do any good.

I should say that, before that, I was in a reformatory and I was married to a queen there and when I got out, me and this queen was married on the streets for a long time. And just before I got busted I was also living with this queen. Then we—this queen and I—met other queens. I've been around queens most of my life. That's why I can usually tell the difference between a queen and a punk.

How old were you when you started hanging out with queens?

My best buddy in school was a homosexual, a queen. And we was going to junior high together, that's where I met him. He was studying to be a beautician and we got together and had a few times together, done a few things together. That was the first time. Then I started standing on the street corners. I shined shoes when I was a kid too, and I met several of them from here and there. I met several of them in New Orleans. I tramped and went to New Orleans. There are a number of gay places in New Orleans that I'd go to. Most of my life I've been and messed with them.

I guess I just feel better around them than I do a lot of people because you very seldom hear in the paper where a boy gets a man busted, but a lot of times you hear a woman gets a man busted behind something. If a queen loves you she don't care what you do and what you have; if she loves you that's all there is to it. It's not like a punk. A punk loves you for what you have. If a queen loves you they'll do anything in the world for you. Like I said before, whether you're a something or a nothing they're going to be with you, but it's not going to be just because you're here, it's because they want to be with you. You make plans. I have made several plans with my wife [Roger] for when I discharge. We've made several plans because we've figured that if we'd met each other a long time ago we'd never have come here.

She gets out fourteen months and thirteen days before me. And I believe she'll be there, waiting for me. I have a lot of faith in it because I'd put a lot of faith in a queen before I would a woman. She will be here and I intend to go to work. She will work too and we're gonna go to California and live, because it's not as bad in California as it is in Texas.

In Texas if they catch a homosexual and a person—actually you're both homosexual but they just consider one of you homosexual. If they catch a homosexual and a bull living together they can send them back to the penitentiary for unnatural sex acts. But in California it's not like that. Unless you're caught right out in the open.

When I come to jail the first time I was young and I don't look too bad and there were several of them that said, "Little boy, who you belong to?" I told them I didn't belong to nobody. I'd always been taught that if you fight, things like that don't happen. But that's not right because I fought and got my face messed up. I had to have plastic surgery and I still got turned out. I had a wire stuck to my throat. I say a wire, I mean a big piece of long straight wire with a point on it and them telling me to do it or die. And I'm afraid I'm gonna die. You meet people that say all the time, "I'd rather die first." And I said it myself, but when it come to either doing or dying, I just had to do it.

At first I just had to trick, and then it was eat them up too. One to one only then, but somebody went out and snitched on us. And when they snitched on us they called me up. I pleaded that I was homosexual to keep these people from getting into trouble because I don't believe in snitching. What happened when I come out of the tank with my face all messed up, the warden told me if I didn't snitch on what had happened he was going to put me back in there. And I didn't tell him what had happened so he put me back in there. I was really scared then.

They started to put me in solitary confinement at county jail, but when they saw where I'd been burned with cigarettes, and I had big burn marks on me from where they mixed Dutch Cleanser and bleach and lye soap, they knew what happened. They put me in the hospital tank.

The guards don't watch those places very well, do they?

In jail it's not that they don't watch it very well. You've got twenty-five to thirty people in a clique and you just can't whip a clique. Even they can't whip a clique.

But I was lucky in that I ended up with one person somehow, and I wouldn't have nothing to do with anybody else. Being with four or five of them is not right. But I have seen them, some guys, have to take on the whole place every time they're in there.

When you came up here were there people who had known what had happened to you in the jail?

Yes, there was. But I got that straight on the farm with an aggie, a hoe. I wasn't uptight because I didn't have to fight five or six or seven or eight or fifteen or twenty of them at one time. I just took a swing at a couple of them with an aggie, and they decided they'd better leave me alone.

In here, it's the same as on the street in a lot of ways. It's mostly just being lonely. When it first gets started, it's somebody to have conversation with, and do things with, and somebody to set around and talk with, and eat with, and do different things with. Discuss things about what you've done on the streets. It's like that that things get started—just loneliness is what it is.

Which are you talking about—the punk, bull, queen, or husband? Or
  all of them?

All of them, 'cause you have to look around before you know
who is which. I'm talking about your queens or turnouts and also the
bulls. You have to be around one a while before you know exactly
what they are.

  And how do you know what they are?

The bull talks about different things he's done on the streets and
your turnout talks about "give me this" or "give me that," "I'd like to
have this" or "I'd like to have that." And your queen, well, it's not always "give me." By the motions you can also tell, or the acts. The way
they act, the way they talk, the things they do, the stories that they tell.

Your punk talks about all the women he's made love to and all
the fights he's been into and everything like that. But he'd go to bed
with you either way. The punk is just trying to make it, that's all there
is. He figures somebody else will take up for him if he gets into
trouble. He can jump on somebody else and someone will take up for
him.

Marriages are something different. It's like on the streets when
you're with a woman quite a bit. A queen is actually a woman, really.
Just the one difference. She has the same actions as a woman. You
feel better being around her just like you would with a woman. So if
you like this person just like a woman, well, outside you would nine
times out of ten marry such a person, to have this person be with you
all the time and also to have somebody to talk to or somebody to listen to, and it's the same in here. To have help when you need to write
a business letter and you're not smart, they help you out. That's the
way it is with me. Then you make plans. You spend most of your time
together. Every place you go, this queen is with you, and they consider
you man and wife and usually you give them a ring and look out after
them and things like that.

But mostly it's just to have somebody. To be wanted in here, the
same as out there.

  How do other convicts react to the people in a marriage, a husband
  and a queen?

You don't run across too many people that look down upon it in
a penitentiary except maybe your bosses and things like that. Other
convicts are like us in some ways. If they had a chance to get married,
nine times out of ten they would get married too. It's a world of its
own. It's just like out there, you have to take what you can get. There

if you're married to a woman they don't say anything. In here, you're married to a queen and they don't say anything because a queen in here is the same as a woman out there.

You have to have trust in this person, this person has to have trust in you. It's just like with a woman except you don't go through the whole matrimony bit in a church, but it's the same thing. What's yours is hers and what's hers is yours. You help each other and you look out for each other and things like that.

And then you don't feel lonely. You feel like you've got just a little more freedom. You've got just a little bit more than anybody else's got. You've got something that maybe somebody else hasn't got. And you don't worry about nobody but this person and yourself. You don't worry about nobody else and what people think.

Do people make out on the side? Will a husband make out with other queens?

Some will and some won't. That's just like on the streets. Some will and some won't. I'd say that really it's less so than on the streets because you're so close to your own queen, your own wife. If you're gonna do it you get a divorce, and if you think enough of this person you don't want a divorce.

And what about the queen? How does being married change her behavior?

The queen feels the same way that you do except that she's not running around with people who would tell the Man the first time you've done something with them.

Now there's some people that won't do any of this at all, that won't have anything to do with punks or queens. That's because they're scared because they figure if they get caught they're gonna lose their good time. They're gonna go to solitary or something like that.

You think that's what holds most of the others back?

Definitely. You see a man who comes down with three or five years and hasn't been locked up before, nine out of ten of them will do it. Because it's something that's hard to do without. A man with three years, he's scared of losing his good time, but still, if he gets a chance where he won't get caught and the person won't say anything, then he'll go ahead and do it.

Is there any difference in what happens in a showdown with a queen or punk?

No. With a queen, now, it's really both ways 'cause if you're married to her she's your wife and with your wife anything goes, right? And then it's according to how long a showdown you have. If it's a punk, it's subject to be most anything because she figures she's gonna make something out of it. She'll sometimes say, "Oh, I won't do that," but if they think they're gonna make something out of it or you're gonna help them make that time, then, yeah, they'll do anything too.

It's a lot easier on the farms than in a prison like this. On the farms if you're married you can give the building tender a carton of cigarettes or so and he can move your wife in with you. Or you can buy you a showdown at breakfast time. That's because when everybody goes to breakfast, you and this queen or punk, you two won't go to breakfast. Then when everybody else is at breakfast you two go into a cell, usually the building tender's cell. See, in this place they bring us our food in our cells, we never get out of here, but down there, everybody went to breakfast who wanted to go eat. If you didn't want to eat you didn't have to go to breakfast. They counted you out when you went to breakfast to find out who went to breakfast, but a lot of them stayed in and slept and wouldn't go to breakfast. That was the time.

Al and Jerry: "When you can't get wine, get whiskey . . ."

JERRY: Ordinarily I would say that the man who plays the active role most of the time doesn't *always* play the active role. Ordinarily. Myself, I can't distinguish between the two of them. I don't know the difference. But when it's practiced extensively, everybody experiments, I guess.

The heavyweight champion in Nashville, I can't think of his name, Bobby something, I was talking to him in quarantine in Nashville and then this young boy came in and I was talking to him. The boy's name was Joe. He said, "One of the first things I'm going to do is I'm going to get me a kid."

And he's about seventeen years old. Almost as smooth and slick as some other people that you see around pretty close here, and I said, "Joe, knock that off. Boy, you'll be done *on* one before long at all, talking like that."

"What do you mean!" He bristled up with his 105 pounds, whatever it was, ready to fight, and I called Bobby over.

I said, "Bobby, come on over here." He comes over, and he's a hairy, muscular, broad-shouldered one-eyed ugly bastard, he's a nasty bastard. I said, "Bobby, you tell me that you had a boy when you were here before."

"Yeah, yeah," he says, "I love him too. Love him like a wife."

"Well," I says, "look, tell Joe here what happened after the first three or four years."

"Well, shit, I just got to love him more."

I said, "How would you manifest this love? What did you do for the boy?"

"Well, suck his peter a little every once in a while."

And this little boy, he just backed off. Poor little Joe, he backed off and he was just aghast.

I was transferred about two months later down to another unit in Tennessee and this little Joe had been down there about a week ahead of me. He was already in the hole. He was caught sitting on a fellow's lap. The fellow was sitting on the shitbowl and had, well, as much prick as he could manage up the boy. The boy says, "We were just playing," but they threw him in the hole anyhow.

I think that if that is very strong in a person's mind one way, it's at least in a smaller degree in their mind the other way. I think that there's very little difference in one fruit and another.

So you consider both participants fruits?

Yes, when it's an extensive thing. When they are beyond the experimental stage. When they've found out what it is and don't quit. They'll go further.

AL: Just sitting here thinking about it now, it does seem that guys who been in here a long time, they do often turn queer.

You mean really queer?

Yeah. From my own experience, most of the guys that come in here who are going to do it do it in a year or so. They either had some experience someplace before, some other joint, or on the street, or were leaning just a little toward that homosexual side to begin with. I believe that after a guy's here a length of time, say five, six, seven years, or longer, some of them longer than the others, that you're tempted to these young boys. Now I don't think you got to be a fruit or anything like that. And after a while you fall in love, I guess eventually a guy would do that just like he would with a woman, which he'd be tempted to do with a boy too.

JERRY: You can develop a strong affection for a fellow in the penitentiary. A man that you've lived closer to than you would on the outside, you can become very involved in his problems and so forth. If you happened to have these leanings, I can see where it would almost be inevitable.

I knocked off some ass in the boy's detention hall in Peoria, Illinois, too many years ago to tell about. I found that, afterward, it was a humiliating experience. I have had a little feminine asshole since. I haven't been tempted toward the male asshole since. Now I have had a bit of head since then, a bit of head, yes. You know that expression? A blowjob.

Since then, personally, just speaking for myself, I feel that is a thing to stay away from before I start to like it. We all have our feminine characteristics unless we're stone flat animals, and I think it's better to manifest my feminine characteristics through music or something of that nature. I don't knock it for the other guy if that's the play the other guy wants to make. Another guy's life, whether he ruins it completely or not, is none of my business—unless he asks me for some help.

AL: Something interesting here, to me anyway: I've seen a lot of these guys meet these young kids and fall in love with them and really get hooked up. That's even worse than on the streets with a woman or something. But nine times out of ten, after they cell with the guy a while, after this relationship goes on for a while, they quit it. As a mutual agreement. It just wears out, I guess. They may still cell together, like good friends, but I guess the passion there, whatever it was, just wears itself out and they just say to hell with it.

Do they go and get another punk?

Usually no, not until the young guy goes home or something like that. Of course now, some guys, they'll pick up one of these kids here and it's almost like a woman in the streets, they're just like whores. Then when the guy's in the cell with them a while they just start to getting kind of tired of them or they get to squabbling a bit among themselves and just move out and get somebody else.

JERRY: And sometimes they sell them, the stud will. And the young boy is resigned to the fact that he's pussy and that's it. Whoever is fucking him is the guy who's taking care of him, he's happy. He figures there's no other way.

He figures he can't fight this big guy and all that bullshit. He wouldn't have to whip him, though, he'd just have to *fight* him. That's all it would take. But the boy doesn't know this, he's afraid for his life.

And I think nobody knows better than an old con that one of these guys wouldn't actually hurt the boy. He might slap him around but he wouldn't hurt him. Not if the boy wanted to fight about it.

AL: Some of these old things are on the lookout. They watch the new hall's line. And you see them come down for commissary and change clothes. If there's some particular guy in there with real smooth skin, brown eyes, and so forth, and young, they'll say, "Man, you see what's coming in H Hall?" When he comes into the dining room some particular guy will look him up. The general approach is to find out what his name is and what time he's doing, then the guys will start trying to impress him with their reputation and things like that.

JERRY: And they'll say, "Is there anything you need? If you need anything, just tell them to ask for old Joe. Everybody knows me."

AL: Then they'll judge how the guy's reacting toward it. If he's suspicious or if he's real strong they'll leave him alone. Some of the kids, they just fall right into it. I think, nowadays, most of these kids coming in here, they don't consider anything wrong with it. A lot of these kids will come up from the reformatory and they'll talk about these punks and they'll say, "Well, I know a lot of good people that's playing that game." They think it's all right to be a punk. It ain't.

I'll tell you something. When I first come here them punks was looking at me and I didn't even want them speaking to me, you know. Some time later, I was walking on the yard out there and a little kid I knew, he was going with another guy out there, and that was the only guy that he ever played that business with. He's a pretty nice kid, a lot of sense, quiet, kept to himself. And, just out of curiosity, I asked him, "What do you do this for?"

And he said, "Well, that guy's got a life sentence, he's been here seven or eight years and he ain't never going to get out of here and," he said, "that's the only thing I can do for him."

He was sincere about it. And I kinda took a little different opinion of him then.

The guy went ahead and did his time and went on out of here.

JERRY: Well, it's generous, I'll say that. That's a feeling attitude. It's beautiful. Christ.

There's one lad down in the tag plant who's supposed to be a real bad-ass of a stud. I did time with him in El Reno and he was the queen of El Reno. *The* queen. I mean the flat stone queen. Why his reputation hasn't followed him I'll never know. I'll never spread his name around. First place, I'm not interested in the guy, and second place, there's no sense hurting people.

We've even had situations here where they'd stand in line for a boy. I mean, form a *line*, the boy is in a little cubbyhole and one guy takes a crack and comes out and the boy says, "Next," and the next one comes in and takes a crack and so forth. This is where it gets to be ridiculous. I can see where at a weak moment a guy can get worked up and fuck up, see, but that standing in line is pretty cold. It's like you're buying tickets to a theater.

That's even cold with a woman.

AL: It's even colder than that: usually the guy don't even get paid. Not guys like that. Now some do. They get friendship or cigarettes or candy bars. There's no standard price. They got some big hustlers in the colored hall that work just like on the streets.

JERRY: Yeah. This one boy I was mentioning, he's real proud of his situation. He'll stand right to you, face to face, and tell you in the same breath that he's a bad man, that he has the best ass in A Hall, and, by God, they pay good prices for it. And, from what I hear, they pay good prices.

What's a good price?

He gets from five packs to a carton of cigarettes. When you turn a dozen tricks in a damn night that adds up to quite—

—a lot of smoking.

Yeah. He can't smoke them all. He just lives good. You buy a lot of food and things, which isn't a bad deal either. Some way to buy a lot of food—but no thanks.

AL: If they're the type of people that did that on the streets, they're regular homos, they haven't lost any respect here, you know. But the kids that come in here and turn punks, they're looked down on.

So an outside homosexual has better status here . . .

JERRY: By all means: you have a sonofabitch who tries to act like you do and then turns tricks. But a person who just happens to have a different psychological makeup from you and has brought it in, jeez, we all have psychological problems, and as a matter of fact with one pair—Sugar and Bill—it doesn't seem to be a problem. I wish I had as good a relationship with my wife as they have together.

Usually, a guy doesn't really think down inside of him that he's just a strong out-and-out homo. He rationalizes and says, "Now circumstances made it necessary to do this, I have no women, what was I supposed to do?" It seems that masturbation has lost its appeal in the youthful age and so forth, and there's still a strong sex urge. Well, it goes someplace.

AL: I think this here is a temporary thing. You know, when you can't get wine, get whiskey.

Sugar: "French is quick and clean and efficient . . ."

Being as aggressive as I am, I've indoctrinated people to accept it. Not to become homosexual. I would never ever endeavor to even want to make anyone homosexual. There are too many frustrations and heartaches in life because of the ostracism, because of the prejudice. But to accept homosexuality as merely a diversion, to respect homosexuality particularly in this type of society for what it can give you, for what it can do for you, rather than merely take it as an animal thing and drop it and show disrespect for something that has pleased you, something that has given you satisfaction and release and pleasure. To show disrespect for it is just a huge hypocrisy. Really.

Do you find many of the inmates coming around to that line of thinking?

Yes. Many of them have. They balked at first and a lot of them have been very afraid, but the ones who talked the loudest against homosexuality in this society just as outside in society, are the ones that have the most to hide. They, too, several of them, have come around to my way of thinking.

I resent the term "punk." A punk is a weak person most generally, one who is turned out because he's weak or because he seeks security from other aggressive persons.

The first year I was here I didn't open up at all. We were what you might say, "casing the joint." I was strictly taboo, I was strictly untouchable for the first year. My own choice. Until we could consider the attitudes, until we could see the lay of the land, so to speak. One month the attitude will be this and the next it will be something else. This is all instigated by the administration simply because they are running around in circles constantly with new rules and this and that and the other, they really don't know what they're doing. So the inmate can hardly be expected to know what he's doing or even to make up his own mind. He's treated that way consistently. But when I did open up, I found that about seven out of ten people who came to me were the men who could place all the blame on me but who wanted to be strictly with me the passive homosexual, they wanted me to be aggressive.

Did they come to you for fellatio or sodomy?

Both, either one, but mostly sodomy. They continue their role as man because I don't spread any word, you know. But they're protected when they come to me. It is automatically assumed I am always the passive one, but instead I am the—well, I'm a pleasure-giver, I give you whatever pleasure you desire, and when they decide to be the passive homosexual I turn into the aggressive homosexual, and their character and personality are protected because they can place all the blame on me because it is automatically assumed that I have been passive. That they just came up there for a quick trick or a blowjob from me.

I get a great deal of pleasure out of both, but I don't get the *same* pleasure, not at all. I mean, I am basically completely feminine. To be aggressive is a novelty to me rather than a sensual satisfaction. Particularly when it's a real man.

When a man, when a stud has a punk, neither are considered homosexual. It's the most ambiguous statement there is. But they don't consider themselves homosexual at all—because they're not like me, they're not like Bill. If you're not an out-and-out queen—in other words, if you act like a man during the day, we call them gangsters by day and gunmolls by night, well, you're not considered a homosexual, not even in the eyes of this administration. They know you're carrying on a homosexual affair, but it just isn't the same. Their prejudices are all directed toward overt homosexuals, those who don't give a damn what people think. I don't mean exhibitionists, but just like me, merely an overt homosexual.

This jewelry, it's from my kids in here, from the guys that I've gone with. Except for my graduation ring. I'm a cross between a mother and a mistress to all of them. I have a one-inch by one-half-inch turquoise handmade by the Zuñi Indians and I have a 1908 dime pounded around a mound of silver and my graduation ring—it's Egyptian goldstone set in white gold, and I have a class ring of 1955 and I've got some paste diamonds set in platinum and I have a hand-made—it's a joint-made ring—stainless steel with an initial on it. And two solitaire diamonds.

The administration doesn't say anything about your wearing those rings?

Yes. But nothing they can do anything about. Rings are legal. You're allowed to wear jewelry. They don't like the idea. They think it's exhibitionistic. But it's simply because they don't understand that a guy gives me a ring and then when he sees me he wonders where the ring is. And if I'm not wearing it . . .

See, this is a thing they don't even try to understand. Nobody tries to understand anything. They merely jump to conclusions. And wander around, stagger around. Presumptions.

Do they say anything about your red socks?

No. There's a lot of people wear red socks. Well, not so much anymore because I . . . I started the saying: "You know what kind of people wear red socks." So as a consequence of that I've gotten four-teen pair of red socks given to me.

I was a graphologist in a carnival. We had a booth where we ana-lyzed handwriting. It was sort of one step up from being a Gypsy for-tune-teller. I dressed as a woman, always. Since I was thirteen, except for my army days and my prison days.

How long were you actually in the army?

I was in the army for fifteen months.

Didn't that get kind of tacky?

Well, at the time I went in the army they were taking anything. It was 1943 to 1945. I didn't do basic training. I was in my third week of basic training and they told me I was entirely too much, so they put me in the medical corps and I was in the dispensary there for about eight months and then they put me in medical school. And then I had a fight in medical school, so I was kicked out instead of the instigator being kicked out. I broke his jaw. With a ring, not my fist. I used to wear a big solid silver ring. This was Camp Hood, Texas. It's now Fort Hood.

So I told my commanding officer—with whom I was going at the time—that I couldn't tolerate this being kicked out of medical school, so I was leaving. And he says, "Well, you can't leave," and I said, "Well, I am leaving." There wasn't much he could do about it. I was going out with him, as I said. My sergeant drove me down to Dallas and I went to work at the Le Rendezvous on North St. Paul in Dallas as a cocktail waitress and all the guys used to come down to see me. They knew where I was, but no one ever got me for AWOL or desertion or anything else. And so from there I went to New Orleans.

Bill and I were legally married. We were coming from New Orleans to California, to Long Beach, and driving through Yuma we stopped a few minutes after three in the morning and we saw these neon signs all over the place: MARRIAGE 24 HOURS A DAY. So we stopped at the justice of the peace, this little one. And you just go in. You're supposed to have a blood test and you're supposed to have all the other stuff, you know, the license and everything like that, but the justice of the peace can make out all of that right there for a $20 bill under the counter. Which is what it cost us to get married. But he didn't even ask the sex or anything else, he just assumed we were man and—male and female. We'll be married fifteen years on Memorial Day.

I had so many female hormones prior to my discharge from the army that I didn't shave. I didn't have any hair on my chest, I had just fuzz on my arms and legs. But they were going to cure me of homosexuality in Letterman General Hospital. And they gave me what then was a rather new thing—male hormones. And it just made a growth of hair and it deepened my voice. But outside of that it didn't do anything.

They didn't change my outlook. I'm as much psychologically a homosexual as I am physiologically a homosexual. All sex is a psychological thing, it really is. At least sensual desires are. A psychological thing.

Are you promiscuous?

Completely. All homosexuals are.

Why?

Probably a more profound taste for variety, a more profound need for variety. I don't think it's enough to explain it as a feeling of insecurity because of social ostracism. It's merely a taste for variety, and the more variety you have the larger your taste develops. Until you're completely promiscuous. You're more promiscuous than anything else.

Do you or Bill feel jealousy when the other is mixed up with someone?

Not at all, not at all. There's too much love involved. After fifteen years I know that no one can replace me and certainly Bill knows that no one can replace him. No one ever has. No one can come up to his intellectual ability, or potential even. And I've certainly never found anyone that can come up to my talent.

I was also in a Federal institution—Terminal Island in California. I got five years for embezzlement but it was reduced to eighteen months because court procedures were so . . . erroneous.

On the East Coast and West Coast it's an openly accepted thing, and even when it's not openly accepted it is certainly tolerated with no hypocrisy whatsoever. It is really tolerated, particularly in the institutions. The Midwest, well, it's at least a hundred, a hundred and fifty years behind. And I've heard that in some Federal institutions, and in the Georgia state prison, they certainly don't condone homosexuality, but they certainly practice it from your entrance into the institution. They tell you to get an old man if you're a homosexual or get yourself a kid if you're not a homosexual and settle down. It's the best way to do time. They actually do. I've heard the story too many times from too many different sources. It's the administrations that tell you to do that, not the inmates. They still don't condone it on paper, the same as this institution. This place has a fabulous system on paper, but none of it is put in practice.

How often do you manage to have sexual intercourse here?

In here it's, very luckily, four times a week. With four different partners.

What about the average convict who participates?

Once a night, at least once a night.

So you have less sex than the average convict does?

Ours is a matter of convenience. Most of the homosexuals and the punks are kept in one-man cells where it's not so convenient; most of the affairs that are going on are in two-man cells where it's a completely convenient thing. But they can't possibly stop it. It'd be impossible to stop it. It'd be impossible to even slow it down. [A loud scream echoed over from the long hallway in the cellblock fifteen yards away.]

Someone just got it, huh? Sounded like it, didn't it. It's normal procedure in here. Just had one over a racial thing. But last July, not even a year ago, there were twenty-nine stabbings in thirty days. Just for the month of July. Peter Rabbit and his committee came in, staggered around, strutted around, and didn't do anything. Nothing. Nothing whatsoever. This is a political regime. There isn't anything one can do against it; there isn't even anything that one can do for it. It's strictly political appointments, all over the place.

How many of these knifings would you say resulted from conflicts over sexual affairs?

Relatively none. Mostly it's gambling, a racial thing. But mostly it's gambling. Any money owed. If you borrow, or if you gamble your money and you don't pay your debts. That's the biggest thing and the quickest and easiest way to get it. But sexually if a punk changes his mind or a queen changes her mind, that's it.

My first sex experience in prison. The first time I was fifteen and it was in Oakland, California. I was put in the juvenile detention home and my only one experience there was a gangbang or gang rape until I passed out. I spent three months in the hospital after that and required seven stitches. In the beginning four people held me down and they began to bang me and then I lost count and lost consciousness and everything and I woke up in the hospital. That was my first experience and I was only doing thirty days. They were all near my age, from thirteen to seventeen.

Does this strike you now as being fairly young for this kind of conduct?

Not fairly young. It was fairly vicious though.

The next time I was arrested was in New York City. I was nineteen and was sent for eighteen months to the county jail at Rikers Island for prostitution and female impersonation. They have a whole wing set aside strictly for homosexuals, for strictly the overt homosexuals. And at that time there was such a mixture in the cell block of men who admitted being homosexual merely to get over in the block with the homosexuals. I had no adverse experience there at all. They were all very happy. New York is a very progressive state, it always has been.

And then I was sent to the San Bruno county jail in San Francisco. That was for prostitution again and for possession of knockout drops. I only did six months there and I was arrested once again in San Francisco on the same charge. At that time I was wanted as a deserter from the army, so I escaped a prison sentence in California, because it was my second offense, by going to Letterman General Hospital at Fort Scott, Presidio, San Francisco, and obtaining my discharge.

They had drafted you even though they knew you were homosexual?

Oh, yes. I showed up for the draft in a silver lamé shirt and black slacks and really long hair and it was bleached, but they took me right straight on in. They swore me in that same day, right after my physical, whereas everyone else was given a three-week reprieve before they reported to be sworn in. See, I had been drafted in 1942, late in 1942, and I showed up for the draft in 1943. Because I was traveling and I didn't even know I had been drafted. It wasn't an evasion, it was just simply I had no idea I was drafted.

What were you doing those years?

I was working in shows in restaurants and nightclubs.

When did you first start working as a female impersonator?

Billed as a female impersonator when I was seventeen, but I worked as a female impersonator prostitute from the time I was thirteen. That's when I left home.

On stage were you always billed as a man impersonating a woman or were you ever billed as a woman?

I've been billed as a woman. I traveled with the carnival and I worked for Pete Fountain. That's where I met Bill. I was stripping then. At that time I was billed as a woman. Paraffin injections for the breasts and an elastic band for a gaff.

Describe the gaff.

You put a piece of Kleenex around the penis, just back of the head, and cinchknot with three-quarter-inch elastic. You cinchknot as tight as you can possibly cinchknot it. And bring all of your equipment, testicles and penis both, down between your legs and then push the testicles up into the stomach, into the lower abdomen, and bring everything else as tight as you possibly can up between the crack of your ass. Then you tie the elastic again so that there's another knot right at the base of your spine and the remaining elastic goes around your waist as tight as you can possibly cinch it. So that you're stripped completely. You can show absolute nakedness except you have to wear a back panel. They can never see your rear end at all. No, you never float around and you can only leave it on for about ten minutes, otherwise it cuts off your circulation.

I did that one time I guess for about twenty-five minutes and I swelled up and it turned black and it was a terrible mess for a long time, about three weeks.

Isn't it painful?

Yes, but you can become accustomed to it. This is like anything else. If you wore a ring in your nose you would eventually become accustomed to it.

The gaff with the elastic band makes the appearance of a vagina. The testicles up in the abdomen produce the pelvic bulge of the vagina, and the empty bag, the bag which is now empty, brought forward, produced the lips of the vagina. And everything else is so tight that they can get in—

How far?

Two or three inches.

How do you explain that?

Well, they don't actually go in, it's just merely the appearance of going in. They're actually only between your legs.

And they don't notice?

No. And I've had men kiss it and never know the difference.

I can see that, but I wonder about actually inserting the penis.

Once a man gets an erection he's very apt to stick it into anything and not really care, as long as it gives the appearance.

Especially working with a carnival. We had a regular show where we stripped and then we had a blowoff where we did dirty songs and rubbed around on the men and things like that. I only did one song, "Room Two Hundred and Two." It's been years ago. Let's see, it's:

> Room two hundred and two
> Where the walls keep talking to you
> I'm gonna tell you everything that was said
> Turn out the lights and go to bed
>
> Two old whores walking down the street
> No hats on their heads and no shoes on their feet
> Too old to fuck and too proud to suck
> Just two old whores, shit out of luck.

And it goes on and on like that, in the same vein. And each time you sing the "Room two hundred and two." And you're rubbing around on them and it's real filthy, that's all it is. It wasn't very appealing even to me. But it was to them.

At that time we were accepting tricks for $10 and $20. A quick French trick for $10 and if they wanted to stand up and perform the act, it was $20. Since it's only between your legs, of course, my panel was always full, my shoes were full, everything else was full. Because they didn't know where they were coming. Or going. Or anything else. Is that too frank? Like I say, once you get a man excited, he doesn't much care.

Was this mostly small towns?

Not always. We played the state fairs. Phoenix State Fair and Sacramento State Fair in California and the Diamond Jubilee in Penticton, British Columbia, and the Fourth of July in Prince Ruppert, B. C. That's the last northern outpost. Through Oregon and Washington we were cut down quite a bit; we couldn't give the blowoff and we couldn't strip all the way and things like that.

Was this covered by paying off the local police?

Yes. The advance man, he explains as much as is absolutely necessary about the girl show and then they either make dictations—leave on your bras and leave on your panties or delete the blowoff or something like that—or they say "All the way. Who cares."

Why do you call it a blowoff?

Because it's an extra added filthy attraction. Where you actually arouse the men. And the word "blowoff" comes from a blowjob. You don't usually have sex. I mean even the real broads don't have sex. You usually just give a quick blow. It's quicker and cleaner and easier and no douches afterward and all that sort of stuff. Like I said, when we'd stand up and do it, it goes all over the place. Down our legs and shoes and everything. It was so messy. And French is quick and clean and efficient.

How many girls would take part in it?

We had seven. Four of the seven were like me, the other three were real broads.

And no one ever picked up on it?

No. Half of your burlesque queens are—queens. Well, they are. Homosexuals. They've even got a new operation now where they slice under the breast and put in a plastic cup. That parafin can cause skin cancer, it's rather dangerous, and you can't handle them because you get them all out of shape anyhow. I never kept it up.

Well, if you have a trick, doesn't the guy want to feel you up?

No. Because most prostitutes, most whores, don't want to be felt up around the breasts because it makes them baggy and saggy and they lose all of their shape and form completely.

Is that true or is that bad folklore?

That's true. Too much handling makes them floppy. They want to suck on them and play with them and all that stuff, it wrecks them, ruins them. Besides, most prostitutes are interested in one thing: trick the guy and get rid of him. Feeling around takes time. Just get on and get off, or do the thing and get through.

Do you have friends who are prostitutes?

Yes.

Do they know you're a male?

Some of them do. Some never have known.

How do they react?

I'm merely one of their horde, one of their battalion, whatever you want to call it.

They have no adverse reaction?

Oh no. That's why a prostitute makes the best wife once she decides to settle down. She has the broadest understanding, the deepest feeling, everything. She's lived, in other words. Now she knows how to settle down, how to make a man happy, she knows how to build a home. She isn't a novice. At anything.

Have you ever been discovered?

The closest I came was an attempted rape. But I got away from him. I was working on the carnival then, too, and he invited me to a Saturday night dance. He had been in all week. He invited us all to dinner, but then he singled me out and he invited me to the dance. And we were wandering up through this rocky mountain road, supposedly going to this barn dance, and he just stopped all of a sudden and turned into an utter savage beast. He knocked me around quite a bit. I slid down and broke both my knees open, broke my heels. He broke his leg. Falling after me. And I ran on down the country road back toward town. And he turned around and came back and picked me up. And he took me—I rode on the running boards—back into town. He was in no condition to do anything then.

You told me you worked as a prostitute.

I never worked for free; I've always gotten paid. When I worked, I averaged twenty tricks a day. I've never done anything for free. The most I ever made was $3,200 for one trick and the least I ever made was sixty-seven cents for one trick.

Would you mind telling me how those two figures were arrived at?

Well, the $3,200 was a traveling collection man, something, he had to do with collections and this was a Friday night and he had not gotten to the bank. He had a briefcase full of cash and checks and money orders and things like that. But the cash amounted to $3,200. And he became, oh, God, gregarious. What other word is there? And we were both enormously drunk and he took all the money out of the briefcase and stuffed it in my purse. And he decided that he was going to quit his job anyway. And so I got paid $3,200 for one night. He didn't change his mind. He actually quit the firm for which he was working; he went to jail, too.

And the least I ever made . . . When we needed money, I'd go out on Highway 40. Our home is in San Francisco, so any time we ran out of money or were short like that, I would go out on Highway 40 and go with nothing but truck drivers. As a woman of course. I mean I'd thumb. And they'd stop and ask where I was going and I'd say, "Well, I'm going just as far as you'll let me go, honey." Right away, they knew. So I usually charged $5 for a real quick trick. That's French only, just French. One time I went out and charged $1 an inch and I got more $10 bills from five- and six-inchers than could possibly be imagined. One time I was soused rather (but I've never gotten drunk. I just get loaded and that's it. I mean I never stagger around or anything like that) and I decided I was just going to take whatever came. Before I always turned down truck drivers who didn't have the $5 bill. I'd decided I'd just take whatever came. And I made $1.94. Made $4. Made sixty-seven cents. That was the time I accepted a trick for sixty-seven cents. That was all he had on him. But most generally I charge $5 or $10. And that's just for French only.

Bill: "This homosexuality is how you test a man's manhood in here . . ."

At least half participate. That's trying to be fair both ways. It's quite a secretive thing. Everybody doesn't put their business on the streets so it's kind of difficult to tell.

The other half, part of them, they absolutely do not participate. They don't want anything to do with it. They're more or less neutral. The more intelligent people consider it to be everyone's own prerogative, their own business. The other part of that half are inclined to be a little bit antagonistic, depending on how much they're covering up.

It's hard to take an accurate percentage because so many people have the front up in here, and generally this front is a sexual front. You have, for example, what you call a prison jocker. He's constantly trying to impress people with the sexual conquests he had outside with women. Consequently, one of the first things he does is get himself a kid in here, or kids, as many as he can, you know. He's evidently trying to prove himself to be a man. But you would be surprised at the number that are not just strictly aggressive homosexuals once they get started. It seems there was a latent thing in the beginning anyway and they just gradually brought out these tendencies to where it's a passive-aggressive situation.

As in any prison, there is a very sharp and defined difference between homosexual types. There's the all-out homosexual, or what they call a queen. And then you have the youngsters who, sometimes by pressure, fear, or because they need commissary and money, submit to homosexuality when in reality they don't enjoy it, they feel guilty. They're pretty well protected. They try to hide it. Their daddy tries to hide it for them. But queens are something else. An all-out homosexual—as Sugar—they're in for a lot more criticism and abuse than the kid because the kid, during the daytime and on the yard and in the lines, swaggers and tries to play the gangster role just like the big tough ones. Whereas the queens don't, they don't put up any front.

This homosexuality is how you test a man's manhood in here. Most of the guys try to keep their reputation clear, they don't want this reputation. If they have a kid they want it understood that this is strictly a one-way proposition.

You know, it might not be so in the beginning, but pretty soon this guy becomes very attached emotionally and becomes very jealous. This leads to fights, true, but the kid has a lot to do with that if he doesn't know how to conduct himself and he insists on being belligerent just because he has a protector. That's why a lot of the kids submit anyways, because they need a protector. And if they capitalize on the fact that they have a protector it becomes a bad and nasty situation.

But I'd say if it's a normal one, one I consider to be a normal situation, I'd say it does a lot of good. I feel there's an awful lot of tension builds up in a man doing time with no sexual release, and the hand won't do it.

It's hard to say who's doing what. You'd be surprised. Some of it that you would swear is a strictly aggressive type is what they call flip-flop.

Costs. Cigarettes are all the medium of exchange in here, there's no cash. The cost would vary, depending on how attractive the individual was. They work from a couple of packs to five. And to a permanent upkeep, supplying all the cigarettes and coffee and watch, ring, just anything else they need.

If a kid has made a few enemies they might be likely to force him. But that's rare. Most generally it's a matter of talking to them. Most of them need a protector and there are a few that will make themselves so annoying that the kid will submit to someone he likes rather than put up with some of this belligerence from other people. There's so much pressure in a society like this anyways that sometimes for a young kid like that it's a little too much for him. He has to go somewhere and he will submit to someone he likes.

They have a saying whenever somebody is too strongly a wolf. They say, "Well, he's nothing but a punk out for revenge."

Here's the peculiar thing about this society. A person's reputation in here is pretty important because you can't escape from your associates. A punk or homosexual, either one is not considered to be a man in this society. Consequently they try to hide as much as they possibly can and sometimes this description may be accurate. Maybe some of the wolves have been punks at some time or another. But I think a big percentage of the time it's just that they're trying to prove to everybody that they are a man.

Other things on that. Not showing fear is one. Payment of debts is something, especially gambling debts—if you don't pay your debts you lose reputation and you might get seriously hurt. Of course most especially a snitch has a hard way to go in most places. No one likes him. The administration doesn't even like him as far as that is concerned. But I would say that probably the most severely punished is a snitch.

As far as overall reputation goes, the man that pays his debts and someone knows that this fellow will pay back, he's all right. And if he knows he doesn't have to watch what he says or does in their presence, knows he won't snitch, this insures him to be a good person. And of course who you associate with has a bearing. If you associate with someone that's got a bad reputation there's going to be an element that does talk about you to a certain extent.

There are some, you always have some in an institution, a group that will keep themselves aloof from the overall population. They don't have too much to do with anybody. I try to be one of these. I have a lot of acquaintances, but I have very few friends, you know. Mainly because friendship in here can fall out over the slightest thing.

It can fall out over a pack of cigarettes or a candy bar. They become important things. Most of the guys in here don't have any money, they don't have any razor blades. If they are not on a job and don't earn any money in here, they don't have anything. They can't get a toothbrush, toothpowder, razor blades, or anything. Consequently, commissary is a means of exchange and it's an important thing. If somebody beats somebody out of a dollar, it's about like beating someone out of fifty outside.

How much of a debt is enough to get hurt for?

Two packs on up.

How much is enough to get killed for?

Two packs on up.

It depends on who you owe it to. Some people, it doesn't matter what the amount was, it's the principle.

In general, the ones that rise up and become most influential in a prison are the ones that have quite a bit of money. Three or four hundred dollars in prison is a lot of money. If someone has a constant amount of $300 or $400 on the books in the treasury office he is generally considered to be a pretty big man. You buy a lot of prestige in here.

What you were busted on has something to do with that, too. Like the size of the robbery you've done. Someone who was arrested for stealing a car to joy-ride around town, why, he isn't considered to be anything. He really can't caper, in other words, he doesn't know how to thieve, he just stole the car and drove it around a few blocks. Whereas the guy that hit a supermarket and at one time he had in his possession $20,000—even if it was five minutes or two days—he's considered to be a good operator, because he was willing to go out after the big stuff. I'll agree that it doesn't make much sense, but that's the consensus.

Now you take child-molesters or people who were arrested for incest, they are definitely not associated with. There might be a few exceptions, but in prison they hate a child-molester more than anything in the world, short of a snitch. I think they put him just about on the same level.

What sort of treatment does a child-molester get?

First of all, nobody will talk to him, and they won't have anything to do with him. He can possibly do his sentence and nobody will hurt him physically as long as he doesn't try to force his friendship or acquaintance on any particular individual unless it's asked for. But if he tries to make himself one of the fellows he's going to be slapped down right away, because they don't like it. There's a consensus in here among us that a person like that doesn't belong in a prison, he belongs in a state hospital.

And rape. Strange as it may seem, the biggest percentage of the population don't think it's necessary and they don't like rapos either.

They have a tendency to think, well, he must not be much of a man, he can't make a conquest on his own ability if he has to go out and take it.

Maxwell: "It's the talk of the whole farm about me getting screwed in the garden . . ."

Every farm has a queen of the farm. And I'm the queen of this one. And what I say goes. I mean, I don't care. I don't care if I tell some boy to get out there and shit in the hall. He's going to do it.

Why?

What I say goes.

Why?

I'm not conceited, but I'm just it, I mean . . .

What I meant is, is it because you'll crack somebody's head if they don't do it, or what?

Somebody else will.

See, I got better stuff than most people around here. And I know how to use it. And I don't snitch on everybody. And every chance I get, I'm going to get me some peter. And the other ones, nobody else here is that way. They always too scared or they're afraid somebody's going to see them or they're going to run and tell if they get in a mess. I never do.

You were telling me before about officers asking you about kinds of sodomy you'd never heard of.

Yeah. Anvil sodomy.

Anvil sodomy?

Something like that. They call it something like that.

And what is that?

Supposed to be when you get fucked in the back. And I never heard of that, anvil sodomy. And then oral sodomy. To me, I thought that was just talking somebody into it or something. It's supposed to be when you have it in the . . .

Well, what do you usually call a blowjob?

A blowjob.

Okay.

That's what *we* call it. *They* call it oral sodomy.

And what do you call what they call anal sodomy?

Anal sodomy?

Uh, anvil sodomy?

Oh. We call that a brownie queen. In prison they call it under-yonder and round-brown. Everything you can think of. Anything they can think of.

Last week I was caught out in the garden with this guy I've been going with. We was just laying there and we was knocking it right off. And this other queen was on the other side of me and this punk was on the other side of us. And they kept hollering that the boss was coming and I wouldn't get up and so the boss went right up to us and just stopped and looked at us and just kept looking at us and so when we finished we just got up and didn't even look at him and walked off. And nothing was said about it. And then this guy that's over the garden come up here and asked me in front of the boss that seen me if I'd done anything and I said, "No," and the boss didn't say nothing. Then this morning it's the talk of the whole farm about me getting screwed in the garden.

The boss didn't put you on report for it?

No.

Why not?

They can't prove it.

But he saw you doing it.

He's one person. We have thirty-two people. Thirty-two people say I didn't do nothing. What's he going to do, what's his word? His word isn't nothing, not against thirty-two people. See, we take up petitions here to take care of people we like.

You mean if he tried to put you on report for that and everybody in the squad said you weren't doing it, they wouldn't pull you in? They'd believe the squad?

They'd believe the squad. They might put us in the shitter [solitary], but I wouldn't get into too much trouble. But I don't know: he's a good boss anyway. He wouldn't tell. Everybody here knows how bad I need men, they know how bad it is. They give me a break every once in a while.

This boy that I was with, him and this other boy hogged this Mexican that wasn't a punk. They threw him in the shitter and took all his good time.

What happened to the guy who got hogged?
Nothing.
I mean—
He's just the laughing-stock, that's all. Well, the ones that fucked him say he wasn't no good anyway.

This poor little old guy, he couldn't speak English and he couldn't talk anyway and they had a belt around his neck choking him and one of them fucked him and then he took the little boy's hat and wiped his peter off on it and put the hat back on the little boy's head. And this other one, this boy that'd already fucked him, held him down while this other boy was going to fuck him. And the boss come up and caught them. So the little boy just went over there with his pants down and started crying and telling the boss what happened.

But he disappeared after that. About a week or two after that, that little boy that got fucked disappeared. They said he discharged, but he didn't. We don't know what happened to him. You never know around this place.

Some of the bosses here, they call them dried-ups, they just get here and some of them are homosexuals theirself. I'm supposed to be getting investigated now about a boss. One night they was here and everybody in the gal block knew about it and he called me out. And then we slipped one time in the field and said something about it and I had to go in front of a bunch of bosses and tell them about it. But I wouldn't tell his name. That's the way it is down here; you just don't tell nobody's name you go with.

If they catch a boss jacking off down here they put him in the picket away from everybody. They believe that if he'd jack off he'd try and make somebody.

I'm kidded a lot because too many people knew me, you know, they know about me. And out in the field they always asking if I'd let a horse fuck me, something like that. The bosses always kidding me about it. If I want to grab this nigger, if I want to be in their squad and let all these niggers make me and something like that.

They caught one colored queen down here. She had fifteen guys in about an hour. That's the truth.
She got fucked or was blowing?
She got fucked. She was pretty raunchy.
Sounds like she was pretty sore, too. Where did that happen?
In the chicken house out in the garden. It was when she was in the line and she was one that was lucky enough to get in the line. They walked in on her last one. And it was a bit late then.

How did she manage to get away with fifteen guys for that long?
I don't know how. I think she was one on the streets. She was pretty hefty. I mean, she wasn't little or nothing. And they just all talked her into it. I mean, she was peter-crazy anyway. There's a lot of them that way.

You know most of the punks, they don't take it in the ass at all. They just give hand-jigs or they'll give blowjobs. There's punks all over the place in the gal tank. They'll stick their hands around the bars at night when everybody's gone to bed and give each other hand-jigs. That's pretty popular around here and all over the farm.

Doesn't that leave kind of a mess in the walkway?
It makes dark black splotches on the floor. But the bosses haven't caught on what it is yet.

I thought punks were willing to take it in the ass.
Not exactly. They take it in the ass, but it hurts. It's too much to go into about that, but they just don't like to take it in the ass. Someone like me, well, I'm used to it. I've been doing it for about ten years.

How old are you now?
Nineteen. My cousin used to screw me when I was five. I've been getting screwed ever since.

You were five?
Yeah. I've had a lot of experience.

That's pretty young.
It is, but I don't know. I didn't like it to start with. When I got a little older I was scared to tell. You know how it is when you're that young. But then I got to liking it. And then when I was twelve I just left home. I went to New Orleans then. I started stripping when I was fourteen. And in New Orleans it's easy to turn a $100 trick. You figure if you can turn one that good and don't know nothing, then you try to find a little bit more experience. That's why I always try to find some new little gimmick that I could show somebody.

Such as, well, like I said awhile ago, about the way they just lay still, most of these convicts here. Well, they like you to squeeze yourself up, you know, so it would be tighter. They call it puckering up. And they like to put it in and bring it out and you just all the time squeezing on it. And you do it on your back and on your head. Most guys, I mean, I never did it standing up or something like that. Here all they do is you just stand up and bend over and spread your cheeks and that's it. Here you don't really have to have any experience, you just have to have a hole.

No well-developed skills?

No. Most of them, they go a month or two without having anybody anyway. Doesn't take them but about two or three minutes anyway and they got a climax.

Do you ever get a stud turning into a punk?

Yeah. One here, that other queen you know here, her old man, well, he had some whores on the street and he couldn't hustle them good enough so he started giving blowjobs. And suddenly everybody's wanting to be giving *her* blowjobs.

That does get ambiguous.

It does, it does. It gets ridiculous. I mean, I've been to bed with people here and in the county jail too, and if anybody starts moving their hand around in front of me, boy, that's it. I don't have nothing else to do with them.

Does that happen often?

Oh, very often. 'Cause in the penitentiary they feel nobody's gonna know about it. And they feel that if you get your climax, well, you'll give him a better climax. And then you'll keep coming back to the same one over and over 'cause they giving you something some of the others aren't giving you.

All the punks go both ways, the queens don't. That Mexican queen, she don't want anybody to know she's got a peter so she takes chewing gum and tapes the peter between her legs. Of all things: chewing gum. All the queens they let their fingernails grow out. It's very hard to do. And we polish them with toothpaste. It makes them shine like fingernail polish. We shave our eyebrows and that is against the rules. And every once in a while we score a mascara pencil. When they check our cells we always have to take it and stick it up our butt so we can hide it. They never give us a finger wave here [anal inspection], it's against the rules. Can't nobody touch punks.

Do you think many guys who are punks in here would be queens on the streets if they knew how or were up to it?

Oh, they would. I know what you mean.

There's one here that I was in county jail with. He was my flunky. He cleaned up after me and everything. And he wanted to act what we call nelly, you know, act real feminine. I been trying to teach him because he wants to be that way on the streets. But you just can't teach somebody that way. He just has to be a personality. And somebody that's real muscular and everything, they look funny when they act feminine. Makes a fool out of them. And here it's the same way.

They got this other queen here, she's a Spanish queen. She's really nothing—just dirt trash. And she'll priss real bad, you know.

She'll hold her hand up and everything and sling her head and act real high and snooty, but everybody just makes fun of her.

If somebody makes fun of me I'm liable to jump on them. I broke my nose that way. This guy out in the garden come up and grabbed hold of my ass. He was just going to get some right there in front of everybody. And so we started fighting and he knocked my nose clean off almost. He broke his hand and I also stabbed him with a stick and he was going to kill me with an aggie, and it all wound up that he got a lay-in for two months and I just had to go before the committee.

Is that the day you "stepped on a hoe"?

That was the day I stepped on a hoe. I told the story about it and then everybody found out, 'cause you know how it is around here. I can't do anything without somebody's going to snitch.

I looked at your folder and saw you stepped on a hoe and that reminded me of people falling over a locker box in the service.

It was terrible. He went in that morning and said that a boy throwed a hoe at him and hit him on his hand and broke it. And I went in that afternoon and I told them that I stepped on a hoe and it hit me on the nose.

Then the next day I went out there and this captain beat me on my nose for about a half hour with a pencil. Telling me about telling lies to an officer and insubordination and whatever it is they usually call it. But I couldn't help it. They was mad 'cause I went in there where they had made some pictures of my nose and I didn't know what it was, and I kept picking them up and I was looking at all of them and I went in too many of the things and exposed all the film and so I had that against me too. And besides telling a lie.

If you don't want to do it, you don't do it. I mean everybody says you can get screwed, that anybody can get screwed with enough people ganging up on them. But they wouldn't give in if they didn't want to. They have a punk up there in the punk tank for protection 'cause all these twelve guys rushed at him in the county jail where I was at and he got a razor blade and cut one of 'em's feet clean off. Sliced another one's head half open. He didn't get fucked. But these other punks, they do it because they just want everybody to leave them alone or they like it. They're just peter-crazy, that's why they're a punk. They walk around and gaze at everybody's peter. They would be that way on the street if they had half a chance. They just don't want nobody to know or to find out about it because everybody looks down upon it. Here we're called trash and scabs and scum and everything before everybody.

There are punks that want to be, that are punks already and they're just trying to hide it. It's mostly the kind of boys where they'd be just walking home or something or they'd be standing waiting for the bus and, well, it's just coincidence or something, but some queers can always pick them up and give them money or something, let them drive their car or keep 'em with 'em, let 'em live with them, and they just get used to it. I mean they like it but they act like they don't, and they use a girl as a front so nobody will know about it.

These other punks that are turned out in a jail that don't like it, they usually are these little small-town boys that in their family their mother didn't allow nobody to say nothing about sex. Or they been going with a girl or they're married. Men are supposed to be superior, women are supposed to be inferior, and queers are just supposed to be something that nobody's ever heard of. A lot of them has read and heard that a queer is the lowest form alive, that it's cheaper than a wino. But I haven't seen one yet that didn't have the money. I haven't seen one yet that wasn't better than anybody. 'Cause all queers have a superior feeling.

Punks just can't learn. They just don't have the ability to think like queens do. A punk doesn't have the ability. They feel inferior 'cause they think somebody's messed over them. They—

Are they right?

They're right. There's one here that got a divorce from his wife because when he was in the county jail four people hogged him. Four men hogged him and he's a great big boy too. And he wouldn't do it again, but once they've had that try, they wonder what it would be like the next time, if they could make it better to them, that's what I think.

Who got the divorce, him or his wife?

His wife did. But he let her. He wouldn't have let her go through with it, but he didn't think he could face her while he was here that way.

I'd say about 2 percent of them that are punks here do it when they go out. Because everybody here would fuck a punk and everything else, but when they get out, it's just like it didn't happen. They forget about it.

A guy that's been a punk for a few years, it's no problem for him to go straight back to women?

No, 'cause that's all they think about is women. It's like all these old queers you see around bus stations. They don't go out every night, it's just every once in a while they have to go out and get it out of their system. That's the way these punks are. They won't go out there and just be punks all their lives. Just every little once in a while they have to run out and get their satisfaction from that. And they don't think about it.

That's what causes most of these mental disturbances, businessmen are especially that way. And they just try to act like it don't even happen. They never tell anybody. 'Cause all the punks, every punk that's in our tank has a jack picture, every one of them.

A jack picture?

Some picture of a woman. Some of them have just the head of a woman but they jack off with it anyway. It's terrible.

There's some guys don't bother about punks because they work in the cow stalls. They have quite a few chickens die every once in a while. And they have the pigs. You can hear the pigs' screams all the time, and the only time they holler is when somebody's trying to fuck them. And the horses. . . . They got one mule out there that they say got more pussy than some prostitute on the street. They fuck that poor old mule till he sags everywhere. It's terrible.

I was held one time for three days. They picked me up. I was standing on the street corner in Georgia. In Georgia they don't even know things like me exist. Down right in the South. And I was standing there and I had blue hair to my shoulders and I had on my sister's clothes. And I was just standing up there. And everybody knew I was a boy. They knew my sister and they knew who I was. And so they picked me up and throwed me in jail and tried to book me with sodomy. They went through my billfold and called up everybody, and everybody swore they didn't even know who I was. So after three days of investigation they had to let me go.

I tried to hang myself one time. It didn't work 'cause the rope broke. And then I tried to poison myself one time and I used iodine. It said on the bottle it was poison, you know? And I took that but it didn't do nothing but give me sinus trouble.

And then I drank some tetrachloride and all it did was take my breath away, you know, tetrachloride that they use for cleaning floors. It had "poison" on it and all it did was give me lung trouble and I had to go to the doctor and get nerve pills for that.

And then I tried to take sleeping pills, and I woke up.

And then I cut my wrist one time and that didn't work either 'cause they got me to the doctor too quick.

And then I jumped in the river, I was trying to drown myself. And then I had to think, my makeup all got smeared that I had on,

and so I started screaming for somebody to come help me get out
'cause I didn't want to drown. I just hate for anybody to find me with
my makeup all smeared. It's terrible.

What other ways have I tried it. I had two accidents. One time I
just ran into a building and that hurt my lover more than it did me.
The next time I run into a car and it didn't work either. I didn't get
hurt that time. I just got some traffic tickets.

Did your lover know you were trying to commit suicide?

Oh, yeah. I was trying to talk him into it. We used to get up late
at night when we thought our sugar daddy was asleep, and me and
him, he'd sit on the sink and I'd sit on the stove and we had a razor
blade and we'd cut ourself. And then I thought up a good idea of
powdered glass. And so we drank it and nothing happened. I don't
know why. I mean it's supposed to kill you, but nothing happened. It
makes you feel stupid.

Why were you so unsuccessful?

I thought I wanted to, you know, but I didn't really. I wanted,
being the way I am, I just wanted to see what everybody would think
when it was in the papers that I'd committed suicide. And I wanted to
be here after I was dead to hear what everybody said, you know. Yes-
terday I read in the paper where this go-go girl from San Antonio was
fixing to jump from a building and she got headlines. I thought about
doing that, you know, but it wouldn't never work; I always got too
scared.

And then there was the house.

What about the house?

I went in somebody else's house and sat down in the middle.
They had a den, a family room, a living room, dining room, and I got
right in the middle, it was the den of the house. And I went around to
all the other rooms around it and I set fire to it. And so the house is
burning like crazy and it wasn't even getting close to me. I heard the
sirens and I took off and run. I didn't want them to find me there.

I just couldn't never make it. But one of these days I'll make it.

How old were you when you first tried suicide?

I was about thirteen. I got messed up with this guy who was too
old for me. And I didn't know enough of what was going on. So he
jilted me and it tore me up, so I tried to commit suicide then. I tried to
take sleeping pills. Not sleeping pills, they was some kind of pills that
he had. And it didn't work. I was real serious about it then. These
other times I was trying to commit suicide I wasn't. I wasn't sure why
I wanted to do it.

Why were you trying to kill yourself?

It's like this. I mean, well, I had all these family problems to start with.

Your own family or your homosexual family?

My own family. 'Cause everybody didn't want to have nothing to do with me 'cause I was a homosexual, except my sister. And I kept going with all these boys and everything and I just couldn't get satisfied with them. I mean, I fell in love with them and they'd say they fell in love with me and all they was trying to get was money that I was getting from my sugar daddies. It used to tear me up and I'd always try to find another one. And then I fell for my brother-in-law. And, it's terrible, I fell for my brother-in-law and he used to go out with me all the time.

And then, when I got put in the county jail in Houston, the police come up to me and told me he killed my sister. And that was nothing, just every boy I've had something to do with he's always done something against me, you know.

Did he really kill your sister or were the police hassling you?

Oh yes, he killed my sister. And he was trying to file suit against me for a $500 phone bill that I'd run up when I was in Georgia. He was trying to file suit against me and he was in jail for murdering my sister. And they was going to take me back to Georgia and everything, but he signed a confession. It's been about nine months ago.

What happened to him?

They still got him. I guess they got him in jail for murder. It's nothing he can do. She was always fussing him and she found out about me.

And then this later lover, I've had him three years and I was living with him two months. I quit stripping and working and everything, you know, I was really geared behind him. And two months after I was living with him he decided to go with somebody else that was younger than I was. They called me an old faggot! [Maxwell was nineteen at the time of this interview.] That's 'cause I used to get out in the daytime, but I tried to make myself believe I wasn't doing anything against him. But I was always going out and going to bed with anybody that would pick me up. I went for that. And he found out about me and then I couldn't make him live with me. So I was getting more sugar daddies and I was having to go to bed with more men then to get more money to keep him. And it didn't work. He just run off and left.

Explain to me the relationship between your lovers and your sugar daddies. You were talking before and saying that the current one of each knew each other.

One of my sugar daddies is manager of the F—— company in Houston; the other sugar daddy owns a furniture company. And they're on some kind of council there.

Are these guys that you have homosexual affairs with for money?

No. I get lovers and I go to bed with my lovers. And my lovers go to bed with my sugar daddy. See, I always sell all my lovers to my sugar daddy. When I wasn't going to bed with them. 'Cause most men, most older men, they don't like to go to bed with somebody that's feminine. They like to go to bed with somebody that's butch. I mean, somebody that likes to do, you know, the man part, 'cause most of these sophisticated men like to play like women every once in a while. It's dainty and it's sick. It looks terrible to see a grown man acting like a woman, then running around in social circles.

There's no way I can change. Doctors and everybody say you can change, but there's no way you can change. I mean, I can get jobs. I can work in nightclubs and all this, but still, I'm a homosexual. I'm never satisfied. I always want more. I don't know, I can go to bed with one boy and get right up and I want to go to bed with somebody else.

When you're making out well on the streets how many times a day will you go to bed with somebody?

Making out well? It sounds like I'm a whore, but about ten or eleven times. Something like that.

Will you have orgasms each time?

Oh, no. People tell me I'm crazy 'cause I have a belief that all my sex organs are in my butt. And I don't have to have an orgasm. They call me a mortar.

Hermaphrodite?

They call me that. Well, I get pleasure out of somebody else getting pleasure. That's the way it goes. I wouldn't feel like I was cheating on my lover unless I got an orgasm from going to bed with somebody else.

Do you have orgasms when you get fucked in the ass?

Every once in a while. Sometimes, I just go to bed with people just to be going to bed with them. 'Cause I'm peter-crazy. Sometimes I go to bed with somebody 'cause I'm hot for them. If I'm walking down the street or something and somebody picks me up, I'll go to bed with him. Unless they're nelly; I can't stand anybody that's feminine.

On the street I had two whores that lived with me. They slept in one bed and I slept in another one. And one night we all got drunk and we all went to bed together. And the next day I got up and I was sick and I stayed sick for a long time. I just can't stand them.

You lived with two whores. But I thought you said you can't stand women?

I can't. I feel sorry for women. Everybody calls a woman a broad and I don't like it. I'll call down anybody about that because I respect women. But I just don't like them. I hate them.

I like lesbians, now. Me and lesbians get along real good. Because I know where they stand, and they know where I stand.

Why do you hate women?

I just do. My mother was a whore. And I just grew up knowing nothing but females. And I just hate them. I never did like them. I don't know. They, just to me they seemed like some creepy substance. Like most straight people think that queers are creepy. I just can't stand females in the same way.

They give me too much competition. What's a man want with me when he can get a woman? I mean, you know, some people are that way.

Do you know your father?

I don't have one. Oh, I had one, but I'm illegitimate. My mother, she was married seven times and she had seven kids, except she wasn't married when she had the seven. It was always in between the marriage.

Not very tactful timing.

No. And my grandmother, she's a lesbian. She's terrible.

Is your family from Georgia too?

No. My grandmother's in France. She was born in France. She came over here and I don't know where she's at now. I haven't seen her in two or three years.

How come you haven't tried to commit suicide since you've been in here?

In here? Well, in the street I had a lot of competition, in here I don't. I'm the cock of the walk and I know it. So it's easy.

Every once in a while I get depressed. I'll get busted too much. I'm always standing on the wall [waiting for disciplinary action] for not having a belt on, having somebody else's shoes on or prissing too much, or for arching my eyebrows, having my fingernails too long, or something like that. And I just get perturbed about it. I get depressed. But I don't know why, I'm just satisfied I guess for the time being.

But you don't like being in prison?

No. To me it's just a new experience. I took trips everywhere all over the world and there's always a new experience. I always want to get back, but I never know where I'm getting back to. In here, it's the same way, it's just a new experience. I won't be here that long—and I see these people that's got life.

When I get out I'll get drunk, and then when I get drunk I get sympathetic, you know. And that's when I try to commit suicide.

You sort of try.

Sort of try. I don't think I can go . . . One of these days I'll go all the way, I guess. That's when I get old.

Big Sal: "I take the blood and I wipe it on me . . ."

A friend of mine was on death row and this girl here says, "I know you're thinking about that goddamned dago out there, and I hope she dies."

Baby, when she said that, I knocked fire from her ass. I hit her and she went all the way across the hall. I was on to her and we got in a fight and I went to ice [solitary]. I stayed up there forty-five days. I didn't eat the whole time I was up there. I couldn't eat. I just blocked myself off.

See, in isolation, you don't have nothing to do. You lay there and sleep or think. I kept my light out all the time. They don't have lights now in ice, though, just a hole. And I slept on the floor and I laid there. I couldn't eat that unseasoned food they give you right out of a can, and it's not even heated. And I don't like vegetables in the first place. So it was just mental torture, that's all, torment and torture, that's all it was. I just lay up there and I finally blocked myself off from everybody that didn't give a damn about me. And I cut a little bit when I was up there, bled myself. I don't know whether it's a sexual kick that I get out of it or what.

I take this little weapon I made me and I stick it into my artery and it flows like a river, man. I fill up cups on top of cups and watch it, and I dig a kick out of it. And there's other little things I found to do.

What?

Now that's getting real personal. I ain't going to tell you that. But the bleeding, that's just like I'm taking out a part of my soul. You're taking out part of your soul and you're seeing it in your hand. *Do you think about that when it's flowing?* Yes. I sit there and I think about it. And I think about what I'd like to do to somebody. Then I take the blood and I wipe it on me and I think about some gal that appeals to me, maybe, you know? And I wipe it on me. And I love her. It's just a kick. *How far does it go? Do you have orgasms when you do it?* Yes. Oh, yeah. And I rub it on my trim and I get my kicks.

But I got away from it. I couldn't do it after about a month ago. I couldn't even get no sexual kick out of it. I kept trying and trying it. I did this years ago and I got a kick out of it. I was showed and it was planted in my mind that I could do it. Well, that's all sex is anyway. It's all in your goddamned mind.

I was in Rusk [Texas mental hospital] for a while, then I fell back out on stud row. This little old butch gal, no, she's not a butch, she's a lesbian, she definitely isn't a butch, she's been with this gal here for four years but they've never had no kind of sex because this other gal has never participated in gay life whatsoever. She claims she's never been in love before, but now she says she's in love with this gal; I can't see how in the hell does she know it's love if she's never been in love. How does she know what love is? So this lesbian and I, we got real friendly. We got to talking about books and things, like a regular conversation. Finally, Mary says one night, "Sal, ain't you getting down with nobody in the shop for a kick?"

I told her, "No, honey." So we started digging each other in a roundabout way. I knew she did the same thing I did, bleed herself. And I told her, "Mary, what do you dig out of lighting the candle?" That's what we called it, "lighting the candle."

And she told me, "If you never have tried it, you don't know."

And I told her, "Who said I haven't tried it?"

And we started having this conversation.

I asked her, "Do you feel like . . . tell me what you feel? I promise you I'll tell you exactly what I feel if you tell me first." So I got her to tell me. Hers is a self-torture because she killed her father. That's why she's here. She was in the Air Force and she's trying to get away from herself. They've given her blood transfusions here and everything else for it. A lot of people thought when I started was when I started messing with her, but it wasn't. I've been doing it on and off since the early forties. But really and truly, I did it heavier since I've had this life sentence on me. Then I stopped digging this sexual kick behind it. I started doing it because, I don't know, I didn't want to die, but yet I didn't want to go through all this waking up every morning and seeing the goddamn four walls.

Were you cutting yourself enough that you might have bled to death?

Yeah. If I'd a did it every night I would have. As it was, I'd walk down the hall and everything would start turning black. I'd have to hold the wall for a few minutes till I could get myself back. I came down from 197 pounds to 155 pounds. I'm five foot nine and before I started getting my weight back I started looking like a walking skeleton for a while. My people was writing the warden, asking what in the hell was wrong with me. They was all shook up because I looked sick. I looked like death warmed over.

When you were shooting outside, would you light the candle too or would you just take junk?

I just took junk. That was my crutch.

Do you dig fucking with men as much as with women?

No. I can't get my kicks out of this fucking a man. I can't. He could pump all day long, but I wouldn't get a sexual kick. I don't know, I've analyzed it this way: I think it's because the first time that I really ever busted my nuts was with this woman schoolteacher. A woman. She loved my body. And that was it.

You never busted your nuts with a man? Even if he goes down on you?

No. I do now. When a man loves my body, goes down on me and everything, then I get my kicks. If he knows what his business is. Hell, I've had some experts, believe me. Everybody says that the Frenchmen is the best. Bullshit.

Gay people, I guess they're my favorite kind of people. Because I know what a lonely life it is. And that's one reason I would not turn nobody out in gay life.

But here, a girl can be here two weeks and the officials already got it planned how they're with somebody. If I walk down the hall over three or four times with one girl, I'm fucking her, or I'm trying to fuck her, or something. But you know what? These country idiots around here, if they'd only snap. These little old playing things about "I'm mama and you're daddy," they're just children. And if they would put them in a goddamn cell together and just tell them, "There you are, play house." There's going to be a little fighting, maybe, because when mama wants daddy to get down, that's where it stops, right there.

There isn't a girl in here that wouldn't lay down and make a spread and get their pussy ate. There isn't a girl in here that wouldn't do it. The oldest goddamn woman. Because women are women, and if they know it's safe and they don't have to—I'll say it like this—if they didn't have to kiss after the deal went down, they'd lay down. That's the majority of them in here. But as far as really being involved, there isn't even a third that would actually stick with it.

It's a status thing?

Yeah. So they can say they was in with the in-crowd, you know. I'll show you an example. This little old girl came in, oh, she made me sick. She never messed in homosexual activities in her life. Her husband was over here at the Walls. A little farm girl now, mind you. Okay. She landed up in one of the wards and some of the girls wanted their pussy eaten. So they ribbed this girl. So she says, "I've never done that before. I never heard of that before." Now she admitted to this. I was in Rusk when she came in and she started all this bullshit. When I came back they had cut off her hair, she was wearing a duck, she was out there on stud row. And she was walking hard, you know? Playing like she was a goddamn man. Even the butch broads that I know don't put it out like that. They may even dress in drag, but they still don't walk like a man. They don't imitate a man in no way. So she says, "I don't know you."

And I looked at her. Now, I am a crazy bitch and I'll say what I think to anybody. I don't care. I just looked at her and I told her, "No, and you never will get to know me." And I sit there and I watched TV. This went on for about a month. I didn't talk to her and she didn't talk to me. We recced together and we didn't talk.

She says, "Sal, I want to know what is it about me you don't like."

I told her, "Had you ever been with a girl before?"

She said, "No."

I said, "You're married, huh?"

"Yeah."

I said, "When you get home, are you planning on living with your husband?"

She said, "Well, I imagine so." She's got her plans, but she's playing because everybody wanted her to. See the picture? And then she says, "Why?"

And I said, "You know what? Your old man, if he's any kind of man, ought to kick the dog shit out of you." And I just got up and walked out. We didn't talk no more. And about two weeks before she went home she told somebody, "You know what? I don't think I'm going back to my husband. I think I'm going to go home and live with Kathryn." This little old gal that she had met in here. And Kathryn didn't know anything about homosexuality at all when she came in here. When she came in, somebody asked her to play and she told them, "Oh, no. My mother and daddy would be disappointed." She was a little old farm gal. But when she got out both of them was madly in love with each other.

That first girl, I hope her old man's kicked the shit out of her.

A lot of girls get turned out like that, right in here. If they really wanted to help, the people who run these places, they'd spot people like myself and Betty, the different girls that really participate in homosexuality in the street, the ones that really and truly lived it, and they would put them in a place all their own, don't even let them work with the other ones. If they lived that life and know what it's about and everything, then put them all together. That's their world.

Just like dope addicts. They ought to put all the dope addicts together. And put all the ones that never shot dope in another wing and never let them come in contact with each other. I have seen so many little young gals come in here and when they got out they wanted to shoot dope because they heard about what a big kick it was, what a thrill they'd get, and stuff like that.

See, these officials around here, they don't want to help you. They don't help you. They don't give a damn. It's nothing off of them. They got a job, and the girls see that. They holler rehabilitation. Shit. They got it. Isolation or a threat every time you turn around. It just makes you hard.

I'm indifferent to most people. I take them or leave them and it wouldn't bother me if they dropped dead. There's that girl that passed by before and a couple of others, I can count them on one hand, the ones that really amount to anything or matter to me. But the rest of them—I'm indifferent. But the warden says I'm the most well-liked person on the camp. But really and truly, they don't like me. The only reason they act like they do is because I'm Big Sal. That's right. And I know it. If I don't like somebody and they get on my shit list, my friends are not going to like them either. That's all it is. It's just a fucking dog-eat-dog, that's all. That's all this kind of life is. And I'm tired of it. I really am.